USING STATISTICAL METHODS IN
SOCIAL SCIENCE RESEARCH
WITH A COMPLETE SPSS GUIDE

USING STATISTICAL METHODS IN SOCIAL SCIENCE RESEARCH WITH A COMPLETE SPSS GUIDE

Second Edition

Soleman Hassan Abu-Bader
Howard University

LYCEUM
BOOKS, INC.

Chicago, Illinois

Richard Hull is an artist living and working in Chicago. His work can be found in many private and public collections. He teaches at the School of the Art Institute of Chicago. The drawing is "Untitled," 2010, 19 × 13", crayon on paper.

© 2011 by Lyceum Books, Inc.

Published by

LYCEUM BOOKS, INC.
5758 S. Blackstone Avenue
Chicago, Illinois 60637
773-643-1903 fax
773-643-1902 phone
lyceum@lyceumbooks.com
www.lyceumbooks.com

Previously published by Lyceum Books, Inc., as *Using Statistical Methods in Social Work Practice: A Complete SPSS Guide*

SPSS is a registered trademark of IBM, Inc.
233 South Wacker Drive, 11th Floor
Chicago, Illinois 60606
www.spss.com

6 5 4 3   11 12 13 14

ISBN 978-1-935871-02-6

Book and cover design by Tim Kaage.
Printed in the United States of America.

Library of Congress Cataloging-in-Publication Data

Abu-Bader, Soleman H., 1965–
    Using statistical methods in social science research with a complete SPSS guide / Soleman H. Abu-Bader. — Rev. ed.
        p. cm.
    Previously published under title: Using statistical methods in social work practice.
    Includes bibliographical references and index.
    ISBN 978-1-935871-02-6 (pbk. : alk. paper)
    1. Social service—Statistical methods. 2. SPSS (Computer file) I. Abu-Bader, Soleman H., 1965– Using statistical methods in social work practice. II. Title.
    HV29.A28   2011
    005.5'5—dc22

                                                            2010042480

To my wife, Buthaina, and children, Nagham, Layanne, and Samer,
with love and appreciation

Contents

Preface to the First Edition

Consider the following research questions:

1. Does the physical health of elderly people significantly affect their levels of depression?

2. Are there statistically significant differences between the levels of anxiety of parents who have an autistic child and parents who do not have an autistic child?

3. Are there statistically significant differences between BSW, MSW, and PhD child welfare workers with regard to their levels of burnout?

4. Do battered women who participate in stress management skills therapy significantly decrease their levels of stress after they complete the therapy?

5. Are people of color more likely to seek mental health services than white people?

6. Which set of factors best predicts self-esteem among welfare recipients: gender, race, marital status, age, education, physical health, mental health, or social support?

These are examples of the many research questions that face social sciences researchers, administrators, and practitioners every day. The purpose of these questions is twofold: (1) to find whether a relationship exists among the variables under study, and (2) to better plan and develop a treatment therapy or intervention that helps clients to improve their day-to-day lives.

For example, if statistical analysis shows that physical health significantly affects levels of depression among elderly people, this could help gerontological therapists to plan their treatments with the elderly accordingly. Moreover, if social services practitioners were able to predict the levels of self-esteem among welfare recipients based on multiple conditions, such as recipients' gender, race, marital status, or other factors, they could select and provide appropriate treatment to consumers who are predicted to be at greater risk of low self-esteem.

How do researchers statistically examine these questions? The answer lies herein. This is a book on data analysis for social sciences practitioners, such as social workers, psychologists, health care providers, etc. There are already many outstanding data analysis and statistical textbooks, and this book is not intended to compete with them. *Using Statistical Methods in Social Science Research with a Complete SPSS Guide* is a comprehensive book that provides step-by-step descriptions of the processes practitioners will need to organize, summarize, analyze, interpret, and make sense of their data.

My intention is to provide a work that is academically sound but written for social sciences students with no statistical background. During my seven years of teaching research methods and data analysis for diverse graduate students in Utah, Kansas, and Washington, D.C., I have become aware that most social sciences students fear statistics, formulas, and numbers. My impression is that there is a growing need among students for a statistical book that helps them evaluate their practice, while refraining from applying major mathematical formulas and calculations.

Using Statistical Methods in Social Science Research with a Complete SPSS Guide is the answer for this growing need. This book targets undergraduate and graduate social sciences students. The book can be used as a main textbook for statistics and data analysis courses or as a supplement text for research methods or program evaluation courses that cover statistical methods.

The book is organized in twelve chapters. Each chapter is divided into two main parts: the first part discusses the theoretical background of the topic under discussion, and the second part presents practical examples with step-by-step examination of a specific problem, how to analyze it, and how to interpret and write the results. Each chapter also includes a detailed discussion of the use of SPSS in computing appropriate statistics.

Chapter 1 reviews major methodological terms, specifically, terms related to data analysis. These terms include variables, levels of measurement, hypotheses, reliability, validity, descriptive and inferential statistics, and types of relationships between variables.

Chapter 2 introduces the Statistical Package for the Social Sciences (SPSS) and SPSS syntax file. The chapter discusses how to start SPSS, create variable names, labels, value categories, and SPSS templates. The chapter also discusses how to enter data in SPSS, clean, recode variables, and compute total scores for a scale.

Chapter 3 and chapter 4 discuss descriptive statistics. Chapter 3 discusses the frequency distribution table, including absolute frequency, cumulative frequency, absolute percentage, and cumulative percentage. The chapter then presents three different graphs: bar graphs, histograms, and stem-and-leaf plots. Chapter 4 discusses measures of central tendency, measures of variability, and percentiles, and presents the boxplot chart.

Chapter 5 discusses various types of distributions. The chapter discusses the properties of normal distributions and skewed distributions and then discusses methods of data transformations. The chapter also discusses the properties of standard scores and how to use a z score table.

Chapter 6 introduces the process in hypothesis testing. The chapter discusses the differences between one-tailed and two-tailed research hypotheses, errors in hypothesis testing, levels of significance, and confidence interval. The chapter then compares parametric and nonparametric tests, presents methods for selecting the appropriate statistical test, and discusses the steps in hypothesis testing.

Chapter 7 presents Pearson's product-moment correlation coefficient and Spearman's *rho* correlation. The chapter discusses the purpose of these tests, defines the coefficient of determination, discusses the assumptions underlying Pearson's correlation, and presents the scatterplot. The chapter then presents two practical examples illustrating the use of SPSS and interpreting and writing the results of Pearson's correlation.

Chapter 8 presents the independent *t*-test and the Mann-Whitney *U* test. The chapter discusses the purpose of these tests, presents methods of data evaluations, and discusses the assumptions of the independent *t*-test and the Mann-Whitney *U* test. The chapter also presents two practical examples illustrating the use of SPSS and interpreting and writing the results of the independent *t*-test.

Chapter 9 presents the dependent *t*-test and Wilcoxon signed ranks test. The chapter discusses the purpose of these tests, type of data used with them, assumptions of the tests, and presents two practical examples illustrating the use of SPSS and interpreting and writing the results of the dependent *t*-test.

Chapter 10 presents the one-way analysis of variance (ANOVA) and the Kruskal-Wallis *H* test. The chapter discusses the purpose of these tests, presents methods of data evaluations, and discusses the assumptions of the one-way ANOVA and Kruskal-Wallis *H* tests. The chapter then discusses the use of post hoc tests, such as the Bonferroni, Scheffe, Tukey, and Tamhane's T2. The chapter also presents two practical examples illustrating the use of SPSS and interpreting and writing the results of the one-way ANOVA.

Chapter 11 presents the contingency table and chi-square test of association. The chapter discusses the purpose of the chi-square test, the difference between observed and expected frequencies, the type of data used with the test, and the assumptions of the chi-square test of association. The chapter then discusses the difference between the *phi* and Cramer's *V* coefficients. The chapter also presents two practical examples illustrating the use of SPSS and interpreting and writing the results of a contingency table and the chi-square.

The final chapter (chapter 12) presents the multiple regression analysis. The chapter discusses the purpose of multiple regression analysis, the regression equation, and presents the major coefficients produced by multiple regression analysis. The chapter then discusses the assumptions of multiple regression analysis and the process in selecting the variables to be entered in the analysis. The chapter then discusses the differences between forward, stepwise, and backward regression methods. Finally, the chapter presents a practical example illustrating the use of SPSS and interpreting and writing the results of the multiple regression analysis.

Data Files

This book does not require the use of mathematical formulas or a paper and pencil to compute the statistics. Instead, this book uses the Statistical Package for the Social Sciences (SPSS) computer program to organize, summarize, and analyze the data. This program was chosen because it is the most popular software and is available in most university computer labs. Users of other statistical software can still greatly benefit from this book because it provides a detailed discussion of the process of organizing and summarizing data, selecting the appropriate test, understanding the statistics, writing the conclusion, and presenting the results in summary tables. SPSS is only a tool used in this book to compute statistics. The same statistics can be computed by other software, such as SAS and Excel (see References for Users' Guide for SAS and Excel).

Seven data files that can be used with SPSS, SAS, Excel, and other computer programs may be obtained from the Lyceum Books Web site: www.lyceumbooks .com. These files include *Anxiety*, *Elderly*, *Job Satisfaction*, *Mental Health*, *PTSD*, *Welfare*, and *Well-Being*. Appendix A describes each study and presents the name, label, range of scores, and value labels for each variable in each data file (see chapter 2 for more on these terms).

Preface to the Second Edition

I am pleased with the reception of the first edition of this book and very grateful for the many ideas and suggestions for the second edition. Where possible, I incorporated these suggestions to improve the quality of the book and to benefit a wide range of undergraduate and graduate social science disciplines. These changes and additions are as follows:

1. I have updated all SPSS screens and figures based on the SPSS versions 18.0 and 19.0 throughout the chapters.

2. I have added four new SPSS data files. They are Anxiety, Mental Health, PTSD, and Well-Being, and I have added new practical examples throughout the chapters.

3. In chapter 1, I have presented additional methodological terms, including mathematical concepts, quantitative and qualitative variables, population and sample, and the Kuder-Richardson 20 (KR20) reliability coefficient.

4. In chapter 2, I have added a discussion on computing and interpreting the reliability coefficient in SPSS.

5. I have introduced additional statistics and graphs, including class-interval frequency distribution, exact-limit frequency distribution, and frequency polygon in chapter 3, and mean deviation in chapter 4.

6. I have introduced two additional methods for evaluating normality of distributions, including the Pearson's skewness coefficient and the normal Q-Q plots in chapter 5.

7. I have defined power and effect size and how they impact sample size in chapter 6.

8. I have provided sample size tables for all statistical tests discussed in chapters 7 through 12.

9. Finally, I have introduced three additional statistical techniques: the one-sample case *t*-test in chapter 8, the one-way analysis of covariance in chapter 10, and the chi-square goodness-of-fit test in chapter 11.

I hope this new edition will benefit social science students, faculty, and practitioners in organizing, analyzing, and reporting data and efficiently evaluating practice. This text is especially important because practice and program evaluations have a significant role in the development and advancement of social science research and professions.

ACKNOWLEDGMENTS

Many people helped make this new edition possible. First, thank you to all my data analysis and advanced statistics graduate students for their feedback and suggestions for improving this edition and making it student-user friendly. I would also like to thank the faculty of Howard University School of Social Work for their support. I am especially thankful to Dr. Sandra Edmonds Crewe, Dr. Fariyal Ross-Sheriff, Dr. Jacqueline Smith, and Dr. Cudore L. Snell for their continuous support and encouragement.

I would like to extend my special thanks to the reviewers, Thomas O'Hare of Boston College and John McNutt of the University of Delaware, whose suggestions improved this new edition. I am also thankful to copy editor Jennifer Barrell for reviewing and editing this edition. Finally, a special thank you goes to my wife, children, and family abroad for their love and support.

Overview of Research Methodological Terms

LEARNING OBJECTIVES

1. Understand basic mathematical concepts
2. Understand variables and constants
3. Understand quantitative and qualitative variables
4. Understand types of variables and levels of measurement
5. Understand null and alternative hypotheses
6. Understand reliability and validity of instruments
7. Understand descriptive and inferential statistics
8. Understand relationships between variables

INTRODUCTION

Perhaps you already have learned about the research process and research design in introductory research courses. You may know about selecting and defining researchable social/health science-related concepts (e.g., self-esteem, self-perception, attitudes toward homosexuality, anxiety, depression, etc.), levels of measurement, research questions and hypotheses, probability and nonprobability sampling methods, psychometric properties (reliability and validity), and data collection methods. However, you probably have not covered in depth and detail how to prepare and code data for entry in a statistical computer program; enter, clean, and analyze the data; and interpret and write the results. Data analysis methods, interpretations, and discussion of the results are the next, and central, steps in the research process.

Using Statistical Methods in Social Science Research is all about data analysis methods. It includes a step-by-step discussion of data analysis, starting with preparation of data for entry in a statistical program such as the Statistical Package for the Social Sciences (SPSS) and ending with selection of appropriate statistical techniques to analyze the data and discuss and present the results. However, because data analysis is a continuation of the research process, basic mathematical concepts and research methodological terms will be reviewed, especially those that are significant to data analysis, including: variables and constants, quantitative and qualitative variables, types of variables and levels of measurement, research hypotheses, population and sample, reliability and validity, descriptive and inferential statistics, and relationships between variables.[1]

BASIC MATHEMATICAL CONCEPTS

Statistical analysis depends heavily on mathematical operations. While this book uses mathematical operations and statistical formulas at the minimum, students should be exposed to the basic mathematical operations utilized in statistical calculation.

Mathematical operations include everything from basic mathematic calculations to complex modeling algorithms. The following describes some basic mathematical operations:

Summation

Summation refers to "the sum of" and is symbolized by the Greek capital letter sigma (Σ). For example, suppose you want the sum of X_1, X_2, . . . , X_{10}, then you can write this as $\Sigma(X_1$ to $X_{10})$.

As a general rule, the summation operation is written as the following:

$$\sum_{i=1}^{N} X_i = X_1 + X_2 + \ldots + X_N$$

That is, the sum of X_i, whereas X goes from "i" to "N." The "X" represents the numbers for the summation, the "i" represents the first X in the summation, and the "N" represents the last X in the summation.

Example: If $X_1 = 2$, $X_2 = 4$, $X_3 = 6$, $X_4 = 8$, $X_5 = 10$, $X_6 = 12$, $X_7 = 14$, and $X_8 = 16$, then the sum of X_1 to X_4, for example, can be written as

$$\sum_{i=1}^{4} X_i = 2 + 4 + 6 + 8 = 20$$

---

[1]For more discussion of the research process, research design, and methodological terms, see Fortune & Reid (1999), Rubin & Babbie (2011), and Weinbach & Grinnell (2010).

That is, the sum of X, whereas X goes from 1 to 4. You may also write the sum of X_5 to X_8 as

$$\sum_{i=5}^{8} X_i = 10 + 12 + 14 + 16 = 42$$

That is, the sum of X, whereas X goes from 5 to 8.

General Mathematical Rules

First rule: Multiplying each number (X_i) by a constant (C) in a summation is the same as multiplying the sum of the numbers by the constant. That is,

$$\sum_{i=1}^{N} CX_i = C \sum_{i=1}^{N} X_i$$

Example: Multiplying 3 (constant) by X_1 to X_4 in the previous example (X_1 = 2, X_2 = 4, X_3 = 6, X_4 = 8) is the same as multiplying 3 by the sum of X_1 to X_4. That is,

$$\sum_{i=1}^{4} 3(X_i) = (3 \times 2) + (3 \times 4) + (3 \times 6) + (3 \times 8) = 60$$

$$3 \sum_{i=5}^{4} X_i = 3(2 + 4 + 6 + 8) = 3 \times 20 = 60$$

Second rule: The sum of X values in one group and the sum of Y values in a second group are the same as if you add each X value to each corresponding Y value and then sum all these values together. That is,

$$\sum_{i=1}^{N} (X_i + Y_i) = \sum_{i=1}^{N} X_i + \sum_{i=1}^{N} Y_i$$

Example: If X_1 = 2, X_2 = 4, X_3 = 6, X_4 = 8 and Y_1 = 3, Y_2 = 5, Y_3 = 7, Y_4 = 9, then the sum of X_i and the sum of Y_i is the same as the sum of $(X+Y)_i$. That is,

$$\sum_{i=1}^{4} X_i + \sum_{i=1}^{4} Y_i = (2 + 4 + 6 + 8) + (3 + 5 + 7 + 9) = 44$$

$$\sum_{i=1}^{4} (X_i + Y_i) = (2 + 3) + (4 + 5) + (6 + 7) + (8 + 9) = 44$$

Order of Mathematical Operations

Basic mathematics involves several operations, including addition, subtraction, multiplication, and division. In addition, these operations involve parentheses and exponents.

When more than one operation is involved, you should follow these steps:

1. Perform the operations inside the parentheses.
2. Perform the operations for the exponents.
3. Perform the operations for multiplications and divisions.
4. Perform the operations for additions and subtractions.

Example: Solve the following problem:

$$X = \sqrt{25} + (7 + 8)^2 - 3*(2 + 6) \div 2^2$$

1. Operate inside the parentheses; that is,

$$X = \sqrt{25} + (15)^2 - 3*(8) \div 2^2$$

2. Solve the exponents; that is,

$$X = 5 + 225 - 3*(8) \div 4$$

3. Perform the multiplications and the divisions; that is,

$$X = 5 + 225 - 24 \div 4 = 5 + 225 - 6$$

4. Finally, perform the additions and then subtractions; that is,

$$X = 230 - 6 = 224$$

VARIABLES AND CONSTANTS

Variables

The main purpose for conducting any statistical analysis is to examine if relationships exist among two or more variables under investigation and whether these relationships can be generalized to the population from which the sample is drawn. Variables are, thus, anything that can vary among subjects, events, or objects, such as the following:

1. GENDER: An individual can be male or female.

2. RACE: An individual can be white, African American, Native American, Hispanic, or other.

3. AGE: An individual can be eighteen years old, twenty-five, twenty-eight, thirty, thirty-six, and so on.

4. INCOME: An individual can earn $20,000, $26,500, $37,800, $50,000 a year, and up.

5. EDUCATION: An individual can have ten years of education, twelve, sixteen, or eighteen years of education. *Or*, an individual can have a high school diploma, two-year college degree, undergraduate degree, graduate degree, or other degrees.

6. LEVEL OF ANXIETY: An individual can be very anxious, somewhat anxious, somewhat not anxious, or not at all anxious. *Or*, an individual can have an anxiety score of 25 on a scale that ranges between 10 and 30, with higher scores indicating greater levels of anxiety.

7. LIFE SATISFACTION: An individual can be very satisfied with life, somewhat satisfied, somewhat not satisfied, or not at all satisfied.

Variables can be classified in two groups, quantitative and qualitative.

Quantitative variables.   These are variables that are measured using numerical values and, thus, have numerical meanings. They are also known as *continuous variables* or *continuous data*. Example of quantitative variables include annual income, number of years of education, number of hours of exercise, age, weight, height, IQ, levels of life satisfaction, levels of depression, etc.

Qualitative variables.   These are variables that are classified into groups or categories. They are also known as *categorical* variables or *discrete* variables. Examples of qualitative variables include gender, race, religious affiliation, eye color, political party, etc. While in statistics these categories are assigned numerical values (e.g., 1 = male and 2 = female), these values have no numerical meanings. In a sense, you can label males as 0, 1, or 2, and females can be assigned any other value.

There are four types of variables: independent, dependent, extraneous, and control.

Independent variable.   This is a variable that researchers can control or manipulate according to the purpose of the study. It is a variable believed to cause an outcome. For example, if you believe that a higher level of education leads to more annual income, then level of education will be the independent variable. If you believe better physical health leads to a lower level of depression, then physical health will be the independent variable. Also, if you believe that there are differences between Caucasian, African American, Hispanic, and other college students with regard to their body mass index (BMI), then race will be the independent variable.

Dependent variable.   This is a measure of the effect of the independent variable. It is dependent upon the occurrence of the independent variable. In other words, it is the outcome of the independent variable. Annual income is the dependent variable in the first example above, level of depression is the dependent variable in the second example, and BMI is the dependent variable in the third example.

Extraneous variable.   This represents an alternative explanation for any relationship observed between the independent and dependent variables. It is a third variable that is not part of the analysis, but is believed to influence the relationship between the independent and dependent variables under study.

Extraneous variables are considered major threats to the internal validity of longitudinal research studies. While many factors may influence internal validity (that is, the manipulation of the independent variable is responsible for the changes in the dependent variable), researchers have identified at least nine possible sources of threats to internal validity. These include history, maturation, testing, instrumentation, statistical regression, selection, attrition, ambiguity about the direction of causal influence, and diffusion or imitation of treatment.[2]

In the above examples, the relationship between education and annual income could also be affected by an individual's gender. The relationship between physical health and level of depression could also be affected by an individual's age. Also, the relationship between race and BMI could be affected by an individual's number of hours of exercise per week. Gender, age, and number

---

[2]For more on threats on internal validity see Bloom, Fischer, & Orme (2006) and Rubin & Babbie (2011).

of hours of exercise could thus be viewed as extraneous variables that may influence the relationship between education and income, physical health and levels of depression, and race and BMI, respectively.

Control variable.   This is a variable that researchers assume has an effect on the dependent variable. In a sense, it is an extraneous variable that researchers can statistically control to determine its effect on the dependent variable. To do so, researchers first treat it as a control variable (also called covariance) and then choose the appropriate statistical technique (such as partial correlation, hierarchical multiple regression analysis, or analysis of covariance) to examine the relationship between the independent and dependent variables while controlling for the effect of this control variable. For example, if researchers collect data on gender, age, and number of hours of exercise, respectively, they can statistically control for their effect on the dependent variables. Thus, gender will serve as a control variable, or covariance, in the first example, age will serve as a control variable in the second example, and number of hours of exercise will serve as a control variable in the third example.

To control for the effect of gender on the relationship between education and annual income, for example, researchers may also conduct two separate statistical analyses, one for men and another for women. To control for the effect of age on the relationship between physical health and levels of depression, researchers may recode age into young, middle, and old, and then conduct three separate analyses, one for each category. Also, to control for the effect of the number of hours of exercise on the relationship between race and BMI, researchers may recode number of hours of exercise into a number of categories, such as 0–5, 6–10, 11–15 hours, etc., and then conduct separate analyses, one for each category.

Yet, researchers must first show that the "control" variable is significantly correlated with the dependent variable in order to treat it as a control variable and then conduct the appropriate statistical analysis to control for its effect on the relationship between the independent and dependent variables. If no significant correlation exists between the control and dependent variables, then it could be treated as a second independent variable.

Constants

Unlike variables, constants are anything that do not vary among the subjects, events, or objects under study. A constant is a characteristic that all participants under investigation have in common. For example, if all people were Christian, then religion would be treated as a constant. But since there are several religious groups, such as Christians, Muslims, Jews, Buddhists, and others, religion is not a constant but a variable. The speed of light, on the other hand, is a constant; it remains steady. In geometry, π (Greek small letter pi) is a constant because it is a fixed value: 3.14. To compute the area of a circle, square the radius (which is a variable) then multiply it by π (area = $r^2 \times \pi$). In regression analysis (see chapter 12), the "a" in a regression equation is a constant.

LEVELS OF MEASUREMENT

Variables are classified under four levels of measurement: nominal, ordinal, interval, and ratio. Table 1.1 summarizes the levels of measurement and their characteristics.

Nominal

Nominal variables are those variables with attributes that are exhaustive and mutually exclusive. To be exhaustive, every participant in the study *must* be classifiable according to one of the variable's attributes (categories, groups). For example, a person can be a Christian, Muslim, Jew, or Other. If "Other" is not one of the attributes of religion, then you may not represent participants who are Buddhist or those who have no religious affiliation. Mutually exclusive means that you must classify every participant in *one and only one* of the variable's attributes. In other words, an individual cannot be classified in more than one attribute: a person can be male, female, or transgender but not more than one attribute; someone can be Christian or Muslim but not both. Thus, nominal variables are those variables whose attributes can be classified in qualitative categories, or discrete groups.

Examples: gender (attributes: male, female); race (attributes: white, African American, Hispanic, Native American, other); religion (attributes: Christian, Jewish, Muslim, Buddhist, no preference, other); hair color (attributes: black, brown, red, other); political party (attributes: Democratic, Republican, independent, other); country of birth (attributes: U.S., France, China, Lebanon, other).

Ordinal

Variables measured on the ordinal level are those variables whose attributes have the characteristics of nominal variables (mutually exclusive and exhaustive) and can be rank-ordered. Rank-ordered means that one attribute is greater or less

Table 1.1: Characteristics of Levels of Measurement

Level of Measurement	Exhaustive/ Mutually Exclusive	Rank Order	Equal Distance	Absolute Zero
Nominal	X			
Ordinal	X	X		
Interval	X	X	X	
Ratio	X	X	X	X

than another attribute. However, it is impractical to precisely state how much greater or how much less one attribute is from another.

Examples: Five-point Likert scale (attributes: 1 = very dissatisfied, 2 = dissatisfied, 3 = neither satisfied nor dissatisfied, 4 = satisfied, 5 = very satisfied); grading system (attributes: A, B, C, D, F); people standing in a line (attributes: 1st, 2nd, 3rd, etc.); dress size (attributes: S, M, L, XL, XXL).

Interval

Variables measured on the interval level are those variables whose attributes have the characteristics of ordinal variables (mutually exclusive, exhaustive, and rank-ordered) plus have an equal distance. This indicates that the distance between the first and second attributes is the same as the distance between the second and third, third and fourth, and so on.

Examples: Fahrenheit temperature (attributes: 80°, 70°, 60°, etc.); percentile rank (attributes: 50th, 40th, 30th, 10th, etc.); IQ score (attributes: 110, 100, 90, 80, etc.).

Ratio

Variables measured on the ratio level are those variables whose attributes have the characteristics of interval variables (mutually exclusive, exhaustive, rank-ordered, and equal distance) plus have an absolute zero. In other words, a zero point is possible. For example, if someone has zero income, this means he or she has no income, but if someone has zero IQ, this does not mean he or she has no intelligence.

Examples: Age[3] (attributes: 10, 15, 25, 36, 45 years old, etc.); weight (attributes: 50 pounds, 60, 80, 95, 120, 150, etc.); annual salary (attributes: $20,000, $25,000, $30,000, $45,000, etc.); number of years of education (attributes: 6, 8, 12, 14, 15, 16, 20, etc.).

If feasible, collecting data using interval or ratio levels of measurement is recommended because interval or ratio variables can always be recoded into ordinal or nominal variables. However, it is impossible to recode nominal or ordinal variables into interval or ratio variables. That is, it is possible to recode a higher level of measurement to a lower level, but not the opposite.

Example: If you are interested in participants' ages, you may ask them to report their actual age at their last birthday. In this case, age is defined as a ratio level of measurement, which is appropriate for all parametric statistics (see chapter 6). You can also recode age into young, middle, or old, which becomes an ordinal level of measurement. Or you could recode it into two groups: less than thirty years and thirty years or older. In this case, age is treated as a nominal level of measurement.

---

[3] If age is defined as young, middle, and old, then it will be treated as an ordinal level of measurement.

Why and how to determine the level of measurement of a variable. Levels of measurement play a fundamental role in choosing the appropriate statistical test. While we have discussed four levels of measurement, interval and ratio levels of measurement are both treated the same way in data analysis. Therefore, we refer to the two levels as interval or higher. As discussed in chapter 6, one assumption for utilizing any parametric test (such as the Pearson's correlation or the independent t-test) is that the dependent variable is measured at the interval level or higher. Parametric tests also make assumptions about independent variables. For example, while the Pearson's correlation and the dependent t-test require that the independent variable be measured at the interval level of measurement or higher, the independent t-test and one-way analysis of variance require independent variables to be measured at the nominal level.

Determining the level of measurement of a variable is not as straightforward as it may seem. In general, a variable that only consists of mutually exclusive and exhaustive categories or discrete groups is measured at the nominal level of measurement. For example: gender (male or female); race (white, African American, Hispanic, Native American, other); religion (Christianity, Islam, Judaism, other); sickness (Do you consider yourself sick? Yes, No).

A variable measured by a single item on a three-, four-, five-, or seven-point Likert scale is usually considered an ordinal variable. For example: Overall, how satisfied are you with the services you receive? 1 = not at all satisfied, 2 = not satisfied, 3 = satisfied, 4 = very satisfied; Compared to this time last year, how would you rate your health now? 1 = much worse, 2 = worse, 3 = same, 4 = better, 5 = much better; Letter grading system: 1 = A, 2 = B, 3 = C, 4 = D, 5 = F.

A variable measured by a scale (number of items) and a total score is computed to generate a scale score, or a variable that requires an exact numeric value usually measured at the interval level or higher (ratio). For example, the total scores in the CESD and Rosenberg Self-Esteem Scale (appendix A) are considered interval variables. Actual income, actual age, number of years of education, number of children at home, and number of years off of welfare are all measured at the interval level or higher (ratio).

RESEARCH HYPOTHESES

A hypothesis is an assumption about the relationship among two or more variables under investigation. It provides the general framework for the investigation and describes the problem and the variables being tested. There are two types of hypotheses: null and alternative.

Null Hypothesis (H_o)

A null hypothesis always assumes *no statistically significant* relationships among the independent and dependent variables or *no statistically significant* differences among groups (independent variable) with regard to the dependent variable. Researchers usually seek to *reject* the null hypothesis. It is denoted by H_o.

Examples:

H_{o1}: There is no statistically significant relationship between number of hours of exercise per week and body mass index (BMI) among college students.

H_{o2}: There is no statistically significant difference between male and female college students with regard to their BMI.

Alternative Hypothesis (H_a)

The alternative hypothesis, also known as *research hypothesis*, always assumes *statistically significant* relationships among the independent and dependent variables or *statistically significant* differences among groups (independent variable) with regard to the dependent variable. Researchers usually seek to support (not reject) the alternative hypothesis. It is the complement of the null hypothesis and can be supported *only* by rejecting the null hypothesis. It is denoted by H_a.

Examples:

H_{a1}: There is a statistically significant relationship between number of hours of exercise per week and body mass index (BMI) among college students.

H_{a2}: There is a statistically significant difference between male and female college students with regard to their BMI.

In statistics, researchers *always* examine the null hypotheses, although their interest is the alternative hypotheses.

PSYCHOMETRIC PROPERTIES OF AN INSTRUMENT

The aim of empirical research is to generate data from a sample that correctly reflect the true information about the population from which the sample's participants are recruited. However, the only way to have *complete* true information about the population is by studying all members of the population, which is not feasible due to many reasons, such as time, resources, reaching subjects, and others.

Reliability and Validity

Reliability.   Reliability is the extent of random variations or random errors in the results of a study. It refers to whether a particular measure or test applied repeatedly to the same subjects or objects would yield the same results each time. In other words, reliability relates to the consistency of a measure or test over time. Reliability, however, does not ensure accuracy.[4] For example, illegal immigrant employees might or might not lie about their immigration status when asked. While the statement is reliable, the answer may not be accurate.

---

[4]For more on reliability and scale development, see DeVellis (2003).

Reliability coefficients range between 0 and 1. The closer the coefficient is to 1, the more reliable the measure is, with less random errors. How close to 1 must a reliability coefficient be? While interpretations of reliability coefficients may vary from one researcher to another, as a general guideline, a reliability coefficient greater than .80 is considered excellent, .70 to .80 is considered very good, .60 to .69 is considered acceptable, and a reliability coefficient less than .60 is considered weak due to the high proportion of random errors. The relationship between reliability and random errors can be expressed in the following equation:

$$\text{Reliability} = 1 - \text{Random Error}$$

There are a number of reliability coefficients. These include inter-observer/inter-rater reliability coefficient, test-retest reliability coefficient, equivalence reliability coefficient, and internal consistency reliability coefficient.

Inter-observer/inter-rater reliability refers to whether two or more observers or raters are consistent in their rating of certain behaviors of subjects. For example, a teacher and a social worker may be asked to observe and rate a school-age child on a certain behavior. The greater the number of agreements between the two (teacher and social worker), the higher the reliability coefficient.

The *test-retest reliability coefficient*, also known as the stability coefficient, refers to whether a test yields similar results every time it is repeated with similar objects or subjects. In this case, researchers administer the same test to the same/similar subjects in two separate occasions. The higher the relationship between the two occasions, the higher the reliability coefficient.

The *equivalence reliability coefficient*, also known as the parallel-forms or alternate forms reliability coefficient, refers to whether one test (form 1) produces similar results as another, well-known test (form 2) measuring the same concept. For example, you may administer a newly developed test of depression (form 1) to a sample of one hundred battered women. At the same time, you may administer the well-know CESD depression scale (Center for Epidemiological Studies of Depression) (form 2) to the same sample. The higher the relationship between the two tests (forms), the higher the reliability coefficient of form 1.

The *internal consistency reliability coefficient* is perhaps the most used form of reliability. It assesses the extent to which measuring items are homogeneous. The assumption is that if items measure the same concept, then the correlations among items, also known as *inter-item correlation coefficients*, should be high.

Unlike previous reliability coefficients, internal consistency reliability coefficients can be assessed simply by administering the measuring test on only one occasion without the need for multiple raters/observers or forms. Then, researchers may utilize one of the following three methods to compute the reliability coefficient:

1. SPLIT-HALF METHOD: Researchers may split the number of measuring items in two equal subsets using various methods (e.g., randomly assign items to each set, odd items versus even items, rank-order items based on their difficulties, etc.) and then examine the correlation between the two sets.

2. CRONBACH'S ALPHA (α) COEFFICIENT: This is the most used method of estimating the internal consistency reliability coefficient of a measuring test. Here, Cronbach's alpha is computed using the following formula:

Cronbach's Alpha Formula

$$\alpha = \frac{K}{K-1} * (1 - \frac{\Sigma \sigma_i^2}{\sigma_x^2})$$

α = Cronbach's alpha
K = Number of items in the test
$\Sigma \sigma_i^2$ = The sum of the variance of item 1, 2, . . . , i
σ_x^2 = The variance of all items

---

3. KUDER-RICHARDSON 20 (KR20) RELIABILITY COEFFICIENT: This is a special case of Cronbach's alpha coefficient. It is most appropriate with dichotomous/binary items (e.g., yes/no; true/false; agreement/no agreement). In this case, KR20 is computed using the following formula:

Kuder-Richardson 20 Formula

$$KR20 = \frac{K}{K-1} * (1 - \frac{\Sigma PQ}{\sigma_x^2})$$

K = Number of items in the test
σ^2 = The variance of all items
P = Proportion of correct answers (correct answers/K)
Q = Proportion of incorrect answers (1 − P)

Finally, table 1.2 summarizes these coefficients and describes the source of random errors for each type of reliability, data collection methods for evaluating the coefficient, and the statistical techniques used to compute the coefficient.

Validity. Validity refers to whether the observed scores in a study precisely reflect the true scores of the concept or variable under investigation. In other words, validity answers this question: Does the instrument measure what it intends to measure? For example, a measure of employee job satisfaction is valid if it accurately measures only job satisfaction and not another concept. In

Table 1.2:   Comparison of Reliability Coefficients

Reliability Coefficient	Source of Random Error	Data Collection Methods	Statistical Computation[a]
Stability Coefficient	Change in subject's scores due to *multiple raters*.	Rater 1, wait, rater 2 (same subjects, same test, two raters).	Compare number of agreements among raters.
	Change in subject's score due to *time*.	Test, wait, retest (same subjects, same test, two occasions).	Compute the correlation between scores from time 1 and time 2.
Equivalence Coefficient	Change in subject's score due to *content sampling* (from test 1 to test 2).	Give test 1, give test 2 (same subjects, two tests, one occasion).	Compute the correlation between scores of test 1 and test 2.
Internal Consistency Coefficient	Change in subject's score due to *content sampling* or *flawed items*.	Give one test to one sample (one test, same subjects, one occasion).	1. Divide items into two equal subsets and compute the correlation between the scores of the two subsets. 2. Compute Cronbach's alpha, or 3. Compute KR20

[a]Statistical computation of reliability is more complicated than it looks in table 1.2. For more on this, see Crocker & Algina (1986).

the previous example of the illegal immigrant, the question was reliable, however the true score may not be valid as the response may not be truthful. Thus, an instrument can be reliable but not necessarily valid.

Validity can be improved when researchers control variables that may affect the dependent variable. There are four types of validity: face validity, content validity, criterion-related validity, and construct validity.

Face validity refers to whether an instrument *appears* to measure what it intends to measure. A life-satisfaction scale has face validity if it appears to measure only life satisfaction and not other concepts. Researchers can assess face validity simply by sharing items (instrument) with experts in the field in which the instrument will be used (mental health, education, social work, etc.) and asking for their feedback.

Content validity refers to whether an instrument measures all possible dimensions of the concept or variable under investigation. A depression scale will measure a person's mood, as well as interest or pleasure in activities, excessive sleep, fatigue, stress, feelings of worthlessness or guilt, ability to concentrate, or suicidal thoughts. Content validity is also assessed by sharing the instrument with professionals and experts who will assess whether the instrument covers all facets (dimensions) of the concept under study. In addition, researchers may conduct a pilot study to assess the content validity of their instrument by administering the instrument to subjects (N > 30) from the population being studied. Feedbacks from experts and subjects help researchers to edit, revise, add new items, and/or delete ambiguous ones.

Criterion-related validity refers to whether an instrument can predict concurrent criterion (*concurrent validity*) or future criterion (*predictive validity*). For example, a written driving test that predicts how well a person will drive soon after passing the written test demonstrates concurrent validity; a GRE score that predicts how well a student will do in future graduate studies demonstrates predictive validity. Concurrent validity is assessed by examining the relation between the construct and concurrent criterion. Predictive validity is assessed by examining the relation between the construct and future criterion.

Construct validity refers to whether an instrument has high correlation with existing instruments that measure the same construct (*convergent validity*) or has low correlation with instruments that measure other constructs (*discriminant validity*). For example, a new self-esteem scale is said to have convergent validity if it is highly correlated with, for example, the Rosenberg Self-Esteem Scale (Royse, 1999), a well-known standardized scale. The new scale is said to have discriminant validity if it has low correlation with, for example, the Life Satisfaction Index (Wood, Wylie, & Sheafor, 1969), also a well-known standardized scale. Convergent validity is assessed by examining the relation between the construct measured by the new instrument and the same construct as measured by an existing instrument. Discriminant validity is assessed by examining the relation between one construct and another as measured by a different instrument.

Well-developed instruments should establish at least content validity and construct validity (one does not replace the other) and also have a high reliability coefficient.

POPULATION AND SAMPLE

As stated earlier, the main purpose of scientific research is to examine the relationships between two or more variables and whether these relationships can be generalized to the population.

To achieve this purpose, researchers first decide on the population to which generalization will be made, select a sample from that population, and then collect data from the sample.

Population is, thus, defined as a collection of all objects or subjects to which generalization of the study results will be made. A sample is defined as a subset of the population from which study data will be collected.

As a general rule, a sample must be *representative* of the population to which generalization of the results will be made. In fact, this is an assumption of all inferential statistical techniques, parametric and nonparametric (discussed in chapter 6 and beyond). Researchers usually assume representativeness by utilizing a probability sampling method to select participants for their studies. These methods include simple random sampling, systematic random sampling, stratified random sampling, or cluster random sampling.

Sometimes, however, researchers rely on a nonprobability sampling method (purposive sampling, convenience sampling, quota sampling, or snowball sampling) to recruit subjects for their studies.[5] This may raise questions about the representativeness of the sample and the generalizeability of the results. In such cases, researchers may utilize various statistical techniques (one-sample case t-test, chi-square goodness-of-fit test, etc.) to compare the sample characteristics (e.g., age, gender, race, education, etc.) with those of the population to which generalization will be made (some of these techniques will be discussed in later chapters).

Finally, when representativeness of a sample is established either through probability sampling methods or statistical analysis, researchers feel greater confidence on their study results and its generalizeability. On the other hand, when representativeness cannot be established or is questionable, researchers should be cautious when making conclusions about the study results and its generalizeability.

DESCRIPTIVE AND INFERENTIAL STATISTICS

Descriptive Statistics

Descriptive statistics describe, characterize, or classify data by summarizing them into understandable terms without losing or distorting information.

Descriptive statistics include: summary tables, graphs (bar graphs, histograms, boxplots, stem-and-leaf plots, and others), frequencies, percentages, measures of central tendency (mean, median, mode), and measures of variability (range, variance, standard deviation).

Example: Descriptive statistics summarize the number of males and females in a study, the mean (average) age, the most frequent score for a specific variable (mode), and the percentage of whites and non-whites in a study.

Inferential Statistics

Inferential statistics consist of parametric statistical techniques such as the Pearson's correlation, Student's t-tests, or analysis of variance, and nonparametric statistical techniques like Spearman's *rho*, Mann-Whitney U, Wilcoxon signed ranks, and Kruskal-Wallis H tests, which are used to make generalizations about population characteristics by studying a sample selected from a given population. Researchers then make inferences from the statistics of a sample to the parameters of a population.

Statistics describe the characteristics of a sample selected from a population. They are symbolized by Roman letters. Example: $\overline{X}$ = mean, S^2 = variance, SD = standard deviation, and r = correlation coefficient.

---

[5]For more discussion on probability and nonprobability sampling methods, see Rubin & Babbie (2011).

Parameters describe the characteristics of the population from which a sample is drawn. They are symbolized by Greek letters. Example: μ (mu) = mean, σ^2 (sigma squared) = variance, σ (sigma) = standard deviation, and ρ (rho) = correlation coefficient.

CORRELATIONS BETWEEN TWO VARIABLES

Statistical analyses examine the relationships or correlations among independent and dependent variables. These relationships can be positive, negative, curvilinear, or no correlation.[6]

Positive (Direct) Correlation

A positive correlation occurs when an increase in the independent variable leads to an increase in the dependent variable, or a decrease in the independent variable leads to a decrease in the dependent variable. In other words, it occurs when both variables move in the same direction at the same time. For example, in the Elderly data file (see appendix A), the greater the level of emotional balance among the elderly is, the higher the level of self-esteem. This demonstrates a significant positive (direct) correlation between emotional balance and self-esteem (see figure 1.1).

Figure 1.1:   Scatterplot for Emotional Balance and Self-Esteem

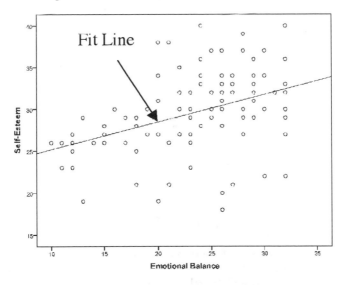

6Correlation between two variables does not necessarily indicate that one variable causes the other variable to occur. For conditions of causality, see chapter 7.

Figure 1.1 illustrates the relationship between emotional balance and self-esteem. The fit line runs from the lower left side to the upper right side, indicating a positive relationship.

Negative (Inverse) Correlation

A negative correlation occurs when an increase in the independent variable leads to a decrease in the dependent variable, or vice versa. In other words, both variables move in the opposite direction at the same time. For example, in the Elderly data file, the higher the level of emotional balance among the elderly, the lower the level of depression. This demonstrates a significant negative (inverse) correlation between emotional balance and depression (see figure 1.2).

Figure 1.2:   Scatterplot for Emotional Balance and Depression

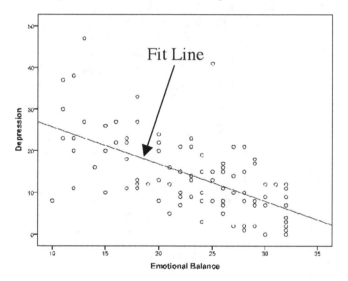

Figure 1.2 illustrates the relationship between emotional balance and depression. The fit line runs from the upper left side to the lower right side, indicating a negative relationship.

Curvilinear Correlation

A curvilinear correlation occurs when the relationship between the independent and dependent variables changes at certain levels. In other words, two variables could have a positive correlation at one time, but later become negative. For example, physical ability among individuals increases until a certain age and then it begins to decrease as they become older (see figure 1.3).

Figure 1.3: Scatterplot for Age and Physical Ability

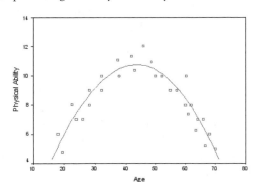

Figure 1.3 shows a curvilinear relation between age and physical ability. From birth until about the mid-forties the variables have a positive correlation, then the correlation is negative from about the mid-forties until death.

No Correlation

No correlation occurs when a change in the independent variable has no effect on the dependent variable. For example, in the Elderly data file, a change in the level of economic resources among the elderly neither increases their level of life satisfaction nor decreases it. This demonstrates that no significant correlation exists between the two variables (see figure 1.4).

Figure 1.4: Scatterplot for Economic Resources and Life Satisfaction

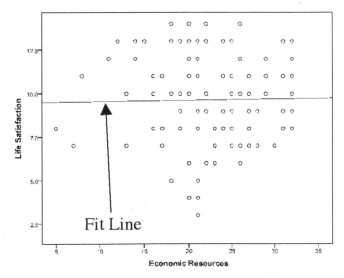

Figure 1.4 illustrates the relationship between economic resources and life satisfaction. The fit line runs parallel to the X axis, which indicates that no correlation exists between the two variables.

SUMMARY

This chapter defined the main research methodological terms used in data analysis. Data analysis employs a variety of statistical techniques to organize, summarize, and test hypotheses regarding relationships between dependent and independent variables at different levels of measurement.

Chapter 1 defined constants and variables, discussed different types of variables, and outlined levels of measurement. Null and alternative hypotheses, reliability and validity of instruments, the use of descriptive and inferential statistics, and types of relationships between variables were also discussed.

Chapter 2 will introduce SPSS and describe its role in data analysis. You will learn how to create an instrumentation codebook, start SPSS, and create variable names, labels, value categories, and SPSS templates, as well as the process of data cleaning, data recoding, and creating total scores. The chapter will end with a discussion of how to compute the Cronbach's alpha reliability coefficient for a scale.

PRACTICAL EXERCISE

Review a *current* empirical-research-based article in a professional social science/health care journal in your area of interest and answer the following questions. Attach the article along with your answers.

1. Summarize the article's main purpose, methods, and major findings.
2. What are the null and alternative hypotheses?
3. What are the independent and dependent variables under study?
4. What are their levels of measurement?
5. Which instrument(s) were used to measure the dependent variable(s)?
6. Discuss the reliability and validity of the instrument(s).
7. Discuss the statistical methods (descriptive or inferential) used to analyze the data.
8. Discuss the relationships among the dependent and independent variables and their directions.
9. Discuss the strengths and limitations of this study.
10. In your judgment, what could be done differently?

CHAPTER 2

Creating SPSS Data Files

LEARNING OBJECTIVES

1. Understand SPSS and syntax files
2. Understand how to create an instrumentation codebook
3. Understand how to start SPSS
4. Understand how to create variable names, labels, and value categories
5. Understand how to create SPSS templates
6. Understand the data cleaning process
7. Understand how to recode data
8. Understand how to compute total scores for a scale
9. Understand how to compute Cronbach's alpha for a scale

INTRODUCTION

Statistics has traditionally been a tough subject for social science and health care students (social work, psychology, sociology, nursing, etc.). Many experience anxiety about statistics, especially about memorizing mathematical formulas or using a paper and pencil to create graphs, calculate means, or compute complex analyses, such as correlation, analysis of variance, covariance, regression, or others.

Today, students still need to be able to do simple calculations, but most of the data analyses and statistical tests are conducted by computer programs. This means you can focus more on understanding the rationale for using a specific statistical test, utilize the computer to run the test statistic, and learn to read and make sense of the results, as well as understand the theoretical application of the test, while focusing less on memorizing the mathematical and statistical formulas. This technology reduces anxiety over statistics, and students are more apt to apply it in their practice.

Many computer programs are available for data analysis. They may be used for small data sets and simple calculations or for more advanced and complex analysis with larger data sets. The most popular computer program used in the social sciences is the Statistical Package for the Social Sciences (SPSS).[1] Other popular statistical software programs include SAS and Excel (Gilmore, 2004; SAS Publishing, 2001; Walkenbach, 2007).

This chapter introduces SPSS for Windows and SPSS syntax file. It discusses how to prepare data for entry in SPSS, start the program, and create variable names, labels, value categories, and templates. Chapter 2 also discusses how to enter data in SPSS, check data for errors, recode negative scores to positive scores, and compute total score for a particular scale. Finally, the chapter discusses how to compute a scale's reliability coefficient.

ABOUT THE SPSS PROGRAM

This book utilizes SPSS for Windows Version 18.0 as the main software to organize, describe, and analyze data. While some may use older versions of SPSS, most of the SPSS 18.0 commands discussed here are the same as those of SPSS 15.0 to 17.0. All SPSS syntax commands in this book still can be used with earlier versions of SPSS. Also, since the completion of this book, IBM has released SPSS Version 19.0. It is, however, identical to Version 18.0 except that it provides some extra options that do not impact our SPSS screens or discussion of how to utilize the SPSS in data analysis (e.g., SPSS 19.0 has an extra option for *Direct Marketing* in the main menu and *Bootstrap* in some dialog boxes). IBM SPSS Version 19.0 is used in chapters 10, 11, and 12 for clarification.

SPSS for Windows was chosen because it is a powerful statistics program that can run most bivariate and multivariate statistics. It is the most widely used statistical program in academic and professional organizations worldwide.

Like much Windows software (Microsoft Word, Excel, or PowerPoint, for example), SPSS for Windows has simple toolbar and dialog boxes that enable users to easily run most kinds of statistical analysis.

SPSS Main Toolbar

The SPSS main toolbar (see figure 2.1) provides easy access to all buttons and functions available in the SPSS program. Use the mouse to scroll up and down or click on the appropriate button to complete the analysis or employ any other function. The *File* menu allows users to open new and existing data files or SPSS syntax files, save files, and many other options.

Figure 2.1:   SPSS Version 18.0 Main Toolbar and Dialog Boxes

---

[1]When IBM acquired SPSS, Inc., in 2009, it changed SPSS to PASW (Predictive Analytics SoftWare). SPSS 19.0 was released under a new name, IBM SPSS Statistics 19.

To open a new data file, click on *File*, then on *New*, then on *Data*. A new SPSS "Data Editor" screen will open.

To open an existing SPSS data set, click on *File*, then on *Open*, then on *Data*. A new "Open Data" dialog box will open. In the *Look in* drop down menu, choose the directory where the data set is located, click on the file name, then on *Open*. This is the same method used to open a Word or PowerPoint file.

The *Analyze* menu allows users to run frequency tables; compare means; run correlations, regression, reliability, and nonparametric tests; and complete many other functions.

SPSS Syntax File

Another way to run statistical analysis in SPSS is using the SPSS syntax file.[2] This is the SPSS programming language, a text file composed of statistical commands that instruct the program to run a specific analysis. For example, you may instruct SPSS to run a frequency table for a specific variable, say gender, simply by typing the command frequency gender in the SPSS syntax text file (you must add a period at the end of each syntax; i.e., *frequency gender.*). This instructs SPSS to run a frequency table for the variable gender. You may also instruct SPSS to run a frequency table and measures of central tendency (see chapters 3 and 4) for age by typing this command in the SPSS syntax text file: *frequency age/statistics = mean, median, mode, sum.* This command (frequency) and subcommand (/statistics)[3] instruct SPSS to run a frequency table for age and the mean, median, mode, and sum for age.

Use of the SPSS syntax file is most appropriate when the same data are collected frequently from new subjects that require a new analysis. In this case, it is recommended to create and save a syntax file for the original data set and reuse it when new data are added. You may use the same syntax file commands with a different SPSS data set, but change the variable names. For example, you can use the above syntax (frequency age/statistics = mean, median, mode, sum) to request a frequency table and measures of central tendency for the variable "depression" from another data set. In this case, substitute "age" with "depression."

A third advantage (not available in the SPSS main toolbar) is that you can save all your functions in a syntax file. This enables you to add, edit, or rerun the analysis. A fourth advantage is that a syntax file created with SPSS Version 18.0, for example, can be used with SPSS Version 10.0, while the SPSS Version 10.0 main toolbar may not be the same as that of Version 18.0. You are able to use all syntax commands discussed in this book with earlier versions of SPSS. Finally, you can use SPSS syntax to run more advanced and complex statistics that can-

---

[2]The SPSS syntax file is not available in the SPSS Student Version.

[3]Each subcommand must start with a slash (/). Each command and subcommand must end with a period (.) and be in a separate line. All commands and subcommands can be lowercase or capitals. Variable names must be spelled exactly as they appear in the SPSS data file.

not be utilized using the SPSS main toolbar, such as canonical correlation analysis (Abu-Bader, 2010).

The SPSS main toolbar is the main method to run descriptive and inferential statistics and other analyses. The SPSS syntax commands for each function appear throughout the book, presented in boxes. To use them, this book illustrates how to open a new SPSS syntax file, type syntax commands, and run them.

CREATING AN INSTRUMENTATION CODEBOOK

Data are usually collected using existing instruments or instruments constructed specifically for a particular study. Participants in a study are asked either to write their answers for each question (open-ended question) or circle one or more answers that best describe their views or attitudes (closed-ended question) about specific issues. For example, the Welfare Survey (appendix B) asks participants to complete the month, day, and year for the question "When were you born?" It also asks them to circle male or female for "What is your gender?" and circle their race for the question "What is your race?"

For these three questions and those remaining, two things must happen before they can be entered into an SPSS file: each question must be given a name, and each categorical value (such as "male" and "female") must be given a numerical value. All questions, items, and categories included in any questionnaire must be given a code prior to data entry in SPSS.

Most statistical software is the same; that is, the first step in preparing data for entry in SPSS is creating an instrumentation codebook. This codebook consists of letters, numbers, or other characters that are then entered into an SPSS data file. For example, "What is your gender?" may be named "gender" or "sex," while "male" and "female" may be coded as "1" for male, and "2" for female. These codes follow guidelines set up by SPSS programmers.

SPSS Guidelines for Variable Names and Labels

1. Each question included in the questionnaire represents a variable that will be entered in SPSS.

2. Each variable should be given a name before it is entered in an SPSS file.

3. In SPSS 18.0 (also versions 12.0 and newer), variable names can be up to *sixty-four* characters. However, in older SPSS versions (11.0 and earlier), variable names cannot be more than eight characters.[4]

4. Each variable must have a different name.

5. Variable names must start with a letter. For example, the name VAR2 is acceptable, but 2VAR is not.

---

[4] If you try to open an SPSS file that was created with SPSS Version 18.0 or 19.0 using SPSS version 11 or earlier, only the first eight characters of the variable name will appear.

6. Variable names cannot include spaces, slashes [forward (/) or backward (\)], or hyphens (-). For example, variable names such as VAR 2, VAR/2, VAR\2, or VAR-2 are not acceptable.

7. Variable names can contain periods (.) and underscores (_). For example, VAR.2 and VAR_2 are acceptable.

8. Each name can be assigned a label that is not constrained to these conditions. Usually the labels are the same as the questions. In the SPSS data view screen, only the variable names are visible, yet it is easy to access the variable labels.

Value Categories

In chapter 1, we defined variables as concepts consisting of attributes (groups) that differ in quantity or quality among the subjects, events, or objects under study. Attributes identify categorical variables; for example, the attributes for gender are typically male and female, and the attributes for race are African American, white, Hispanic, Native American, and other. When attributes of a variable are expressed in words, they are called *value categories*.

Because quantitative statistical analysis is based on numerical values, all value categories must be converted into numerical values. For example, for a variable with two categories, you may assign "1" for the first category and "2" for the second category (1 = male, 2 = female). Or you may assign "0" for the first category and "1" for the second category (0 = male, 1 = female). Once you assign a value, you must consistently enter the same value category throughout the file.

Recommendations for value categories.   If the variable consists of two groups, assign "0" to one group and "1" to the other group. This is especially important in multiple regression analysis (see chapter 12), which requires that categorical variables and dichotomous variables (nominal variables with only two groups) be recoded to dummy variables, that is, "0" and "1." Also, when the value categories consist of negative and positive values such as "agree vs. do not agree," "yes vs. no," or "never vs. always," assign "0" to the negative value and "1" to the positive value (0 = Do not agree, 1 = Agree; 0 = No, 1 = Yes; 0 = Never, 1 = Always, etc.).

If the variable consists of more than two groups, assign "1" to the first group, "2" to the second group, "3" to the third group, and so on. You may use "0" later on if you want to compare one group versus all the others. In this case, you may recode all other groups to "0" and the other group to "1." For example, let's say that the variable race was coded as 1 = White, 2 = African American, 3 = Native American, 4 = Asian, and 5 = Other. Now you are interested in comparing whites versus all other groups. In this case, you may recode "2," "3," "4," and "5" to "0," and keep White as "1." If you were interested in comparing African Americans versus all others, then you may recode "1," "3," "4," and "5" to "0," and "2" (African Americans) to "1."

Identification Numbers

Each questionnaire should be assigned an ID number. This is especially important in case an error occurs during data entry in SPSS (for example, you accidentally enter "99" instead of "9," or "0" instead of "1"). If participants provide their Social Security numbers or phone numbers, then you may use these numbers as ID numbers. If no ID numbers were provided, you may create your own. Say you collected data from two hundred subjects; you may assign ID numbers starting from 001 to 200. Although it is only for identification purpose, ID will be entered in the SPSS file and will be treated as a variable.

You may use ID numbers to go back to the instrument, locate, and correct the errors. For example, in a study that examines depression among three hundred elderly people who are sixty-five years of age or older, you notice that the age of one subject is forty-five. By finding the ID number for this subject, you can go back to that instrument and check the age, and if the subject is indeed forty-five, you may decide to delete that entry from the analysis, because the study covers only age sixty-five or older.

PRACTICAL EXAMPLE

The instrument in appendix B is used as an example to create variable names, value categories, labels, and assign missing values. The instrument was sent to two hundred former welfare recipients in Prince George's County, Maryland. Of two hundred, 107 completed and returned the instruments. No Social Security or other identification numbers were collected. The following describes the process for preparing the instrumentation codebook.

For the purpose of data entry, a new variable called "ID" is created for each instrument. This ID number will range from 1 to 107 (total number of completed surveys).

Using SPSS guidelines previously discussed, assign a variable name for each question. It is recommended to designate a name that is easy to remember. Then, assign value categories for categorical variables, such as gender, race, level of education, and so on. Table 2.1 summarizes the variable names and value categories for all items in appendix B.

STARTING THE SPSS PROGRAM

Starting SPSS may differ from one computer to another. It will also depend on the Windows configurations set up by the administrator for computers where SPSS is installed. There are two ways to access SPSS.

Table 2.1:   Welfare Survey—Instrumentation Key

Question/Label	Variable Name	Value Categories, if any
ID #	ID	none (ID ranges between 1 and 107)
When were you born?	DOB	mm/dd/yy: two digits for the month/two digits for the day/and two digits for the year (example: July 1, 2002 = 07/01/02). Although you may choose a different format (e.g., dd-mm-yyyy), you must stay consistent with whatever format you choose.
What is your gender?	Gender	0 = Male 1 = Female
What race are you?	Race	1 = African-American 2 = Asian or Pacific Islander 3 = Hispanic 4 = Native American 5 = White 6 = Mix or multiracial 7 = Other, (Please specify):
How many years of education do you have?	Educat	No value categories are needed for variables measured at the interval or ratio level of measurement.
Do you receive government assistance to help pay for your housing?	House	0 = No 1 = Yes
a. IF YES, what type of housing assistance?	House_A (indicating it depends on the previous item)	1 = Section 8 2 = Public housing 3 = Other, (Please specify):
How would you describe your physical health?	P_Health (P for physical)	1 = Excellent 2 = Very good 3 = Good 4 = Fair 5 = Poor
CESD Scale: (The next 20 items represent the CESD scale. In this case we will assign CESD1 for the first item, CESD2 for the second item, until CESD20)	CESD1 CESD2 .... CESD20	0 = Rarely or none of the time 1 = Some or a little of the time 2 = Occasionally 3 = Most or all of the time *These values apply for all 20 items.*

1. In Windows, click on *Start*, click on *All Programs*, click on *SPSS Inc*, and click on *PASW 18.0 Statistics* or *IBM SPSS Statistics 19* (or follow the same steps if you have an earlier version of SPSS).

2. If there is an SPSS shortcut icon on the desktop, double-click on the icon.

These steps will open a new SPSS spreadsheet called "SPSS Data Editor" (see screen 2.1.A). Depending on the computer configuration, a dialog box called "PASW Statistics 18.0" will open (see screen 2.1.B) or "IBM SPSS Statistics" (if you use SPSS 19.0). If this dialog box opens, click on *Cancel* to close it. (You may check *Don't show this dialog in the future*, see screen 2.1.C). There are two tabs in the lower left corner of the SPSS spreadsheet: *Data View* and *Variable View* (see screen 2.1.D). These tabs allow you to switch between the data view screen and variable view screen.

Screen 2.1:   SPSS Data Editor Main Dialog Box

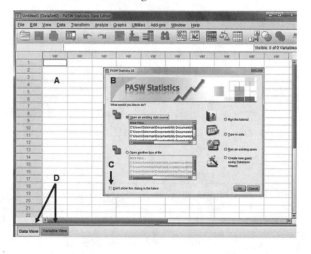

Variable View

Before entering data in the SPSS spreadsheet, first define the variables in the study. Transfer the information created in the instrumentation codebook to the variable view screen (see screen 2.2) by clicking on the *Variable View* tab.

Each row in the variable view screen represents a variable; each column represents a variable property, which allows you to define and edit all variables in the study, according to their type (numeric, date, string, and so on), width, decimals, label, value (for categories), missing values, column width, alignment, and level of measurement.

The following describes the steps for creating variable names and their properties for the instrument described in table 2.1:

Screen 2.2:   SPSS Variable View Dialog Box

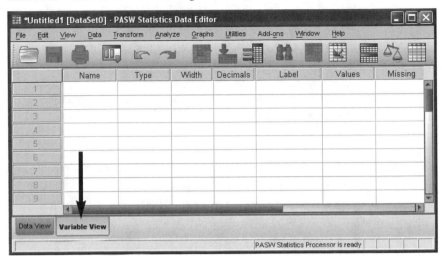

1. ID: To enter the first variable name in the codebook, double-click on the first row under "Name," type "ID", and click on *Tab* (or *Enter*) on the keyboard.

    a. Double-click on the gray box under "Type" (first row). The default for *Type* in SPSS is *numeric*. Because ID is a numeric (1 to 107), leave as is and click *OK*.

    b. The default for *Width* is "8." Only the first eight characters of the variable name will be visible. ID numbers in this case have a maximum of three characters (001 to 107). If necessary, change this to more or less than eight. Here, keep all variables at eight characters.

    c. The default for *Decimals* is "2." Only the first two decimal places of the variable value will be visible. For example, a zero value will appear as .00 and 3.7522 will appear as 3.75. If necessary, change *Decimals* to more or less than two. Keep the decimals at two places.

    d. Double-click on the first box under "Label" to type a label for a variable. Because it is clear what ID stands for, there is no need to create a label for ID; leave this box empty.

    e. There is no need to create *Values* or assign *Missing data* for ID. (SPSS treats empty cells as missing by default.)

    f. To change the column for ID (SPSS default is 8), click on the first box under "Columns" and click the up arrow to increase the width or down arrow to decrease it. Columns represent the number of digits or characters that will be visible in the data view screen. If you change *Columns* to 3, then only the first three digits or characters for the variable will be visible. Leave this box as the default.

g. To align data for ID, click on the first box under "Align" and click on the down button to align data to the left, right, or center. By default, all information will be aligned right.

h. Because ID is used here to identify subjects, treat it as a nominal variable. To replace *Scale* (SPSS default), click on the first box under "Measure," and click on *Nominal*. Notice that there are three levels of measurement: nominal, ordinal, and scale (interval or higher).

2. DOB: To enter the second variable name, double-click on the second row under *Name*, type "DOB", and hit the tab key.

a. Double-click on the second row under "Type." Because this is a date, change *Numeric* (SPSS default) to *Date*.

b. Click on the gray box next to *Numeric*. A new dialog box called "Variable Type" will open (see screen 2.3).

c. Select *Date*. A list of formats will open. Find and click on the one you preselected. Click on *mm/dd/yy* and click on *OK* (notice that *Type* for DOB has changed to *Date*).

d. Leave default for remaining cells as is.

Screen 2.3:   SPSS Variable Type Dialog Box

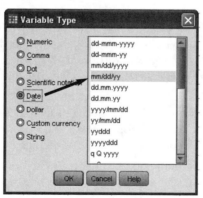

3. Gender: To enter the third variable name, double-click on the third row under "Name," type "Gender", and press tab on the keyboard.

a. Double-click on the third row under "Type." Because this is a numeric variable (0 = male, 1 = female), leave *Type* as is.

b. Leave default for *Width* as "8."

c.   Double-click on the third row under *Decimals*. You can type "0", or use the up and down arrows to change the "2" to "0". We will change this to "0" because if we leave it, any value that is "0" will appear as ".00". (We may leave it as is . . . this will not affect any of the analyses).

d.   There is no need to create a label for gender.

e.   Because gender is a nominal level of measurement, assign value categories. The values for gender are 0 = male and 1 = female. To assign value categories, click on the third row under *Values* and click on the gray box next to *None* (SPSS default).

f.   A new dialog box called "Value Labels" will open (see screen 2.4).

Screen 2.4:   SPSS Value Labels Dialog Box

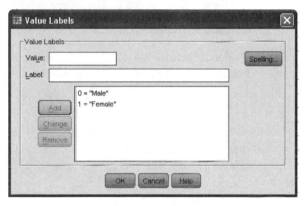

g.   Type "0" in the *Value* box and type "male" in the *Label* box.

h.   Click on *Add* to confirm the assignment of "0" for male. Click on *Add* each time you add or edit a label.

i.   Type "1" in the *Value* box, type "female" in the *Label* box, and click on *Add* to confirm the assignment of "1" for female.

j.   Click on *OK*.

k.   MISSING: By default, SPSS for Windows treats empty boxes as missing cases. You do not need to create missing values. However, some researchers may assign values such as "9," "99," "999," or something else, to represent missing data. To assign missing values for Gender, click on the third row under *Missing* and click on the gray box next to *None*. A new dialog box called "Missing Values" will open (see screen 2.5).

l.   Check *Discrete missing values*.

m.   Type "9", "99", "999", or whatever you choose.

n. Click on *OK*.

o. Gender is a nominal variable. Under the "Measure" column, change the level of measurement from *Scale* to *Nominal* (as discussed above).

Screen 2.5:   SPSS Missing Values Dialog Box

4. Race: To enter the fourth variable name, double-click on the fourth box under "Name," type "Race", and press the tab key on the keyboard.

a. Leave the default for *Type*, *Width*, *Decimals*, and *Label* as is.

b. Click on the fourth row under *Values* and click on the gray box. A new dialog box called "Value Labels" will open (see screen 2.6).

c. Type "1" in the *Value* box, type "African American" in the *Label* box, and click on *Add* to confirm the assignment of "1" for African American.

d. Repeat step c to assign values to all other races.

e. Click on *OK*.

Screen 2.6:   SPSS Value Labels Dialog Box

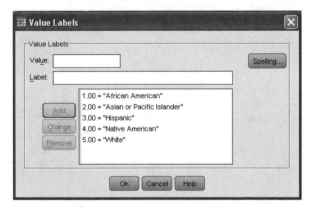

f. You may leave *Missing* as is or assign values as discussed above.

g. Change *Scale* to *Nominal* under *Measure*.

5. Educat: To enter the fifth variable name, double-click on the fifth row under *Name*, type "Educat", and hit tab on the keyboard.

    a. Leave the default for *Type*, *Width*, and *Decimals* as is.

    b. Double-click on the fifth row under *Label* and type "Number of years of education". This will serve as a label for the variable Educat.

    c. Assigning value categories is inappropriate because this is a continuous variable, interval, or higher level of measurement. (Subjects can have any number of years of education.)

    d. Because education is measured here at the ratio level (interval or higher), leave *Scale* as is under "Measure."

6. House: Use the same steps used for Gender to create this variable. It is important to create a label for this variable because there are too many interpretations for House. For example, you may label it as "Receive government assistance to pay for housing."

7. House_A: Repeat the same steps to create this variable. You may label it as "If yes to House, what type of assistance?"

8. P_Health: Repeat the same steps used in Race to create a variable name for P_Health. You may need to add a label, such as "How would you describe your physical health?"

9. CESD Scale. For the next twenty items, start by typing "CESD1" in the ninth row under "Name" and "CESD2" in the tenth box under "Name." Continue in this manner until you type "CESD20" in the twenty-eighth row.

10. Double-click in the *Values* box associated with CESD1 (ninth row under "Values") to create value categories for CESD1. Use the same steps used for Gender or Race to create these labels.

11. After creating values for CESD1, click on the box containing these values (ninth box under "Values").

12. Click on the right mouse button and select *Copy*.

13. While holding the left mouse button, click on the *Values* box for CESD2 and scroll down until you reach the *Values* box for CESD20. This will highlight all the *Values* boxes for CESD items 2 to 20.

14. Point the mouse anywhere in the highlighted area, click on the right mouse button, and select *Paste*. This will paste values to all selected items. This function is called *SPSS template*. It simplifies the process for creating value categories, especially when many items have the same one. Items don't have to appear in order. You can copy and paste value categories anywhere in variable view (see screen 2.7).

15. Save your work often.

Screen 2.7:   SPSS Variable View File

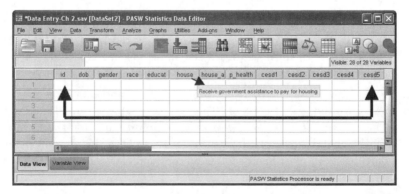

	Name	Type	Width	Decimals	Label	Values	Missing	Columns	Align	Measure
1	id	Numeric	8	2		None	None	8	Right	Nominal
2	dob	Date	8	0		None	None	8	Right	Nominal
3	gender	Numeric	9	0		{0, Male}...	9, 99, 999	5	Right	Nominal
4	race	Numeric	8	2		{1.00, African-Am...	None	6	Right	Nominal
5	educat	Numeric	8	2	Number of year...	None	None	7	Right	Scale
6	house	Numeric	8	2	Receive govern...	{.0, No}...	None	8	Right	Nominal
7	hous_a	Numeric	8	2	If yes to HOUS...	{1.00, Section 8}...	None	8	Right	Nominal
8	p_health	Numeric	8	2	How would you ...	{1.00, Excellent}...	None	8	Right	Ordinal
9	cesd1	Numeric	8	2		{.0, Rarely or non...	None	8	Right	Ordinal
10	cesd2	Numeric	8	2		{.0, Rarely or non...	None	8	Right	Ordinal
11	cesd3	Numeric	8	2		{.0, Rarely or non...	None	8	Right	Ordinal
12	cesd4	Numeric	8	2		{.0, Rarely or non...	None	8	Right	Ordinal
13	cesd5	Numeric	8	2		{.0, Rarely or non...	None	8	Right	Ordinal

Data View

The next step is to enter all data collected from participants. Click on the *Data View* tab at the lower left corner in the main SPSS screen (see screen 2.7). A new spreadsheet with all the variable names, starting with ID and ending with CESD20 will appear in the top row (see screen 2.8). In SPSS data view, each row represents a single case or a single observation, and each column represents a variable or an item being measured. To view the label for a specific variable, point the mouse on the specific variable name but don't click on it. For example, to view the label for House, pointing the mouse on House will cause the label to appear (see screen 2.8). Double-clicking on the variable will open variable view for this and other variables.

Screen 2.8:   SPSS Data View Screen

The following describes steps for data entry in SPSS:

1. Enter the ID number for the first case in the first row under "ID." Order is not important in data entry. That is, you may first enter case number 15, then number 11, followed by 3, and so on. Let us start with case number 3.

2. Enter "3" in the first row under "ID." Once a value is entered in the first row and first column (ID), all columns associated with this case fill with dots (.). These dots (SPSS default) represent missing values and will remain missing unless they are replaced with valid data; otherwise, they will be excluded from future analysis.

3. Click on the first row under "DOB." Type, for example, "02/28/85" in the first box under "DOB." If the date does not appear, check that you are using the format you chose for *Date*.

4. If case number 3 is female, type "1" in the first row under "Gender."

5. Enter remaining data for case number 3.

6. Save your work after each case.

7. Enter data for your next subject, for example, case number 7.

8. After finishing this data entry, you may sort cases by ID (or any other format). Click on *Data* on the SPSS main toolbar, scroll down, and click on *Sort Cases*. A new dialog box called "Sort Cases" will open. Click on *ID*, and click on the arrow between the two boxes to move *ID* under *Sort by*.

9. Click on *OK*. This will sort cases by ID number; case number 3 will be first, followed by case number 5, and so on (see screen 2.9).

10. You can also sort cases by ID (or any other variable) simply by clicking on *ID* to highlight the entire column, right-click on the mouse, and click on *Sort Ascending* (or *Sort Descending*).

Screen 2.9:   SPSS Data View File

	id	dob	gender	race	educat	house	house_a	p_health	cesd1	cesd2	cesd3	cesd4	cesd5	cesd6	ces
1	3.00	02/28/78	1	2.00	12.00	.0	1.00	4.00	3.00	2.00	3.00	2.00	1.00	.0	
2	5.00	03/12/76	0	4.00	10.00	1.00	3.00	1.00	1.00	1.00	2.00	1.00	2.00	1.00	1
3	7.00	10/10/83	1	3.00	8.00	.0	.	2.00	.0	.0	.0	.0	.0	.0	
4	11.00	11/12/80	0	1.00	10.00	1.00	1.00	3.00	2.00	2.00	1.00	2.00	3.00	2.00	2
5	14.00	07/07/75	2	1.00	7.00	1.00	2.00	3.00	1.00	3.00	1.00	2.00	2.00	2.00	2
6															

Data View   Variable View

PASW Statistics Processor is ready

Data Cleaning

Sometimes, especially if you have a large sample size, you may make errors in data entry. For example, your intention is to click on "0" (male) for Gender, but you click on "9" because it is nearby on the keyboard. Or you may enter "4" instead of "3" for CESD items. Errors will significantly affect your analysis, so it is necessary to clean your data before conducting any descriptive or inferential analyses. The following describes steps for data cleaning:

1. Run frequencies for all variables in the study. Click *Analyze* in the SPSS main toolbar, click *Descriptive Statistics*, and then click *Frequencies* (see screen 2.10).

Screen 2.10:   SPSS Analyze Toolbar

2. A new dialog box called "Frequencies" will open (see screen 2.11). While holding the left mouse button down, click on *ID* in the variables list box (left box), scroll down, and highlight all variables. You may also clean them one by one or every five variables, especially if you have many variables. Click on the arrow button between the two boxes to move variables into the *Variable(s)* box. Make sure the *Display frequency tables box* is checked (SPSS default).

3. Click on *OK*.

Screen 2.11:   SPSS Frequencies Dialog Box

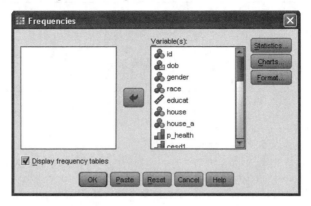

SPSS frequencies output.   The following is the SPSS output displaying the frequencies for all variables. Because the process for data cleaning is the same, we will only check frequency tables for ID (see table 2.2), DOB (see table 2.3), Gender (see table 2.4), and CESD10 (see table 2.5).

This study requires a different ID number for each case. Table 2.2 shows that no duplicate ID numbers exist, thus indicating no errors in ID.

If participation in the study was limited to welfare recipients eighteen years or older, then the latest year of birth should be 1992. Anyone born after 1992 should not be included in this study. Table 2.3 shows that the youngest person

Table 2.2:   Frequency Table for ID

		Frequency	Percent	Valid Percent	Cumulative Percent
Valid	3.00	1	20.0	20.0	20.0
	5.00	1	20.0	20.0	40.0
	7.00	1	20.0	20.0	60.0
	11.00	1	20.0	20.0	80.0
	14.00	1	20.0	20.0	100.0
	Total	5	100.0	100.0	

Table 2.3:   Frequency Table for Date of Birth (DOB)

		Frequency	Percent	Valid Percent	Cumulative Percent
Valid	07/07/75	1	20.0	20.0	20.0
	03/12/76	1	20.0	20.0	40.0
	02/28/78	1	20.0	20.0	60.0
	11/12/80	1	20.0	20.0	80.0
	10/10/83	1	20.0	20.0	100.0
	Total	5	100.0	100.0	

Table 2.4:   Frequency Table for Gender

		Frequency	Percent	Valid Percent	Cumulative Percent
Valid	0 male	2	40.0	40.0	40.0
	1 female	2	40.0	40.0	80.0
	2	1	20.0	20.0	100.0
	Total	5	100.0	100.0	

in the study was born in 1983 (twenty-seven years old), which indicates that DOB entries are accurate.

Gender was coded "0" for male and "1" for female. Any value that is neither "0" nor "1" (unless it is a missing value) is inaccurate and must be corrected.

Table 2.4 shows that two participants were male, two were female, and one was labeled "2," thus indicating an error. To clean the error, follow these steps:

1. Open the SPSS data view file.
2. Click on the variable *Gender*. This will highlight all data in this category.
3. Click on *Edit* in the SPSS main toolbar.
4. Scroll down and select *Find*. A new dialog box called "Find and Replace - Data View Column: Gender" will open (see screen 2.12).
5. Type "2" in the box labeled *Find* and click *Find Next*.

Screen 2.12:   SPSS Find and Replace Dialog Box

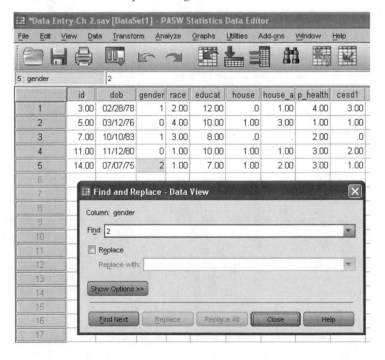

Table 2.5:   Frequency Table for CESD10

		Frequency	Percent	Valid Percent	Cumulative Percent
Valid	.00 Rarely or none of the time	1	20.0	20.0	20.0
	1.00 Some or a little of the time	1	20.0	20.0	40.0
	2.00 Occasionally	1	20.0	20.0	60.0
	3.00 Most or all of the time	1	20.0	20.0	80.0
	4.00	1	20.0	20.0	100.0
	Total	5	100.0	100.0	

6. The number "2" under Gender will appear.

7. Find the case number associated with this "2," in this case, ID number 14.

8. Go back to instrument number 14 and confirm the gender for this participant. Let us say it was female.

9. Return to SPSS data view file and double-click on "2," delete it, and type "1".

10. Save your file. Repeat steps if there are other errors under Gender.

CESD items were coded as "0," "1," "2," or "3." As with Gender, any other value is inaccurate and will need to be corrected.

Table 2.5 presents the frequency for CESD10. It shows one participant with a score of 4. This score is outside the possible range, and represents an error. To clean this error, follow the same steps used to clean Gender.

Finally, because data entry is so time-consuming and computer failure is always possible, it is recommended that you save the clean SPSS data file in the hard drive as well as on an external drive or disk.

Recoding Values

A scale is a set of items where some items are positively worded and others are negatively worded. For example, the CESD scale (appendix B) is used as a screening tool to gauge frequency of depressive symptoms in the preceding week. The scale consists of twenty items measured on a four-point Likert scale. Of them, items number 4, 8, 12, and 16 ("I felt that I was just as good as other people," "I felt hopeful about the future," "I was happy," and "I enjoyed life") are positively worded: higher scores in these items indicate less depression, while higher scores in the remaining sixteen items indicate greater depression. To be sure all items indicate the same direction (that higher scores indicate greater depression), the scores for items 4, 8, 12, and 16 must be reversed before any further statistical analysis. In this case, reverse a score of 3 to 0, 2 to 1, 1 to 2, and 0 to 3. This procedure is referred to in SPSS as Recode.

Two methods may be used to run SPSS commands: SPSS main toolbar and SPSS syntax file.

1.   To use the SPSS main toolbar to recode values of above items, follow these steps:

    a.   Open the SPSS data file with the variable(s) you wish to recode.

    b.   Click on *Transform* and scroll down to *Recode into Same Variables* (see screen 2.13).

Screen 2.13:   SPSS Transform-Recode Dialog Box

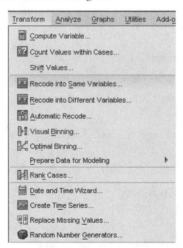

    c.   A new dialog box called "Recode into Same Variables" will open (see screen 2.14). From the variables list in the left box, scroll down and click on *CESD4*, then click on the arrow button to move it into the *Numeric Variables* box.

Screen 2.14:   SPSS Recode into Same Variable Dialog Box

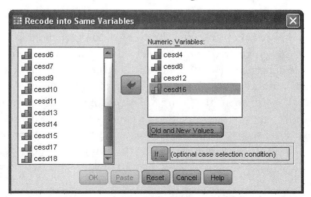

d.   Repeat step c to move CESD8, CESD12, and CESD16.

e.   Click on *Old and New Values*. A new dialog box called "Recode into Same Variables: Old and New Values" will open (see screen 2.15).

f.   Type "3" in the *Value* box under "Old Value." Type "0" in the *Value* box under "New Value."

g.   Click on *Add* to confirm this recode. This will transfer the old and new values in the *Old . . . New* box.

h.   Repeat steps f and g to recode "1" to "2", "2" to "1", and "3" to "0".

i.   Also, click on *System-missing* under "Old Value" and "New Value," and click on *Add* to keep missing values as is.

j.   Click on *Continue*, and then click on *OK*.

Screen 2.15:   SPSS Recode into Same Variable Dialog Box

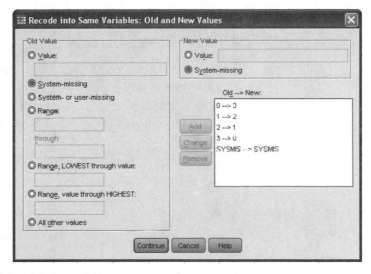

2.   To use the SPSS syntax file, follow these steps:

a.   Open the SPSS data file that contains the variable(s) you wish to recode.

b.   Click on *File* in the SPSS main toolbar and click on *New*.

c.   Click on *Syntax* (see screen 2.16). A new SPSS syntax file will open.

d.   Type the following SPSS syntax exactly:

RECODE CESD4 CESD8 CESD12 CESD16 (0 = 3) (1 = 2) (2 = 1) (3 = 0).

e.   Highlight this syntax.

Screen 2.16:   SPSS Syntax Main Toolbar

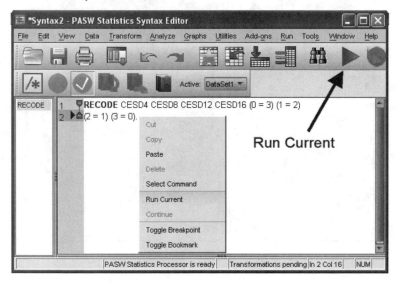

f.   Click on the right mouse button and click on *Run Current* (see screen 2.17). You may also click on the arrow button on the toolbar at the top right of the screen.

Screen 2.17:   SPSS Syntax Screen

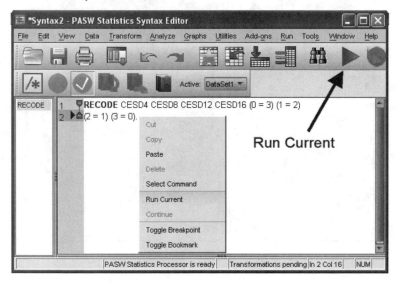

After all recodes are completed, save this file in a new SPSS data file (for example, SPSS Welfare Analysis). This ensures that you have access to two files: the original SPSS raw data file and the new SPSS data file on which future analysis will be conducted.

Remember: You can use the *Recode* function to combine groups, change categorical values, and other changes. For example, if Race was defined as 1 = White, 2 = African American, 3 = Hispanic, 4 = Native American, you can compare whites against all others by creating a new variable using the *Recode* function. Recode "2," "3," and "4" to "0" (0 = Non-Whites) and keep "1" (Whites) as "1" in a new variable (for example, Race_Rec). The syntax file for this would read as follows:

> RECODE RACE (1 = 1) (2 = 0) (3 = 0) (4 = 0) INTO RACE_REC.
> EXECUTE.

Computing a Total Score for Scale

Many social constructs are measured using a scale, which is a set of items or questions. The scores for these items are generally summed to generate a total score for the specific construct. For example, the potential total score for the CESD scale ranges from 0 to 60, where higher scores indicate greater levels of depression. A score of 16 is generally used as a cutoff score, indicating high levels of symptoms, or clinical depression. Researchers may collect information on multiple items to measure depression, but they are usually most interested in the total score.

Like most SPSS functions, you can use the SPSS main toolbar or the SPSS syntax file to compute a total score. To compute the total score for the CESD in our example, follow these two methods:

1. To use the SPSS main toolbar, follow these steps:

    a. Open the SPSS data file that contains the scale items you wish to tally to compute a total score.

    b. Click on *Transform* (see screen 2.13 above).

    c. Click on *Compute Variable*. A new dialog box called "Compute Variable" will open (see screen 2.18).

    d. Type the name of the new variable you want to create in the *Target Variable* box in the upper left corner of the "Compute Variable" dialog box. In this case, name it CESD.

    e. Under *Function Group* (see screen 2.18.A) click on *All*. Scroll down under *Functions and Special Variables* (see screen 2.18.B) and click on *SUM*.

    f. Click on the arrow button next to *Functions and Special Variables* (see screen 2.18.C) to move this function into the *Numeric Expression* box (see screen 2.18.D).

    g. Scroll down under *Type & Label* (see screen 2.18.E) and highlight CESD1.

    h. Click on the arrow button in the right side of *Type & Label* (see screen 2.18.F) to move CESD1 to replace the first "?" in the *Numeric Expression* box.

    i. Repeat steps g and h to replace the second "?" with CESD2.

    j. Repeat these steps until you have moved all twenty CESD variables.

    k. Make sure there is a comma (,) between each CESD item (see screen 2.18).

    l. Click on *OK*.

Screen 2.18:   SPSS Compute Variable Dialog Box

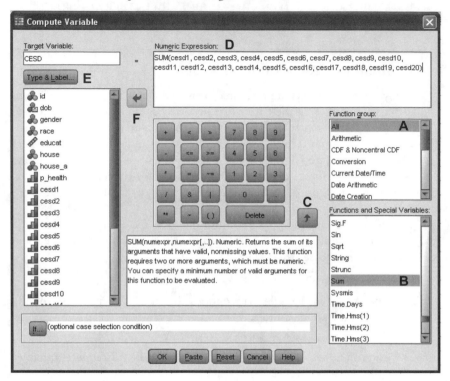

2.   To use the SPSS syntax file to compute a total score, follow these steps:

   a.   Open the SPSS data file that contains the scale items you wish to tally
        to compute a total score.

   b.   Click on *File* in the SPSS main toolbar.

   c.   Click on *New* and click on *Syntax* to open a new SPSS syntax file.

   d.   Type the following syntax exactly:

        COMPUTE CESD = SUM (CESD1, CESD2, CESD3, CESD4, CESD5,
        CESD6, CESD7, CESD8, CESD9, CESD10, CESD11, CESD12,
        CESD13, CESD14, CESD15, CESD16, CESD17, CESD18, CESD19,
        CESD20).

        EXECUTE.

        Note: If all items to be summed are sorted in order in the SPSS data
        view screen and no other items are between them, simply type:

        COMPUTE CESD = SUM (CESD1 TO CESD20).

        EXECUTE.

   e.   Highlight this syntax.

   f.   Click on the right mouse button and click on *Run Current*. You may
        also click on the arrow button located in the toolbar at the top of the
        screen (see screen 2.17 above).

Both SPSS methods will create and add a new variable called CESD to the SPSS data file. This file will be located in the last column in the data view screen (see screen 2.19).

Screen 2.19:   SPSS Data View File

Computing Cronbach's Alpha Reliability for Scale

While reliability analysis is beyond the scope of this book, we will demonstrate how to examine the Cronbach's alpha (see chapter 1) for a particular scale. Recall that reliability issues must be addressed during the research design process and selecting a measurement instrument. Thus, at this stage of the research process, data analysis, it is assumed that the instrument chosen has been used by others and has shown some reliability. Some instruments, however, may not be as reliable in the study as in the original studies for which they were designed. Therefore, it is recommended that the internal reliability consistency coefficient among items for each scale in the study be examined.

How to compute Cronbach's Alpha in SPSS.   Before you run reliability analysis, data need to be error-free, and all negative items must be recoded as discussed above. To examine the Cronbach's alpha coefficient for the CESD scale in our example, follow these two methods:

1. To use the SPSS main toolbar, follow these steps:
    a. Open the SPSS data file that contains the scale items you wish to compute the reliability coefficient.
    b. Click on *Analyze*, click on *Scale*, and then click on *Reliability Analysis* (see screen 2.20). A new dialog box called "Reliability Analysis" will open (see screen 2.21).
    c. Scroll down in the *Variables List* box and highlight CESD1.
    d. While holding down the *Control* button on the keyboard, click on *CESD2, CESD3, . . . , CESD20*. This highlights all CESD items.

Screen 2.20:   SPSS Analyze-Scale Reliability Dialog Box

Analyze	Graphs	Utilities	Add-ons	Window	Help

Reports	▶
Descriptive Statistics	▶
Tables	▶
Compare Means	▶
General Linear Model	▶
Generalized Linear Models	▶
Mixed Models	▶
Correlate	▶
Regression	▶
Loglinear	▶
Classify	▶
Dimension Reduction	▶
Scale	▶
Nonparametric Tests	▶
Forecasting	▶
Survival	▶
Multiple Response	▶

cesd8	cesd9	cesd10	cesd11
.0	.0	4.00	3.00
2.00	.0	.0	.0
1.00	1.00	1.00	1.00
3.00	3.00	3.00	1.00
3.00	2.00	2.00	2.00

Reliability Analysis...

Multidimensional Unfolding (PREFSCAL)...

Multidimensional Scaling (PROXSCAL)...

Multidimensional Scaling (ALSCAL)...

e.   Click on the middle arrow to move all twenty items in the *Items* box.

f.   Make sure that *Alpha* appears in the *Model* box. This is the Cronbach's alpha reliability coefficient. If not, click on the drop down arrow in the *Model* box and choose *Alpha*. (You may choose other methods of reliability, such as Split-half reliability).

g.   Type a scale name in the *Scale Label* box (for example: CESD - Depression Scale) (see screen 2.21).

h.   Click on *OK*.

Screen 2.21:   SPSS Reliability Analysis Dialog Box

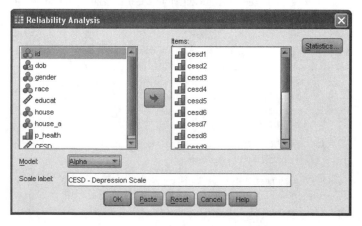

2.   To use the SPSS syntax file to compute a reliability coefficient, follow these steps:

    a.   Open the SPSS data file that contains the scale items you wish to tally to compute a reliability coefficient.

    b.   Click on *File* in the SPSS main toolbar.

    c.   Click on *New* and click on *Syntax* to open a new SPSS syntax file.

    d.   Type the following syntax exactly:

RELIABILITY

/VARIABLES=CESD1 CESD2 CESD3 CESD4 CESD5 CESD6 CESD7 CESD8 CESD9 CESD10 CESD11 CESD12 CESD13 CESD14 CESD15 CESD16 CESD17 CESD18 CESD19 CESD20

/SCALE ('CESD - DEPRESSION SCALE') ALL

/MODEL=ALPHA.

Both of these methods produce two output tables, table 2.6 and table 2.7.

Table 2.6 displays the number of valid cases (n = 4), number of cases excluded due to missing value(s) (n = 1), and total number in the study (N = 5). Note, this is only an example, and ideally the sample size generally is larger than five cases and depends on a number of criteria (see chapter 6).

Table 2.7 reports the Cronbach's alpha reliability coefficient for the CESD scale utilized in our study and the number of items composing the scale. In this example, the Cronbach's alpha coefficient is .86 (.856), indicating an excellent internal consistency reliability among the twenty items (N of Items) composing the CESD scale (see chapter 1). *Note*: If the reliability coefficient was low, a negative value, or cannot be computed, check data for errors and check if all

Table 2.6:   Case Processing Summary Table

	Case Processing Summary		
		N	%
Cases	Valid	4	80.0
	Excluded[a]	1	20.0
	Total	5	100.0

a. Listwise deletion based on all variables in the procedure.

Table 2.7:   Reliability Analysis

Reliability Statistics	
Cronbach's Alpha	N of Items
.856	20

negative items were recoded properly. If problem continues to exist, check items for content flaws.

SUMMARY

This chapter introduced the SPSS program, SPSS main toolbar, and SPSS syntax file. The chapter discussed the importance of creating an instrumentation code-book prior to data entry. This codebook defines variable names, types, and labels, and assigns numerical codes for categorical values.

The process of transferring these codes in SPSS files using two SPSS com-puter screens was described. The variable view screen shows where variables and their categories are defined and edited, and the data view screen is where data are entered.

Next, the chapter discussed the importance and the practical steps for data cleaning, recoding items, and computing total scores for a scale. Finally, chapter 2 discussed how to compute the internal reliability consistency coefficient in SPSS.

Chapter 3 presents methods for organizing and summarizing data. The chapter will discuss frequency tables and graphs, including the bar graph, his-togram, and stem-and-leaf, and how to use SPSS to create frequency tables and graphs.

PRACTICAL EXERCISE

A mental health researcher was interested in the levels of self-esteem among first-(not U.S. born) and second-generation (U.S. born) older immigrants from Africa, the Middle East, and Asia. For this purpose, the researcher collected data from a random sample of forty subjects who identified themselves as either first- or second-generation immigrants. All participants were asked to answer six per-sonal and demographic variables (D1 to D6):

1. D1: Age, actual age.

2. D2: Gender: M = male, and F = female.

3. D3: Ethnicity: AF = African, ME = Middle Eastern, AS = Asian.

4. D4: U.S. born: Y = yes, N = no.

5. D5: Health in general: How would you rate your physical health? 1 = Very Poor, 2 = Poor, 3 = Fair, 4 = Good, 5 = Very Good.

6. D6: Education: What is your highest level of education? GD = Graduate Degree, CD = College Degree, HS = High School Diploma.

Participants also were asked to complete the Rosenberg Self-Esteem Scale (appendix C). This scale consists of ten items (E1 to E10), where participants rated their general feelings about each item on a four-point Likert scale (1 = strongly disagree, 2 = disagree, 3 = agree, and 4 = strongly agree). E1, E3, E4, E7, and E10 were positively worded, and all others were negatively worded. A total score was computed for each subject, ranging from 10 to 40, with higher scores indicating greater self-esteem. Table 2.8 displays the data:

Table 2.8:   Immigrants' Self-Esteem Raw Data

#	D1	D2	D3	D4	D5	D6	E1	E2	E3	E4	E5	E6	E7	E8	E9	E10
1	50	F	ME	Y	VP	GD	4	2	3	4	1	1	3	1	1	3
2	50	F	ME	N	G	GD	4	2	3	4	1	1	3	1	1	3
3	50	M	AF	N	P	HS	4	1	3	3	1	1	3	1	1	4
4	50	M	ME	Y	F	HS	3	1	3	3	1	2	4	3	1	4
5	51	F	ME	Y	P	CD	3	2	4	3	3	2	4	1	2	3
6	51	F	ME	Y	P	CD	4	1	4	3	1	1	4	1	1	4
7	52	F	AF	Y	VG	GD	2	2	2	2	2	2	2	2	2	2
8	52	F	AF	N	VP	HS	4	1	4	4	1	1	4	1	1	4
9	53	M	ME	Y	P	HS	3	1	3	3	3	4	3	3	2	3
10	53	F	ME	Y	P	HS	3	1	3	3	3	4	3	3	2	3
11	54	F	ME	N	P	CD	2	1	4	4	1	1	4	1	1	4
12	54	M	AF	Y	VG	CD	3	2	3	3	2	3	3	2	3	3
13	54	F	AF	N	F	HS	4	1	4	2	4	1	3	1	1	4
14	55	M	ME	N	VP	HS	4	1	4	4	1	1	4	1	1	4
15	55	M	AF	Y	P	HS	4	1	4	4	1	1	4	1	1	4
16	55	F	AS	Y	VP	HS	4	2	3	3	1	1	4	1	1	4
17	56	F	AF	N	P	CD	3	2	3	3	1	2	3	3	1	4
18	57	M	ME	N	VP	GD	4	1	4	4	1	1	4	1	1	4
19	57	M	ME	N	P	CD	1	3	3	3	1	3	3	1	1	3
20	58	F	ME	N	VP	HS	4	1	4	4	1	1	4	1	1	4
21	60	F	AS	N	F	HS	3	2	4	4	1	2	4	1	1	3
22	61	M	AF	N	G	CD	2	1	3	3	1	1	3	1	1	3
23	61	M	AS	Y	P	CD	3	2	3	3	2	2	3	1	3	4
24	61	F	AS	N	P	HS	3	3	4	3	2	3	4	1	1	3
25	61	M	AF	Y	P	HS	3	2	4	4	1	2	3	3	2	3
26	62	M	AF	Y	F	GD	2	3	2	2	2	2	2	3	3	2
27	63	F	AS	N	F	GD	4	1	3	1	3	3	3	1	1	3
28	63	F	ME	Y	P	HS	4	1	4	4	1	1	4	1	1	4
29	64	M	AS	Y	P	CD	3	2	4	3	2	2	3	3	2	3
30	65	M	AS	N	F	GD	4	1	3	3	3	2	3	4	1	2
31	65	M	AS	N	VG	HS	1	4	4	4	1	2	4	1	1	4
32	65	F	AS	N	F	HS	3	1	4	4	1	1	4	1	1	4
33	66	F	ME	N	F	HS	4	1	4	2	1	1	4	1	1	4
34	66	M	AS	N	F	HS	3	1	4	4	1	1	4	1	1	4
35	67	M	AS	Y	G	HS	4	1	4	4	1	1	4	1	1	4
36	71	F	AS	N	F	CD	4	1	4	4	1	1	4	1	1	4
37	75	M	AS	Y	G	GD	2	3	3	2	2	2	3	3	2	3
38	78	M	AF	Y	G	GD	3	2	3	3	3	3	2	1	2	3
39	80	F	AF	Y	G	GD	2	2	3	3	2	3	3	3	2	3
40	92	M	AF	Y	VG	HS	4	1	4	1	1	3	4	1	1	4

Instructions:

1. Create a new SPSS data file. In the variable view screen, define each variable's name, its type, decimals, label, values, and its measure.

2. In the data view screen, enter the raw data.

3. Check data for entry errors and save your file as "Chapter 2 Raw Data."

4. Examine Cronbach's alpha reliability for the Rosenberg Self-Esteem Scale. What is the reliability coefficient? Is there any problem with this coefficient? If yes, what?

5. Now, recode (reverse) scores for the positive self-esteem items.

6. Compute total score for self-esteem and save your clean file as "Chapter 2 Clean Data."

7. Re-examine Cronbach's alpha reliability for the Rosenberg Self-Esteem scale. What is the reliability coefficient? Is there a difference between this coefficient and that in question 4? If yes, why?

8. Run frequency tables for all variables using the clean data file and save it as "Chapter 2 Output."

Note: Submit to your instructor your clean data file, output file, and your answers for questions 4 and 7.

Data Organization and Summary: Frequency Tables and Graphs

LEARNING OBJECTIVES

1. Understand absolute frequency distribution table

2. Understand class-interval frequency distribution table

3. Understand exact-limits frequency distribution table

4. Understand bar graph, histogram, frequency polygon, stem-and-leaf plot, and their uses

5. Understand how to utilize SPSS to create frequency distribution tables and graphs

DATA SET (APPENDIX A)

Job Satisfaction

Well-Being

INTRODUCTION

The aim of empirical research is to examine the characteristics of a population and how they are related. Researchers select representative samples from the population to which generalizations will be made, then collect data from subjects who agree to participate in surveys or interviews (face-to-face, or via telephone or Internet).

After data are collected, they are coded, entered into statistical software such as SPSS, and checked for data entry errors. Some items may need to be recoded to ensure that all scale items progress in the same direction. The last step in preparing data for statistical analysis is to compute the total scores for scales and subscales (see chapter 2).

Now the process of data analysis and interpretation begins. The first step is to organize and summarize data in a way that is easy to understand and interpret. Two simple ways to accomplish this are frequency distribution tables and graphs.

This chapter discusses frequency distribution tables and their components, then presents three types of graphs. You will also learn how to work with SPSS to create frequency distribution tables and graphs.

FREQUENCY DISTRIBUTION TABLES

A frequency distribution is an arrangement of values (attributes) that shows the number of times (frequency) a given value (score) or group of values occurs. It details how the research sample or population's values are distributed.

For example, a frequency distribution may show the frequency of males and females for Gender (dichotomous variable, nominal level of measurement); frequency of whites, African Americans, Native Americans, Hispanics, or others for Race (categorical variable, nominal level of measurement); and the number of participants who are thirty, forty, fifty, or sixty years old for Age (continuous variable, ratio level of measurement). A frequency distribution may also show the frequency of participants who are between twenty-one and twenty-five years old, or between twenty-six and thirty years old for Age (21–25, 26–30, 31–35, etc.); or who make between $11,000 and $20,000, or between $21,000 and $30,000 for Income ($11,000–$20,000, $21,000–$30,000, $31,000–$40,000, etc.)

There are three types of frequency distributions: absolute frequency distribution, class-interval frequency distribution, and exact-limits frequency distribution.

Absolute Frequency Distribution

This distribution reports the frequencies and percentages of the actual score or value for each subject. It has four components:

1. ABSOLUTE FREQUENCY (f): This refers to the actual (observed) number of times each score or value occurs. It is symbolized by a lowercase italic f. The sum (Σ or sigma) of all frequencies will always equal the number of valid cases in the study ($\Sigma f = N$).

2. CUMULATIVE FREQUENCY (cf): This refers to the number of cases at and below a given score or value. It is symbolized by lowercase italic cf. The cumulative frequency distribution for the maximum score will always equal the total number of valid cases in the study (N).

3. PERCENTAGE (%): This refers to the percentage of cases for each score or value. The sum of all percentages will always equal 100 percent.

4. CUMULATIVE PERCENTAGE ($c\%$): This refers to the percentage of cases at and below a given score or value. The cumulative percentage distribution for the maximum score is always 100 percent.

How to create a frequency distribution table. The first step is to arrange the raw data (observed scores) in an array. In this case, scores must be arranged from the lowest value (minimum score) to the highest (maximum score).

Example: The following are levels of life satisfaction (see raw data 3.1) for fifty subjects. Scores range between 10 and 50, with higher scores indicating greater levels of satisfaction:

Raw Data 3.1

32	22	40	31	28	34	34	36	36
26	38	38	36	32	32	30	30	26
26	33	28	31	31	32	34	34	32
27	32	40	35	33	41	40	26	31
24	24	31	42	32	40	41	31	27
27	38	36	30	24				

To create a frequency distribution table, first arrange scores in an array by sorting from lowest to highest (see array data 3.1).

Array Data 3.1

22	24	24	24	26	26	26	26	27
27	27	28	28	30	30	30	31	31
31	31	31	31	32	32	32	32	32
32	32	33	33	34	34	34	34	35
36	36	36	36	38	38	38	40	40
40	40	41	41	42				

The next step is to construct a table with five columns, shown in table 3.1.

1. In the first column, under X, enter the life satisfaction scores as they appear in the array data starting with the minimum score (22) and ending with the maximum score (42). Enter each score only one time.

2. In the second column, under f, enter the number of times each score occurs. Remember, the sum of all frequencies (Σf) must equal the total number of subjects in the study; in this case, 50.

3. In the third column, under cf, enter the total number of students at and below each score. For example, the cf for the score 22 is 1 because only one subject has a life satisfaction score of 22 or below. The cf for the score 26, for example, is the number of subjects who scored 26 plus the number who scored less than 26; that is, $4 + 3 + 1 = 8$. The cf for 31 is the number of subjects who scored 31 plus the number of students who scored less than 31; that is, $6 + 3 + 2 + 3 + 4 + 3 + 1 = 22$.

Remember, the *cf* for the maximum score (in this case, 42) is equal to the number of subjects in the study (N); in this case, 50. In other words, all subjects scored 42 or less.

4. In the fourth column, under %, enter the percentage of times that each score occurs. To compute percentage, divide the number of times a score occurs (*f*) by the total number in the sample (N). In our example, the percentage of subjects who scored 22 is 1/50 = .02, or 2 percent. The percentage who scored 30 is 3/50 = .06, or 6 percent, and the percentage who scored 32 is 7/50 = .14, or 14 percent.

Formula: $\% = f/N$

f = frequency

N = sample size

QUESTION: What percentage of subjects scored 31 in table 3.1?

ANSWER: $\% = f/N = 6/50 = .12$ or 12 percent

5. In the fifth column, under *c*%, enter the total percentage of subjects at or below each score. For example, the c% for 22 is 2 percent because only 2 percent of subjects scored 22 or below; the c% for 26 represents the percentage of subjects who scored 26 plus the percentage who scored less than 26; 8 percent + 6 percent + 2 percent = 16 percent. (You can also compute

Table 3.1: Frequency Distribution Table

X	f	cf	%	c%
22	1	1	2.0	2.0
24	3	4	6.0	8.0
26	4	8	8.0	16.0
27	3	11	6.0	22.0
28	2	13	4.0	26.0
30	3	16	6.0	32.0
31	6	22	12.0	44.0
32	7	29	14.0	58.0
33	2	31	4.0	62.0
34	4	35	8.0	70.0
35	1	36	2.0	72.0
36	4	40	8.0	80.0
38	3	43	6.0	86.0
40	4	47	8.0	94.0
41	2	49	4.0	98.0
42	1	50	2.0	100.0
Total (Σ)	50		100.0	

X = score (life satisfaction); *f* = frequency; *cf* = cumulative frequency; % = percentage; c% = cumulative percentage *c*% by dividing the *cf* for 26 by N; 8/50 = .16, or 16%.) The c% for 28 is the percentage of subjects who scored 28 plus the total percentage of students who scored less than 28; that is, 4 percent + 6 percent + 8 percent + 6 percent + 2 percent = 26 percent (or, divide the *cf* for 28 by N; 13/50 = .26, or 26%).

Remember, the c% for 42 (maximum score) is 100 percent. In other words, 100 percent of subjects scored 42 or less. To compute c%, divide the cumulative frequency (*cf*) by the total number of cases in the study.

Formula: c% = *cf*/N

cf = cumulative frequency

N = sample size

QUESTION: What is the cumulative percentage for a score 35 in table 3.1 (in other words, what percentage of subjects scored 35 or less)?

ANSWER: c% = *cf*/N = 36/50 = .72 or 72 percent

How to create a frequency distribution table in SPSS.   For this purpose, we will use the variables of marital status (MStatus) and age (Age) from the *Job Satisfaction* data file as a practice example. As taught in chapter 2, two methods may be used to run a frequency distribution table: the SPSS main toolbar or an SPSS syntax file.

To create a frequency table in SPSS, follow these steps:

1. Open the SPSS *Job Satisfaction* data file.

2. Click on *Analyze*, click on *Descriptive Statistics*, and click on *Frequencies* (see screen 3.1). The dialog box "Frequencies" will open (see screen 3.2).

Screen 3.1:   SPSS Analyze Toolbar

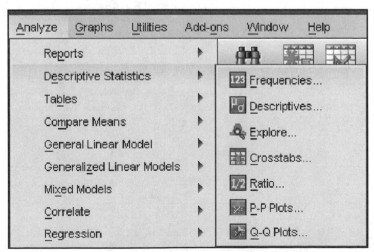

Screen 3.2:   SPSS Frequencies Dialog Box

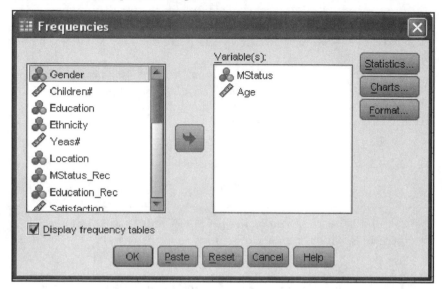

3.   From the variables list (left box), scroll down and click on *MStatus*.

4.   Click on the arrow button between the two boxes to move *MStatus* into the *Variable(s)* box.

5.   Repeat steps 3 and 4 to find and move *Age* into the *Variable(s)* box.

6.   Make sure that the box in the right side of *Display frequency tables* is checked (SPSS default).

7.   Click on *OK*.

SPSS Syntax for Frequency Distribution

Frequency MStatus Age.

The following tables describe the SPSS output. They include Statistics (see table 3.2) and Frequency tables (see table 3.3.A and table 3.3.B). The Statistics table summarizes the number of valid and missing cases for each variable in the analysis; in this example, marital status and age.

Table 3.2:   Statistics

Statistics		MStatus	Age
N	Valid	218	215
	Missing	0	3

Table 3.3.A: Frequency Table for Marital Status

		Frequency	Percent	Valid Percent	Cumulative Percent
			MStatus		
Valid	1 Married	141	64.7	64.7	64.7
	2 Single	47	21.6	21.6	86.2
	3 Divorced	30	13.8	13.8	100.0
	Total	218	100.0	100.0	

As shown in table 3.2, there are 218 valid cases for marital status and 215 for age. In other words, all subjects (MStatus: Valid = 218, Missing = 0) reported their marital status, but three failed to report their ages (Age: Valid = 215, Missing Age = 3).

The frequency table shows the frequencies, percentage, valid percent, and cumulative percentages for each score (value) in each variable. There is one frequency table for each variable in the analysis; in this case, one table for marital status and one for age.

Unlike in table 3.1, SPSS does not produce the cumulative frequency distribution. Instead, SPSS produces two columns for percentage: *Percent* and *Valid Percent*. Percent represents the percentage of times each score (value) occurs, assuming there are no missing cases. Valid Percent represents the percentage of times each score (value) occurs when taking into account only cases with no missing scores (values). If there are no missing cases, then the Percent and Valid Percent will be identical. It is recommended to report the Valid Percent.

Table 3.3.A shows that 141 participants are married (64.7%), forty-seven are single (21.6%), and thirty are divorced (13.8%). Notice that both Percent and Valid Percent are equal in this case. This is because there are no missing values. Remember that the sum of all frequencies is equal to the total sample size (N = 141 + 47 + 30 = 218), and the total percentage is 100 percent.

Table 3.3.B shows the lowest age is twenty-two and the maximum score is sixty-two. Four subjects (1.9%) are twenty-two years old, ten subjects (4.7%) are forty-two years old, and two subjects (.9%) are sixty-two years old. The Cumulative Percent shows that 13 percent are twenty-five years old or younger, 34 percent are thirty years old or younger (that is, 100% − 34% = 66% are older than thirty years), 84.7 percent of subjects are forty-five years old or younger (that is, 100% − 84.7% = 15.3% are older than forty-five years), and all subjects, 100 percent, are sixty-two years old or younger.

Class-Interval Frequency Distribution

In table 3.1 above, we displayed all actual scores observed from all fifty subjects. Sometimes, however, presentation of all observed scores can be lengthy and time-consuming, especially with very large samples and scales with wide ranges (e.g., 1 to 100).

Table 3.3.B: Frequency Table for Age

		Age		
		Frequency	Percent	Valid Percent	Cumulative Percent
Valid	22	4	1.8	1.9	1.9
	23	4	1.8	1.9	3.7
	24	9	4.1	4.2	7.9
	25	11	5.0	5.1	13.0
	26	10	4.6	4.7	17.7
	27	11	5.0	5.1	22.8
	28	7	3.2	3.3	26.0
	29	5	2.3	2.3	28.4
	30	12	5.5	5.6	34.0
	31	9	4.1	4.2	38.1
	32	7	3.2	3.3	41.4
	33	12	5.5	5.6	47.0
	34	8	3.7	3.7	50.7
	35	5	2.3	2.3	53.0
	36	9	4.1	4.2	57.2
	37	7	3.2	3.3	60.5
	38	6	2.8	2.8	63.3
	39	6	2.8	2.8	66.0
	40	5	2.3	2.3	68.4
	41	8	3.7	3.7	72.1
	42	10	4.6	4.7	76.7
	43	7	3.2	3.3	80.0
	44	4	1.8	1.9	81.9
	45	6	2.8	2.8	84.7
	46	1	.5	.5	85.1
	47	5	2.3	2.3	87.4
	48	3	1.4	1.4	88.8
	49	5	2.3	2.3	91.2
	50	2	.9	.9	92.1
	51	2	.9	.9	93.0
	52	2	.9	.9	94.0
	53	3	1.4	1.4	95.3
	54	1	.5	.5	95.8
	55	2	.9	.9	96.7
	56	2	.9	.9	97.7
	57	1	.5	.5	98.1
	58	1	.5	.5	98.6
	61	1	.5	.5	99.1
	62	2	.9	.9	100.0
	Total	215	98.6	100.0	
Missing	System	3	1.4		
Total		218	100.0		

As an alternative, researchers may reduce the number of scores by grouping several scores into one group of scores, or an interval of scores. For example, instead of reporting subjects' actual scores of life satisfaction in table 3.1, we may group the scores into several intervals of five scores each (21–25; 26–30; 31–35; 36–40; 41–45; and 46–50) and then report the frequencies and percentages for each interval. This method of reducing observed scores into intervals is known as *class intervals*. Table 3.4 displays a class-interval frequency table for the data presented in table 3.1.

As it is shown in table 3.4, each class interval has two limits, *lower limit* (LL) and *upper limit* (UL). In table 3.4, 21 is the LL and 25 is the UL in the first interval, 26 is the LL and 30 is the UL in the second interval, and so on. The distance between the lower limit and the upper limit is called the *interval width*. In our example, the interval width equals 5; that is, there are 5 units between the LL and UL. For example, the interval 21–25 includes the scores of 21, 22, 23, 24, and 25; the interval 36–40 includes the scores of 36, 37, 38, 39, and 40. In other words, all class intervals have equal width. As a recommendation, class widths should be odd numbers (3, 5, 7, etc.) which makes it easier to compute the *midpoint* for each interval. For example, the midpoint for the first interval (21–25) is 23 and for the fourth interval (36–40) is 38.

While grouping several scores into a small number of intervals makes large data files easier to manage and report, we may not be able to know the actual score for each subject in the study or the exact number of subjects who have similar scores. Furthermore, with class intervals, researchers assume that the midpoint represents the true score of all subjects within a specific interval, which could be misleading. Also, the distinction between an upper limit of one interval and a lower limit of the next interval may be ambiguous, especially when a comparison of intervals on certain variables is conducted (e.g., comparing subjects 21–30 years old, 31–40, and 41–50 years old with regard to their physical health).

Table 3.4:   Class-Interval Frequency Table

X	f	cf	%	c%
21–25	4	4	8.0	8.0
26–30	12	16	24.0	32.0
31–35	20	36	40.0	72.0
36–40	11	47	22.0	94.0
41–45	3	50	6.0	100.0
Total (Σ)	50		100.0	

X = Class Interval (life satisfaction); *f* = frequency; *cf* = cumulative frequency; % = percentage; c% = cumulative percentage. Notice that by grouping the life satisfaction scores into class intervals, we reduced the number of rows from sixteen in table 3.1 to only five rows in table 3.4.

Exact-Limit Frequency Distribution

As stated, we use class intervals to reduce a large number of observed scores into several intervals with equal widths. These scores represent continuous data. Yet, class intervals result in discontinuity between intervals' limits, thus producing *discrete* data. For example, in table 3.4, there is a break between the interval 21–25 and 26–30, between 26–30 and 31–35, and so on. The question is, then, what happens to participants who score, for example, 25.4, or 30.7?

To maintain the continuity of large data, we could reduce these data into *exact-limit class intervals*. In a sense, exact-limit intervals are the same as class intervals, but their limits extend a half unit below each lower limit and a half point above each upper limit. In our class intervals in table 3.4, the exact limit for the first interval (21–25) is 20.5–25.5, the exact limit for 26–30 is 25.5–35.5, and so on. Table 3.5 is the same as table 3.4, but it displays the exact limits of the class intervals.

How to create class intervals and exact limits in SPSS.   The steps for creating class-interval and exact-limit frequency tables are the same as we discussed earlier under frequency distribution table (see screens 3.1 and 3.2). However, before we run these frequency tables, we need to group the actual scores into class interval or exact-limit intervals. This is done in SPSS through the SPSS *Transform Recode into Different Variables* commands.

For this purpose, we will use the age (Age) variable from the Job Satisfaction data file to create class intervals. As we saw earlier in table 3.3.B, age ranges between twenty-two and sixty-two. Therefore, we will create intervals with width of seven units as follows: 21–27; 28–34; 35–41; 42–48; 49–55; 56–62. You could create intervals with a five-unit width or any other width.

To create these intervals in SPSS, follow these steps:

1.   Open the SPSS Job Satisfaction data file.

2.   Click on *Transform*, scroll down, and click on *Recode into Different Variables* (see chapter 2, screen 2.13).

Table 3.5:   Exact Limits Class Interval Frequency Table for Life Satisfaction

X	f	cf	%	c%
20.5–25.5	4	4	8.0	8.0
25.5–30.5	12	16	24.0	32.0
30.5–35.5	20	36	40.0	72.0
35.5–40.5	11	47	22.0	94.0
40.5–45.5	3	50	6.0	100.0
Total (Σ)	50		100.0	

X = Exact Limit (life satisfaction); *f* = frequency; *cf* = cumulative frequency; % = percentage; c% = cumulative percentage.

3. A new dialog box called "Recode into Different Variables" will open (see screen 3.3). From the variables list in the left box, scroll down and click on *Age*, then click on the arrow button to move it into the *Input Variable-Output Variable* box.

4. Type CL_Age (that is, Class Interval for Age) in the *Name* box under "Output Variable" (see screen 3.3). You may type a label for this variable in the *Label* box. Type "Class Interval for Age."

5. Click on the *Change* button under *Output Variable* to confirm your request, that is, to change *Age* to *CL_Age*.

6. Click on *Old and New Values*. A new dialog box called "Recode into Different Variables: Old and New Values" will open (see screen 3.4).

7. Click on *Range* under *Old Value*, type "21" in the first *Range* box (see screen 3.4.A), type "27" in the *Range Through* box (see screen 3.4.B), and then type "1" in the *Value* box under *New* Value (see screen 3.4.C).

8. Click on *Add* (see screen 3.4.D) to confirm this recode. This will transfer the range and new values in the *Old . . . New* box (21 thru 27 . . . 1).

9. Repeat steps 7 and 8 to create all class intervals as shown in screen 3.4.

10. Click on *Continue*, and then click on *OK*.

To create exact-limit class intervals, follow the same steps above. You need, however, to type the exact limits in the "Recode into Different Variables: Old and New Values" box as shown in screen 3.5.

Screen 3.3:   SPSS Recode into Different Variables Dialog Box

Screen 3.4:   SPSS Recode into Different Variable: Old and New Value Dialog Box
(Class Intervals)

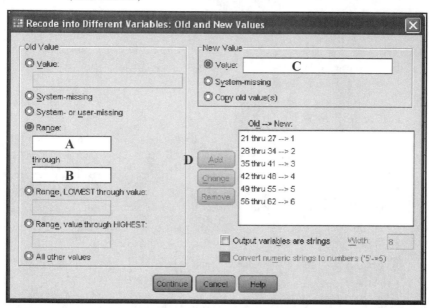

Notice that in screen 3.5 all intervals extend from xx.51 to xx.50. This is needed to prevent any SPSS execution's problems due to overlaps between intervals. For example, someone with a score 27.50 may fall in the interval 20.50–27.50 or 27.50–34.50.

Screen 3.5:   SPSS Recode into Different Variable: Old and New Value Dialog Box
(Exact Limits)

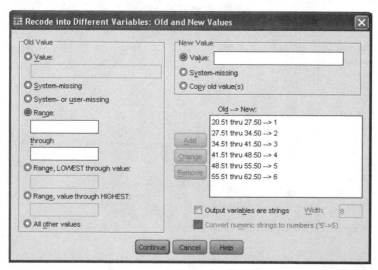

SPSS Syntax for Recode into Different Variables—Class Intervals

RECODE Age (21 thru 27=1) (28 thru 34=2) (35 thru 41=3)
(42 thru 48=4) (49 thru 55=5) (56 thru 62=6) INTO CI_Age.

VARIABLE LABELS CI_Age 'Class Interval for Age'.

EXECUTE.

SPSS Syntax for Recode into Different Variables—Exact Limits

RECODE Age (20.51 thru 27.50=1) (27.51 thru 34.50=2)
(34.51 thru 41.50=3) (41.51 thru 48.50=4) (48.51 thru 55.50=5) (55.51
thru 62.50=6) INTO ELCL_AGE.

VARIABLE LABELS ELCL_AGE 'Exact Limits Class Interval for Age'.

EXECUTE.

The execution of these commands creates the variables CI_AGE and ELCL_AGE and places them at the last two columns in the SPSS data view file (see screen 3.6).

Next, you may want to assign value labels to the six new class intervals or exact-limit class intervals. To assign value labels for these intervals, for example for CI_AGE, click on the *Variable View* tab on the main SPSS data screen (see chapter 2, screen 2.2), locate the CI_AGE variable in the variable Name column (usually at the end), and follow the instruction discussed in chapter 2 for assigning value labels (see chapter 2, screen 2.4). In our example, use these value labels: (1 = 21–27; 2 = 28–34; 3 = 35–41; 4 = 42–48; 5 = 49–55; and 6 = 56–62). These are shown in screen 3.7.

Now that we created class intervals and exact-limit intervals for age and assigned the appropriate value labels, we will run frequency tables for both intervals for age. To run frequency tables, simply follow the steps discussed above under "How to Create a Frequency Distribution Table in SPSS." Tables 3.6.A

Screen 3.6:   SPSS Data View File

Screen 3.7:   SPSS Value Labels for CI_AGE

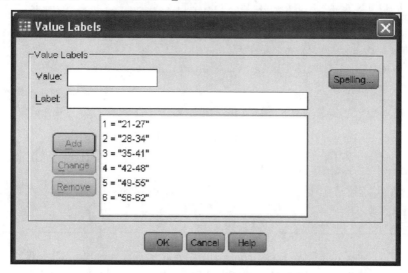

and 3.6.B display the class-interval and exact-limit frequency distributions for age.

These tables are similar to table 3.3.B. The difference between the two, however, is that tables 3.6.A and 3.6.B report the class intervals and exact limits, respectively, for the actual ages of participants reported in table 3.3.B. However, both tables 3.6.A and 3.6.B have fewer rows (six rows) compared to table 3.3.B (thirty-nine rows). Still they show the number for missing cases (Missing = 3).

Lastly, we recommend that you present a summary table displaying the frequencies and percentages for each class interval and exact-limit intervals along with their midpoints as shown in table 3.7.

Table 3.6.A: Frequency Table for Age with Class Intervals

		CI_Age Class Interval for Age			
		Frequency	Percent	Valid Percent	Cumulative Percent
Valid	21–27	49	22.5	22.8	22.8
	28–34	60	27.5	27.9	50.7
	35–41	46	21.1	21.4	72.1
	42–48	36	16.5	16.7	88.8
	49–55	17	7.8	7.9	96.7
	56–62	7	3.2	3.3	100.0
	Total	215	98.6	100.0	
Missing	System	3	1.4		
Total		218	100.0		

Table 3.6.B: Frequency Table for Age with Exact Limits

				Valid	Cumulative
		Frequency	Percent	Percent	Percent
Valid	20.5–27.5	49	22.5	22.8	22.8
	27.5–34.5	60	27.5	27.9	50.7
	34.5–41.5	46	21.1	21.4	72.1
	41.5–48.5	36	16.5	16.7	88.8
	48.5–55.5	17	7.8	7.9	96.7
	55.5–62.5	7	3.2	3.3	100.0
	Total	215	98.6	100.0	
Missing	System	3	1.4		
Total		218	100.0		

ELCI_Age Exact Limits Class Interval for Age

Table 3.7:   Class Intervals and Exact Limits Summary Table for Age

Class Intervals	Exact Limits	Midpoint	f	cf	%	c%
21–27	20.5–27.5	24	49	49	22.8	22.8
28–34	27.5–34.5	31	60	109	27.9	50.7
35–41	34.5–41.5	38	46	155	21.4	72.1
42–48	41.5–48.5	45	36	191	16.7	88.8
49–55	48.5–55.5	52	17	208	7.9	96.7
56–62	55.5–62.5	59	7	215	3.3	100.0
Total (Σ)			215		100.0	

GRAPHIC PRESENTATIONS OF DATA

Presentation of data in frequency distribution tables is sometimes discouraged if the audience is not familiar with basic statistics and won't understand what these tables represent. In this case, it is more helpful to present the data in a way that will communicate to the average person.

Graphic presentation is another way to organize data. Graphs can help visualize data. Unlike frequency distribution tables, however, graphs do not give detailed information and can be misleading as different people interpret them based on their own understanding.

While there are many types of graphs, only five commonly used styles are introduced in this book. This chapter presents the bar graph, histogram, frequency polygon, and stem-and-leaf plot. The boxplot chart is introduced in the following chapter.

Bar Graph

A bar graph is used to display the frequency or percentage of cases under value categories (discrete data); that is, variables that are measured at the nominal level of measurement. These variables have values that represent categories with no intrinsic ranking, such as gender, race, marital status, religious affiliation, or political party affiliation.

A bar graph can be useful to display the frequency or percentage of cases for variables measured at the ordinal level. These variables have values that represent categories with intrinsic ranking, such as the five-point Likert scale (1 = strongly disagree, 2 = disagree, 3 = neither agree nor disagree, 4 = agree, 5 = strongly agree).

In a bar graph, the Y axis represents the frequency or percentage of cases associated with each category, and the X axis represents the value categories. To construct a bar graph, draw the same number of vertical bars as the number of categories associated with the nominal variable: draw four bars to represent four race categories and two bars to represent two gender categories. All bars should have equal width, and they should not touch each other, as the categories are mutually exclusive. Figure 3.1 is an example of a bar graph representing three body mass index (BMI) categories: normal weight, overweight, and obese. The graph shows that the majority of subjects are considered normal weight (n = 93), followed by overweight (n = 62), and obese (n = 27). Notice that the three bars are the same width and do not touch each other, indicating that these are three mutually exclusive groups.

How to create a bar graph in SPSS.   To illustrate this, we will create a bar graph for body mass index (Weight) from the Well-Being data file. As with frequency distribution tables, there are two ways to generate bar graphs: the SPSS main toolbar and SPSS syntax file.

Figure 3.1:   Bar Graph for Body Mass Index

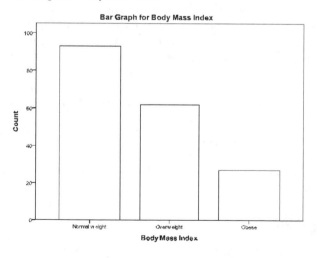

To create a bar graph for BMI, follow these steps:

1. Open the SPSS Well-Being data file.
2. Click on *Graphs*, *Legacy Dialog*, and *Bar* (see screen 3.8).

Screen 3.8:   SPSS Graphs—Legacy Dialogs Main Toolbar

3. Click on *Simple* (SPSS default) in the "Bar Charts" dialog box (see screen 3.9). Make sure that *Summaries for groups of cases* under "Data in Chart Are" is checked (SPSS default). If not, check it.
4. Click on *Define*. A new dialog box, "Define Simple Bar: Summaries for Groups of Cases" opens (see screen 3.10).
5. Find and highlight *Weight* in the variables list and click on the arrow button in the left side of *Category Axis*.
6. Check *N of cases* under "Bars Represent" to request frequencies, *% of cases* to request percentage, or other options.
7. To add a title to the graph, click on *Titles*. A new dialog box called "Titles" will open (see screen 3.11). Type the title (e.g., "Bar Graph for Body Mass Index") in the *Line 1* box.

Screen 3.9:   SPSS Bar Charts Dialog Box

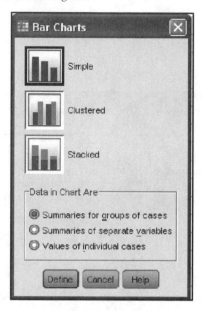

Screen 3.10:   SPSS Bar Charts Dialog Box

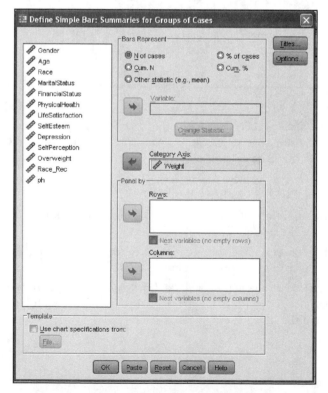

8. To create bar charts for different groups (e.g., BMI by gender), click on the grouping variable (e.g., gender) and move it in the *Rows* box under the "Panel by" box.

9. Click on *Continue*, then *OK*.

We can also create bar charts in SPSS using the Analyze, Descriptive Statistics, and Frequencies commands. We will discuss this in the next chapter.

SPSS Syntax for Bar Chart (Frequency)

GRAPH

/BAR(SIMPLE)=COUNT BY WEIGHT

/TITLE='Bar Graph for Body Mass Index'.

SPSS Syntax for Bar Chart (Percentages)

GRAPH

/BAR(SIMPLE)=PCT BY WEIGHT

/TITLE='Bar Graph for Body Mass Index'.

Screen 3.11:   SPSS Bar Charts: Titles Dialog Box

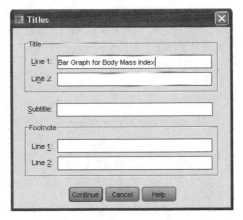

Figure 3.1 (above) and Figure 3.2 display two bar charts for body mass index. The first bar graph (figure 3.1) presents frequencies for each BMI category (normal weight, overweight, and obese). The second bar graph (figure 3.2), which is identical to the first, presents percentages for each BMI category (51%, 34%, and 15%, respectively).

Histogram

A histogram is used to graphically display a distribution of scores or values for continuous data, usually variables measured at the interval or ratio levels of

Figure 3.2:   Bar Graph for Body Mass Index (Percentages)

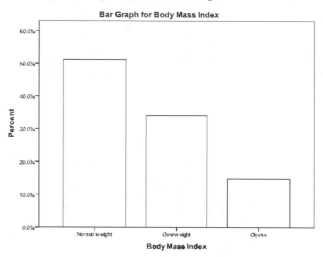

measurement. As we discussed in chapter 1, interval variables have values that represent ordered categories with equal distance between values; for example, IQ scores or Fahrenheit temperatures. Ratio variables share the above properties plus have a fixed zero; for example, age, years of education, or annual income.

A histogram, like a bar graph, uses the Y axis to display frequency of cases for a given score and the X axis to display scores (see figure 3.3). Unlike a bar graph, the bars in a histogram touch each other, indicating continuous data.

Figure 3.3:   Histogram for Autonomy at Work

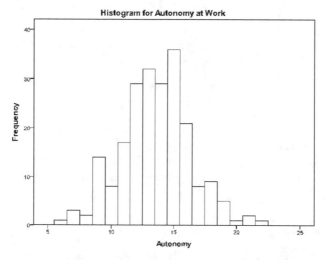

To construct a histogram, draw a vertical bar for each score, class interval, or exact-limit interval. All bars should have equal width and connect to each other.

How to create a histogram in SPSS.   To illustrate this, we will create a histogram for autonomy at work (Autonomy) from the SPSS Job Satisfaction data file.

To create a histogram in SPSS, follow these steps:

1. Open the SPSS Job Satisfaction data file.

2. Click on *Graphs*, *Legacy Dialog*, and *Histogram* (see screen 3.8 above).

3. Scroll down in the variables list, click on *Autonomy* in the "Histogram" dialog box, then click on the top arrow button to move *Autonomy* in the *Variable* box (see screen 3.12).

Screen 3.12:   SPSS Histogram Dialog Box

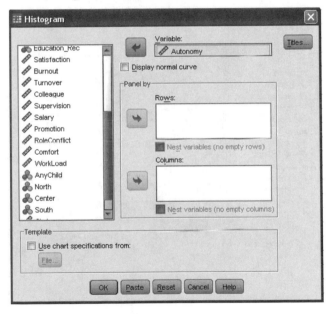

4. Click on *Titles*, type "Histogram for Autonomy at Work," and click *Continue* (see screen 3.11 under "Bar Chart").

5. You can also check the box next to *Display normal curve* to examine the shape of the distribution (see chapter 5).

6. To create histograms for different groups (e.g., autonomy by gender), click on the grouping variable (e.g., gender), and move it in the *Rows* box under the "Panel by" box (see screen 3.13).

7. Click *Continue*, then *OK*.

SPSS Syntax for Histogram

GRAPH

/HISTOGRAM=Autonomy

/TITLE='Histogram for Autonomy at Work'.

SPSS Syntax for Histogram by Grouping Variable:

GRAPH

/HISTOGRAM=Autonomy

/PANEL ROWVAR=Gender ROWOP=CROSS

/TITLE='Histogram for Autonomy at Work by Gender'.

Screen 3.13:   SPSS Histogram by Grouping Variable Dialog Box

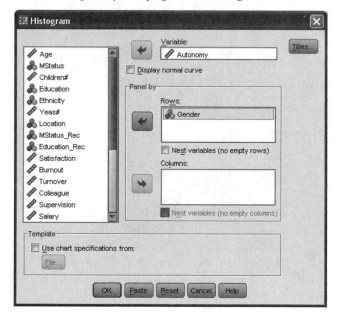

Figure 3.3 above displays a histogram for autonomy at work produced by SPSS. It shows seventeen bars of equal width representing seventeen continuous values for autonomy (minimum = 6 and maximum = 22). The highest bar represents the most frequent score (mode, see chapter 4); the shortest bar represents the least frequent score.

Figure 3.4 displays a histogram for autonomy at work by gender produced by SPSS. It compares the distribution of males with the distribution of females

Figure 3.4:   Histogram for Autonomy at Work by Gender

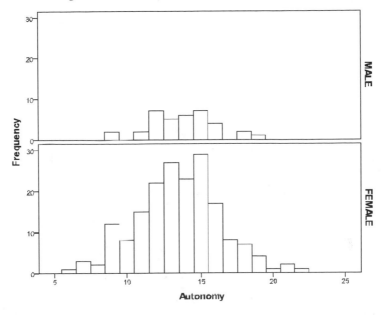

with regard to their scores on autonomy at work. This is of importance for selecting the appropriate statistical test(s) since some (*t*-tests, analysis of variances, etc.) require that the distributions of groups under comparison should be normal. We will discuss this in subsequent chapters.

Frequency Polygon

Another way to graphically display continuous data is in a frequency polygon. In a frequency polygon, it is assumed that the midpoints accurately represent the class interval or the bars in histograms. These midpoints are then connected together to visually display the shape of the distribution of a given variable.

To create a frequency polygon for a specific variable, first create a histogram as discussed above and then identify and mark the midpoint for each bar or class interval on the histogram. Next, using a pencil and ruler (or a computer program), connect these midpoints with straight lines. Figure 3.5 displays a frequency polygon for workload from the Job Satisfaction data.

How to create a frequency polygon in SPSS.   To illustrate how to utilize SPSS to create a frequency polygon, we will use the variable workload (Workload) from the Job Satisfaction data file, so we can compare it with figure 3.5.

Figure 3.5:   Frequency Polygon for Workload

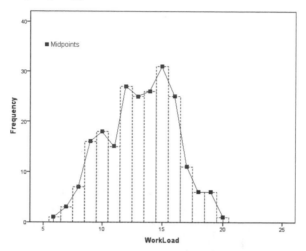

To create a frequency polygon in SPSS, follow these steps:

1. Open the SPSS Job Satisfaction data file.
2. Click on *Graphs* and click on *Chart Builder* (see screen 3.14). A new dialog box called "Chart Builder" will open (see screen 3.15).

Screen 3.14:   SPSS Graphs—Chart Builder Main Toolbar

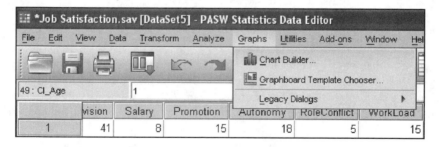

3. Click on *Gallery* (SPSS default), scroll down under *Choose from*, then click on *Histogram*. This displays four types of histograms in the right box.
4. Double click on the third graph from left. This activates the X axis and Y axis boxes under the "Chart preview uses example data" box. It also opens a new dialog box for "Element Properties" (we will not use this dialog box here).
5. Scroll down in the *Variables* box and click on *Workload*.
6. While holding the right mouse button down, drag *Workload* in the X axis box. A preview of the frequency polygon will be displayed in the *Chart preview uses example data* box (see screen 3.16).
7. Click on *OK*.

Screen 3.15:   SPSS Chart Builder Dialog Box

SPSS Syntax for Frequency Polygon

Note: You must type all as is in the SPSS syntax file. Only replace Workload with the name of the variable for which the frequency polygon will be created.

GGRAPH

/GRAPHDATASET NAME="graphdataset" VARIABLES=WorkLoad MISSING=LISTWISE REPORTMISSING=NO

/GRAPHSPEC SOURCE=INLINE.

BEGIN GPL

SOURCE: s=userSource(id("graphdataset"))

DATA: WorkLoad=col(source(s), name("WorkLoad"))

GUIDE: axis(dim(1), label("WorkLoad"))

GUIDE: axis(dim(2), label("Frequency"))

ELEMENT: area(position(summary.count(bin.rect(WorkLoad))), missing.wings())

END GPL.

Screen 3.16:   SPSS Chart Builder Preview

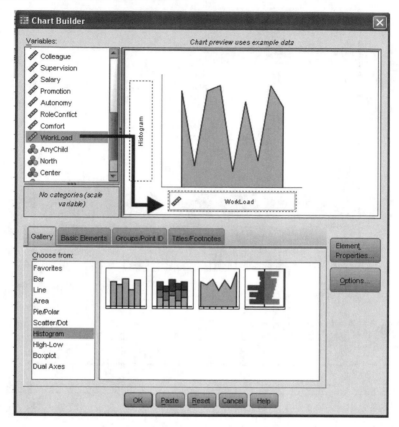

Next, you may or may not want to add grid lines to the graph. To do so, follow these three steps:

1. Point the mouse anywhere on the chart and double click on it. This will open the "Chart Editor" dialog box (see screen 3.17.A).
2. Right-click on the Chart Editor, scroll down, and click on *Show Grid Lines* (see screen 3.17.B). This adds grid lines to the chart. You can also add grid lines simply by clicking on the grid lines button on the upper right side of the Chart Editor main menu (see screen 3.17.C). *Note:* You may use the Chart Editor to edit different aspects of the chart, such as colors, titles, and others.
3. Close the "Chart Editor" dialog box.

Figure 3.6 displays a frequency polygon for workload produced in SPSS. Notice that the shape of the distribution in figure 3.6 is identical to that in figure 3.5, which was manually produced.

Screen 3.17:   SPSS Chart Editor Dialog Box

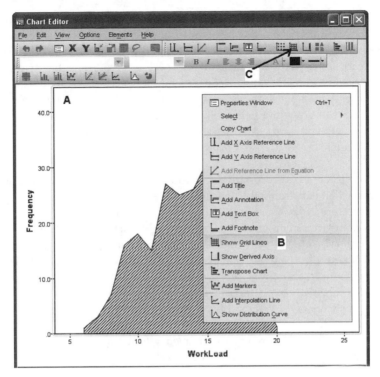

Figure 3.6:   SPSS Frequency Polygon for Workload

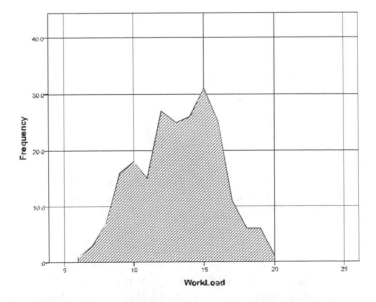

Stem-and-Leaf Plot

Like a histogram, a stem-and-leaf plot displays the distribution of scores or values for continuous data. In a stem-and-leaf plot, each observed score or value is subdivided into two components: the leading digits (stem) and the trailing digits (leaf). A stem-and-leaf plot shows each value, a group of values (class intervals), frequency for each value, frequency for each class interval, and the total sample size. A stem-and-leaf plot is especially useful for comparing two or more groups under one variable (e.g., comparing males and females with regard to their levels of depression). Another advantage of a stem-and-leaf plot is if it is turned counterclockwise, it will form a histogram.

How to create a stem-and-leaf plot.   To illustrate this, we will use the Life Satisfaction data from table 3.1. In these data, the minimum score is 22 and maximum score is 42.

To construct a stem-and-leaf plot, first decide on the stem, then on the leaf. In this example, use the tens digits for the stems and the ones digits for the leaves. For example, the tens digit for the score of 22 is 2, and becomes the stem, and the ones digit, also 2, will serve as the leaf; the tens digit for the score of 30 is 3, and becomes the stem, and the ones digit, 0, will serve as the leaf; the tens digit for the score of 41 is 4, and becomes the stem, and the ones digit, 1, will serve as the leaf; and so on.

The next step is to present the frequency for each group of scores. Figure 3.7 displays a stem-and-leaf plot for these data.

Figure 3.7:   Stem-and-Leaf Plot for Life Satisfaction

Frequency	Stem	Leaf
13	2	2 4 4 4 6 6 6 6 7 7 7 8 8
30	3	0 0 0 1 1 1 1 1 1 2 2 2 2 2 2 2 3 3 4 4 4 4 5 6 6 6 6 8 8 8
7	4	0 0 0 0 1 1 2
Total = 50		

This graph provides the following information:

1.   Minimum score = 22 (stem = 2 and leaf = 2).

2.   Maximum score = 42 (stem = 4 and leaf = 2).

3.   CLASS-INTERVAL FREQUENCY: Thirteen subjects scored between 22 (stem = 2 and leaf = 2) and 28 (stem = 2 and leaf = 8), thirty subjects between 30 (stem = 3 and leaf = 0) and 38 (stem = 3 and leaf = 8), and seven subjects scored between 40 (stem = 4 and leaf = 0) and 42 (stem = 4 and leaf = 2).

4.   INDIVIDUAL FREQUENCY: The exact frequency for each score. One subject scored 22 (the number 2 appears one time under Leaf with a Stem of 2); three people scored 24 (the number 4 appears three times under Leaf with a Stem of 2); four subjects scored 36 (the number 6 appears four times under Leaf with a Stem of 3); and so on.

5. SAMPLE SIZE: N – 50. This represents the sum of all frequencies.

6. SHAPE OF THE DISTRIBUTION: Rotating this graph counterclockwise 90° will produce a histogram displaying the same data as shown in figure 3.8.

Figure 3.8:   Stem-and-Leaf Plot for Life Satisfaction—Counterclockwise

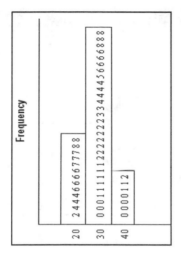

How to create a stem-and-leaf plot in SPSS.   To illustrate this, we will create a stem-and-leaf for age (Age) from the SPSS Job Satisfaction data file (see table 3.3.B).

To create a stem-and-leaf plot in SPSS, follow these steps:

1. Open the SPSS Job Satisfaction data file.

2. Select *Analyze*, click on *Descriptive Statistics*, then click on *Explore* (see screen 3.18).

Screen 3.18:   SPSS Analyze, Descriptive Statistics Toolbar

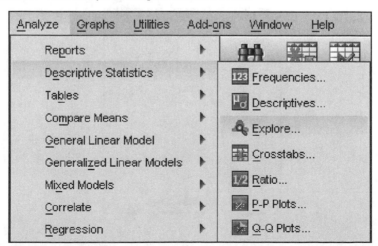

3. Scroll down in the variables list in the "Explore" dialog box, click on *Age*, then click on the top arrow button to move it into the *Dependent List* (screen 3.19).

Screen 3.19:   SPSS Explore Dialog Box

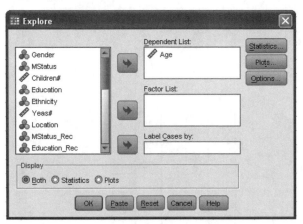

4. *Note:* To create different analyses or plots for different groups (e.g., males and females), move the grouping variable (e.g., Gender) in the *Factor List* box.

5. Check *Plots* under "Display" in the lower left corner.

6. Click on *Plots* in the upper right corner to open the "Explore: Plots" dialog box (see screen 3.20).

7. Make sure the *Stem-and-Leaf* box under "Descriptive" is checked (SPSS default). You can also request a histogram by checking the *Histogram* box under "Descriptives" and a boxplot under "Boxplots."

Screen 3.20:   SPSS Explore: Plots Dialog Box

8. Choose *None* under "Boxplots" (see chapter 4).

9. Click *Continue*, then *OK*.

SPSS Syntax for a Stem-and-Leaf Plot

EXAMINE AGE

/PLOT STEMLEAF.

The execution of these commands results in two tables and one plot: case-processing summary, descriptive statistics, and a stem-and-leaf plot. We will discuss the first two in the next chapter. Figure 3.9 displays a stem-and-leaf plot for age.

As it is shown in figure 3.9, each interval of scores (20–29, 30–39, 40–49, etc.) is divided into two halves: 20–24 and 25–29 (there are two stems for 2s, two stems for 3s, etc.). The score of 20–24 falls under the first grouping for the 2 stem, while 25–29 falls under the second grouping for the 2 stem. This is useful to reduce the length of rows, especially with large data where many subjects fall within a specific interval (e.g., 20s, 30s, etc.).

In this example, the stem-and-leaf plot shows that seventeen participants are between twenty-two and twenty-four years old (first row: frequency = 17, stem = 2, and leaf = 2, 3, 4), forty-four participants are between twenty-five and twenty-nine (second row: frequency = 44, stem = 2, and leaf = 5, 6, 7, 8, 9), forty-eight participants are between thirty and thirty-four, and so on. This is the same information presented in table 3.3.B.

Figure 3.9:   Stem-and-Leaf Plot for Age

```
Frequency    Stem & Leaf

  17.00    2 . 22223333444444444
  44.00    2 . 555555555556666666666777777777778888888899999
  48.00    3 . 00000000000011111111122222223333333333344444444
  33.00    3 . 555556666666667777777788888899999
  34.00    4 . 0000011111111222222222233333334444
  20.00    4 . 5555556777778889999
  10.00    5 . 0011223334
   6.00    5 . 556678
   3.00    6 . 122

Stem width:    10
Each leaf:   1 case(s)
```

SUMMARY

This chapter discussed two methods for summarizing, organizing, and presenting data: frequency distribution tables and graphs.

Frequency distribution tables summarize the frequency for each score or group of scores, cumulative frequency, percentage, and cumulative percentage.

Three types of frequency distributions were discussed, absolute frequency distribution, class-interval frequency distribution, and exact-limit frequency distribution.

Graphs are used to visually display the distribution of scores. Four types were discussed: bar graphs, histograms, frequency polygons, and stem-and-leaf plots. A bar graph is used to illustrate the distribution of categorical data. The histogram and frequency polygon display the shape of a distribution for continuous data. A stem-and-leaf plot illustrates both the frequency and the shape of a distribution for continuous data.

SPSS methods of computing and creating frequency tables and graphs were discussed in detail throughout.

Chapter 4 presents the next step in data organization and summary: measures of central tendency, variability, and percentiles, as well as the boxplot chart and its use in data description. The chapter will outline the steps involved in computing these measures and creating boxplot charts in SPSS.

PRACTICAL EXERCISES

Part 1: Use a pencil and paper to do the following:
The following are the final scores of basic statistics for forty students:

68	65	75	73	80
68	65	76	82	80
86	66	88	75	81
70	67	79	75	74
72	68	100	82	82
72	76	91	96	84
84	89	94	100	88
86	90	96	80	82

The following grading system was used to determine final grades:

A = 96–100	A– = 91–95	B = 86–90	B– = 81–85
C = 76–80	C– = 71–75	D = 66–70	F = 61–65

1. Develop a frequency distribution table and construct a histogram for the raw data.
2. Develop a frequency polygon on top of the histogram you developed in question 1.
3. In one table, create a class-interval, exact-limit, and midpoint frequency distribution using the grading system.
4. Construct a bar graph for the class-interval frequency distribution.
5. Construct a stem-and-leaf plot for the raw scores.

Part II: Access the SPSS clean data file you created in chapter 2 and answer the following questions:

1. Describe participants (frequencies and percentages) in the study based on gender, age, birthplace, race, education, and physical health (run frequency tables for these variables and discuss them).

2. From the variables in question 1, choose one categorical variable and one continuous variable. For each one, create either a bar graph or a histogram, as appropriate. What information do they convey?

3. Create a class-interval frequency distribution table of five-unit width for age. Begin with age fifty. What information does it convey?

4. Create a histogram for self-esteem by gender. What information does it convey?

5. Create a stem-and-leaf plot and frequency polygon for self-esteem. What information do they convey?

Note: You may copy and paste all your SPSS tables and graphs to a word-processing document by right-clicking on the SPSS table or figure, select *Copy*, then point the mouse on the word document where you want to paste the output, right-click on the mouse, and click on *Paste*. Then you can edit tables and resize figures for neat presentations of outputs.

Descriptive Statistics: Measures of Central Tendency, Variability, and Percentiles

LEARNING OBJECTIVES

1. Understand measures of central tendency
2. Understand measures of variability
3. Understand percentiles
4. Understand boxplot charts
5. Understand outlier cases
6. Understand how to use SPSS to run these measures and charts

DATA SET (APPENDIX A)

Job Satisfaction

Mental Health

INTRODUCTION

Chapter 3 presented two methods for organizing and summarizing research data: frequency distribution tables and graphs. These are two useful methods that visually show how samples' characteristics and scores are distributed, but they do not describe where the values or scores of variables are centered. For example, a mental health researcher who examines levels of anxiety among sexually abused young females might like to know which level of anxiety score appears the most, falls at the middle, or is average.

This chapter presents three measures of central tendency that provide information about the point around which a distribution's values are clustered: the mode, median, and mean. Four measures of variability describe the dispersion of each value or score from the mean: range, mean deviation, variance, and standard deviation. Percentiles and boxplot charts are also discussed.

To understand these statistics and chart, consider the raw data presented in table 3.1 (see chapter 3). These are as follows (see raw data 4.1):

Raw Data 4.1

32	22	40	31	28	34	34	36	36
26	38	38	36	32	32	30	30	26
26	33	28	31	31	32	34	34	32
27	32	40	35	33	41	40	26	31
24	24	31	42	32	40	41	31	27
27	38	36	30	24				

MEASURES OF CENTRAL TENDENCY

Mode

The mode is the simplest measure of central tendency. It is the most frequently occurring score in a distribution. As advantages, the mode is simple to figure out; it is the most occurring score. Also, it is not affected by outlier scores, the extremes at either end of the distribution, which may demand special consideration.

On the other hand, unlike other measures of central tendency (mean and median), one disadvantage of the mode is that a given distribution may include more than one mode. A distribution with one mode, which is desired, is called *unimodal*. A distribution with two modes is called *bimodal*, and a distribution with three or more modes is called *multimodal*. Another disadvantage of the mode is that it does not provide information about the variation of scores.

QUESTION: What is (are) the mode(s) in raw data 4.1?

ANSWER: To determine the mode in our example, first arrange the scores in an array, from low to high (see array data 4.1), and then count the number of times (frequency) each value occurs.

Evaluating these data shows that the value 32 occurs seven times, followed by 31, which occurs six times. Therefore, 32 is the mode. Also, you may find the mode simply by looking at the absolute frequency (f) column in table 3.1 (see chapter 3). Table 3.1 shows that 32 is the most frequent score; it occurred seven times, the highest frequency.

Array Data 4.1

22	24	24	24	26	26	26	26	27
27	27	28	28	30	30	30	31	31
31	31	31	31	*32*	*32*	*32*	*32*	*32*
32	*32*	33	33	34	34	34	34	35
36	36	36	36	38	38	38	40	40
40	40	41	41	42				

Median

The median is a value in a distribution below and above where half of the values fall; that is, two halves. The median thus divides an array of values into two equal groups. Like the mode, median is not affected by outlier scores.

To determine the median, first arrange raw data in an array. If the distribution has an odd number of cases, the median will be the middle score; that is, the score for the middle case. If the distribution has an even number of cases, the median will be the sum of the two middle scores divided by two.

QUESTION: What is the median in raw data 4.1?

ANSWER: Since there are fifty cases in these data, the median will be the sum of the two middle scores divided by two. Looking at array data 4.1, we found that the two middle scores (case #25 and case #26) are 32 (case #25) and also 32 (case #26). Thus, the median is 32 + 32/2 = 32.

Mean

The mean is the most reported measure of central tendency. It is the arithmetic average of the scores in a distribution: the sum of all values (ΣX) divided by the number of cases (N). The main disadvantage of the mean, unlike the mode or median, is that it is very sensitive to outlying scores. Data should be carefully evaluated for outlying scores before a decision is made to report the mean. In such cases, the mean may not be appropriate to report. The symbol for the population mean is μ (mu) and the sample mean is $\overline{X}$ (X bar).

Mean Formula

$$\overline{X} = \frac{\Sigma fX}{N}$$

$\overline{X}$ = Mean
Σ = Sum of
f = Frequency
X = Score
N = Number of cases

QUESTION: What is the mean score for raw data 4.1?

ANSWER: First, arrange data in a frequency table, presenting the scores and their absolute frequencies (see table 4.1). Second, add a third column to present the product of multiplying each score (X) by its frequency (f). Third, sum the values in the fX column together (that is, ΣfX). Finally, divide this sum by the number of cases in the study (N). That is,

$$\overline{X} = \frac{\Sigma fx}{N} =$$

$$\frac{22 + 72 + 104 \ldots + 42}{50} = 32.28$$

Table 4.1:   Frequency Distribution Table

X	f	fX
22	1	22
24	3	72
26	4	104
27	3	81
28	2	56
30	3	90
31	6	186
32	7	224
33	2	66
34	4	136
35	1	35
36	4	144
38	3	114
40	4	160
41	2	81
42	1	42
Total (Σ)	50	1614

X = score (life satisfaction), f = frequency; fX = score × frequency

Another way to compute the mean without creating a frequency table is simply by summing all fifty scores in raw data 1 (i.e., 32 + 22 + 40 + . . . + 24 = 1614) and then dividing the sum by 50 (i.e., 1614/50 = 32.28).

MEASURES OF VARIABILITY

Range

The range is the simplest measure of variability. It is the number of units on a distribution of scores that include the maximum and minimum scores. For example, the number of units on a scale of 1 to 10 is ten (1, 2, 3, 4, 5, 6, 7, 8, 9, and 10; there are ten values). The number of units on a scale of 25 to 33 is nine (25, 26, 27, 28, 29, 30, 31, 32, and 33; there are nine values). A range is defined mathematically as:

Range Formula

Range = (Maximum Score − Minimum Score) + 1

QUESTION: What is the range for raw data 4.1?

ANSWER: To find the range, first arrange the data from low to high, find the minimum and maximum scores, then apply them in the range formula as follows:

Raw Data 4.1: Range = (42 − 22) + 1 = 21

Mean Deviation

In the previous section, the mean was defined as the average score of a distribution of continuous data. However, while the mean may represent a distribution, especially when no outlier scores exist, it does not tell how far, on average, each case is above or below the mean. To accomplish this, the mean deviation of a distribution may be computed.

A mean deviation is a measure of variability that describes the dispersion of scores around the mean. It is the *average* (mean) deviations (distances) of scores from the mean. Mean deviation is symbolized as *MD*.

To compute the mean deviation of a distribution, first compute the deviation of each score from the mean by subtracting the mean from each score, that is, $(X - \bar{X})$. Next, sum the *absolute values* of all deviations; that is, $\Sigma |X - \bar{X}|$. Then, divide the sum of deviations by the number of cases.

Note: The absolute values are used to reflect the distance for each score from the mean. The +/− signs only indicate if a score is above or below the mean. Also, the sum of $(X - \bar{X})$ is zero.

Mean Deviation Formula

$$MD = \frac{\Sigma |f(X - \bar{X})|}{N}$$

MD = Mean Deviation
Σ = Sum of
f = Frequency
X = Score
$\bar{X}$ = Mean
N = Number of cases

QUESTION: What is the mean deviation for the data in table 4.1?

ANSWER: To find the mean deviation for these data, first add two new columns; $f(X - \bar{X})$ and $|f(X - \bar{X})|$. (*Note:* We multiply by f to account for all cases with similar scores. If each score appears one time, ignore f); sum all $|f(X - \bar{X})|$, then divide it by N as shown in table 4.2.

Table 4.2:   Calculation of Mean Deviation

X	f	fX	f(X − X̄)	|f(X − X̄)|
22	1	22	1 × (22 − 32.28) = −10.28	10.28
24	3	72	3 × (24 − 32.28) = −24.84	24.84
26	4	104	4 × (26 − 32.28) = −25.12	25.12
27	3	81	3 × (27 − 32.28) = −15.84	15.84
28	2	56	2 × (28 − 32.28) = −8.56	8.56
30	3	90	3 × (30 − 32.28) = −6.84	6.84
31	6	186	6 × (31 − 32.28) = −7.68	7.68
32	7	224	7 × (32 − 32.28) = −1.96	1.96
33	2	66	2 × (33 − 32.28) = 1.44	1.44
34	4	136	4 × (34 − 32.28) = 6.88	6.88
35	1	35	1 × (35 − 32.28) = 2.72	2.72
36	4	144	4 × (36 − 32.28) = 14.88	14.88
38	3	114	3 × (38 − 32.28) = 17.16	17.16
40	4	160	4 × (40 − 32.28) = 30.88	30.88
41	2	81	2 × (41 − 32.28) = 17.44	17.44
42	1	42	1 × (42 − 32.28) = 9.72	9.72
Total (Σ)	50	1614	Zero	202.24

X = score (life satisfaction); f = frequency; fX = score × frequency; $f(X - \bar{X})$ = deviations; $|f(X - \bar{X})|$ = absolute deviations

The mean deviation for this distribution is as follows:

$$MD = \frac{\Sigma|f(X - \bar{X})|}{N} = \frac{202.24}{50} = 4.04$$

That is, participants in the life satisfaction study are 4.04, on average, above, or below the mean of 32.28.

Variance

Another measure of variability is the variance. It is a statistic that measures how spread out a distribution of scores is from the mean. The more spread out a distribution is, the greater the deviation is from the mean.

Mathematically, the variance is defined, unlike the mean deviation, as the average (mean) of the sum of squared deviations around the mean. The symbol for the variance in a population is σ^2 [sigma (lowercase for Σ) squared] and in a sample it is S^2.

To obtain the variance, follow these steps:

1. Compute the mean $\bar{X}$ for the data as discussed above.
2. Compute how far each score deviates from the mean as with mean deviation; that is, $(X - \bar{X})$.
3. Unlike mean deviation, where absolute values are used, square each deviation, that is, $(X - \bar{X})^2$.
4. Sum all squared deviations. This is called *sum of squares of deviations*, or simply *sum of squares*, and is symbolized as *SS*; that is, $SS = \Sigma (X - \bar{X})^2$. It is widely used in inferential statistics such as *t*-tests and analysis of variances.
5. Finally, divide the sum of squares by (N – 1).

Variance Formula

$$S^2 = \frac{\Sigma f(X - \bar{X})^2}{N - 1} = \frac{SS}{N - 1}$$

S^2 = Variance
Σ = Sum of
f = Frequency
X = Score
$\bar{X}$ = Mean
SS = Sum of Squares
N = Number of cases

Remember: The sum of all deviations is always zero; that is, $\Sigma (X - \bar{X}) = 0$ (see table 4.2).

QUESTION: What is the variance of life satisfaction scores presented in table 4.2?

ANSWER: To compute the variance, first add another column to the table for the squared deviation $f(X - \bar{X})^2$ as shown in table 4.3. Next, compute the mean (if you did not do it) and subtract it from each raw score to compute each deviation. Then, square each deviation and multiply it by the frequency for the corresponding score to account for all similar scores. Finally, sum all squared deviation and divide it by 49 (i.e., N – 1 = 50 – 1 = 49). (*Note:* Follow the summation and mathematical operations rules discussed in chapter 1).

The mean and variance for this distribution are as follows:

$$\text{Mean} = \bar{X} = \frac{\Sigma fX}{N} = \frac{1614}{50} = 32.28$$

$$\text{Variance} = S^2 = \frac{\Sigma f(X - \bar{X})^2}{N - 1} = \frac{1278.16}{50 - 1} = 26.08$$

Table 4.3:   Steps of Calculating the Variance and Standard Deviation

X	f	fX	$SS = f(X - \bar{X})^2$
22	1	22	$1 \times (22 - 32.28)^2 = 105.68$
24	3	72	$3 \times (24 - 32.28)^2 = 205.68$
26	4	104	$4 \times (26 - 32.28)^2 = 157.76$
27	3	81	$3 \times (27 - 32.28)^2 = 83.64$
28	2	56	$2 \times (28 - 32.28)^2 = 36.64$
30	3	90	$3 \times (30 - 32.28)^2 = 15.60$
31	6	186	$6 \times (31 - 32.28)^2 = 9.84$
32	7	224	$7 \times (32 - 32.28)^2 = .56$
33	2	66	$2 \times (33 - 32.28)^2 = 1.04$
34	4	136	$4 \times (34 - 32.28)^2 = 11.84$
35	1	35	$1 \times (35 - 32.28)^2 = 7.40$
36	4	144	$4 \times (36 - 32.28)^2 = 59.36$
38	3	114	$3 \times (38 - 32.28)^2 = 98.16$
40	4	160	$4 \times (40 - 32.28)^2 = 238.40$
41	2	81	$2 \times (41 - 32.28)^2 = 152.08$
42	1	42	$1 \times (42 - 32.28)^2 = 94.48$
Total (Σ)	50	1614	1278.16

X = score (life satisfaction); f = frequency; fX = score × frequency; SS = sum of squares; $\bar{X}$ = Mean

Standard Deviation

Standard deviation is the most-used measure of variability. Always reported along with the mean, it indicates how closely scores in a distribution cluster around the mean. The larger the standard deviation is, the larger the variability around the mean. It is measured in the same units as the mean. For example, if the mean age is 25 years, a standard deviation could be ±5 years.

The standard deviation is most appropriate when data approach a normal distribution (see chapter 5). In this case, 68.26 percent of subjects will fall within ±1 standard deviation of the mean, 95.44 percent of subjects fall within ±2 standard deviations of the mean, and 99.74 percent of subjects will fall within ±3 standard deviations of the mean. We return to this in the next chapter when we discuss normal distribution and z scores.

Mathematically, standard deviation is the square root of the variance ($S = \sqrt{S^2}$). The symbol for the standard deviation for a population is σ and for a sample is SD.

As with any value produced by the square root, standard deviation is always reported with + and − signs, which indicate that a given score in a distribution can be above or below the mean.

QUESTION: What is the standard deviation for the data in table 4.2?

ANSWER: Calculating the standard deviation is a simple one, especially since we already calculated the variance. To calculate the standard deviation, simply compute the square root of the variance. Thus, the standard deviation for the data in table 4.2 is as follows:

$$SD = \sqrt{S^2} = \sqrt{26.08} = \pm 5.11$$

We will return to standard deviation in more detail in the next chapter when we discuss normal distribution and z scores.

MEASURES OF CENTRAL TENDENCY AND VARIABILITY TO REPORT

The three measures of central tendency each provide different information about the distribution. However, the type of data, their levels of measurement, and their distribution will determine what is most appropriate for reporting and interpreting.

With nominal variables, the mode is the only measure of central tendency to report.

Example: If the variable Race is classified as 1 = White, 2 = African American, 3 = Hispanic, 4 = Native American, and 5 = Other, it is meaningless to report the median or the mean. However, if we found that the majority of participants in a study, for example, are African American, then we can safely report that the mode is African American, or 3, the categorical value associated with it.

With ordinal data, both the mode and the median could be reported.

Example: We asked fifty subjects to rate their physical health on a five-point Likert scale (1 = poor, 2 = fair, 3 = good, 4 = very good, 5 = excellent). Seven subjects rated their physical health as 1, eight as 2, ten as 3, fifteen as 4, and ten as 5. Here, the mode is 4 because 4 is the most frequent score (fifteen subjects chose 4); the median is 3.5, the middle score in an even number of cases (twenty-five subjects, or 50%, chose 3 or less; twenty-five subjects, or 50%, chose 4 or above).

With interval or ratio data, the mean could be reported along with the mode and median. However, the mean is very sensitive to outlier cases. For example, if we asked ten undergraduate students their ages and found that nine of them were between eighteen and twenty-four and the tenth student was thirty-six, this increases the mean from where it should be to a higher score. If this student was fourteen, then the mean would be lower than it should be. In either case, the mean is not a good representation of the data. The researcher may want to treat this case as missing and report the mean for the nine students within a normal range.

Unlike measures of central tendency, measures of variability (mean deviation, variance, and standard deviation) describe the spread of a distribution of continuous scores around the mean. Therefore, it is recommended to report them, especially standard deviation, alongside (perhaps in parentheses) the mean. It is also recommended to report the minimum and maximum scores to indicate the range of scores. Minimum and maximum can also be reported with ordinal data.

PERCENTILES

A percentile is a score, or a group of scores (class interval) in a distribution, at or below which a given percentage of cases is found. It is symbolized by the capital letter P with a subscript number indicating the percentile desired. For example, P_{35} indicates the 35th percentile; 35 percent of cases fall at or below the given score. The 50th percentile (P_{50}) is the score that 50 percent of cases fall at or below. This is also called the median (median = 50th percentile).

Example: If John's score on a statistics test was 85 and he is told he is at the 64th percentile, then 64 percent of John's classmates scored at or below 85 and 36 percent scored higher than 85; that is P_{64} = 85.

To find the percentile for a specific score in a distribution, locate the cumulative percentage (c%) in a frequency distribution table (see chapter 3). The cumulative percentage for a given score represents the percentile for this score.

For example, using table 3.1 (in chapter 3), someone with a score of 27 on the life satisfaction scale falls at the 22nd percentile (P_{22}); that is, 22 percent of participants scored at or below 27. A participant who scored 34 falls at the 70th percentile; that is 70 percent scored at or below 34; 22 percent and 70 percent are the cumulative percentages for 27 and 34.

Quartiles

The quartiles are the 25th, 50th (median), and 75th percentiles, symbolized by Q1, Q2, and Q3, respectively. Quartiles divide a distribution of scores into four equal parts.

To find a quartile, first find the median, the 50th percentile, which divides a distribution into equal groups. Treat each half as a separate distribution. For all scores below the median, find the middle point. This will be the 25th percentile. Now, locate the middle point for all scores above the median. This is the 75th percentile.

QUESTION: What are the quartiles for the raw data 4.1?

ANSWER: To compute the quartiles for these data, arrange them from low to high in an array. Next, split them in two equal sets each with twenty-five cases (there are fifty total cases) as shown in array data 4.2. Then find the median for each set as we discussed under the median. Since each set has an odd number of cases (twenty-five cases), then the median is the score associated with the middle case (case #13) in each set. These are 28 (set 1) and 36 (set 2). In other words, the 25th percentile is 28, and the 75th is 36. Remember, the median, the 50th percentile, is 32.

Array Data 4.2

Set 1								
22	24	24	24	26	26	26	26	27
27	27	28	28	30	30	30	31	31
31	31	31	31	32	32	32		

Set 2

32	32	32	32	33	33	34	34	34
34	35	36	36	36	36	38	38	38
40	40	40	40	41	41	42		

You may also locate the quartiles simply by looking at table 3.1 (see chapter 3) under cumulative percentages. Notice in table 3.1 that 26 percent of participants scored 28 or less, which includes the bottom 25 percent. That is, 28 is the 25th percentile. We follow the same principle to locate the 50th (median) and 75th percentiles; the 50th percentile is 32 (c% = 58%) and the 75th percentile is 36 (c% = 80%).

Interquartile Range

Interquartile range is defined as the distance between the 75th percentile (Q3) and the 25th percentile (Q1). It is symbolized by IQR. It is computed by subtracting the 25th percentile from the 75th percentile.

Interquartile Formula

$IQR = Q3 - Q1$

IQR = Interquartile range
$Q3$ = 75th percentile
$Q1$ = 25th percentile

QUESTION: What is the interquartile range for the raw data 4.1?

ANSWER: To compute the interquartile range for these data, simply subtract the 25th percentile value from the 75th percentile value we identified above as follows:

$$IQR = Q3 - Q1 = 36 - 28 = 8$$

That is, the distance between the 25th and 75th percentiles is 8 units.

HOW TO RUN MEASURES OF CENTRAL TENDENCY AND VARIABILITY IN SPSS

To demonstrate the use of SPSS to compute measures of central tendency (mean, median, and mode), variability (range, mean deviation, variance, and standard deviation), percentiles (including quartiles), we will use the variables gender (Gender) and emotional balance (EB) from the SPSS Mental Health data file as an example. Notice we have two variables in which the first (Gender) is categorical and the second (EB) is continuous.

To run measures of central tendency, variability, and percentiles for these variables (and others) in SPSS, we use the *Analyze*, *Descriptive Statistics*, and *Frequencies* commands (we may also use the *Explore* commands) as follows:

1. Open the SPSS Mental Health data file.
2. Click on *Analyze*, click on *Descriptive Statistics*, then click on *Frequencies* (see chapter 2, screen 2.10). A new dialog box called "Frequencies" will open (see screen 4.1).

Screen 4.1:   SPSS Frequencies Dialog Box

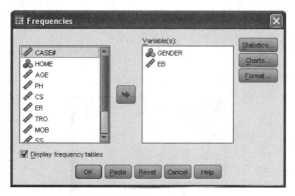

3. Scroll down in the variables list, click on *Gender*, and click on the arrow button between the two boxes to move *Gender* in the *Variable(s)* box.
4. Repeat step 3 and move *EB* in the *Variable(s)* box
5. Click on *Statistics* in the upper right side of the "Frequencies" dialog box to open the "Frequencies: Statistics" dialog box (see screen 4.2).

Screen 4.2:   SPSS Frequencies: Statistics Dialog Box

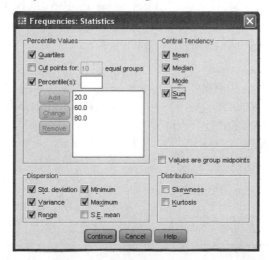

6.   Check *Mean*, *Median*, *Mode*, and *Sum* under "Central Tendency."

7.   Check *Quartiles* under "Percentile Values" to get the 25th, 50th, and 75th percentiles. You may also check *Percentile(s)* to request a specific percentile. Let us request the 20th, 60th, and 80th percentiles. After you check the *Percentile(s)*, type "20" in the *Percentile(s)* box and click on *Add*. Type "60," and click on *Add*. Then type "80" and click on *Add*.

8.   Check *Std. Deviation*, *Variance*, *Range*, *Minimum*, and *Maximum* under "Dispersion."

9.   Click on *Continue* to return to the "Frequencies" dialog box.

10.   You can also click on *Charts* to request a chart. A new dialog box called "Frequencies: Charts" will open (see screen 4.3).

Screen 4.3:   SPSS Frequencies: Charts Dialog Box

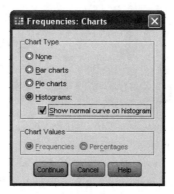

SPSS Syntax for Measures of Central Tendency, Variability, Percentiles, and Charts

FREQUENCIES VARIABLES=GENDER EB

/NTILES=4

/PERCENTILES=20.0 60.0 80.0

/STATISTICS=STDDEV VARIANCE RANGE MINIMUM MAXIMUM MEAN MEDIAN MODE SUM

/HISTOGRAM NORMAL

/ORDER=ANALYSIS.

Note: You may request other percentiles simply by typing them next to the *Percentiles* command. Or, you may request analysis for other variables by typing the variable names next to the *Frequencies Variables* command.

11.   If you have a categorical variable like gender, you may check *Bar charts* or *Pie charts*. For continuous variables like emotional balance, you may request a histogram. Here we have one categorical variable and one continuous variable, and thus we cannot choose both *Bar chart* and *Histogram*. However, for learning purposes, check *Histograms* and check *Show normal curve on histogram* (we already discussed in chapter 3 how to create these graphs using the *Graphs* menu).

12.   Click on *Continue*, then click on *OK*.

The execution of these SPSS commands produces one general statistics table, one frequency table for each variable entered in the analysis, and one graph for each variable. Here, only the statistics table is discussed, as chapter 3 addressed how to interpret and report frequency tables and graphs.

Table 4.4 reports the number of valid missing cases and displays measures of central tendency (mean, median, and mode), variability (standard deviation, variance, range, minimum, and maximum), sum of scores, and percentiles (including quartiles) for the variables gender and emotional balance.

Table 4.4 shows that all 155 subjects reported their gender (missing = 0) compared to 149 subjects who complete the emotional balance scale (missing = 6).

Next, the table shows that the mean, median, and mode for gender are .52, 1.00, and 1, respectively. Recall that with categorical variables the only measure of central tendency to be reported is the mode. Thus, while SPSS computes all statistics, you should only report those appropriate measures. For emotional balance, the mean, median, and mode are 19.58, 20, and 23, respectively.

Table 4.4:   Descriptive Statistics for Gender and Emotional Balance

		Statistics	
		Gender	Emotional Balance
N	Valid	155	149
	Missing	0	6
Mean		.52	19.58
Median		1.00	20.00
Mode		1	23
Std. Deviation		.501	5.701
Variance		.251	32.501
Range		1	24
Minimum		0	8
Maximum		1	32
Sum		80	2918
Percentiles	20	.00	14.00
	25	.00	15.00
	50	1.00	20.00
	60	1.00	21.00
	75	1.00	23.00
	80	1.00	23.00

Table 4.4 then reports measures of variability for both variables. Again, since gender is a categorical variable, the standard deviation and the variance, which is always to be reported with the mean, are not appropriate. The standard deviation and variance for emotional balance are 5.701 and 32.501, respectively. Recall that the standard deviation is the square root of the variance ($\sqrt{32.501}$ = ±5.701).

The range is next reported for both variables. In SPSS, range is computed as the maximum minus the minimum score. For gender, the range is 1 (that is, $1 - 0 = 1$), and for emotional balance, it is 24 (that is, $32 - 8 = 24$). Both minimum and maximum scores are then presented. In this example, minimum for gender is 0 (male) and maximum is 1 (female). Emotional balance ranges between 8 and 32 (see Mental Health in Appendix A).

The table then reports the sum of scores (this is ΣfX). Again, this is appropriate only for continuous data where it is used to compute the mean and other statistics. Table 4.4 shows that the sum of scores for emotional balance as 2,918. Dividing this number by the valid cases produces the mean; that is, $\frac{2918}{149}$ = 19.58.

Lastly, the table displays the three quartiles (25th, 50th, and 75th) and those percentiles we requested. Notice that the 50th percentile for emotional balance is the same as that of the median.

As you may notice, the table does not report the interquartile range or the mean deviation. To compute the interquartile range, simple subtract the 25th percentile (15) from the 75th percentile (23). That is, $23 - 15 = 8$. Interquartile range, however, can be generated through the SPSS *Explore* commands.

On the other hand, to compute the mean deviation, create a new variable for the absolute deviation scores using the *Transform and Compute* command.

To compute the absolute deviations for emotional balance in SPSS, open the "Compute Variable" dialog box by clicking on *Transform and Compute* (see screen 4.4).

Screen 4.4: SPSS Compute Variable Dialog Box

Type "EB_AbsDev" (Absolute Deviations for EB) in the *Target Variable* box, type "ABS(EB-19.58)" in the *Numeric Expression* box, and click *OK*. The ABS is the command for absolute, and 19.58 is the mean score for emotional balance (see table 4.4).

This creates a new variable called "EB_AbsDev" in the SPSS data view file, which is the absolute deviation for each subject on the emotional balance scale. To compute the mean deviations, use the SPSS *Analyze, Descriptive Statistics*, and *Frequencies* commands discussed above and request the mean for this new variable.

SPSS Syntax for Computing Absolute Values for
Emotional Balance Deviations

COMPUTE EB_AbsDev=ABS(EB-19.58).
EXECUTE.

Table 4.5 displays the statistics for the emotional balance deviations. The table shows that the mean deviation is 4.6124.

BOX-AND-WHISKER PLOT

A box-and-whisker plot, simply known as a boxplot, was created by John Tukey in 1977 as an exploratory graphical presentation that illustrates the spread of a distribution of continuous data. It visually displays five measures of central tendency and variability. These measures include the median (P_{50}), the range (minimum and maximum), and quartiles (Q1 and Q3). Boxplot is also useful to identify unusual or outlying scores in a distribution. In addition, boxplots are used to compare measures of central tendency and variability between groups (e.g., males vs. females). A boxplot does not, however, provide as much information as a histogram or a stem-and-leaf plot.

Figure 4.1 displays a boxplot for levels of depression among participants in the Mental Health data file. The figure shows both quartiles (Q1, Q2, and Q3) and ranges of scores (minimum and maximum). The figure shows that 25 percent

Table 4.5: Descriptive Statistics for Mean Deviation

Statistics		
		EB_AbsDev
N	Valid	149
	Missing	6
Mean		4.6124
Minimum		.42
Maximum		12.42

Figure 4.1:   Boxplot for Levels of Depression

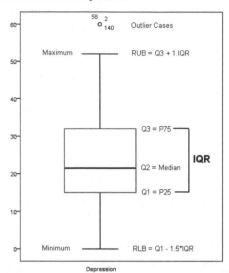

of subjects scored at or below 15 (Q1), 50 percent scored at or below 21 (Q2 or median), and 75 percent scored at or below 32 (Q3). The figure also shows that levels of depression range between 0 (minimum) and 52 (maximum). The figure also shows that three cases (2, 58, and 140) are considered outlier scores.

Outlier Cases

As we said earlier, outliers are unusual scores that fall at either end of a distribution of continuous data. There are two types of outlier cases; minor outliers and extreme outliers.

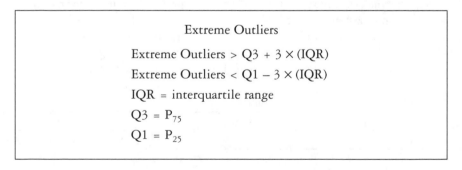

Extreme Outliers

Extreme Outliers $> Q3 + 3 \times (IQR)$

Extreme Outliers $< Q1 - 3 \times (IQR)$

IQR = interquartile range

$Q3 = P_{75}$

$Q1 = P_{25}$

A score is considered an extreme outlier if it is more than or less than three times the interquartile range (IQR). That is, any score greater than (Q3 + 3 * IQR) or less than (Q1 − 3 * IQR) is considered an extreme outlier. Recall that IQR is the distance between Q1 and Q3.

A score is considered a minor outlier if it is more than or less than one and a half times the interquartile range (IQR). That is, any score greater than (Q3 + 1.5 * IQR) or less than (Q1 − 1.5 * IQR) is considered a minor outlier.

Minor Outliers

Minor Outliers > Q3 + 1.5 × (IQR)

Minor Outliers < Q1 − 1.5 × (IQR)

IQR = interquartile range

Q3 = P_{75}

Q1 = P_{25}

Reasonable boundaries.   To identify and account for outlier cases in a boxplot, it is necessary that we adjust both minimum and maximum scores since, by default, they contain all cases observed in a study including outliers. Therefore, to account for those outliers at the upper end, we adjust the maximum score to reasonable upper boundary (RUB) and the minimum score to reasonable lower boundary (RLB) as follows (also see figure 4.1):

Reasonable Boundaries

RUB = Q3 + 1.5 × (IQR)

RLB = Q1 − 1.5 × (IQR)

RUB = Reasonable Upper Boundary = Adjusted Maximum

RLB = Reasonable Lower Boundary = Adjusted Minimum

Minor outliers are usually identified in a boxplot by small dots or circles as shown in figure 4.1. Extreme outliers are identified with asterisks. When no outlier cases exist, the actual minimum and maximum scores are used instead of the RUB and RLB.

How to construct a boxplot.   We will construct a boxplot for our raw data 4.1. Recall that we have fifty scores on life satisfaction. To construct a boxplot for these data, follow these steps:

1. Identify the quartiles for these data. Recall that we already identified these quartiles as 28 (Q1), 32 (Q2), and 36 (Q3) (see the "Quartiles" section above).

2. Compute the interquartile range and both reasonable upper and lower boundaries as follows:

$$IQR = Q3 - Q1 = 36 - 28 = 8$$
$$RUB = Q3 + 1.5 \times (IQR) = 36 + 1.5 * 8 = 36 + 12 = 48$$
$$RLB = Q1 - 1.5 \times (IQR) = 28 - 1.5 * 8 = 28 - 12 = 16$$

That is, any score that is greater than 48 or smaller than 16 is considered an outlier. Recall, however, that raw data 4.1 range between 22 and 42, which fall within the RUB and RLB. That is, the data have no outlier cases and, therefore, we should use the actual minimum and maximum scores.

3. Now list the five measures for constructing the boxplot: minimum (22), Q1 (P_{25} = 28), Q2 (median = 32), Q3 (P_{75} = 36), and maximum (48).

4. To construct the boxplot, first draw a line parallel to the X axis to convey the minimum score (22). Second, draw a line of the same length to convey the maximum score (42). Third, draw three lines parallel to the X axis but slightly longer than the previous two lines to convey Q1, median, and Q3. Fourth, connect the ends of these three lines to form a rectangle. Fifth, connect the midpoint of the minimum with Q1 and another line to connect the midpoint of the maximum with Q3. Figure 4.2 illustrates this boxplot.

How to create a boxplot in SPSS.   For this purpose we will use the Job Satisfaction data file to create two boxplots, one for workload (Workload) and another for levels of burnout (Burnout) by gender (Gender).

Figure 4.2:   Boxplot for Life Satisfaction (raw data 4.1)

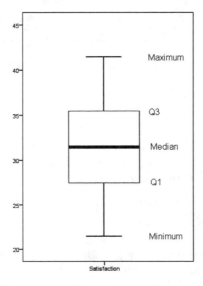

To create a boxplot for workload, follow these steps:

1. Open the SPSS Job Satisfaction data file.

2. Click on *Graphs*, *Legacy Dialog*, and *Boxplot* (see chapter 3, screen 3.8). A dialog box called "Boxplot" will open (see screen 4.5).

Screen 4.5:   SPSS Boxplot Dialog Box

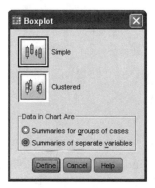

3. Click on *Simple* (SPSS default) and check *Summaries of separate variables* under "Data in Chart Are."

4. Click on *Define*. A new dialog box called "Define Simple Boxplot: Summaries of Separate Variables" will open (see screen 4.6).

Screen 4.6:   SPSS Define Simple Boxplot: Summaries of Separate Variables Dialog Box

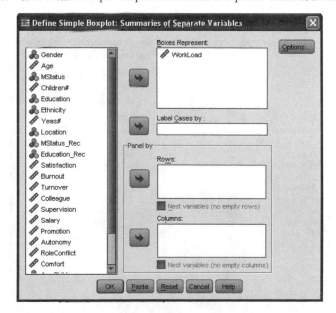

5. Scroll down in the variables list and click on *WorkLoad*, then click on the upper arrow button to move it into the *Boxes Represent* box.

6. If you want to create separate boxplot charts for different groups (e.g., gender), then move Gender (or the grouping variable) into the *Rows* box under "Panel by." (If, however, you want separate boxplots on one chart for a side-by-side comparison, then continue on to the next section of this chapter.)

7. Click on *OK*.

SPSS Syntax for Boxplot

EXAMINE VARIABLES=WorkLoad

/PLOT=BOXPLOT.

To create a boxplot for burnout by gender, follow these steps:

1. Follow steps 1 and 2 above and check *Summaries for groups of cases* under "Data in Chart Are" (see screen 4.5).

2. Click on *Define*. A new dialog box called "Define Simple Boxplot: Summaries for Groups of Cases" will open (see screen 4.7).

3. Scroll down in the variables list, click on *Burnout*, and click on the upper arrow button to move it into the *Variable* box.

4. Scroll down in the variables list, click on *Gender* (grouping variable), and click on the second upper arrow button to move it into the *Category Axis* box.

Screen 4.7:   SPSS Define Simple Boxplot: Summaries for Groups of Cases Dialog Box

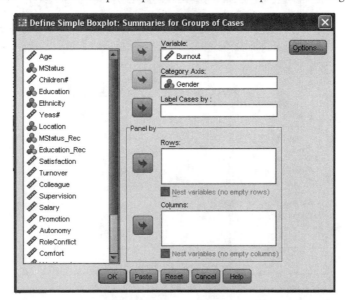

5. If you want to compare burnout by gender and, for example, by a third grouping variable, say ethnicity (Arabs vs. Jews), you can move *Ethnicity* into the *Rows* box under "Panel by."

6. Click on *OK*.

SPSS Syntax for Boxplot

EXAMINE VARIABLES = *Burnout BY Gender*

/PLOT=BOXPLOT.

Note: We can also create boxplots for separate variables or separate groups through the SPSS *Analyze, Descriptive Statistics, Explore* (see chapter 3, screen 3.18) commands as we discussed under stem-and-leaf plot. Here, we move Burnout in the *Dependent List* box and Gender in the *Factor List* box (see chapter 3, screen 3.19). Make sure that *Factor levels together* under "Boxplots" is checked (SPSS default) in the "Explore Plots" dialog box (see chapter 3, screen 3.20).

The execution of these commands produces two tables, Case Processing Summary and Descriptives, and a boxplot for the variable workload and same for burnout by gender.

Table 4.6 reports the number of valid, missing, and total cases in the analysis. In our example, all 218 participants complete the workload scale (Missing = 0).

Table 4.7 (it is not available through the *Graphs, Legacy Dialog, Boxplot* menu) reports measures of central tendency (mean and mode) for workload, measures of variability (variance and standard deviation), minimum and maximum, range, and interquartile range. We already discussed these measures. In addition, the table reports the 95 percent confidence interval and both skewness and kurtosis coefficients. These will be discussed in the next two chapters.

In addition, table 4.7 reports the 5 percent trimmed mean. This represents the mean for the distribution if the lower 2.5 percent and upper 2.5 percent of cases are deleted. A difference between the actual mean and the 5 percent trimmed mean indicates that there are some outlier cases. When both are identical, as in table 4.7, this indicates that no outliers exist.

Table 4.6: Case Processing Summary for Workload

	Case Processing Summary					
	Cases					
	Valid		Missing		Total	
	N	Percent	N	Percent	N	Percent
Workload	218	100.0%	0	.0%	218	100.0%

Table 4.7:   Descriptive Statistics for Workload

Descriptives			Statistic	Std. Error
WorkLoad	Mean		13.21	.195
	95% Confidence	Lower Bound	12.82	
	Interval for Mean	Upper Bound	13.59	
	5% Trimmed Mean		13.21	
	Median		13.00	
	Variance		8.266	
	Std. Deviation		2.875	
	Minimum		6	
	Maximum		20	
	Range		14	
	Interquartile Range		4	
	Skewness		–.116	.165
	Kurtosis		–.559	.328

Figure 4.3 displays the boxplot for workload. The Y axis displays the scores for workload. The figure shows that the minimum score was 6 and maximum score was 20; the 25th, 50th, and 75th percentiles are 11, 13, and 15, respectively; there were no outlier cases.

Table 4.8 (case processing summary), table 4.9 (descriptive statistics), and figure 4.4 (boxplot) display the SPSS output for burnout by gender. Table 4.7 shows the number of valid, missing, and total participants in the job satisfaction study who completed the burnout scale by gender. In this case, all male

Figure 4.3:   Boxplot for Workload

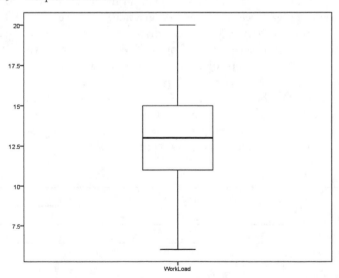

Table 4.8:   Case Processing Summary for Burnout by Gender

Case Processing Summary

| | | \multicolumn{6}{c}{Cases} | | | | | |
| | | Valid | | Missing | | Total | |
	Gender	N	Percent	N	Percent	N	Percent
Burnout	Male	36	100.0%	0	.0%	36	100.0%
	Female	182	100.0%	0	.0%	182	100.0%

participants (n = 36) and female participants (n = 182) completed the scale (Missing = 0).

Table 4.9 reports measures of central tendency, variability, range, skewness, and kurtosis for burnout for males and females. The table shows that levels of burnout among females range between 8 and 49 compared to 11 and 45 among

Table 4.9:   Descriptive Statistics for Burnout by Gender

Descriptives

	Gender			Statistic	Std. Error
Burnout	Male	Mean		24.03	1.198
		95% Confidence	Lower Bound	21.60	
		Interval for Mean	Upper Bound	26.46	
		5% Trimmed Mean		23.69	
		Median		23.00	
		Variance		51.685	
		Std. Deviation		7.189	
		Minimum		11	
		Maximum		45	
		Range		34	
		Interquartile Range		11	
		Skewness		.702	.393
		Kurtosis		.755	.768
	Female	Mean		21.08	.446
		95% Confidence	Lower Bound	20.20	
		Interval for Mean	Upper Bound	21.96	
		5% Trimmed Mean		20.78	
		Median		20.00	
		Variance		36.220	
		Std. Deviation		6.018	
		Minimum		8	
		Maximum		49	
		Range		41	
		Interquartile Range		6	
		Skewness		1.050	.180
		Kurtosis		2.656	.358

Figure 4.4:   Boxplot for Burnout by Gender

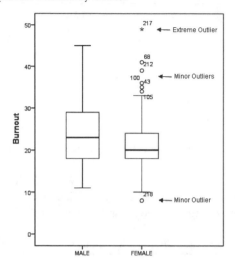

males. Also, the table shows that the interquartile range (Q3 – Q1) among males is greater than that among females (11 and 6, respectively). Moreover, there are some differences between the mean and the 5 percent trimmed mean, especially among males (24.03 vs. 23.69); thus indicating some outlier cases.

Figure 4.4 displays two boxplots in one graph for burnout: one for males and another for females. This graph confirms the statistics displayed in table 4.9. The graph shows that the range of burnout among males is longer than that among females, and so is the interquartile range. Furthermore, the boxplots show that the median among males is greater than that among females.

More important, figure 4.4 reports all minor and extreme outlier cases. Unlike table 4.9, which indicated some outlier cases based on the mean and 5 percent trimmed mean, figure 4.4 displays the case number of all cases with minor outliers and extreme outliers. As shown in the figure, there is one female (case #217) with extreme high burnout. Five more females (Cases #105, 43, 100, 212, and 68) have minor high burnout. On the other hand, one female (case #218) reported minor low burnout. Finally, figure 4.4 shows no outlier cases among males.

SUMMARY

Chapter 4 presented two measures of data description. Measures of central tendency are mode, median, and mean. The mode is the most frequent score in a distribution; the median is the score in a distribution that 50 percent of scores fall at or below; the mean is the average score. Measures of variability consist of the range, mean deviation, variance, and standard deviation. The range is the number of units in a distribution; mean deviation is the average distance of scores from the mean; variance is the sum of the squared deviations around the mean; standard deviation is the square root of the variance.

The chapter also presented the percentile, a point in a distribution at or below which a percentage of cases fall. Chapter 4 next discussed quartiles and interquartile range. Quartiles represent 25th, 50th, and 75th percentiles which divide a distribution to four equal parts. Interquartile range is the distance between the 75th and 25th percentiles. Then, boxplot was discussed. A boxplot visually displays measures of central tendency and variability. How to utilize SPSS to compute measures of central tendency, variability, and percentile, and boxplot construction were also presented.

Chapter 5 discusses the properties of normal and skewed distributions, methods of data transformation into normal distributions, and the properties of standard scores (z scores).

PRACTICAL EXERCISES

Part I: Use a pencil, paper, and the data from Part I in chapter 3 and answer the following questions:

1. Compute measures of central tendency and variability.

2. Compute the range, quartiles, and interquartile range.

3. Compute the reasonable boundaries.

4. Are there any outlier cases? Why?

5. Construct a boxplot. Explain what information it conveys.

Part II: Access the SPSS Welfare data file (appendix A) and answer the following questions:

1. Report the appropriate measures of central tendency and variability for age (Age), marital status (MStatus), physical health (PHealth) and levels of depression (CESD).

2. Compute the mean deviation for self-esteem (Esteem). Write the SPSS syntax.

3. What are the quartiles, interquartile range, and the 33rd and 66th percentiles for self-esteem (Esteem)? Discuss what these measures convey.

4. Run a boxplot for depression (CESD) based on education (Education). Discuss what this plot conveys.

5. Run a boxplot for levels of social support (Support) using the SPSS syntax or *Explore* commands. Discuss what the plot and the summary and descriptive tables convey.

Note: You may copy and paste all your SPSS tables and graphs for each question into your word-processing document or save all your SPSS outputs in one SPSS file.

CHAPTER 5

Normality of Distributions, Data Transformations, and Standard Scores

LEARNING OBJECTIVES

1. Understand normal distributions

2. Understand skewed distributions

3. Understand measures of skewness and normal probability plots

4. Understand data transformations process

5. Understand standard scores (z scores)

6. Understand how to use SPSS to evaluate distributions, conduct data transformation, and compute z scores

DATA SET (APPENDIX A)

Elderly

Job Satisfaction

INTRODUCTION

The previous chapter raised the issue of outlier cases that could severely affect the mean score as well as measures of variability (range, mean deviation, and standard deviation). Outlier cases can also significantly affect the shape of the distribution of scores.

The importance of a normal distribution is based on two assumptions: first, many social science constructs, such as life satisfaction, self-esteem, or anxiety in the real world approach a normal distribution. Statisticians refer to this as the central limit theorem (CLT), which indicates the following:

> As the sample size (N) increases, the sampling distribution of the mean for simple random samples of N cases, taken from a population with a mean equal

to μ and a finite variance equal to σ^2, approximates a normal distribution. (Hinkle, Wiersma, & Jurs, 2003, p. 164)

According to the CLT, the distribution of mean scores taken from a sufficiently large number of samples tends to approach a normal curve even if the distribution of the original mean scores may not be normal. In general, as sample size increases, the quicker a distribution becomes normal. Statisticians have shown that sampling distributions tend to be normal with sample sizes as low as thirty (N=30) cases (Hinkle, Wiersma, & Jurs, 2003).

Second, as will be seen in the following chapters, parametric statistical techniques like the Pearson's product-moment correlation coefficients, Student's *t*-tests, analysis of variances, and multiple regression analysis require that the dependent variable (measured at the interval level of measurement or ratio) is normally distributed. These statistics use the mean scores to examine the correlations between the independent and dependent variables (see chapter 7 and thereafter). As mentioned in chapter 4, the mean score is most appropriate to represent a population if a distribution has no outlier cases and it approaches a normal curve.

This chapter examines the normal distribution and its properties. Next, the chapter examines both positively and negatively skewed distributions and presents statistical methods to evaluate whether a distribution is considered normal or skewed, as well as methods of data transformation. The chapter then discusses standard scores (z scores) and their uses. In addition, the chapter presents a detailed discussion of the utilization of SPSS in examining the distributions, conducting data transformation, and computing z scores.

NORMALITY OF DISTRIBUTIONS

Normal Distribution

A normal distribution, also known as Gaussian distribution,[1] has the following characteristics:

1. It is unimodal. That is, it has only one mode. (Recall from chapter 3 that a distribution may have one, two, or multiple modes.)

2. It is symmetrical; the left and right halves are mirror images.

3. It is bell-shaped, with its maximum height at the mean of the scores.

4. All measures of central tendency (mean, median, and mode) are equal.

5. It is continuous. That is, there is a value of y (the height) for every value of x, where x is assumed to be a continuous variable (e.g., weight and height).

6. It is asymptotic to the X axis. The farther away from the mean it goes, the closer it gets to the X axis; yet it never touches the X axis. Figure 5.1 displays a standard normal distribution.

---

[1]Named after Carl Friedrich Gauss, a German mathematician and scientist (1777–1855).

Figure 5.1:   Standard Normal Distribution

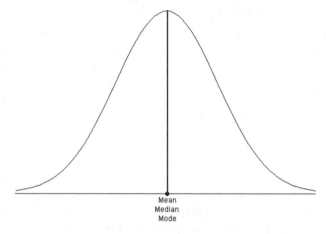

Mean
Median
Mode

In reality, although many social constructs approach a normal shape, they may never have a perfect normal shape. The question is, then, when is a distribution considered normal? A distribution may be considered normal if it is not severely skewed, that is, asymmetrical. An asymmetrical distribution has a mean that is not in the center of the distribution. There are two types of skewed distributions: positive and negative.

Positively Skewed Distribution

Positively skewed distribution is skewed to the right; the right tail is longer than the left. The mean of a positively skewed distribution is greater than the median, and the median is greater than the mode (mode < median < mean). In this distribution, most cases fall to the left (see figure 5.2).

To determine if a distribution is positively skewed, subtract the median from the mean. If the result is a positive value, then the distribution is positively skewed.

Mean – Median = Positive Value

Figure 5.2:   Positively Skewed Distribution

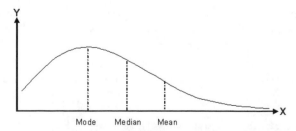

Mode   Median   Mean

Negatively Skewed Distribution

Negatively skewed distribution is skewed to the left; the left tail is longer than the right. The mean is smaller than the median, which is smaller than the mode (mean < median < mode). Most cases fall to the right of the distribution (see figure 5.3).

To determine if a distribution is negatively skewed, subtract the median from the mean. A negative value indicates that the distribution is negatively skewed.

Mean − Median = Negative Value

Figure 5.3:   Negatively Skewed Distribution

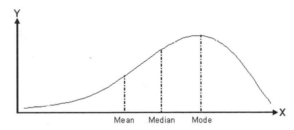

Inspection of Skewness

As discussed above, a distribution can be either normal or skewed; that is, symmetrical or asymmetrical, respectively. The question is, then, how do we examine whether a distribution is skewed, or asymmetrical? Two methods are discussed here: (1) measures of skewness (Pearson's skewness coefficient and Fisher's skewness coefficient), and (2) histogram and probability plots.

Skewness coefficients are measures of the symmetry, or asymmetry, of the shape of a distribution. In general, a normal distribution is symmetric and has a skewness coefficient of 0.

Pearson's skewness coefficient.   Pearson's skewness coefficient was originally introduced by Karl Pearson (Pearson, 1895). It is based on the difference between the mean and the mode in standard deviation units [(Mean − Mode)/Standard Deviation]. However, the formula was revised later to apply the median instead of the mode since samples' modes are often not good estimates of the populations' modes. That is, Pearson's skewness coefficient is calculated by dividing the difference between the mean and median by the standard deviation.

Pearson's Skewness Coefficient Formula

$$Skewness = \frac{Mean - Median}{SD}$$

SD = Standard Deviation

Pearson's skewness coefficient ranges between −1 and +1. In general, a distribution with a coefficient of 0 indicates that the shape of the distribution approaches a normal curve, yet it does not imply a standard normal distribution. According to Hildebrand, skewness coefficients greater than +0.20 or smaller than −0.20 are considered to have severe skewness (Hair et al., 2010; Hildebrand, 1986; Munro, 2005).

Fisher's skewness coefficient.   Fisher's skewness coefficient is based on a more complex formula than Pearson's skewness coefficient.[2] Fortunately, most statistical software, including SPSS, computes both the skewness value and its standard error. Fisher's skewness coefficient is then simply calculated by dividing the skewness value by its standard error.

Fisher's Skewness Coefficient Formula

$$Skewness = \frac{SK}{SES}$$

SK = Skewness Value
SES = Standard Error of Skewness

In general, statisticians have used a 5 percent level of significance (alpha = .05; z = ±1.96) to determine whether a distribution is significantly departed from symmetry and whether it is considered severely skewed. Given an alpha of .05, a skewness coefficient greater than 1.96 indicates that the distribution is significantly skewed to the right (severe positive skewness), and a skewness coefficient smaller than −1.96 indicates the distribution is significantly skewed to the left (severe negative skewness). Other statisticians have used a more liberal approach and used a 1 percent level of significance (alpha = .01; z = ±2.58). That is, with an alpha of .01, a skewness coefficient greater than 2.58 indicates severe positive skewness, and a skewness coefficient smaller than −2.58 indicates severe negative skewness. In other words, a distribution is considered normal if its Fisher's skewness coefficient falls within one of these ranges:

Normal Distribution

Alpha = .05: $-1.96 \leq \frac{SK}{SES} \leq 1.96$

Alpha = .01: $-2.58 \leq \frac{SK}{SES} \leq 2.58$

---

[2]Due to the complexity of their computations, skewness and standard error of skewness (SES) are usually computed by statistical software like SPSS.

Normal probability plots. As we indicated above, both Pearson's and Fisher's measures of skewness are based on the deviation from the mean score. Therefore, they are sensitive to outlier scores and should be interpreted with caution. As an alternative, it is best to refer to the histogram and normal probability plots (also known as *Q-Q plots*) of the distribution to evaluate whether it is severely skewed. Keep in mind, however, that while skewness coefficients may indicate severe skewness, the results of a visual inspection of the distribution may appear to be normal.

Probability plots are used to visually inspect whether or not data approach the shape of a normal curve. If normal, data are clustered on a straight line, stretching from the lower left corner to the upper right corner. Departure from the line indicates the distribution is skewed. In some cases, relying on merely looking at the distribution is more appropriate, especially when extreme outlier cases are present. Thus, first inspect the data for outlier cases (see chapter 4 for outliers and boxplots). Normal probability plots are available in most statistical programs, including SPSS.

Figure 5.4 displays a normal Q-Q plot of physical health from the Elderly data file. The figure shows that almost all points are clustered on the straight line, except one minor deviation on the lower end. Thus, figure 5.4 indicates that the distribution of physical health approaches the normal curve.

Example: To illustrate both Pearson's and Fisher's skewness coefficients, along with histogram and probability plots, we will examine the skewness of both age and depression from the Elderly data file.

Table 5.1 and figures 5.5 to 5.8 display SPSS output for these two variables.

Figure 5.4: Normal Q-Q Plot of Physical Health (Elderly data file)

Table 5.1:   Statistics Table for Age and Depression

		Age	Depression
N	Valid	99	99
	Missing	0	0
Mean		78.27	13.99
Median		78.00	12.00
Mode		83	8
Std. Deviation		8.450	9.110
Variance		71.404	82.990
Skewness		.162	1.100
Std. Error of Skewness		.243	.243
Kurtosis		−.557	1.662
Std. Error of Kurtosis		.481	.481
Minimum		60	0
Maximum		101	47

From table 5.1, use the mean, median, and standard deviation to compute the Pearson's skewness coefficient for each variable. Use the skewness and standard error of skewness to compute the Fisher's skewness coefficient for each variable.

Distribution of age.   First, compute the Pearson's and Fisher's skewness coefficients for age as follows:

Skewness Coefficients for Age

$$Pearson's = \frac{Mean - Median}{SD} = \frac{78.27 - 78.00}{8.45} = 0.03$$

$$Fisher's = \frac{Skewness}{SES} = \frac{.162}{.243} = 0.67$$

RESULTS: Pearson's skewness coefficient is .03, which falls within ±0.20 (notice that both the mean and median are almost identical). Fisher's skewness coefficient is .67, which falls within ±1.96 (or ±2.58). Thus, both skewness measures show that the distribution of age falls within the normal range.

Next, inspect both the histogram and normal Q-Q plot of age. Figures 5.5 and 5.6 display the distribution and normal Q-Q plot of age, respectively. As shown in figure 5.5, the shape of the distribution of age approaches that of a normal curve. Moreover, figure 5.6 shows that data for age are clustered on the straight line with minor deviation, especially one case on the upper end, thus indicating normal distribution.

Figure 5.5:   The Distribution of Age

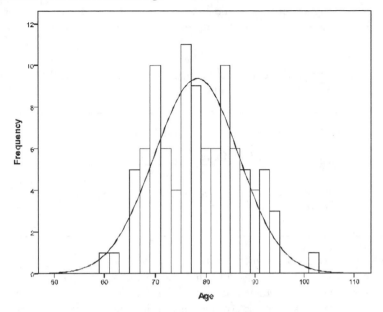

Figure 5.6:   Normal Q-Q Plot of Age

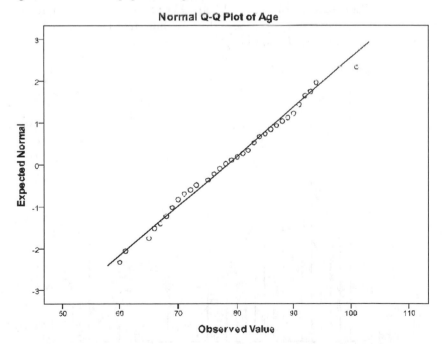

CONCLUSION: The results of both Pearson's and Fisher's skewness coefficients and looking at both histogram and normal Q-Q plot of age show that the distribution of age approaches the shape of a normal curve; one that is not severely skewed.

Distribution of depression.   Compute the Pearson's and Fisher's skewness coefficients for depression as follows:

$$\text{Skewness Coefficients for Depression}$$

$$Pearson's = \frac{Mean - Median}{SD} = \frac{13.99 - 12.00}{9.11} = .22$$

$$Fisher's = \frac{Skewness}{SES} = \frac{1.10}{.243} = 4.53$$

RESULTS: Pearson's skewness coefficient is .22, which falls *slightly* outside ±.20 (notice that the median is smaller than the mean, indicating a positive skewness). Fisher's skewness coefficient is 4.53, which falls outside ±1.96 (and outside ±2.58). Notice that skewness is positive, also indicating positive skewness.

Next, inspect both histogram and normal Q-Q plot of depression. Figures 5.7 and 5.8 display the distribution and normal Q-Q plot of depression, respectively. Figure 5.7 shows that the shape of the distribution of age is skewed to the right (positive skewness). In addition, figure 5.8 shows that many points of

Figure 5.7:   The Distribution of Depression

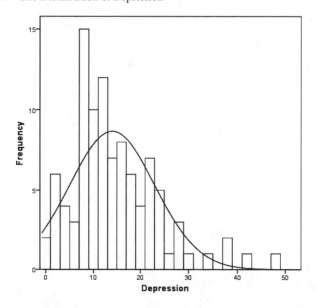

Figure 5.8:   Normal Q-Q Plot of Depression

Normal Q-Q Plot of Depression

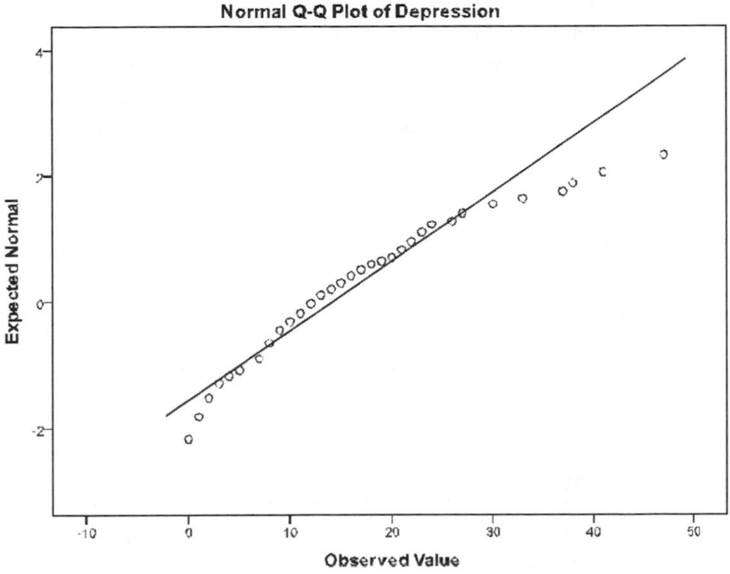

depression scores, especially on the upper end, depart from the straight line, thus indicating severe skewness to the right (positive skewness).

RESULTS: The results of both skewness measures show that the distribution of depression falls outside the normal range, thus indicating severe positive skewness. These results are confirmed by reviewing the histogram and normal Q-Q plot for the distribution of depression.

Data Transformation

Normality of a distribution is one of the assumptions for most inferential statistics, especially parametric tests (see chapter 7 and thereafter). Violation of normality may significantly affect the study results and its conclusion. Therefore, examination of the shape of distributions of variables under study, especially dependent variables, prior to conducting inferential analysis is recommended to ensure that variables are not severely skewed.

Yet, when severe skewness is found, as in the distribution of depression (see figures 5.7 and 5.8), data transformation—converting the raw scores of a variable that is significantly skewed into another type of score—should be considered. This produces a distribution that may approach the shape of a normal curve without affecting the original meaning of the data.

A number of transformation methods are available in SPSS and other statistical software. To transform raw data into another form, two issues must be addressed: (1) the direction of skewness: Is the distribution positively or negatively skewed? and (2) severity of skewness: How severe is the skewness?

If the distribution is negatively skewed, first reverse the raw scores so the distribution becomes positively skewed. Reversing raw scores also reverses the interpretation. If higher scores indicate greater values in the original data, then higher scores will indicate lower values in reversed data (e.g., if higher scores in the original data indicate greater depression, higher scores in reversed data will indicate lower depression). If the original distribution is positively skewed, as in figure 5.5, there is no need to reverse the raw data.

To reverse raw scores, follow these three steps:

1. Find the maximum score for the raw data.

2. Add 1 to the maximum score. This will serve as a constant.

3. Subtract each raw score from the constant.

Reverse Score = (Maximum Score of Raw Data + 1) − Raw Score

Once a distribution is reversed to be positively skewed, the next step is to transform it to one that may produce a distribution that approaches a normal curve. The two common methods of transformation include the square root and the logarithm. Transformation by the square root is generally conducted with distributions that have moderate skewness, while transformation by the logarithm is employed for distributions that are severely skewed. Note, if a transformation by the logarithm is conducted, make sure that the minimum score is greater than zero. If, for example, the minimum score is zero, first add 1 to each raw score, and then conduct a logarithm transformation (Abu-Bader, 2010; Tabachnick & Fidell, 2007).

After a transformation is completed, create a histogram with a normal curve, then run measures of central tendency, variability, and Person's and Fisher's skewness coefficients to evaluate the shape of the transformed distribution and whether another transformation is needed. If the distribution is still severely skewed, try a different method of transformation and evaluate it as you did above.

Example: Recall that the distribution of depression in the previous example has a severe positive skewness. Therefore, before we conduct any further analysis on depression, we will transform it to the square root and, if needed, to the logarithm. Since depression has a positive skewness, there is no need to reverse the raw scores (we only reverse scores if the distribution is negatively skewed).

To conduct a transformation to the square root for depression, simply compute the square root for each raw score. Name the transformed variable SQRTCESD. Table 5.2 displays statistics for both raw scores of depression and the transformed variable. Figures 5.9 and 5.10 display the transformed distribution of depression.

Table 5.2:   Statistics Table for Depression and Square Root of Depression

		Depression	Square Root Depression
N	Valid	99	99
	Missing	0	0
Mean		13.99	3.52
Median		12.00	3.46
Mode		8	3
Std. Deviation		9.110	1.279
Variance		82.990	1.636
Skewness		1.100	−.156
Std. Error of Skewness		.243	.243
Kurtosis		1.662	.551
Std. Error of Kurtosis		.481	.481
Minimum		0	0
Maximum		47	7

Now evaluate whether the distribution of the square root of depression is significantly (severely) skewed. Table 5.2 shows that the distribution of the transformed data has a mean of 3.52, median of 3.46, standard deviation of 1.279, skewness coefficient of −.156, and a standard error of skewness of .243. Use these values to compute the Pearson's and Fisher's skewness coefficients as follows:

Skewness Coefficients for Square Root of Depression

$$Pearson's = \frac{Mean - Median}{SD} = \frac{3.52 - 3.46}{1.279} = .05$$

$$Fisher's = \frac{Skewness}{SES} = \frac{-.156}{.243} = -.64$$

CONCLUSION: Pearson's skewness coefficient is .05, which falls within ±.20. Fisher's skewness coefficient is −.64, which falls within ±1.96. Thus, both skewness measures show that the distribution of transformed depression falls within the normal range. Also, a visual review of the distribution of the square root of depression (figure 5.9) shows that it approaches the shape of a normal curve. In addition, the normal Q-Q plot (figure 5.10) shows that data are clustered on the straight line, although with minor deviations (notice the difference between figures 5.8 and 5.10). In other words, both statistics and visual inspection of the distribution of the transformed depression scores indicate that it appears to be normal. Thus, it is recommended that the square root of depression be used in any future analysis to represent levels of depression.

Figure 5.9:   The Distribution of Square Root of Depression

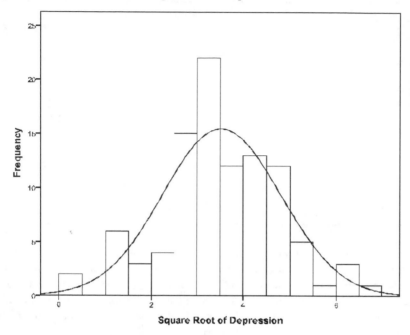

Figure 5.10:   Normal Q-Q Plot of Square Root of CESD (Depression)

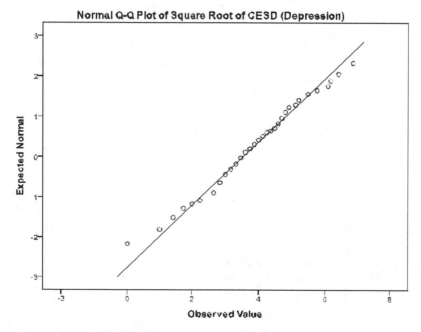

How to Run Measures of Skewness, Plots, and Transformation in SPSS

To illustrate this, we will use the variable supervision (Supervision) from the Job Satisfaction data file. First, run measures of central tendency, variability, Fisher's skewness values, a histogram with a normal curve, and a normal Q-Q plot to evaluate whether a transformation is needed.

To run these measures and graphs in SPSS, follow these steps:

1. Open the SPSS Job Satisfaction data file.

2. Select *Analyze*, click on *Descriptive Statistics*, then click on *Explore* to open the "Explore" dialog box (see chapter 3, screens 3.18 and 3.19).

3. Scroll down in the variables list, click on *Supervision*, and move it in the *Dependent List* box (see screen 5.1). Make sure *Both* is checked under *Display* (SPSS default). This command produces both statistics and plots.

Screen 5.1:   SPSS Explore Dialog Box

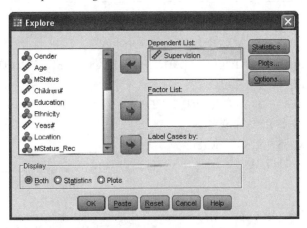

4. Click on *Plots* in the upper right corner to open the "Explore: Plots" dialog box.

5. Check *Histogram* under "Descriptive," and check *Normality plots with tests*. Leave *Stem-and-leaf* under "Descriptive" and *Factor levels together* under "Boxplots" as is (this produces all plots) (see screen 5.2).

6. Click on *Continue* and click on *OK*.

You can run analyses on more than one variable at once. To do so, simply type each variable name after *Supervision*.

The execution of these commands produces three tables and five graphs. For our purpose, we are interested in the descriptive table, histogram, and Q-Q plot. The interpretations of two other graphs, stem-and-leaf and boxplots, were discussed in chapters 3 and 4 and, thus, will not be discussed here.

Screen 5.2:   SPSS Explore: Plots Dialog Box

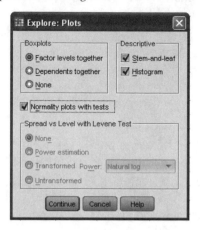

SPSS Syntax for Explore

EXAMINE VARIABLES=Supervision
/PLOT BOXPLOT STEMLEAF HISTOGRAM NPPLOT
/COMPARE GROUPS
/STATISTICS DESCRIPTIVES
/CINTERVAL 95
/MISSING LISTWISE
/NOTOTAL.

Table 5.3 and figures 5.11 and 5.12 display measures of central tendency, measures of variability, and skewness values produced by SPSS, a histogram with a normal curve, and a normal Q-Q plot for supervision.

To evaluate the shape of the distribution of supervision, first use the statistics in table 5.3 to compute Pearson's and Fisher's skewness coefficients as follows:

Skewness Coefficients for Supervision

$$Pearson's = \frac{Mean - Median}{SD} = \frac{54.71 - 58.00}{14.733} = -.22$$

$$Fisher's = \frac{Skewness}{SES} = \frac{-1.293}{.166} = -7.79$$

Table 5.3:   Statistics Table for Supervision

			Statistic	Std. Error
Supervision	Mean		54.71	1.007
	95% Confidence	Lower Bound	52.73	
	Interval for Mean	Upper Bound	56.70	
	5% Trimmed Mean		55.96	
	Median		58.00	
	Variance		217.050	
	Std. Deviation		14.733	
	Minimum		2	
	Maximum		79	
	Range		77	
	Interquartile Range		17	
	Skewness		−1.293	.166
	Kurtosis		2.184	.331

Now, inspect both histogram and normal Q-Q plot for supervision. Figure 5.11 shows that the distribution is skewed to the left (long tail on the left side), thus indicating a negative skewness (also notice that the skewness is negative, −1.293). Also, the normal Q-Q plot shows several points substantially deviate from the straight line with more points in the lower end than the upper end, indicating negative skewness.

Figure 5.11:   The Distribution of Supervision

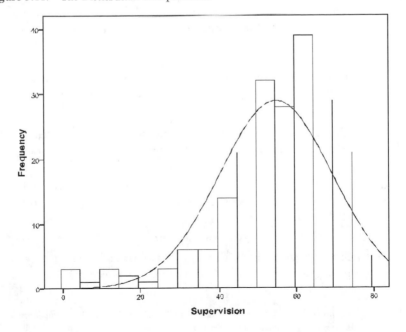

Figure 5.12:   Normal Q-Q Plot of Supervision

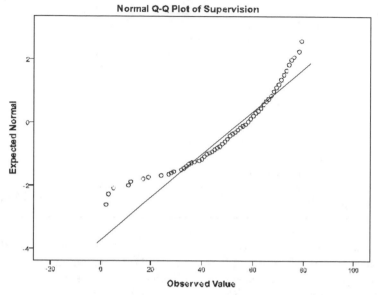

CONCLUSION: Pearson's skewness coefficient for supervision is –.22, which falls slightly outside ±.20. Fisher's skewness coefficient is –7.79, which falls outside ±1.96 (and outside ±2.58). Also, visually reviewing the distribution in figures 5.11 and 5.12 shows that it is severely skewed to the left and thus confirming the results of both skewness coefficients. Therefore, a transformation is needed to try to convert the shape of the distribution of supervision to approach the shape of a normal curve.

Transformation of supervision statistics.   Recall that the supervision distribution shows a significant negative skewness, so two transformations are necessary.

1.   Reverse the raw scores:[3] Add 1 to the maximum score in supervision. This will serve as a constant. The maximum score is 79; thus, the constant is 79 + 1 = 80.

2.   Subtract each raw score from the constant (80). This transforms the distribution from severe negative skewness to severe positive skewness. To do this in SPSS, follow these steps:

    a.   Open the SPSS Job Satisfaction data file.

    b.   Click on *Transform* in the SPSS main toolbar and click on *Compute* to open the "Compute Variable" dialog box (see screen 5.3).

---

[3]Remember that higher scores in the reversed variable will indicate lower quality of supervision, and lower scores will indicate greater quality of supervision.

Screen 5.3: SPSS Compute Variable Dialog Box

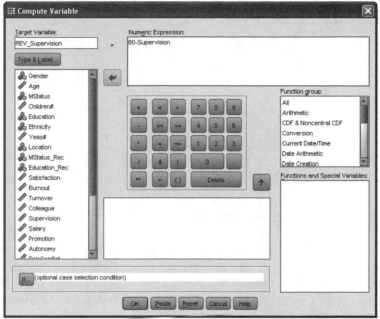

c. Type the name of the new variable in the *Target Variable* box. In this case, type REV_Supervision (reversed supervision).

d. Type the formula you want to use under *Numeric Expression*. In this case, type "80-Supervision."

e. Click on *OK*.

SPSS Syntax for Computing a New Variable

COMPUTE REV_Supervision = 80 − Supervision.
EXECUTE.

---

3. SPSS will create and add a new variable called REV_Supervision to the SPSS data file as discussed in the previous chapters.

4. Run measures of central tendency, variability, skewness, and a histogram for the new reversed variable (REV_Supervision) as discussed above. Table 5.4 displays the statistics, and figure 5.13 displays a distribution with a normal curve for the reversed scores of supervision.

    Notice that the skewness sign for the reversed scores is now positive (1.293) and the mean is greater than the median, which indicates a positive skewness. In addition, applying both Pearson's and Fisher's skewness

Table 5.4:   Statistics Table for Raw and Reversed Scores of Supervision

			Statistic	Std. Error
REV_Supervision	Mean		25.2850	1.00710
	95% Confidence	Lower Bound	23.2999	
	Interval for Mean	Upper Bound	27.2702	
	5% Trimmed Mean		24.0447	
	Median		22.0000	
	Variance		217.050	
	Std. Deviation		14.73261	
	Minimum		1.00	
	Maximum		78.00	
	Range		77.00	
	Interquartile Range		17.00	
	Skewness		1.293	.166
	Kurtosis		2.184	.331

formulas produces the same values as above but with positive signs (Pearson's = .22; Fisher's = 7.79). Moreover, figures 5.13 and 5.14 look the same as the original distribution (figures 5.11 and 5.12) but on the opposite direction, indicating positive skewness. In other words, reversing the scores only reverses the direction of the skewness and does not impact its severity.

Figure 5.13:   The Distribution of Reversed Scores of Supervision

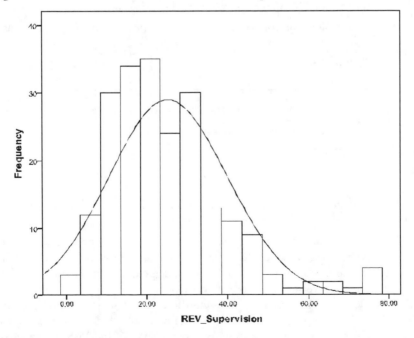

Figure 5.14:   Normal Q-Q Plot of Reversed Scores of Supervision

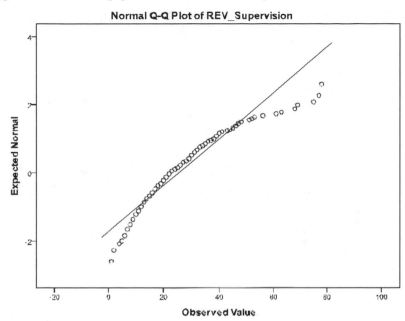

5.   Next, transform the reversed scores (REV_Supervision) to a square root. Use the same methods to transform the variable to a logarithm (log10). To transform REV_Supervision to square root, follow these steps:

a.   Repeat steps 2a to 2c above.

b.   Type the name of the new variable you want to create in the *Target Variable* box (see screen 5.4): SQRT_Super (Square root of supervision).

c.   Select *All* under "Function Group," scroll down under *Functions and Special Variables*, and select *SQRT*.

d.   Click on the arrow button next to the *Functions and Special Variables* box to move *SQRT* into the *Numeric Expression* box.

e.   Scroll down in the variable list, click on *REV_Supervision*, and click on the upper arrow button next to the *Variable List* box to move it in the parentheses after *SQRT* and replace the question mark.

f.   You may simply type "SQRT(REV_Supervision)" in the *Numeric Expression* box instead of following steps c to e.

g.   To transform a variable to the logarithm, type the new variable name in the *Target Variable* box (e.g., LG10_Super), select *All* under "Function Group," click on *LG10* under "Functions and Special Variables," and follow steps d and e above.

h.   Click on *OK*.

Screen 5.4:   SPSS Compute Variable Dialog Box

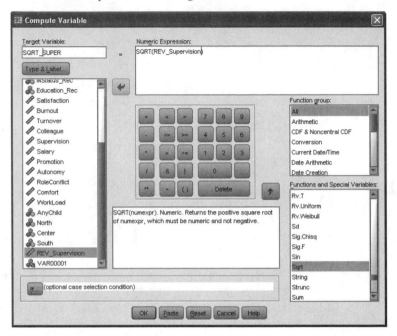

SPSS Syntax for Transformation into Square Root

COMPUTE SQRT_SUPER = SQRT(REV_SUPERVISION).
EXECUTE.

SPSS Syntax for Transformation into Logarithm

COMPUTE LG10_SUPER = LG10(REV_SUPERVISION).
EXECUTE.

These SPSS functions will create and add a new variable called SQRT_
Super in the SPSS Job Satisfaction data file.

Next, we run measures of central tendency, variability, skewness, a histogram with a normal curve, and normal Q-Q plot for the transformed variable to evaluate the skewness of the transformed distribution.

Table 5.5 displays the statistics, and figures 5.15 and 5.16 display the distribution for transformed supervision (SQRT_Super).

Table 5.5:   Statistics Table for Square Root of Supervision (Reversed Scores)

			Statistic	Std. Error
SQRT_SUPER	Mean		4.8246	.09711
	95% Confidence	Lower Bound	4.6331	
	Interval for Mean	Upper Bound	5.0160	
	5% Trimmed Mean		4.7857	
	Median		4.6904	
	Variance		2.018	
	Std. Deviation		1.42063	
	Minimum		1.00	
	Maximum		8.83	
	Range		7.83	
	Interquartile Range		1.78	
	Skewness		.354	.166
	Kurtosis		.447	.331

To evaluate the skewness, we compute both Pearson's and Fisher's skewness as follows:

$$\text{Skewness Coefficients for Square Root of Supervision}$$

$$Pearson's = \frac{Mean - Median}{SD} = \frac{4.825 - 4.690}{1.421} = .10$$

$$Fisher's = \frac{Skewness}{SES} = \frac{.354}{.166} = 2.13$$

Then, we inspect both plots. Reviewing the distribution of the square root of supervision (figure 5.15) shows that it approaches the shape of a normal curve. Furthermore, looking at the normal Q-Q plot (figure 5.16) shows that most of the points are clustered on the straight line, with a few minor deviations on the upper right (minor outlier cases).

CONCLUSION: Pearson's skewness coefficient of the square root of supervision falls within ±.20 (.10). Fisher's skewness coefficient *slightly* falls outside ±1.96 (2.13), yet it falls within ±2.58 (alpha = .01). Reviewing the histogram and normal Q-Q plot shows a normal distribution, perhaps with minor positive deviations (which could explain the slight Fisher's skewness). Therefore, transformation of supervision to square root significantly enhanced the shape of the distribution of supervision, which now approaches the shape of a normal curve. Thus, the square root of supervision should be included in any future analysis instead of the actual raw scores of supervision.

Figure 5.15:   The Distribution of Square Root of Supervision

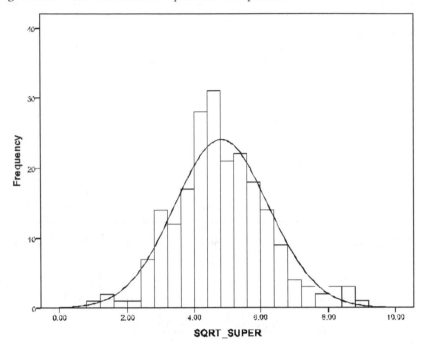

Figure 5.16:   Normal Q-Q Plot of Square Root of Supervision

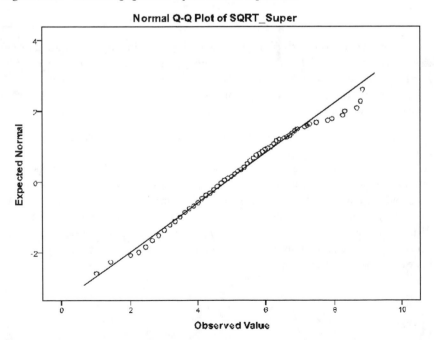

STANDARD SCORES (Z SCORES)

Standard scores, also called z scores, are raw scores converted into standard deviation units. They indicate how many standard deviation units a corresponding raw score, or observation, falls above or below the mean. Standard scores are thus useful to estimate if someone's score is above the mean, on the mean, or below the mean. For example, z scores can be used to determine if John's score on a statistics course is above average, average, or below average score for the course. z scores are also useful to determine the percentile at which a given score falls (see chapter 3 for percentile).

In general, a raw score that is greater than the mean will always have a positive z score. A raw score that is smaller than the mean will always have a negative z score. A raw score that is exactly on the mean will always have a z score of zero.

Properties of Standard Scores

1. The shape of the distribution of standard scores is identical to that of the distribution of the raw scores. That is, converting raw scores to z scores does not change the shape of the distribution of raw scores.
2. The mean of the standard scores is equal to 0, regardless of the mean of the raw scores.
3. The variance of the standard scores is equal to 1.
4. Because the standard deviation is the square root of the variance, the standard deviation of the standard scores is equal to 1 (± 1).
5. The sum of all z scores is equal to 0.

Therefore, by transforming raw scores to standard scores, we transform the original distribution of raw scores to a distribution with an identical shape but with a mean of 0 and a standard deviation of 1.

To illustrate this, we will use SPSS to compare two distributions; the first shows raw data of economic resources (ER) from the Elderly data file and the second shows z scores of the raw data.

The following SPSS output contains three parts: a statistics table (table 5.6), a histogram for economic resources (figure 5.17), and a histogram for z scores for economic resources (figure 5.18).

Table 5.6 shows measures of central tendency, variability, and skewness for the raw scores and z scores of economic resources. The mean score for the z scores is 0 with a variance of 1 (standard deviation = 1). The table also shows that the skewness, standard error of skewness, for both economic resources and its z scores, are identical, therefore the shapes of both distributions are identical. Notice also that the sum of scores of z scores is 0. Recall from chapter 4 that the mean is a function of the sum divided by standard deviation; that is 0/1 = 0.

Figures 5.17 and 5.18 show the distributions for economic resources and the z scores of economic resources, respectively. Both figures appear identical and show slight negative skewness. It is also evident by the difference between the mean and the median, and by the negative skewness coefficients in table 5.6.

Table 5.6:   Statistics Table for Economic Resources

		Economic Resources	Z Score: Economic Resources
N	Valid	99	99
	Missing	0	0
Mean		22.54	.000
Median		22.00	−.0894716
Mode		21	−.25660
Std. Deviation		5.984	1.000
Variance		35.802	1.000
Skewness		−.399	−.399
Std. Error of Skewness		.243	.243
Minimum		5	−2.93062
Maximum		32	1.58179
Sum		2231	.000

Figure 5.17:   The Distribution of Economic Resources

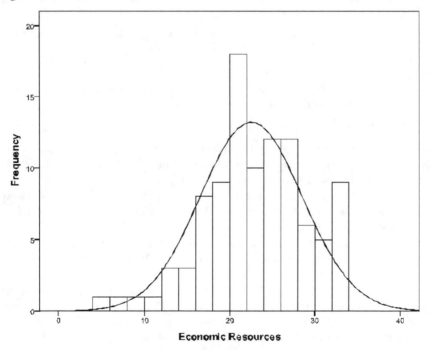

Transformation of Raw Scores to z Scores

Transformation of raw scores to z scores is simple: all you need to know is the mean and the standard deviation for the raw scores (see chapter 4). To convert a raw score to a z score, use the following formula:

z Score Formula

$$Z(x) = \frac{X - \overline{X}}{SD}$$

Zx = Z score for X
X = Raw Score
$\overline{X}$ = Mean
SD = Standard Deviation

Figure 5.18:   The Distribution of the z Scores: Economic Resources

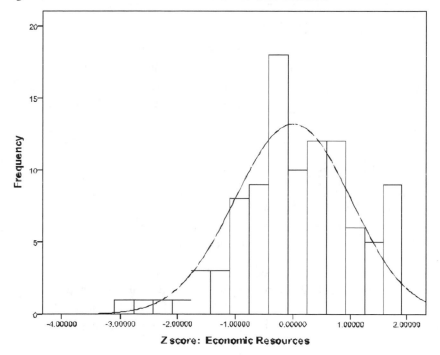

QUESTION: The mean score for a statistics course last semester was 86 with a standard deviation of 3. John's score in this course was 92. What is John's z score?

ANSWER: John's score is greater than the mean; that is, he has a positive z score. John's z score is as follows:

$$Z_{(x = 92)} = \frac{92 - 86}{3} = 2$$

That is, John is 2 standard deviations above the mean.

Why Standard Scores

By knowing the number of standard deviation units each raw score is above or below the mean, as we did for John's score, we can compute the area (percentage) between the mean and each z score, the area between the two z scores, the area above each z score, and the area below each z score. The area at or below which a z score falls is also known as the percentile (see chapter 4). Thus, by computing a z score for each raw score, we can determine the percentile for each subject in a study.

Facts about z Scores and Percentiles

- A positive z score will always have a percentile greater than 50.

- A negative z score will always have a percentile less than 50.

- A z score of zero will always have a percentile of 50 (50% of scores fall below and 50% of scores fall above it). In other words, the percentile for the mean score is always 50.

---

z Scores Table

The z Scores Table (appendix D) presents the area between a z score and the mean, and the area beyond a z score.

Things to Remember

- % beyond a positive z score = % beyond a negative z score
- % below a positive z score = 50% + % between the mean and the z score
- % below a negative z score = 50% − % between the mean and the z score

---

The z Scores Table shows the following information (figure 5.19):

1. 50 percent of the area is above the mean and 50 percent is below the mean (recall that a normal distribution is symmetrical; the left and right halves are mirror images).

2. 34.13 percent is between the mean and 1 standard deviation above the mean; 34.13 percent is between the mean and 1 standard deviation below the mean. That is, 68.26 percent is between ±1 standard deviation.

Figure 5.19:   Normal Distribution for Percentile

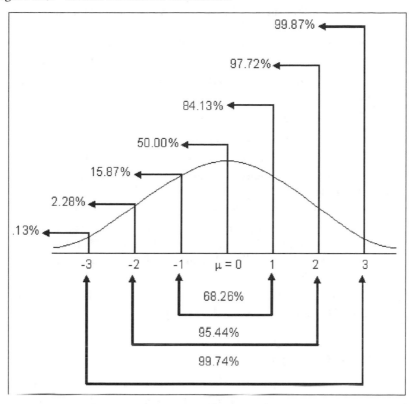

3. 47.72 percent is between the mean and 2 standard deviations above the mean; 47.72 percent is between the mean and 2 standard deviations below the mean. That is, 95.44 percent is between ±2 standard deviations.

4. 49.87 percent is between the mean and 3 standard deviations above the mean; 49.87 percent is between the mean and 3 standard deviations below the mean. That is, 99.74 percent is between ±3 standard deviations.

The z Scores Table (appendix D) contains three columns: z, the area between $\overline{X}$ and z, and the area beyond z:

1. To find the area (percentage) between a specific z and the mean, first locate the z score in the z column, then find the corresponding area in the area between $\overline{X}$ and z column.

   Example: To find the area between the mean and a z score of .45, scroll down to .45 in the z column, then move right to the second column, area between $\overline{X}$ and z. This area is .1736, or 17.36 percent.

2. To find the area below a positive z (the percentile for +z), locate the z score in the z column, find the area between the z score and the mean, then add .50.

    Example: Find the area below (percentile of) a z score of .85.

    a. Find the area between the mean and z of .85. Scroll down to .85 in the z column, then move right to the second column under area between $\overline{X}$ and z. This area is .3023.

    b. Add .50 to .3023. That is, .50 + .3023 = .8023.

    c. A z score of .85 falls at approximately the 80th percentile.

3. To find the area below a negative z (the percentile of –z), locate the z score in the z column, find the area between the z score and the mean, then subtract this area from .50.

    Example: Find the area below (percentile of) a z score of –1.25.

    a. Find the area between the mean and a z of –1.25 (identical to the area between the mean and z of 1.25). Scroll down to 1.25 in the z column, then move right to the second column under the area between $\overline{X}$ and z. This area is .3944.

    b. Subtract .3944 from .50. That is, .50 – .3944 = .1056. A z score of –1.25 falls at approximately the 11th percentile.

PRACTICAL EXAMPLES

QUESTION: On the CESD (depression scale) with a mean of 15 and a standard deviation (SD) of 2, (1) at approximately what percentile will a person with a score of 18 fall? (2) a person with a score of 13?, and (3) what percentage of subjects fall between these two scores?

ANSWER:

1. To solve for a score of 18:

    a. Compute the z score for 18.

    $$Z_{(x = 18)} = \frac{18 - 15}{2} = 1.5$$

    b. Use the z Scores Table to find the area between the mean and a z of 1.50. The z Scores Table shows that the area between the mean and a z of 1.50 is .4332.

    c. Because this is a positive z, add .50 to this area.

    d. Total area below z of 1.50 = .50 + .4332 = .9332.

    e. A score of 18 falls at approximately the 93rd percentile. This means that about 93 percent of subjects have scores at or below 18 and about 7 percent have scores above 18.

2. To solve for a score of 13:

    a. Compute the z score for 13.

    $$Z_{(x = 13)} = \frac{13 - 15}{2} = -1$$

    b. Use the z Scores Table to find the area between the mean and a z of -1.0. This is the same as the area between the mean and a z of 1. The z Scores Table shows that this area is .3413.

    c. Because this is a negative z score, subtract this area from .50.

    d. Total area below a z score of $-1.0 = .50 - .3413 = .1587$, or 15.87 percent (figure 5.19).

    e. Someone with a score of 13 on the CESD scale will fall at approximately the 16th percentile: almost 16 percent of subjects will have scores at or below 13 and about 84 percent will have scores above 13.

3. To solve for percentages of subjects between 13 and 18:

    This includes the area between the mean and a z score of 1.50 (the z score for 18) and the area between the mean and a z score of -1.0 (the z score for 13).

    a. Area between the mean and 1.50 = .4332, or 43.32 percent.

    b. Area between the mean and -1.0 = .3413, or 34.13 percent.

    c. Area between 1.50 and -1.0 = 43.32 percent + 34.13 percent = 77.45 percent. That is, 77.45 percent of participants have scores between 13 and 18 on the CESD scale.

QUESTION: Layanne, a second-year graduate student, took three graduate courses on statistics, psychopathology, and human behavior. Layanne's grades were 85 on statistics, 93 on psychopathology, and 88 on human behavior. Overall, the mean score on statistics was 82 with a standard deviation of 2, the mean score of psychopathology was 95 with a standard deviation of 5, and the mean score on human behavior was 90 with a standard deviation of 4. What appears to be Layanne's strongest graduate course?

ANSWER: To solve this problem, compute the z score for Layanne's grade for each course. The one with the highest z score represents Layanne's strongest area since it falls at the highest percentile. Layanne's z scores are as follows:

$$Z_{(Statistics)} = \frac{85 - 82}{2} = 1.5$$

$$Z_{(Psycho)} = \frac{93 - 95}{5} = -.40$$

$$Z_{(Human)} = \frac{92 - 90}{4} = .50$$

Since Layanne's z score on statistics is the highest (z = 1.5), then statistics appears to be her strongest graduate course, although her grade on statistics was the lowest among the three courses. Notice that psychopathology is her weakest graduate course (lowest z score), although her grade on psychopathology was the highest among the three courses.

How to Create z Scores in SPSS

To illustrate this, compute the z scores for Economic Resources (ER) in the SPSS Elderly data file.

To create z scores in SPSS, follow these steps:

1. Open the SPSS Elderly data file.
2. Click on *Analyze, Descriptive Statistics*, and click on *Descriptives*. A new dialog box called "Descriptives" will open (see screen 5.5).
3. Scroll down in the variables list and move *ER* to the *Variable(s)* box.
4. Check the box of *Save standardized values as variables*.
5. Click on *OK*.

Screen 5.5:   SPSS Descriptives (z Scores) Dialog Box

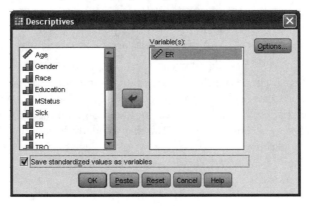

SPSS Syntax for z Scores

Descriptives ER

/save.

A new variable called "ZER" will be added to the SPSS Elderly data set. By default, SPSS assigns a name to the new variable. It is the same name as the original variable, now starting with the letter z, indicating z scores.

Now run measures of central tendency, variability, skewness, and create histograms for both economic resources and z scores of economic resources (see "SPSS output under Properties of Standard Scores" above).

SUMMARY

This chapter discussed normality of distributions and their importance for data analysis. Normal distributions are symmetrical and bell-shaped with their mean in the center. Positively skewed distributions have long tails on the right, and most cases fall on the left; their mean is greater than the median, and the median is greater than the mode. Negatively skewed distributions have long tails on the left, and most cases fall on the right; their mean is smaller than the median, and the median is smaller than the mode.

The chapter also presented two methods to evaluate the shape of a distribution: measures of skewness (Pearson's and Fisher's skewness coefficients) and graphs (histogram and normal Q-Q plots). These methods determine whether a transformation of raw scores is needed. Two transformation methods were presented: square root and logarithm. The chapter also discussed standard scores, their importance, and their use in computing the percentile for each raw score, as well as how to utilize the SPSS toolbar and syntax files to compute measures of central tendency, variability, skewness, data transformation, and how to create z scores.

Chapter 6 introduces the next level of data analysis: inferential statistics. It presents one-tailed and two-tailed research hypotheses, errors in hypothesis testing, levels of significance, and levels of confidence interval. Differences between parametric and nonparametric tests and factors to consider in selecting the appropriate statistical test are covered, along with steps in hypothesis testing.

PRACTICAL EXERCISES

Part I: The following are the number of hours of exercise per week for eighteen students who participated in a healthy weight study:

40	42	44	26	28
34	30	40	32	32
34	32	34	34	36
	36	38	38	

Use a pencil and paper and answer the following questions:

1. Convert raw scores to z scores.
2. Compute mean, median, mode, and standard deviation for the z scores.
3. At approximately what percentile will a student with thirty-two hours of exercise fall?

4. At approximately what percentile will a student with thirty-six hours of exercise fall?

5. What percentage of students exercised between thirty-two and thirty-six hours?

6. Compute the Pearson's skewness coefficient for hours of exercise. Based on this alone, what would you say about the shape of this distribution?

Part II: Access the SPSS Mental Health data file (appendix A) and run measures of central tendency, variability, skewness, histograms, normal probability plots, and z scores for age (Age), physical health (PH), cognitive status (CS), and emotional balance (EB). Use these SPSS outputs to answer the following questions:

1. Evaluate the shape of the distributions of age and emotional balance. Justify your answer.

2. If either one is significantly skewed, what method of transformation would you use to fix their skewness? Use SPSS syntax to run the transformations.

3. Compare the original and transformed distributions. How do the transformed distribution(s) differ from the original distribution(s)? Justify your answer.

4. At approximately what percentile will a person with a score of 22 on the physical health scale fall? Explain.

5. At approximately what percentile will a person with a score of 16 on the physical health scale fall? Explain.

6. What percentage of participants is between sixty-two and seventy-two years old? Explain.

7. Adam participated in the Mental Health survey. He scored 18 on the emotional balance scale (EB), 20 on the physical health scale, and 19 on the cognitive status scale (CS). What does Adam's poorest health area appear to be? Explain.

CHAPTER 6

Hypothesis Testing and Selecting a Statistical Test

LEARNING OBJECTIVES

1. Understand one-tailed and two-tailed research hypotheses
2. Understand errors in hypothesis testing
3. Understand levels of significance
4. Understand power and effect size
5. Understand confidence interval
6. Understand parametric and nonparametric tests
7. Understand the process for selecting a statistical test
8. Understand the steps in hypothesis testing

DATA SET (APPENDIX A)

Welfare

INTRODUCTION

Chapters 3, 4, and 5 introduced and discussed methods of descriptive statistics. Chapter 3 discussed two methods of data organization and summary: frequency tables and graphs. Chapter 4 outlined measures of central tendency and variability. Chapter 5 taught how to evaluate the shape of a distribution and understand standard scores and their importance.

This chapter turns to the study of inferential statistics. As described in chapter 1, the goal of quantitative research is to describe the distribution of the sample characteristics (statistics) and then make a generalization, or inference, from them to the characteristics of the population (parameters) from which the sample is drawn.

For instance, clinicians and therapists want to know if their treatment or intervention is effective with clients, and whether it can be replicated to be successful with other clients in similar settings. Graduate school admissions officers want to know if GRE scores could predict students' success in their graduate programs. Also, mental health researchers want to know the impact of acculturation on levels of stress among refugee clients. These can be determined through inferential parametric and nonparametric statistical techniques, such as Pearson's product-moment correlation coefficient, student t-tests, analysis of variances and covariances, chi-square, and other tests.

This chapter reviews research hypotheses and specifically discusses one-tailed and two-tailed versions. Levels of significance, p value, type I and type II errors, and level-of-confidence intervals are presented, along with parametric and nonparametric tests, selecting a statistical test, and steps in hypothesis testing.

RESEARCH HYPOTHESES

Chapter 1 introduced the null hypothesis and research hypothesis (also known as the alternative hypothesis). The *null hypothesis (H_0)* will predict no significant relationships between independent and dependent variables, while the *alternative hypothesis (H_a)* shows significant relationships between independent and dependent variables.

Why two hypotheses? The main goal of any research study is to find statistical support for the research (alternative) hypothesis, which cannot be supported unless the null hypothesis is statistically rejected. However, that alone will not always provide support for the alternative hypothesis. This will depend on whether the research hypothesis is one-tailed or two-tailed. If one-tailed, two conditions must be met to claim statistical support for the research hypothesis: (1) significant results must be found; that is, there is enough statistical evidence to reject the null hypotheses, and (2) the direction of the results is the same as the direction postulated by the alternative hypothesis.

Example: In the Welfare study, the researcher hypothesized that former welfare recipients who participated in job training would have significantly lower levels of depression than those who did not. The study found significant differences between the two groups; however, the levels of depression for subjects who participated in training were significantly higher than those who did not. The researcher rejected the null hypothesis based on the statistical results, but these results did not support the alternative hypothesis.

One-Tailed Research Hypothesis

A one-tailed research hypothesis, also known as a directional hypothesis, clearly predicts the direction of the relationship between independent and dependent variables. Social science researchers may predict positive (or direct) relationships or negative (or inverse) relationships.

Figure 6.1 compares positive and negative relationships. Positive relationships (see chapter 1) occur when scores in the independent and dependent vari-

Figure 6.1:   Directions of Relationships between Variables

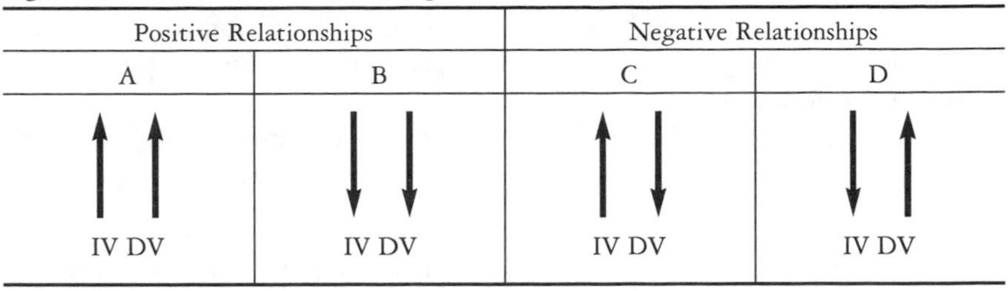

Positive Relationships		Negative Relationships	
A	B	C	D
↑↑	↓↓	↑↓	↓↑
IV DV	IV DV	IV DV	IV DV

IV = independent variable, DV = dependent variable

ables move in the same direction; that is, if the independent variable increases, the dependent variable increases as well (see figure 6.1.A), and vice versa (see figure 6.1.B). Negative relationships occur when scores in the independent and dependent variables go in the opposite directions; if the independent variable increases, the dependent variable decreases (see figure 6.1.C), and if the independent variable decreases, the dependent variable increases (see figure 6.1.D).

Example 1: A clinical social worker who conducts group therapy for battered women wishes to help them increase their self-esteem. To test the effectiveness of the therapy, the clinician conducts an experimental pretest-posttest control group design. Table 6.1 illustrates this experimental design.

Prior to starting group therapy, the clinician may hypothesize two one-tailed research hypotheses (H_a):

H_{01}: There is *no significant* difference between women's level of self-esteem before and after the therapy: $X_1 = X_2$; therapy is ineffective.

H_{a1}: Women's level of self-esteem at the posttest will be *significantly higher* than their level of self-esteem at the pretest: $X_2 > X_1$; group therapy is effective.

H_{02}: There is *no significant* difference between the experimental group and the control group with regard to posttest level of self-esteem; $X_2 = X_4$.

H_{a2}: Posttest level of self-esteem of the experimental group will be *significantly higher* than the control group; $X_2 > X_4$.

To support the first research hypothesis (H_{a1}), the clinician must show that there is a significant difference between pretest and posttest scores of self-esteem and that the posttest scores (X_2) are greater than the pretest scores (X_1).

Table 6.1:   Experimental Pretest-Posttest Group Design

Group	Pretest	Therapy	Posttest
Experimental Group	X_1	Yes	X_2
Control Group	X_3	No	X_4

To support the second research hypothesis (H_{a2}), again the clinician must show a significant difference between the experimental and control groups ($X_2 \neq X_4$) and that the posttest scores of the experimental group are greater than those of the control group ($X_2 > X_4$).

Example 2: In the Welfare study, the researcher examined the impact of social support on clients' levels of depression (CESD). The researcher projected an inverse relationship between the two variables.

H_0: There is *no significant* relationship between social support and levels of depression among former welfare recipients.

H_a: There is a *significant inverse* (or *negative*) relationship between social support and levels of depression among former welfare recipients. In other words, the greater the social support is, the lower the levels of depression.

Example 3: In the same study, the researcher examined the impact of social support on self-esteem and hypothesized a direct (positive) relationship between the two variables.

H_0: There is *no significant* relationship between social support and levels of self-esteem among former welfare recipients.

H_a: There is a *significant direct* (or *positive*) relationship between social support and levels of self-esteem among former welfare recipients. That is, the greater the social support is, the higher the level of self-esteem.

With one-tailed research hypotheses, researchers use words such as *positive, direct, negative, inverse, increase, decrease, higher than, lower than, greater than*, or *less than* to predict the relationships between independent and dependent variables.

Two-Tailed Research Hypothesis

A two-tailed (or nondirectional) research hypothesis does not predict the direction of the relationship between independent and dependent variables. In this case, researchers project a significant relationship between the two variables, but stop short of predicting direction. Therefore, researchers need only to reject the null hypothesis to claim statistical support for the alternative hypothesis.

The following illustrates two-tailed hypotheses for the previous three examples:

Example 1:

H_{01}: There is *no significant* difference between women's self-esteem at the pretest and posttest: $X_1 = X_2$; therapy is ineffective.

H_{a1}: Levels of self-esteem at the posttest will be *significantly different* than levels of self-esteem at the pretest: $X_1 \neq X_2$; therapy is not necessarily effective.

Here, the practitioner does not predict whether therapy will be effective, which may affect the decision of subjects to participate in the therapy.

H_{02}: There is *no significant* difference between the experimental group and the control group with regard to posttest levels of self-esteem: $X_2 = X_4$.

H_{a2}: There is a *significant difference* between the experimental group and the control group with regard to posttest levels of self-esteem: $X_2 \neq X_4$.

Again, the practitioner does not predict which group will benefit from the therapy.
Example 2:

H_0: There is *no significant* relationship between social support and levels of depression among former welfare recipients.

H_a: There is a *significant* relationship between social support and levels of depression among former welfare recipients.

Example 3:

H_0: There is *no significant* relationship between social support and levels of self-esteem among former welfare recipients.

H_a: There is a *significant* relationship between social support and levels of self-esteem among former welfare recipients.

Notice that with two-tailed research hypotheses, researchers do not use words like *positive, direct, negative, indirect, greater than, smaller than*, and others to predict the direction of the relationships between the variables.

ERRORS IN HYPOTHESIS TESTING

Researchers use inferential statistics like Pearson's correlation, *t*-test, chi-square, and others to estimate a population's parameters by studying the statistics of a sample presumed to represent that population. Inferential statistics will also be used to generalize findings from a sample to the population from which it was selected.

Statistics are relied upon to demonstrate the accuracy of conclusions about relationships between independent and dependent variables in the population. Still, two possible errors (type I and type II) can occur (see table 6.2).

Table 6.2:   Errors in Hypothesis Testing

Statistical Decision	H_0 is true	H_0 is false
Reject H_0	Type I error (α)	Correct decision (*Power*)
Do not reject H_0	Correct decision	Type II error (β)

Type I Errors

Type I errors occur when researchers, acting on results of the statistical test, decide to reject the null hypothesis (that no relationship exists between the variables) when, in fact, the null hypothesis is true. In other words, type I errors occur when the null hypothesis is *incorrectly* rejected and should be accepted. It is also known as a false positive and is symbolized as α (Greek lowercase alpha).[1]

Type II Errors

Type II errors occur when researchers decide not to reject the null hypothesis when, in fact, it is false. In other words, these occur when researchers accept the null hypothesis when it should be rejected. This is also known as a false negative and is symbolized as β (Greek lowercase beta).

Correct Decisions

Correct decisions occur when researchers decide to reject a false null hypothesis or not to reject a true hypothesis.

Power.   Power is defined as rejecting the null hypothesis when, in fact, it is false; that is, making the right decision is known as power. Mathematically, power is defined as 1 − beta. That is, the smaller the probability of not rejecting a false hypothesis (beta) is, the greater the probability of rejecting a false hypothesis (power).

In social science research, it is desirable to achieve a power of .80 or higher (or a beta of .20 or less). To achieve this, researchers must carefully decide on a number of issues: the direction of the research hypothesis (one-tailed vs. two-tailed hypothesis); the level of significance (alpha); the sample size; and the effect size (ES) (Cohen, 1988; Hinkle, Wiersma, & Jurs, 2003).

Effect size.   Effect size is defined as the "degree to which a phenomenon being studied (e.g., correlation or difference in means) exists in the population" (Hair et al., 2010, p. 2). In other words, effect size estimates the difference between group means, between the sample's and population's means, or between the dependent and independent variables' statistics in standard deviation units.

Cohen divides effect size in three groups: small (0.2 standard deviation), moderate (0.5 standard deviation), and large (0.8 standard deviation). In general, the larger the effect size is, the more powerful the test. Sample size and effect size will be addressed later in this chapter and in subsequent chapters (Cohen, 1988).

---

[1]Not to be confused with the Cronbach's alpha reliability coefficient (see chapter 1).

Effect Size Formula

$$ES = \frac{\overline{X}_1 - \overline{X}_2}{SD}$$

$\overline{X}_1$ = First mean
$\overline{X}_2$ = Second mean
SD = Standard deviation

Levels of Significance (α)

Levels of significance help determine how close researchers are to making a correct decision by rejecting a false hypothesis or not rejecting a true hypothesis. Levels of significance are also symbolized by the Greek lowercase alpha (α), which refers to the probability of making a type I error. It is the probability that the observed relationships between variables are due to a chance or sampling error.

Researchers choose a level of significance during the research planning prior to collecting and analyzing data. At what level of probability can they claim significant results? Depending on the purpose of the study, they will usually set alpha at .10, .05, .01, or .001.

Traditionally, social science researchers set alpha at .05; that is, the probability of making a type I error is 5 in 100. Medical researchers, for example, whose studies may physically or emotionally risk patients, set alpha lower, usually at .01 (1 in 100) or .001 (1 in 1,000), to reduce errors and avoid harming subjects.

Statistical Significance (p value)

All parametric and nonparametric inferential statistical tests produce a p value. As with alpha, a p value indicates how close researchers are to a correct decision. It refers to the probability that relationships between independent and dependent variables could occur by a chance or sampling error.

Mathematically, a p value ranges between 0.00 (the relationship between variables would never occur by chance) and 1.00 (the relationship between variables definitely occurs by chance). The smaller the p value is, the less probability that the relationship between variables occurs by a chance or sampling error.

Researchers then compare the computed probability level (p value) with the preset level of significance (alpha). If the p value is at or below alpha, they reject the null hypothesis. By doing so, statistical support for the alternative hypothesis may be claimed. If the p value is greater than alpha, they do not reject the null hypothesis or claim statistical support for the alternative hypothesis.

To reject null hypotheses for the three earlier examples, researchers must show the *p* value for each one is at or below .05 (assuming that alpha was set at .05).

One-Tailed and Two-Tailed Rejection Areas

The decision whether to state a one-tailed or two-tailed research hypothesis is made prior to data analysis because this will determine whether a one-tailed or two-tailed statistical test is required.

The word *tail* refers to the ends of a normal curve, where extreme values are usually found. This may indicate significant relationships between the variables under study. Thus, by stating a one-tailed or two-tailed research hypothesis, researchers are predicting that relationships between variables will fall at the right tail or the left (for a one-tailed hypothesis), or at both tails (for the two-tailed hypothesis).

When a two-tailed hypothesis is examined, the rejection area is divided equally between the two ends, the right and left tails (see figure 6.2). This is the level of significance, or alpha (α). If alpha was set at .05, then the total rejection area is 5 percent, which will be divided to two halves of 2.5 percent. If alpha was set at .01, then the total area is 1 percent, and the two halves each equal .5 percent.

Recall from chapter 5 that standard (z) scores represent how far each raw score is above or below the mean, or represent the area above or below a given z score. Alpha, in this case, represents the area of extreme scores (outliers). These areas correspond with a z score, which serves as a cutoff. With a two-tailed hypothesis, researchers reject the null hypothesis if the computed statistic falls beyond the $\pm z$ score; with one-tailed hypotheses, researchers reject the null hypothesis if the computed statistic falls beyond the z score.

To find the z score, use the z Scores Table (see appendix D) as discussed in chapter 5.

1.   Determine the area, or percentage, under each tail. For a one-tailed hypothesis, the area is alpha; for a two-tailed hypothesis, divide alpha by two.

Figure 6.2:   Rejection Area for Two-Tailed Hypothesis

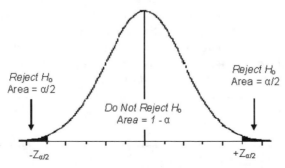

Reject H_0
Area = $\alpha/2$

Reject H_0
Area = $\alpha/2$

Do Not Reject H_0
Area = $1 - \alpha$

$-Z_{\alpha/2}$ $+Z_{\alpha/2}$

2.   Find this area in the Area Beyond z column in the z Scores Table.

3.   Find the z score corresponding with this area in the z column.

Example: If alpha in figure 6.2 was set at .05, then the area in each tail is .05/2, which is .025. Find this area under the Area Beyond z in the z Scores Table. The z score associated with .0250 is ±1.96. In other words, 95 percent of cases will fall between −1.96 and +1.96, and 5 percent of cases will fall beyond these z scores.

Assuming α = .05, a significant result occurs only if the computed statistic falls at or above +1.96 or at or below −1.96. In this case, researchers will reject the null hypothesis. Results will not be significant if the computed statistic falls between −1.96 and +1.96. Researchers in this case will fail to find statistical support for the two-tailed research hypothesis.

When a one-tailed hypothesis is examined, the rejection area falls at one end, at the right or left tail. Figure 6.3 presents the rejection area for a one-tailed hypothesis, predicting a positive (direct) relationship between two variables. Figure 6.4 presents the rejection area for a one-tailed hypothesis, predicting a negative (inverse) relationship between variables.

To find the z score associated with the area at either the right or left tail (figures 6.3 and 6.4), use the same methods as used to find z for the area of .025.

Figure 6.3:   Rejection Area for One-Tailed Hypothesis—Positive Relationship

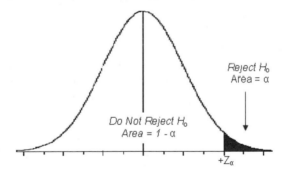

Figure 6.4:   Rejection Area for One-Tailed Hypothesis—Negative Relationship

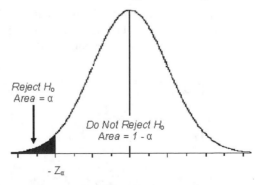

The area under the right or left tail is .05. Locate this area under the Area Beyond z column in the z Scores Table. This area is associated with a z of 1.65.

Assuming α = .05, a significant positive relationship is found only if the computed statistic falls at or above +1.65. A significant negative relationship is found if the computed statistic falls at or below −1.65.

CONFIDENCE INTERVAL

As stated, we study a statistic of a sample to estimate parameters of the population from which the sample is selected, but the sample is only an approximation for the population, and so is the statistic. For example, if, in the Welfare study (N = 107), the mean (statistic) score of depression among former welfare recipients was 15.56 (SD = 10.14) on a scale of 0 to 60, can we be confident that this score accurately reflects the true mean (parameter) score of depression among the population from which the sample was selected?

The only way to be absolutely confident is to study every person in the population who was on welfare, which is impossible. However, we can use the sample data and the level of significance to estimate a range of values that may contain the true depression score for the population, the true population parameter. This range of scores is known as the *confidence interval*.

The confidence interval is a range of upper and lower values, also known as confidence limits, that researchers are confident contain the true population parameter, for example, mean depression.

The *level of confidence* is the degree of confidence that the confidence interval contains the parameter being estimated. Levels of confidence are usually the complement to the levels of significance (alpha). For example, if alpha is set at .05, then the level of confidence will be .95, or 95 percent; if alpha is set at .01, then the level of confidence will be .99, or 99 percent.

Level of Confidence = $1 - \alpha$

α = alpha

While we may compute any level-of-confidence interval, the most reported ones are at 95 percent and 99 percent. They are symbolized by CI_{xx}, where xx represents level of confidence: CI_{95} = a 95 percent confidence interval; CI_{99} = a 99 percent confidence interval.

How to compute the confidence interval

1. Choose the level of confidence: CI_{95} or CI_{99}.
2. Compute the standard error of the mean as follows:

Standard Error Formula

$$SE = \frac{SD}{\sqrt{N}}$$

SE = Standard Error
SD = Standard Deviation
N = Sample Size

3. Use the following formulas to compute the 90 percent, 95 percent, or 99 percent confidence interval:

Confidence Interval (CI) Formulas

$$CI_{90} = \overline{X} \pm 1.65 * (SE)$$
$$CI_{95} = \overline{X} \pm 1.95 * (SE)$$
$$CI_{99} = \overline{X} \pm 2.58 * (SE)$$

$\overline{X}$ = Mean
SE = Standard Error

Remember: The sample statistic (mean) must always fall within the confidence interval.

QUESTION: What are the 99 percent, 95 percent, and 90 percent confidence intervals for levels of depression among former welfare recipients?

ANSWER: The mean score for depression was 15.56 with a standard deviation of 10.14. The sample size (N) was 107.

1. Compute the standard error:

$$SE = \frac{SD}{\sqrt{N}} = \frac{10.14}{\sqrt{107}} = \frac{10.14}{10.34} = .98$$

2. Compute the 99 percent confidence interval:

$$CI_{99} = \overline{X} \pm 2.58 * (SE)$$
$$CI_{99} = 15.56 \pm 2.58 * (.98) = 15.56 \pm 2.53$$

Upper limit = 15.56 + 2.53 = 18.09
Lower limit = 15.56 − 2.53 = 13.03

CONCLUSION: We are 99 percent confident that the interval 13.03 to 18.09 contains the true depression score (parameter) for the population of former welfare recipients.

3. Compute the 95 percent confidence interval:

$$CI_{95} = \overline{X} \pm 1.96 * (SE)$$
$$CI_{95} = 15.56 \pm 1.96 * (.98) = 15.56 \pm 1.92$$

Upper limit = 15.56 + 1.92 = 17.48
Lower limit = 15.56 − 1.92 = 13.64

CONCLUSION: We are 95 percent confident that the interval 13.64 to 17.48 contains the true depression score (parameter) for the population of former welfare recipients.

4. Compute the 90 percent confidence interval:

$$CI_{90} = \overline{X} \pm 1.65 * (SE)$$
$$CI_{99} = 15.56 \pm 1.65 * (.98) = 15.56 \pm 1.62$$

Upper limit = 15.56 + 1.62 = 17.18
Lower limit = 15.56 − 1.62 = 13.94

CONCLUSION: We are 90 percent confident that the interval 13.94 to 17.18 contains the true depression score (parameter) for the population of former welfare recipients from which the sample was selected.

Notice that the 99 percent confidence interval (13.03 to 18.09) is wider than the 95 percent confidence interval (13.64 to 17.48), and that the 95 percent confidence interval is wider than the 90 percent confidence interval (13.94 to 17.18). In other words, the greater the levels of confidence, the wider the confidence intervals. Figure 6.5 compares levels of confidence and their corresponding intervals.

Figure 6.5: Comparison of Level-of-Confidence Intervals

CI_{00}	15.56	
CI_{xx}	———	
CI_{90}	13.94 _____ 17.18	
CI_{95}	13.64 _____ 17.48	
CI_{99}	13.03 _____ 18.09	

The higher the level of confidence is, the wider the confidence interval.

How to compute confidence interval in SPSS.   To illustrate this, we will compute the 99 percent confidence interval for depression (CESD) in the Welfare data file.

To compute confidence interval in SPSS, use the following steps:

1. Open the SPSS Welfare data file.

2. Click on *Analyze*, click on *Descriptive Statistics*, and click on *Explore* to open the "Explore" dialog box (see chapter 3, screens 3.18 and 3.19).

3. Scroll down on the variables list in the left box, click on *CESD*, and click on the top arrow button to move *CESD* into the *Dependent List* box.

4. Check *Statistics* under "Display" to request only statistics. You may leave *Both* checked (SPSS default) to request statistics and plots for the variables under analysis.

5. Click on *Statistics* in the upper right side of the dialog box. A new dialog box called "Explore: Statistics" will open (see screen 6.1). Make sure that *Descriptives* is checked and the *Confidence Interval for Mean* is set at "95%" (SPSS default).

Screen 6.1:   SPSS Explore: Statistics Dialog Box

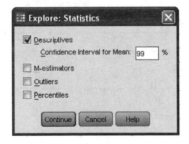

SPSS Explore Syntax

EXAMINE VARIABLES=CESD

/PLOT BOXPLOT STEMLEAF

/COMPARE GROUPS

/STATISTICS DESCRIPTIVES

/CINTERVAL 99

/MISSING LISTWISE

/NOTOTAL.

Note: To request the 95th confidence interval, simply type "95" or "90" instead of "99" next to CINTERVAL.

6. To compute 99 percent, simply change "95%" to "99%." You can request any level of confidence (e.g., 90%). (You may check *Outliers* to request a list of cases with outlier scores and *Percentile* to request the quartiles and 5th, 10th, 90th, and 95th percentiles).

7. Click on *Continue*.

8. Click on *OK*.

Tables 6.3 and 6.4 display the output produced by SPSS (other outputs may include stem-and-leaf and boxplot—this depends on whether you check *Statistics* or *Both* under "Display" in the SPSS "Explore" main dialog box).

Table 6.3 summarizes the number and percentage of valid, missing, and total cases for depression, and table 6.4 summarizes the descriptive statistics for depression, all of which have been discussed (see chapter 4, tables 4.5 and 4.6). This is especially appropriate when the distribution is severely skewed.

Table 6.4 shows that the 99 percent confidence interval for depression ranges between 12.99 (Lower Bound) and 18.13 (Upper Bound). In other words, we are 99 percent confident that the interval 12.99 to 18.13 contains the true depression score for former welfare recipients from which the sample was selected. The table also reports the standard error of the mean (Standard Error = .98), which we computed earlier.

Table 6.3: Case Processing Summary Table for Depression

	Cases					
	Valid		Missing		Total	
	N	Percent	N	Percent	N	Percent
Depression	107	100.0%	0	.0%	107	100.0%

Table 6.4: Descriptive Statistics Table for Depression

			Statistic	Std. Error
Depression	Mean		15.5607	.98007
	99% Confidence	Lower Bound	12.9900	
	Interval for Mean	Upper Bound	18.1315	
	5% Trimmed Mean		14.8982	
	Median		14.0000	
	Variance		102.777	
	Std. Deviation		10.13790	
	Minimum		.00	
	Maximum		47.00	
	Range		47.00	
	Interquartile Range		13.00	
	Skewness		.985	.234
	Kurtosis		.668	.463

SELECTING A STATISTICAL TEST

This section presents and compares a number of statistical techniques for computing a statistic and a p value to examine the null hypothesis. All statistical techniques test whether there is statistical support for the null hypothesis. In other words, by computing the p value, researchers decide to reject or not to reject the null hypothesis.

Parametric and Nonparametric Tests

When data collection is complete and ready for analysis, researchers decide which statistical test is most appropriate. The decision is a critical one because choosing an inappropriate statistical test may lead to inaccurate decisions, interpretations, and conclusions. Researchers must carefully examine their data to ensure certain conditions (assumptions) are met, such as normality of distributions.

The many statistical tests to choose from are grouped into two sets: parametric and nonparametric tests. While each statistical test has its own assumptions and requirements, parametric and nonparametric tests assume that the sample from which data are collected represents the population for which generalizations will be made.

A representative sample is essential to estimate the population's parameters. If a nonrepresentative sample is used, generalization of the results to the population will be questionable. This occurs when the characteristics of the sample (such as gender, race, age, education, or income) significantly differ from the characteristics of the population for which generalizations will be made.

Generally, a sample is presumed to be representative of the population if it is drawn through probability sampling methods, such as simple random sampling, systematic random sampling, stratified random sampling, or cluster random sampling methods. When a sample is selected through nonprobability sampling methods, such as purposive, convenience, or snowball sampling, researchers should compare the characteristics of the sample with those of the population to examine whether they are similar (Rubin & Babbie, 2011). This book introduces two statistical methods researchers may use to compare the characteristics of their samples with those of the population. These are the one-sample case t-test (chapter 8) and the chi-square goodness-of-fit test (chapter 11).

In addition to the above assumptions, parametric tests assume the following:

1. The dependent variable is continuous data, measured at the interval or ratio levels of measurement.

2. The shape of the distribution of the dependent variable should approach the shape of a normal curve. The distribution should not be severely skewed.

3. The sample size should be large enough. This is important because the larger sample size is, the smaller the standard error of the mean, and the greater the statistical power of the test. With a large sample size, the

central limit theorem (discussed in chapter 5) ensures that the distribution of the means approximates a normal distribution. The question is, then, how large is large?

Statisticians have used parametric statistics with sample sizes as small as thirty cases. Yet, different analyses may require different sample sizes. This depends on four criteria: the direction of the research hypothesis (one-tailed vs. two-tailed), level of significance (alpha .10, .05, .01, and .001), power of the test (.80, .90, etc.), and effect size (small, moderate, or large). Once these criteria are established, researchers may use tables,[2] statistical formulas,[3] or computer software such as SPSS Sample Power to calculate the minimum sample size needed for their studies (sample sizes are discussed in subsequent chapters).

Nonparametric tests, also known as *distribution-free tests*, may be used when the assumptions for parametric tests are violated.[4] Nonparametric tests are appropriate when the dependent variable is measured at the ordinal or nominal levels of measurement, when the distribution of the dependent variable is severely skewed, and/or when a smaller sample size is used.

While most parametric tests have corresponding, or alternative, nonparametric tests, parametric tests are more powerful because they provide a better chance of detecting significant results when they exist. If data violate, for example, only the assumption of normal distribution, then the data can be transformed into a normal distribution as outlined in chapter 5. If transformation does not change the shape of the distribution, then a nonparametric test may be undertaken to analyze the null hypothesis.

Consider these factors when selecting a statistical test: (1) sampling method (representativeness), (2) distribution of the dependent variable (normal or not normal), (3) level of measurement (nominal, ordinal, interval, or ratio), and (4) sample size.

General Guidelines for Test Selection

The next five chapters present and discuss bivariate statistical tests used most in social science research. Bivariate tests are used to examine the relationship between two variables, one independent variable and one dependent variable. These include the Pearson's *r* correlation, independent *t*-test, dependent *t*-test, one-way analysis of variance (ANOVA), one-way analysis of covariance (ANCOVA), and chi-square. When the relationship between multiple independent variables and one or more dependent variables is examined, researchers may use multivariate statistics, such as multiple regression analysis (chapter 12), multivariate analysis of variance (MANOVA), multivariate analysis of covariance (MANCOVA), canonical correlation, and others (Abu-Bader, 2010).

---

[2]See Cohen (1988).
[3]See Hinkle, Wiersma, & Jurs (2003).
[4]For a comprehensive discussion on nonparametric tests, see Siegel & Castellan (1988).

Table 6.5 presents a number of bivariate statistical tests. The table shows each parametric test, its corresponding nonparametric test, and the appropriate levels of measurement for the independent and dependent variables. The table also shows the symbol associated with each test.

1. When the independent and dependent variables are interval or higher and are paired observations (measured at the same time; e.g., age and income), the Pearson's *r* correlation may be used. If the dependent variable is ordinal, Spearman's *rho* may be used (see chapter 7).

2. When the independent variable is nominal with two groups (e.g., gender: male and female), and the dependent variable is interval or ratio, the independent *t*-test may be used. If the dependent variable is ordinal, then the alternative nonparametric Mann-Whitney *U* test may be used (see chapter 8).

3. When both the independent and dependent variables are interval or higher, and one is a repeated measure of the other (pretest and posttest), the dependent *t*-test may be used. If one or both variables are ordinal, then the Wilcoxon signed ranks test may be used (see chapter 9).

4. When the independent variable is nominal with three groups or more (e.g., Race: white, African American, Native American, Hispanic, other), and the dependent variable is interval or ratio, the one-way analysis of variance (one-way ANOVA) may be used. If the dependent variable is ordinal, then the alternative nonparametric Kruskal-Wallis *H* test may be used (see chapter 10).

5. When both the independent and dependent variables are measured at the nominal level of measurement, the nonparametric chi-square test of association may be used (see chapter 11). This test does not have a corresponding parametric test, but there are other alternative nonparametric tests such as *phi*, Cramer's *V*, and others.

Remember: For all parametric tests, the shape of the distribution of the dependent variable should approach the shape of a normal curve. In addition,

Table 6.5:   Guidelines for Selecting a Statistical Test

Type	Test	IV	DV	Symbol
Parametric	Pearson's *r*	Interval/ratio	Interval/ratio	r
Nonparametric	Spearman's *rho*	Ordinal or higher	Ordinal	ρ
Parametric	independent *t*-test	Nominal/2 Groups	Interval/ratio	t
Nonparametric	Mann-Whitney *U*	Nominal/2 Groups	Ordinal	z
Parametric	dependent *t*-test	Interval/ratio	Interval/ratio	t
Nonparametric	Wilcoxon signed ranks	Ordinal or higher	Ordinal	z
Parametric	one-way ANOVA	Nominal/3 Groups+	Interval/ratio	F
Nonparametric	Kruskal-Wallis *H*	Nominal/3 Groups+	Ordinal	χ^2
Parametric	none	none	none	none
Nonparametric	chi-square test	nominal	nominal	χ^2

each parametric test has its own assumptions that should be met. These assumptions are discussed in detail in the next chapters. When these assumptions are violated, the alternative nonparametric test may be more appropriate to use to examine the relationship between the variables.

Steps in Testing a Statistical Hypothesis

Most social sciences researchers follow similar steps in testing a research hypothesis. Some are decided during early stages of research design, prior to data analysis. These include the following:

STEP 1: State the null and alternative (research) hypotheses. Research hypothesis can be either one-tailed or two-tailed hypothesis. This is critical because SPSS produces a two-tailed p value for all statistical tests discussed in this book, except Pearson's r correlation. For this test, select one-tailed or two-tailed analysis based on whether the research hypothesis is one-tailed or two-tailed (see chapter 7). In all other cases, divide the computed two-tailed p value by two if the research hypothesis is one-tailed.

STEP 2: Set the criteria for rejecting H_0. Traditionally, social science researchers set alpha at .05 ($\alpha = .05$). Reject the null hypothesis if the p value is equal to or less than alpha (e.g., .05).

STEP 3: Choose the appropriate statistical test to examine the null hypothesis. First, select the most appropriate parametric and nonparametric tests as outlined in table 6.5. Second, review the parametric assumptions (e.g., distribution, level of measurement, homogeneity of variance, sample size) to determine whether they are met. Third, if necessary, transform the data to the square root, logarithm, or other method (as discussed in chapter 5). Based on these evaluations and transformations, choose the appropriate test.

Recommendation: If you choose a nonparametric test, run the corresponding parametric test. If both tests produce the same results (the same conclusion), report the results of the parametric test and indicate that the results of the nonparametric test are consistent with the results of the parametric test.

STEP 4: Compute the test statistic. This is discussed in detail in the following chapters.

STEP 5: Decide whether or not to reject the null hypothesis (H_0). If the computed p value is equal or less than alpha, then reject the null hypothesis. If the computed p value is greater than alpha, do not reject the null hypothesis.

STEP 6: Summarize your findings and present them in readable tables and graphs.

SUMMARY

Chapter 6 discussed the foundation for inferential statistics, essential for all statistical techniques discussed in the remaining chapters. We reviewed null and research hypotheses, the difference between one-tailed and two-tailed research hypotheses, errors in hypothesis testing (type I and type II errors), power and effect size, levels of significance (p value), one-tailed and two-tailed rejection areas, and confidence intervals. The chapter also illustrated how to utilize SPSS to compute confidence intervals.

The chapter then discussed the differences between parametric and nonparametric tests and which factors to consider in selecting appropriate statistical tests. Steps in hypothesis testing were also outlined.

The next chapter introduces a bivariate statistical test, the Pearson's product moment correlation coefficient. Chapter 6 will discuss its purpose, assumptions, coefficient of determination, and the scatterplot. The alternative nonparametric test, Spearman's *rho* correlation, is presented, along with two practical examples and how to compute statistics in SPSS, read the output, and summarize and present results of correlation tests.

PRACTICAL EXERCISES

Part I: Use data from question 1 in chapter 5 and answer the following questions:

1. Compute the 95 percent and 99 percent confidence interval.

2. Explain what these intervals tell you.

Part II: Use the self-esteem data you entered in chapter 2 and answer the following questions:

1. State a null and a one-tailed research hypothesis predicting the relationship between age and self-esteem.

2. What are the independent and dependent variables in question 1 and their levels of measurement?

3. Run a histogram for the dependent variable in question 1 and evaluate its skewness coefficients.

4. Based on your answers for questions 2 and 3, what statistical test appears to be most appropriate to examine the hypothesis in question 1? Why? What is the alternative test?

5. State a null and a two-tailed research hypothesis predicting the relationship between ethnicity and education.

6. What are the independent and dependent variables in question 4 and their levels of measurement?

7. What statistical test appears to be most appropriate to examine the hypothesis in question 5? Why? What is the alternative test?

8. Use SPSS and compute the 99 percent confidence interval for self-esteem. What does this interval tell you?

CHAPTER 7

Bivariate Correlation: Pearson's Product-Moment Correlation Coefficient

LEARNING OBJECTIVES

1. Understand the purpose of Pearson's correlation
2. Understand the coefficient of determination
3. Understand the assumptions underlying Pearson's correlation
4. Understand the scatterplot
5. Understand the alternative nonparametric Spearman's *rho* correlation
6. Understand how to use SPSS to compute statistics and create a scatterplot
7. Understand how to interpret, write, and present results of the tests in summary tables and graphs

DATA SET (APPENDIX A)

Elderly

INTRODUCTION

Previous chapters have reviewed methodological terms and discussed various methods of descriptive statistics, including data organization and presentation, measures of central tendency, variability, percentiles, normal distributions, and measures of skewness. Chapter 6 introduced hypothesis testing, selecting an appropriate statistical test, and steps in hypothesis testing.

This and remaining chapters build on chapter 6. Recall that the purpose of any research study is not only to describe characteristics of a sample, but also to examine if these characteristics can be generalized to the population from which the sample is selected. Can relationships between variables observed in the sample be generalized to the population? For example, a clinical psychologist working with refugees in a local refugees resettlement office may notice that those who are proficient in English experience lower levels of anxiety than those who are less proficient. Or a social worker administrator may notice that social workers in his or her agency with a greater workload tend to experience greater levels of burnout. Do these patterns apply to all refugees or all social workers, respectively?

Here, the psychologist may hypothesize that there is a significant inverse relationship between English proficiency and anxiety among refugees. Or the social work administrator may hypothesize that there is a significant direct relationship between workload and burnout. If these hypotheses prove accurate, they could help both professionals to develop treatment programs or interventions for their respective customers. The psychologist may develop intensive English classes to decrease the refugees' levels of anxiety, and the social work administrator may reorganize employee workloads to decrease the level of burnout.

In these and similar cases, the professionals cannot rely solely on descriptive statistics. Further statistical analysis, inferential statistics, must be conducted.

What type of inferential statistics? Table 6.5 in chapter 6 grouped statistical tests in pairs (one parametric and one nonparametric). The first group included Pearson's r and Spearman's *rho*.

This chapter presents the Pearson's product-moment correlation coefficient and its alternative, Spearman's rank correlation coefficient. It discusses the purpose of these tests, defines the coefficient of determination, discusses assumptions underlying the tests, and presents the scatterplot. Two practical examples are presented, illustrating how to utilize SPSS to compute correlation coefficients, interpret the output, and write and present the results.

PURPOSE OF PEARSON'S CORRELATION COEFFICIENT

The Pearson's product-moment correlation coefficient (or simply known as Pearson's correlation or Pearson's r) is a bivariate parametric test developed by Karl Pearson (1857–1936), a British statistician. It examines the strength and direction of a linear relationship between two continuous variables (one dependent and one independent). The Pearson's correlation coefficient is symbolized by a lowercase Greek letter ρ (rho) to emphasize the relationship between variables in the population and a lowercase English italic letter r to emphasize the relationship between variables in the sample. We, however, study the relationship between variables in a sample (statistic = r) to estimate the correlation in the population (parameter = ρ).

The purpose of Pearson's correlation is to examine whether an increase in the independent variable leads to an increase or decrease in the dependent variable. For example, does an increase in English proficiency lead to a decrease in levels of anxiety among refugees? Or does an increase in workload lead to an increase in burnout among social workers? In these questions, both English proficiency and workload are the independent variables, and both anxiety and burnout are the dependent variables.

Correlation and Causality

Although Pearson's correlation coefficient examines if an increase in variable A leads to an increase or decrease in variable B, it, however, does not examine whether variable A causes the variable B to occur; that is, causality. In order to conclude that variable A causes variable B to occur, three requirements must be demonstrated: (1) the cause (variable A) must precede the effect (variable B) in time; (2) the two variables (A and B) must have empirical correlation; and (3) the correlation cannot be influenced by a third variable. Thus, just because two variables have a high correlation coefficient does not mean that one variable causes the other to occur. In reality, Pearson's correlation only examines the second requirement for causality; empirical correlation. For example, the fact that there is a high correlation between job satisfaction and burnout does not necessary mean that greater job satisfaction leads to lower burnout. It could be the opposite; that is, lower burnout leads to higher job satisfaction

Correlation Coefficient

The Pearson's correlation coefficient, r, ranges between -1.00 and $+1.00$. That is; $-1 \leq r \leq 1$. A correlation coefficient of -1.00 indicates a perfect negative correlation; a correlation coefficient of $+1.00$ indicates a perfect positive correlation. A correlation coefficient of 0 indicates that the two variables are not at all correlated.

The sign (+ or −) of the coefficient indicates only the direction of the relationship. That is, a correlation coefficient between 0 and 1 indicates a positive, direct relationship, and a correlation coefficient between 0 and −1 indicates a negative, inverse relationship.

The absolute value of the coefficient $|\pm r|$ indicates the strength of the relationship between the two variables. For example, a correlation coefficient of $-.65$ is stronger than a correlation coefficient of $.60$ because the absolute value of $-.65$ is greater than the absolute value of $.60$; that is $(|-.65| = .65 > |.60| = .60)$.

Coefficient of Determination

The coefficient of determination measures the strength of the relationship between the two variables. It measures the proportion of variance in the dependent variable that is explained by the independent variable (e.g., anxiety as explained by English proficiency or burnout as explained by workload). In other words, it is the overlap variance between the two variables. It is simply computed by squaring the Pearson's correlation coefficient r.

$$\text{Coefficient of Determination} = r^2$$

Figure 7.1: Venn Diagram—Correlation Between Two Variables

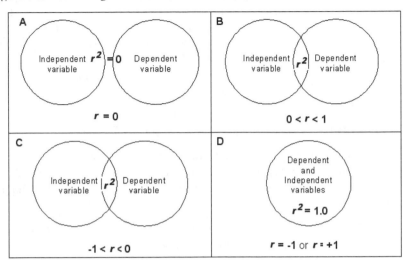

Figure 7.1 contains four Venn diagrams demonstrating different degrees of correlation between two variables. Venn diagram A shows that the two variables are not at all correlated ($r = 0$): the variance in the dependent variable that is explained by the independent variable is zero. Venn diagram B shows a positive correlation between the two variables ($0 < r < 1$). Venn diagram C shows a negative correlation between the two variables ($-1 < r < 0$). In both cases, the independent variable explains some of the variance in the dependent variable (r^2). Venn diagram D shows a perfect correlation between the two variables: the independent variable explains 100 percent of the variance in the dependent variable.

Example: If the correlation between physical health (independent variable) and levels of depression among frail elderly (dependent variable) is $-.40$ ($r = -.40$), then 16 percent of the variance in depression is due to physical health [$r^2 = (-.40)^2 = .16$, or 16%]. How strong is this correlation?

The correlation between two variables may be considered very strong, strong, moderate, weak, or very weak. Table 7.1 displays correlation coefficients in absolute values (e.g., $-.45$ is interpreted the same as $+.45$), coefficient of

Table 7.1: Interpretations of Correlation Coefficients

Interpretation	$|r|$	r^2
Very strong	$r \geq .91$	$r^2 \geq .82$
Strong	$.71 \leq r \leq .90$	$.50 \leq r^2 \leq .81$
Moderate	$.51 \leq r \leq .70$	$.26 \leq r^2 \leq .49$
Weak	$.31 \leq r \leq .50$	$.10 \leq r^2 \leq .25$
Very weak	$r \leq .30$	$r^2 \leq .09$

$|r|$=absolute value of r

determination, and their interpretations. As it is shown, a correlation coefficient of .30 (−.30) or less is considered very weak correlation; .31 to .50 (or −.31 to −.50) is weak; .51 to .70 (or −.51 to −.70) is moderate; .71 to .90 (or −.71 to −.90) is strong; and .90 and above (or −.90 and below) is considered very strong correlation. In our example above, although the correlation between physical health and depression is −.40, it is considered weak correlation since physical health explains only 16 percent of the variance in depression.

ASSUMPTIONS OF PEARSON'S CORRELATION

As discussed in chapter 6, all parametric tests make assumptions about the population from which the sample is selected. In addition, each parametric test requires additional assumptions about the data. The following are the assumptions for Pearson's correlation:

1. The dependent and independent variables must be continuous data and measured at the interval level of measurement or ratio.

2. The dependent and independent variables must be paired observations. Data for both variables must be collected from the same subjects at the same time. For example, to examine the relationship between English proficiency and levels of anxiety among refugees, the psychologist must collect data on both variables from each subject at the same time.

3. The shape of the distributions of the dependent and independent variables must approximate the shape of a normal curve.

   To evaluate the assumption of normality, create histograms with normal curves, normal Q-Q plots, and run measures of central tendency and measures of skewness for both the independent and dependent variables (see chapter 6). If the plots and measures of skewness show severe departure from normality, consider transforming the data to the square root, logarithm, or other transformation methods. If still severely skewed, consider the non-parametric Spearman's *rho* correlation test as an alternative.

4. The sample size should be large enough to conduct bivariate parametric tests such as Pearson's correlation.

   As stated in chapter 6, a sample size as small as thirty cases should be sufficient for parametric tests. Sample size, however, varies from one analysis to another. It depends on the direction of the research hypothesis (one-tailed vs. two-tailed), level of significance (alpha, .05, .01, or .001), power (.80, .90, etc.), and effect size (small, moderate, and large). Therefore, it is recommended that you choose a sample size needed for your analysis based on these criteria. Sample size can be easily calculated using statistical formulas, sample size tables,[1] online calculators, or sample size computer software such as SPSS Sample Power.

---

[1]See Cohen (1988).

Table 7.2:   Minimum Sample Size (Power = .80)

Alpha	Two-Tailed Hypothesis			One-Tailed Hypothesis		
	ES = .10	ES = .30	ES = .50	ES = .10	ES = .30	ES = .50
.050	778	82	26	613	64	21
.010	1160	122	39	996	105	33
.001	1695	178	57	1534	161	52

Table 7.2 displays the minimum sample size needed for Pearson's correlation to detect a significant correlation between two variables in a population with a statistical power .80. We used Cohen's (1988) definition of effect size (small ES, r = .10; moderate ES, r = .30; and large ES, r = .50) to tabulate these sample sizes using SPSS Sample Power version 2.0. Keep in mind that other computer software, online calculators, or statistical formulas may produce slightly different numbers.

Table 7.2 shows that to achieve a power of .80 with a small effect size (ES = .10), and a two-tailed alpha of .05, a minimum sample size of 778 cases is required. On the other hand, we only need eighty-two cases if we choose a moderate effect size (ES = .30), and only twenty-six cases if we use a large effect size (ES = .50). Moreover, these sample sizes will decrease further if we use a one-tailed instead of two-tailed hypothesis, given other factors held constant.

Therefore, the larger the effect size is, the smaller the sample size needed for Pearson's correlation, given that all other factors are held constant. Remember, however, that when small sample sizes are used, power will decrease, and therefore it is best to conduct a power analysis using statistical formulas[2] or computer software such as SPSS Sample Power to determine the power of the study. Also, when a small sample size is used, the nonparametric Spearman's *rho* correlation test may be considered to examine the relationship between the two variables.

SPEARMAN'S RANK CORRELATION COEFFICIENT

The Spearman's rank correlation coefficient,[3] simply known as Spearman's *rho*, is the nonparametric version of the Pearson's correlation coefficient. While Pearson's correlation examines actual raw scores of independent and dependent variables, Spearman's *rho* ranks these scores and then examines whether there is a relationship between the two ranks.

Because Spearman's *rho* does not make assumptions about the population from which the sample is selected, it is appropriate to use when either or both the independent and dependent variables are measured at the ordinal level of measurement, or at interval levels that do not meet the assumption of normality. As with Pearson's correlation, Spearman's *rho* requires the sample to be

---

[2]See Cohen (1988); Hinkle, Wiersma, & Jurs (2003).
[3]Named after Charles Edward Spearman (1863–1945), an English psychologist.

representative of the population and the independent and dependent variables to be paired observations.

Like the Pearson's correlation coefficient, the Spearman's *rho* coefficient ranges between −1 and +1, where the sign indicates the direction of the relationship and the absolute value indicates the strength of the relationship. This Spearman's *rho* coefficient is symbolized by r_s in the sample and ρ in the population.

SCATTERPLOT

A scatterplot (also called scattergram) is a useful graphical presentation of the relationship between two continuous variables (interval or ratio). The Y axis represents the scores of the dependent variable; the X axis represents the scores of the independent variable. Each point in a scatterplot represents two scores, one for the dependent variable (y) and another for the independent variable (x). There should be one point on the scatterplot for each subject in a study. Figure 7.2 is a scatterplot displaying the relationship between cognitive status (independent variable x) and self-esteem (dependent variable y) from the Elderly data file.

The line in figure 7.2 is called the *fit line*. It indicates that there is a linear positive relationship between self-esteem and cognitive status in the Elderly sample: the greater the cognitive status, the higher the self-esteem. A fit line

Figure 7.2:   Scatterplot for Self-Esteem and Cognitive Status

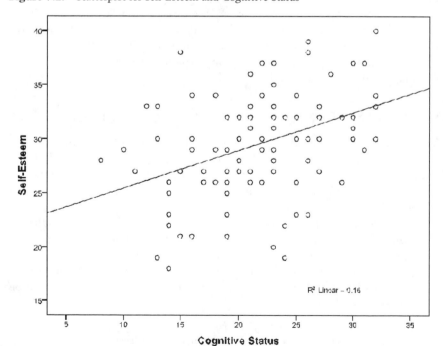

that runs from the lower left side to the upper right side (as in figure 7.2) represents a positive correlation. A fit line that runs from the upper left side to the lower right side represents a negative correlation (see scatterplots in chapter 1). Scatterplot creation in SPSS is addressed later in the chapter.

PRACTICAL EXAMPLES

This book is not about statistical formulas, which are discussed exclusively in many other textbooks.[4] Instead, this book presents and discusses how to utilize SPSS program to run both Pearson's and Spearman's *rho* correlation coefficients and scatterplots.

To illustrate the utilization of Pearson's and Spearman's in hypothesis testing and the utilization of SPSS to compute these tests and graphs, two examples are presented. The first examines the relationship between cognitive status and self-esteem, and the second examines the relationship between physical health and depression. Both examples are from the Elderly study. For each example, follow the steps in hypothesis testing discussed in chapter 6.

Example 1: Positive Correlation

RESEARCH QUESTION: Is there a statistically significant relationship between self esteem (Esteem) and cognitive status (CS) among frail elderly?

Step 1: State the null and alternative hypotheses.

H_0: There is no statistically significant relationship between self-esteem and cognitive status among frail elderly. That is, $r = 0$.

H_a: There is a statistically significant positive relationship between self-esteem and cognitive status among frail elderly. The greater the level of cognitive status among frail elderly is, the higher their level of self-esteem. That is, $r > 0$.

In this one-tailed research hypothesis, cognitive status is the independent variable, and self-esteem is the dependent variable.

Step 2: Set criteria for rejecting H_0.
Set alpha at .05 ($\alpha = .05$). Reject H_0 only if $p \leq .05$.

Step 3: Select the appropriate statistical test.

1. Data for both the independent variable (cognitive status) and the dependent variable (self-esteem) were collected from the same subjects at the same time. They are paired observations.

---

[4]See Hinkle, Wiersma, & Jurs (2003).

2. In this study, the two variables were measured using scales, and total scores were computed for both. That is, total scores for both variables are interval levels of measurement (see appendix A).

    Thus, because cognitive status and self-esteem are paired observations and interval level of measurement (see chapter 6, table 6.5), they satisfy the basic assumptions for either the Pearson's correlation or Spearman's *rho*.

3. To determine which test is more appropriate, evaluate whether the shape of the distributions for both variables approach the shape of a normal curve. To do so, compute Pearson's and Fisher's skewness coefficients and run histograms with normal curves and normal Q-Q plots (see chapter 5) for both variables.

    Table 7.3 and Figures 7.3 to 7.6 display the descriptive statistics, histograms, and probability plots for both cognitive status and self-esteem. Next, compute Pearson's and Fisher's skewness as discussed in chapter 5 and inspect histograms and normal Q-Q plots for both variables. Pearson's and Fisher's skewness coefficients are as follows:

Table 7.3:   Descriptive Statistics for Cognitive Status and Self-Esteem

			Statistic	Std. Error
Cognitive	Mean		21.72	.564
Status	95% Confidence	Lower Bound	20.60	
	Interval for Mean	Upper Bound	22.84	
	5% Trimmed Mean		21.75	
	Median		22.00	
	Variance		31.450	
	Std. Deviation		5.608	
	Minimum		8	
	Maximum		32	
	Range		24	
	Interquartile Range		8	
	Skewness		−.066	.243
	Kurtosis		−.562	.481
Self-Esteem	Mean		29.54	.489
	95% Confidence	Lower Bound	28.56	
	Interval for Mean	Upper Bound	30.51	
	5% Trimmed Mean		29.57	
	Median		30.00	
	Variance		23.721	
	Std. Deviation		4.870	
	Minimum		18	
	Maximum		40	
	Range		22	
	Interquartile Range		6	
	Skewness		−.091	.243
	Kurtosis		−.192	.481

Skewness Coefficients for Cognitive Status

$$Pearson's = \frac{Mean - Median}{SD} = \frac{21.72 - 22}{5.608} = -.05$$

$$Fisher's = \frac{Skewness}{SES} = \frac{-.066}{.243} = -.27$$

Skewness Coefficients for Self-Esteem

$$Pearson's = \frac{Mean - Median}{SD} = \frac{29.54 - 30}{4.87} = -.09$$

$$Fisher's = \frac{Skewness}{SES} = \frac{-.091}{.243} = -.37$$

Pearson's and Fisher's skewness coefficients for both cognitive status and for self-esteem fall within their normal range (±.2 and ±1.96, respectively). Also, inspecting the histograms and normal Q-Q plots for cognitive status (figures 7.3 and 7.4) and self-esteem (figures 7.5 and 7.6) confirms that the shape of their distributions approaches the shape of a normal curve. Therefore, we conclude that data for both variables meet the assumption of normality for Pearson's correlation test.

4. In the Elderly study, ninety-nine participants completed the survey. This sample size is larger than the minimum thirty cases needed for a bivariate

Figure 7.3:   Histogram for Cognitive Status

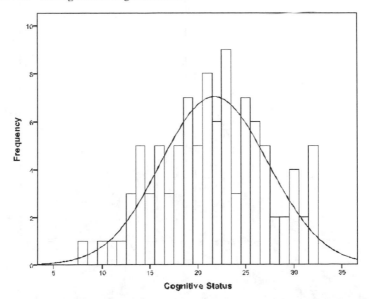

Figure 7.4:   Normal Q-Q Plot of Cognitive Status

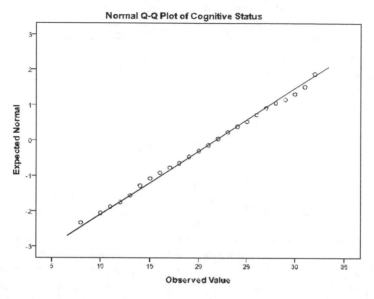

parametric test. It is also larger than the sixty-four cases needed to achieve a power of .80 given a moderate effect size (ES = .30), a one-tailed research hypothesis, and an alpha of .05 (see table 7.2).

Figure 7.5:   Histogram for Self-Esteem

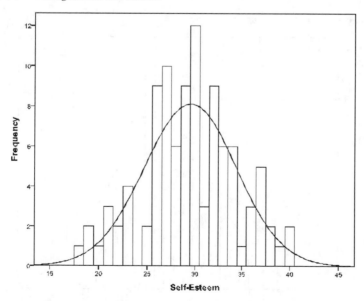

Figure 7.6:   Normal Q-Q Plot of Self-Esteem

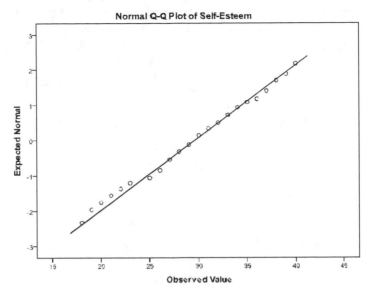

To conclude, the data for both independent and dependent variables in this study satisfied all assumptions for the Pearson's correlation. Now we will utilize SPSS to run the Pearson's correlation. We also will run the Spearman's *rho* to examine whether results of both tests are consistent.

Step 4: Compute the test statistic (using SPSS).
Use SPSS to compute Pearson's correlation and Spearman's *rho* coefficients. Unlike with other statistical tests discussed in subsequent chapters, here both correlation coefficients can be requested simultaneously. In addition, depending on the research hypothesis, the option exists whether to run a one-tailed or two-tailed analysis.

How to compute the Pearson's correlation and Spearman's *rho* coefficients in SPSS.   In this example, the independent variable is cognitive status (CS), and the dependent variable is self-esteem (Esteem). To compute the Pearson's and Spearman's *rho* correlation coefficients in SPSS, follow these steps:

1. Open the SPSS Elderly data file.

2. Click on *Analyze* in the SPSS main toolbar, scroll down, click on *Correlate*, and click on *Bivariate* (see screen 7.1). A new dialog box called "Bivariate Correlations" will open (see screen 7.2).

3. Scroll down in the variable list, click on *CS*, and click on the arrow button between the two boxes to move *CS* into the *Variables* box.

Screen 7.1:   SPSS Bivariate Correlations Main Menu

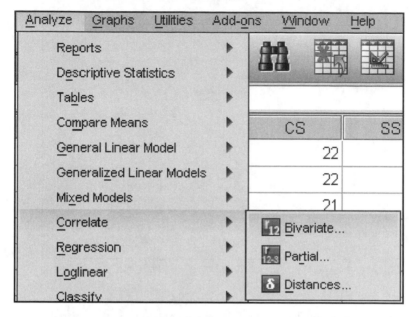

Screen 7.2:   SPSS Bivariate Correlations Dialog Box

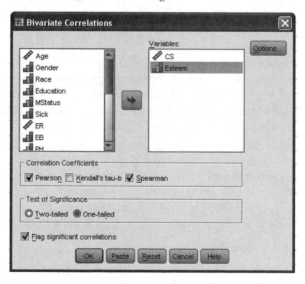

4. Repeat step 3 to move *Esteem* in the *Variables* box. You can add more than two variables to examine their correlations.

5. Make sure that *Pearson* is checked under "Correlation Coefficients" (SPSS default). If not, check it. Also check *Spearman*.

6. For a two-tailed research hypothesis, make sure that *Two-tailed* is checked under "Test of Significance" (SPSS default). For a one-tailed research hypothesis, check *One-tailed*. In this example, check *One-tailed*.

7. Notice that the box next to *Flag significant correlations* is checked. This flags all significant correlations at alpha of .05 with a single asterisk and significant correlations at alpha of 0.01 with two asterisks. You may uncheck this box to remove any asterisk. You may also click on *Options* to request mean and standard deviation for each variable in the analysis.

8. Click on *OK*.

SPSS Syntax for Pearson's Correlation

CORRELATIONS
/VARIABLES=CS Esteem
/PRINT=ONETAIL NOSIG
/MISSING=PAIRWISE.

SPSS Syntax for Spearman's *rho* Correlation

NONPAR CORR
/VARIABLES=CS Esteem
/PRINT=SPEARMAN ONETAIL NOSIG
/MISSING=PAIRWISE.

Note: For two-tailed hypothesis, replace ONETAILE with TWOTAILE next to /PRINT.

Interpreting the output.   Tables 7.4 and 7.5 display the output of SPSS. The first table displays the results of the Pearson's correlation, and the second displays the results of Spearman's *rho* correlation.

Table 7.4:   Results of Pearson's Correlation

		Cognitive Status	Self-Esteem
Cognitive Status	Pearson's Correlation	1	.400**
	Sig. (1-tailed)		.000
	N	99	99
Self-Esteem	Pearson's Correlation	.400**	1
	Sig. (1-tailed)	.000	
	N	99	99

**Correlation is significant at the 0.01 level (1-tailed).

Table 7.4 displays three measures: Pearson's correlation, Sig. (1-tailed), and N. The Pearson's correlation conveys the correlation coefficient *r*. "Sig." conveys the level of significance (*p* value) and "1-tailed" conveys that this is a one-tailed hypothesis. "N" conveys the number of subjects in the study.

The table shows that the correlation coefficient between cognitive status and itself is 1, and the correlation coefficient between self-esteem and itself is 1. This is always the case, that the correlation between a variable and itself is 1, which is useless information. A correlation should always be between two or more variables (e.g., cognitive status and self-esteem).

The correlation between cognitive status and self-esteem is .40 (*r* = .400), the *p* value is .000 (Sig. = .000), and the sample size, N, is ninety-nine subjects. A *p* that is equal to or less than .05 indicates a statistically significant result. Notice that the correlation is flagged with two asterisks, which indicates that this correlation is significant at a .01 level (see explanation at the bottom of table 7.4). In other words, the correlation between cognitive status and self-esteem is statistically significant (*p* < .01). Recall that our alpha is .05 (see step 2).

Table 7.5 displays the results of Spearman's *rho*. Like table 7.4, it has three measures: the Spearman's *rho* correlation coefficient, Sig. (1-tailed), and N. The Spearman's *rho* correlation coefficient conveys the *rho* coefficient. "Sig." conveys the level of significance (*p* value), and "1-tailed" conveys that this is a one-tailed hypothesis. "N" conveys the number of subjects in the study.

Table 7.5 shows that the correlation between cognitive status and self-esteem is .40 (*rho* = .399, round to the nearest decimal), the *p* value is .000 (Sig. = .001), and the sample size is ninety-nine subjects. Because the *p* value is less than .05, the correlation coefficient between the two variables is statistically significant.

Step 5: Decide whether to reject the null hypothesis.

The results of the Pearson's correlation coefficient presented in table 7.4 show a statistically significant relationship between cognitive status and self-esteem (*p* < .05, or in this case, *p* < .01). Therefore, reject the null hypothesis.

Table 7.5:   Results of Spearman's rho Correlation

			Cognitive Status	Self-Esteem
Spearman's *rho*	Cognitive Status	Correlation Coefficient	1.000	.399[**]
		Sig. (1-tailed)	.	.000
		N	99	99
	Self-Esteem	Correlation Coefficient	.399[**]	1.000
		Sig. (1-tailed)	.000	.
		N	99	99

**Correlation is significant at the 0.01 level (1-tailed).

Writing the Results.   When writing the results of Pearson's correlation or Spearman's *rho,* first discuss the normality of distributions and if transformation was conducted. Then, report Pearson's (or Spearman's *rho*) correlation coefficient and the *p* value, as well as the direction and strength (coefficient of determination) of the relationship. You may present results in a Venn diagram or a scatterplot to visually show the relationship between variables. In our example, the results may be summarized as follows:

Prior to examining the relationship between self-esteem and cognitive status among frail elderly, data for both variables were inspected for normality. Measures of central tendency, skewness coefficients, histograms, and normal Q-Q plots ensured that both cognitive status and self-esteem were normally distributed. Therefore, Pearson's correlation test was utilized to examine the null hypothesis.

Note: You may state that "the Spearman's *rho* test was utilized since" normality was violated, transformation was not successful to fix the shape of the distributions, variables were ordinal, and/or sample size was too small.

The results of Pearson's correlation test (or Spearman's *rho*) show a significant positive relationship ($r = .40$, $p < .01$) between self-esteem and cognitive status. In other words, participants who have greater levels of cognitive status tend to experience significantly higher levels of self-esteem than those who have lower cognitive status. These results are supported by the results of Spearman's *rho* test ($r_s = .40$, $p < .01$).

The independent variable (cognitive status) explains, however, 16 percent ($r^2 = .40^2 = 16\%$) of the variance in self-esteem. In other words, 84 percent of the variance in self-esteem is unaccounted for and could be attributed to extraneous variables. Thus, although the two variables have a statistically significant relationship, this relationship is considered weak. Figure 7.7 displays a Venn diagram illustrating the relationship between the two variables. Also, figure 7.2 (shown above) conveys a scatterplot showing the relationship between self-esteem and cognitive status.

Figure 7.7:   Venn Diagram for Self-Esteem and Cognitive Status

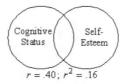

$r = .40$; $r^2 = .16$

How to create a scatterplot in SPSS.   We illustrate how to use SPSS to create the scatterplot in figure 7.2. To create a scatterplot in SPSS, follow these steps:

1.   Open the SPSS Elderly data file.

2.   Click on *Graphs*, *Legacy Dialog*, and *Scatter/Dot* (see chapter 3, screen 3.8). A dialog box called "Scatter/Dot" will open (see screen 7.3).

Screen 7.3:   SPSS Graphs Scatter/Dot Dialog box

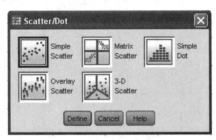

3.   Select *Simple* (SPSS default) and click on *Define*.

4.   A new dialog box called "Simple Scatterplot" will open (see screen 7.4).

Screen 7.4:   SPSS Simple Scatterplot Dialog Box

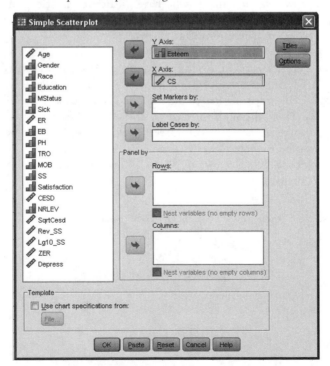

5. Scroll down in the variable list, click on *Esteem* (dependent variable), and click on the top arrow button to move it into the *Y Axis* box.

6. Scroll down in the variable list, click on *CS* (independent variable), and click on the second top arrow button to move it in the *X Axis* box.

7. Click on *OK* (*Note:* You may click on *Titles* to add a title for the scatterplot as we did in chapter 3, screen 3.10).

SPSS Syntax for Scatterplot

GRAPH

/SCATTERPLOT(BIVAR)=CS WITH Esteem

/TITLE = 'Scatterplot for Self-Esteem and Cognitive Status'.

/MISSING=LISTWISE.

The execution of these commands creates a scatterplot for the two variables. These commands, however, do not add a fit line on the graph. To add a fit line, follow these steps:

1. Point the mouse anywhere in the scatterplot and double-click. A new SPSS window called "Chart Editor" will open (see screen 7.5).

Screen 7.5:   SPSS Chart Editor Dialog Box

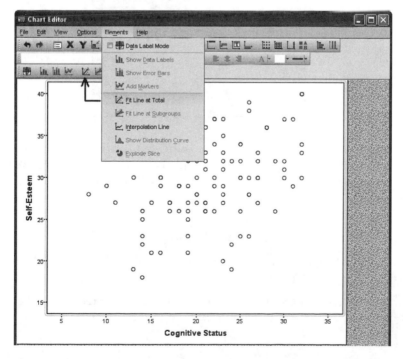

2. Click on *Elements* and click on *Fit Line at Total*. You can also click on the *Fit Line at Total* button at the submenu as seen in screen 7.5.

3. A fit line will be added to the chart. This also opens the "Properties" dialog box (see screen 7.6). It allows you to change the size of the chart, the weight and color, and type of fit line.

4. To end, click on *Close*. Then click on *File* and *Close* in the *Chart Editor* toolbar. Or simply click on the *X* in the upper right corner of the *Chart Editor* to close. This will return you to *Output*.

Screen 7.6:   SPSS Chart Editor Properties Dialog Box

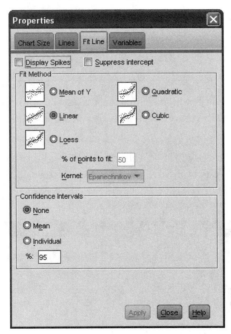

The execution of the SPSS *Graphs* and *Chart Editor* commands creates a scatterplot with a fit line for the two variables. Figure 7.2 (above) displays a scatterplot for self-esteem and cognitive status. Notice that the figure also displays the coefficient of determination (R^2 Linear = .16).

Example 2: Negative Correlation

In this example, the relationship between levels of depression and physical health among frail elderly is examined.

RESEARCH QUESTION: Is there a statistically significant relationship between levels of depression (CESD) and physical health (PH) among frail elderly?

Step 1: State the null and alternative hypotheses.

H_0: There is no statistically significant relationship between levels of depression and physical health among frail elderly. That is, $r = 0$.

H_a: There is a statistically significant negative relationship between levels of depression and physical health among frail elderly. Or, the better the physical health among frail elderly is, the lower their level of depression. That is, $r < 0$.

In this one-tailed research hypothesis, physical health is the independent variable, and depression is the dependent variable.

Step 2: Set criteria for rejecting H_0.
Set alpha at .05 ($\alpha = .05$). Reject H_0 only if $p \leq .05$.

Step 3: Select the appropriate statistical test.

1. Data for both the independent variable (physical health) and the dependent variable (depression) were collected from the same subjects at the same time. They are paired observations.

2. In this study, physical health and depression were measured using well-known standardized scales, and total scores were computed for both variables. These total scores are interval levels of measurement (see appendix A).

    Therefore, since the two variables are paired observations and interval level of measurement (see chapter 6, table 6.5), they satisfy the basic assumptions for either the Pearson's correlation or Spearman's *rho*.

3. To determine which test is more appropriate, evaluate if the shape of the distributions for both variables approach the shape of a normal curve.

    We evaluated the shape of the distribution of depression in chapter 5 (see chapter 5, figures 5.7 and 5.8). Recall that depression was severely skewed and thus was transformed to the square root. The distribution of the square root was normally distributed (see chapter 5, figures 5.9 and 5.10) and will be used in the hypothesis testing instead of the actual raw scores.

    Next, we evaluate the distribution of physical health as we did in the previous example. Table 7.6 and figures 7.8 and 7.9 display the descriptive statistics, histogram, and normal Q-Q plot for physical health.

    Applying the Pearson's skewness formula, we found that the skewness coefficient is .30 [that is, $(15.40 - 14)/4.66 = .30$], which slightly falls outside $\pm.20$. On the other hand, Fisher's skewness coefficient falls within ± 1.96 (that is, $.268/.243 = 1.10$), thus indicating that the distribution is not severely skewed. In addition, inspection of both histogram (see figure 7.8) and normal Q-Q plot (see figure 7.9) of physical health indicates that the shape of the distribution of physical health approaches that of a normal curve, perhaps with slight deviation in the right, which could explain the

Table 7.6:   Descriptive Statistics for Physical Health

			Statistic	Std. Error
Physical	Mean		15.40	.469
Health	95% Confidence	Lower Bound	14.47	
	Interval for Mean	Upper Bound	16.33	
	5% Trimmed Mean		15.30	
	Median		14.00	
	Variance		21.753	
	Standard Deviation		4.664	
	Minimum		7	
	Maximum		26	
	Range		19	
	Interquartile Range		7	
	Skewness		.268	.243
	Kurtosis		−.659	.481

Figure 7.8:   Histogram for Physical Health

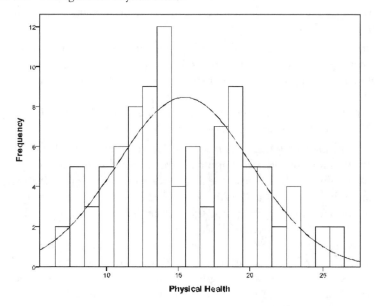

deviation of Pearson's skewness coefficient. Notice that almost all physical health data are clustered on the straight line. Therefore, we conclude that the distribution of physical health meets the assumption of normality.

4. As we said in the previous example, ninety-nine participants completed the survey, which exceeds the minimum requirement for this analysis.

To conclude, the data for physical health and square root of depression satisfied all assumptions for the Pearson's correlation. Again, we will also run the Spearman's *rho* to examine whether results of both tests are consistent.

Figure 7.9:   Normal Q-Q Plot of Physical Health

Normal Q-Q Plot of Physical Health

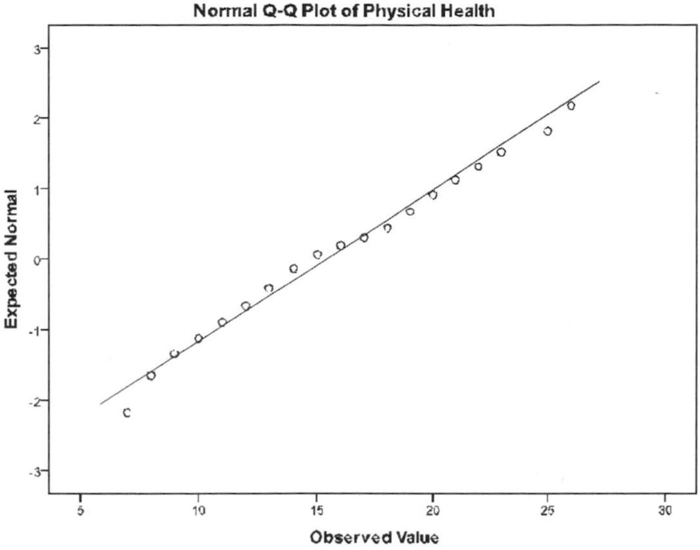

Note: If transformation did not fix the distribution of depression, we would utilize Spearman's *rho* as the *main* test and Pearson's correlation as the alternative test. If both produce similar results, then we still report the results of Pearson's correlation. If their results are different (one significant and the other is not significant), we should report the results of the *main* test, hence Spearman's *rho* correlation.

Step 4: Compute the test statistic.

Follow the same SPSS methods discussed in the previous example to run Pearson's correlation, Spearman's *rho* correlation, and a scatterplot for physical health and levels of depression.

Table 7.7 displays the results of the Pearson's correlation test, and table 7.8 displays the results of the alternative nonparametric Spearman's *rho* correlation test.

Table 7.7 shows that the correlation coefficient between levels of (square root) depression and physical health is −.26 ($r = -.264$), the *p* value is .004 (Sig. = .004), and the sample size is ninety-nine. This indicates a statistically significant negative relationship between depression and physical health.

The results of the Spearman's *rho* correlation presented in table 7.8 are similar to the results of Pearson's correlation presented in table 7.7: $r_s = -.28$ (less than .02 greater than Pearson's *r*), the *p* value is .002 (Sig. = .002), and the sample size is ninety-nine (N = 99). That is, there is a statistically significant negative correlation between depression and physical health.

Table 7.7:   Results of Pearson's Correlation

		Depression	Physical Health
Square root	Pearson's Correlation	1	−.264[**]
Depression	Sig. (1-tailed)		.004
	N	99	99
Physical Health	Pearson's Correlation	−.264[**]	1
	Sig. (1-tailed)	.004	
	N	99	99

**Correlation is significant at the 0.01 level (1-tailed).

Table 7.8:   Results of Spearman's *rho* Correlation

			Depression	Physical Health
Spearman's *rho*	Square Root	Correlation Coefficient	1.000	−.281[**]
	Depression	Sig. (1-tailed)		.002
		N	99	99
	Physical Health	Correlation Coefficient	−.281[**]	1.000
		Sig. (1-tailed)	.002	.
		N	99	99

**Correlation is significant at the 0.01 level (1-tailed).

Step 5: Decide whether to reject the null hypothesis.

The results of Pearson's correlation presented in table 7.7 show a statistically significant relationship between levels of depression and physical health ($p < .01$). Therefore, we reject the null hypothesis.

Writing the results.   As discussed in the previous example, report any violation of normality, transformation, and then the results of the test as follows:

To examine the relationship between levels of depression and physical health among frail elderly, we first inspected the distributions of the two variables for normality. Evaluation of measures of skewness and visually reviewing the histograms and normal Q-Q plots for both variables indicated that physical health was normally distributed. On the other hand, depression had severe positive skewness and thus was transformed to the square root. Evaluation of the distribution of the square root of depression indicated it was normally distributed, and therefore we used the Pearson's correlation test to examine the relationship between (square root) depression and physical health.

Note: If transformation was not successful, you may want to try a different method of transformation, such as logarithm. If still not successful, state that "evaluation of the distribution of the transformed depression did not, however, produce a normal distribution. Thus, the Spearman's *rho* was utilized to examine the relationship between the two variables."

The results of Pearson's correlation (or Spearman's if it was the main test) show a significant negative correlation between depression and physical health ($r = -.26$, $p < .01$), so we rejected the null hypothesis. In other words, participants with better physical health experience significantly lower levels of depression than those with poorer physical health. The results of Spearman's *rho* correlation support these results ($r_s = -.28$, $p < .01$).

These results, however, show that physical health explains about 7 percent [$r^2 = (-.264)^2 = 7\%$] of the variance in depression, thus indicating a very weak correlation. More than 93 percent of the variance in depression is unaccounted for and could be explained by extraneous variables. Figure 7.10 is a Venn diagram describing the relationship between depression and physical health. Also, figure 7.11 displays a scatterplot illustrating the relationship between the two variables. The plot shows a negative, but very weak ($r^2 = 7\%$) linear relationship between the variables; lower depression is associated with better health.

Figure 7.10: Venn Diagram for Depression and Physical Health

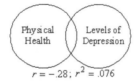

$r = -.28$; $r^2 = .076$

Figure 7.11: Scatterplot for Depression and Physical Health

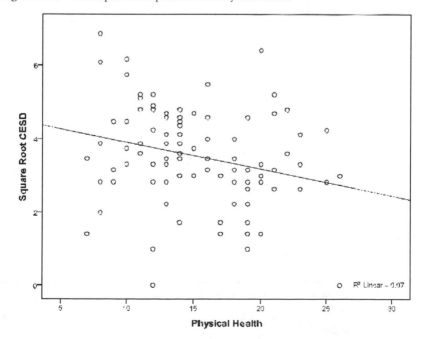

Presentation of Results in Summary Tables

In addition to a write-up and a graph display, results should also be presented in a summary table. There are two types of summary tables. The first presents the correlation coefficients between one dependent variable and a number of independent variables (for example, depression based on physical health, emotional balance, and cognitive status). The limitation of this table is that the relationship between independent variables is not reported. The second type is a correlation matrix, which presents the correlation coefficients between each pair of variables and flags each correlation that is significant with an asterisk.

Tables 7.9 and 7.10 compare these two types of summary tables. Table 7.9 displays the correlation between depression (dependent variable) and four independent variables; physical health, cognitive status, self-esteem, and emotional balance (here we only examined physical health and depression, but for illustration we ran correlations between depression and cognitive status, self-esteem, as well as emotional balance).

Table 7.10 is a correlation matrix. It displays the correlation coefficient between each pair of variables in the analysis. The "1.00" in the diagonal represents the correlation between each variable and itself. Because this is useless, many researchers prefer to report the reliability coefficients (Cronbach's *alpha*) in the diagonal and the mean, standard deviation, and range for each scale, or subscale, at the bottom of the table. Table 7.11, for example, is the same as table 7.10, but it also reports the reliability coefficient (see chapters 1 and 2 for relia-

Table 7.9: Relationship between Levels of Depression (Square Root) and Independent Variables (N = 99)

Variable	r	r^2	p *
Physical Health	−.26	.07	> .010
Cognitive Status	−.25	.06	> .010
Self-Esteem	−.40	.16	> .010
Emotional Balance	−.61	.37	> .010

*One-tailed p.

Table 7.10: Correlation Matrix (N = 99)

	Depression	Physical Health	Cognitive Status	Self-Esteem	Emotional Balance
Depression	1.00				
Physical Health	−.264[**]	1.00			
Cognitive Status	−.313[**]	.027	1.00		
Self-Esteem	−.403[**]	.150	.400[**]	1.00	
Emotional Balance	−.609[**]	.340[**]	.238[**]	.416[**]	1.00

**Correlation is significant at the 0.01 level (1-tailed).

Table 7.11:   Correlation Matrix (N = 99)

	Depression[a]	Physical Health	Cognitive Status	Self-Esteem	Emotional Balance
Depression	.81				
Physical Health	−.264**	.60			
Cognitive Status	−.313**	.027	.77		
Self-Esteem	−.403**	.150	.400**	.82	
Emotional Balance	−.609**	.340**	.238**	.416**	.84
Mean	3.52 (13.99)[b]	15.40	21.72	29.54	23.18
SD	1.28 (9.11)	4.66	5.61	4.87	6.16
Range	0–7 (0–47)	7–26	8–32	18–40	10–32

**Correlation is significant at the 0.01 level (1-tailed).
a. Square Root of Depression.
b. Numbers in parentheses are descriptive statistics for depression raw scores.

bility and reliability analysis) for each scale and their mean, standard deviation, and range observed in the Elderly study at the bottom of the table. (*Note:* Reliability coefficients reported in diagonals are for clarification only and should not be cited as actual scale reliability.)

SUMMARY

The aim of social science researchers is to examine relationships between attitudes, behaviors, feelings, and other characteristics in a sample and generalize these relationships to the population from which a sample is drawn. To accomplish this, researchers utilize various inferential statistical techniques that examine whether relationships observed in a sample fit the population.

This chapter introduced the first pair of inferential statistics discussed in this book, Pearson's product-moment correlation and Spearman's *rho* correlation. The chapter discussed the purpose of the two tests, the coefficient of determination, and the assumptions underlying the statistics. The chapter then discussed the importance of the Venn diagram and scatterplot in visualizing and evaluating the direction and strength of the relationship between two continuous variables.

Two research questions based on real data demonstrated how to state the null and alternative hypotheses, evaluate the test's assumptions, choose the appropriate statistical test, and use SPSS to compute Pearson's and Spearman's *rho* correlation coefficients, create and edit scatterplots, interpret the output, and write and present results in summary tables and graphs.

Chapter 8 will introduce Student's *t*-tests. The chapter will discuss how to use the one-sample case *t*-test to compare a sample's characteristics based on continuous data like age with those of the population. The chapter then will discuss in detail the independent *t*-test and its alternative, the Mann-Whitney *U* test, the purpose of the two tests, and their assumptions. The chapter will present two examples using real social science data to illustrate how to compute the *t*-tests and Mann-Whitney *U* statistics, interpret the output, write, and present the results in summary tables.

PRACTICAL EXERCISES

Part I: Access the Well-Being SPSS data file (appendix A) and examine the following research question:

Are there significant relationships between self-perception of body weight and (a) levels of depression; and (b) life satisfaction among college students?

1. Follow the steps in hypothesis testing and examine each hypothesis (use one-tailed hypotheses). Discuss all steps in detail.

2. Write the SPSS syntax for each transformation, if any.

3. Present the results in a correlation matrix table.

4. Present the results for one pair in a Venn diagram.

5. Create a scatterplot for the second pair of variables.

Part II: Use the self-esteem data you entered in chapter 2 and examine the following research question:

Is there a significant relationship between physical health and levels of self-esteem among older immigrants?

1. Follow the steps in hypothesis testing and examine the hypothesis (use a one-tailed hypothesis). Discuss all steps in detail.

2. Write the SPSS syntax for creating a scatterplot for these variables.

3. Create a scatterplot for the relationship between the two variables using the syntax in question 2.

Independent *t*-Tests: One-Sample Case and Two-Sample Case *t*-Tests of the Mean

LEARNING OBJECTIVES

1. Understand the purpose of the one-sample case *t*-test
2. Understand the purpose of the two-sample case *t*-test
3. Understand the assumptions underlying the test statistics
4. Understand the alternative two-sample case Mann-Whitney *U* test
5. Understand how to use SPSS to compute the test statistics
6. Understand how to interpret, write, and present the results of the tests

DATA SET (APPENDIX A)

PTSD

INTRODUCTION

In social science research, we often are interested in examining attitudes, behaviors, feelings, or other social concepts in a specific group and whether they are similar to those in the general population or other similar groups. For example, as a health care provider, you may want to examine if body mass index (BMI) among one ethnic group is significantly, or not significantly, different from that of the national average. For this purpose, you examine BMI among a sample of 150 subjects representing this specific ethnic group and then compare its BMI to the national average BMI. Figure 8.1.A illustrates this comparison.

Or, as a social work clinician working in a women's shelter that provides mental health counseling for victims of domestic violence, you believe that you have a "magic" therapy to reduce women's severe anxiety. To test your "magic" therapy, you decide to start a ten-week *posttest-only control group design* therapy and randomly assign twenty-five women to the experimental group and another

Figure 8.1:   Group Comparison

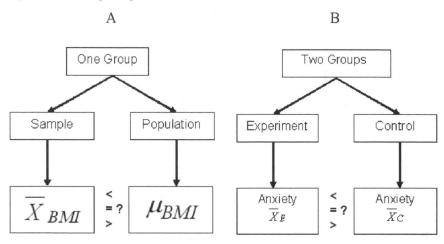

twenty-five to the control group. You then examine the mean score among the experimental group and compare it with that of the control group. Figure 8.1.B displays this design.

In the first example (figure 8.1.A), the health care provider wants to examine if the BMI mean score ($\bar{X}_{BMI}$) among one specific ethnic group is significantly different than the BMI mean score in the general population (μ_{BMI}). In this case, only one variable (BMI) is measured and compared with a known score (population's BMI).

In the second example (figure 8.1.B), the clinician is interested in examining the difference between two groups on one outcome. This example consists of the experiment and control groups and the outcome, level of anxiety. In this case, two BMI scores are measured: one for the experimental group and another for the control group.

In both cases, however, the professionals are interested in examining one thing, if there is a significant difference between the two mean scores: the sample and the population BMI mean scores in the first one, and the experimental and control groups' anxiety mean scores in the second one.

The question is, then, which statistical tests are suitable to examine the differences between each set of means?

This chapter presents two *t*-tests, a one-sample case *t*-test and a two-sample case *t*-test, their purpose, and underlying assumptions. The alternative nonparametric test for the two-sample case *t*-test, the Mann-Whitney *U* test, is also presented. Three examples based on real data illustrate how to use SPSS to compute the statistics and their levels of significance, as well as how to interpret, write, and present the results in summary tables.

STUDENT'S *T*-TESTS

Student's *t*-test is a group of inferential statistical tests developed by William Sealy Gosset in 1908, an English statistician best known by his alias name "Student" (to hide his identity from his company's competitor) after which the *t*-test was named. The purpose of Student's *t*-test is to examine whether a statistically significant difference exists between two mean scores in which one is an observed score and the second is a hypothetical score; the two means are observed scores for two independent groups; or the two means are of repeated measures for the same sample. The first is known as a one-sample case *t*-test, the second is a two-sample case *t*-test, and the third is a two-paired observations *t*-test. This chapter discusses the one-sample case and the two-sample case *t*-test. Chapter 9 discusses the two-paired observations *t*-test.

ONE-SAMPLE CASE *T*-TEST

Purpose

The purpose of the one-sample case *t*-test is to examine if there is a statistically significant difference between the sample and the population on the dependent variable. For example, you may use the one-sample case *t*-test to examine if the number of sexual assaults observed in one county is similar to the overall state sexual assaults reported. This, however, requires that the population's score (e.g., state sexual assaults) is known. Often, the population's score is unknown, which makes the one-sample case *t*-test probably one of the least commonly used statistical tests in social science research.

Using available, known information about the population, social science researchers often use the one-sample case *t*-test to examine if the sample is similar to the population to which generalization will be made. Recall that sample representativeness is an assumption of inferential statistics. For example, you may use the one-sample case *t*-test to compare participants' ages, incomes, or education levels found in your study with those known in the population. An insignificant difference indicates the sample is similar to the population with regard to these characteristics. Otherwise, sample representativeness may not be assumed.

In our earlier example regarding the statistically significant differences between the sample's BMI score and the population's BMI score, the researcher must know the population's BMI score. This can be done by reviewing previous literature on the topic of interest and available data from governmental, educational, and professional organizations, such as the U.S. Census Bureau, U.S. Department of Health and Human Services, National Institutes of Health (NIH), Centers for Disease Control and Prevention (CDC), National Association of Social Workers (NASW), and others.

Mathematically, Student's *t*-tests produce a test statistic called *t* that measures how far apart the two means are in standard deviation units. In the one-sample case, the *t* value is the difference between the sample's mean and the population's mean in standard deviation units (that is, standard errors equal standard deviation divided by the square root of sample size). The larger the *t* value is, the more likely that the difference between the two means is statistically significant. How big *t* should be to be significant depends on the sample size, which determines the critical values and, in turn, the level of significance. Here, we will utilize the SPSS program to compute both the *t* value and the level of significance (*p* value).

ASSUMPTIONS OF ONE-SAMPLE CASE *T*-TEST

Student's *t*-tests, including the one-sample case, are a group of parametric tests and, thus, require the same assumptions as parametric tests. These assumptions include the following:

1. The dependent variable must be measured at the interval or ratio level of measurement. Technically, in a one-sample case *t*-test, only one variable is measured (statistic) and then compared with that of the population (parameter).

2. The shape of the distribution of the dependent variable must approximate the shape of a normal curve.

    To evaluate this assumption, compute measures of central tendency, variability, and skewness, and inspect the histogram and normal Q-Q plot of the variable under study. If skewed, consider transformation. If severe skewness still exists, the results of the one-sample case *t*-test may not be accurate.

3. The sample size should be large enough to compare the sample mean with that of the population.

As with Pearson's correlation test, a sample size as low as thirty cases is generally considered sufficient for the one-sample case *t*-test. Again, however, researchers should choose a sample size based on the predetermined criteria for their study. Table 8.1 displays the minimum sample size needed for the one-sample case *t*-test to achieve a power of .80. We used Cohen's (1988) definition of effect size for two means (Small: ES = .2; Moderate: ES = .50; Large: ES = .80) and the SPSS Sample Power to generate this table.

Table 8.1:   Sample Size for One-Sample Case *t*-Test (Power = .80)

Alpha	Two-Tailed Hypothesis			One-Tailed Hypothesis		
	ES = .20	ES = .50	ES = .80	ES = .20	ES = .50	ES = .80
.050	198	34	15	156	27	12
.010	295	51	22	254	43	19
.001	432	74	33	391	67	29

Table 8.1 shows that a sample size of only thirty-four cases is needed to achieve a power of .80 if we use a moderate effect size (ES = .50) and a two-tailed alpha of .05. On the other hand, a minimum of 198 subjects will be needed for a small effect size (ES = .20) given other criteria are held constant.

TWO-SAMPLE CASE *T*-TEST

Purpose

The two-sample case *t*-test, mostly known as the independent *t*-test, is perhaps the most commonly used bivariate statistical test and the most widely known among social sciences researchers. It is easily interpreted and easy to use by hand and by statistical software.

The independent *t*-test is a bivariate parametric test used to examine the difference between the means of two independent groups observed at the same time (two samples or two groups measured on the same variable) and whether this difference is statistically significant. For example, in the research question regarding whether there is a statistically significant difference between the experimental and control group with regard to levels of anxiety, the variable of group consists of two groups: experimental and control. Group is the independent variable, and anxiety is the dependent variable.

Mathematically, the *t* value of the independent *t*-test is the difference between the means of the two groups in standard deviations units. Again, we will use the SPSS program to compute.

ASSUMPTIONS OF THE INDEPENDENT *T*-TEST

The independent *t*-test makes the same assumptions about the dependent variable as the one-sample case *t*-test. That is, the dependent variable must be measured at the interval or ratio level of measurement and must be normally distributed. When the assumption of normality is not met, consider data transformation. If it is still severely skewed, also consider the nonparametric Mann-Whitney *U* test as an alternative and compare its results with the results of the independent *t*-test. If similar, report the results of the independent *t*-test.

In addition to these two assumptions, the independent *t*-test requires the following four assumptions:

1. The independent variable must be dichotomous; it must consist of two groups or attributes (e.g., Group: experiment or control; Gender: males or females; etc.). If more than two groups are being compared, consider collapsing groups to two groups or utilize the one-way Analysis of Variance or Kruskal-Wallis *H* test (see chapter 10).

2. Data for both groups must be collected at the same time; that is, paired observation (e.g., data on anxiety for the experimental and control groups must be collected simultaneously).

3. The variances of both groups on the dependent variable should be equal. This is known as the assumption of homogeneity of variances, or equality of variances.

    This assumption is evaluated by inspecting the results of the Levene's test of equality of variances produced along with the results of the independent *t*-test. A *p* value greater than .05 (alpha = .05) indicates the assumption is met (some researchers may use alpha of .001 instead of .05). Luckily, we can adjust for violation of this assumption by utilizing alternative formulas. SPSS produces two sets of analyses for the independent *t*-test; one for equal variances and another for unequal variances. We return to this later under interpreting SPSS printout.

4. The sample size should be large enough to compare the means of the two groups.

    Generally, a sample size of thirty cases per group (N = 60) is considered adequate for the two-sample case *t*-test. On the other hand, table 8.2 displays the minimum sample size needed per group for the two-sample case *t*-test to achieve a power of .80. Again, we tabulated these sample sizes using the SPSS Sample Power and Cohen's definition of effect size.

    As shown in table 8.2, to achieve a power of .80, a sample size of sixty-four cases per group (N = 128) is needed for a moderate effect size with a two-tailed alpha of .05, or twenty-six per group (N = 52) for a large effect size and a two-tailed alpha of .05. On the other hand, for a one-tailed alpha of .05, a sample of 102 (51 × 2 = 102) cases with a moderate effect size, or a sample of forty-two (21 × 2 = 42) cases with a large effect size, is needed to achieve a power of .80.

    When a smaller sample size is used, you may conduct power analysis using the actual observed effect size and sample size. If power is not satisfactory (e.g., < .80), consider the alternative nonparametric Mann-Whitney *U* test and compare its results with the independent *t*-test. If still consistent, report the results of the independent *t*-test.

MANN-WHITNEY *U* TEST

The Mann-Whitney *U* test is the nonparametric version of the independent *t*-test. It is the most popular among the four nonparametric tests that examine differences between two groups. In addition to the Mann-Whitney *U*, other

Table 8.2: Sample Size Per Group for Two-Sample Case (Power = .80)

Alpha	Two-Tailed Hypothesis			One-Tailed Hypothesis		
	ES = .20	ES = .50	ES = .80	ES = .20	ES = .50	ES = .80
.050	393	64	26	310	51	21
.010	585	96	39	503	82	33
.001	856	140	57	775	126	51

nonparametric tests include the Kolmogorov-Smirnov Z, Moses extreme reactions, and Wald-Wolfowitz runs.[1]

As with the Spearman's *rho* correlation, the Mann-Whitney U ranks the scores of each group. Unlike Spearman's *rho*, Mann-Whitney U then computes mean rank for each group and examines whether there is a statistically significant difference between the two mean ranks.

The Mann-Whitney U test is appropriate to compare two groups when the dependent variable is measured at the ordinal level, measured at the interval level that does not meet the assumption of normality, or with a small sample size. Mann-Whitney U still requires the sample to be representative of the population and the independent variable to be dichotomous.

PRACTICAL EXAMPLES

To practice the use of the one-sample case and the two-sample case *t*-tests and the Mann-Whitney U in hypothesis testing, we present three examples. The first compares the mean age among a sample of 230 refugees from Asia and Africa and the overall age among refugee population; the second examines levels of PTSD among the refugees based on their country of origin (Asia and Africa); and the third examines the difference between married and not married refugees with regard to their powerful health locus of control. All three examples are from the PTSD data file (appendix A).

Example 1: One-Sample Case *t*-Test

To illustrate the utilization of the one-sample case *t*-test, we use the SPSS PTSD data file to examine if our sample's mean age is similar to a known population's mean age. For this purpose, let us assume that based on available data on refugees, we found that the mean age is forty-six.

RESEARCH QUESTION: Is there a statistically significant difference between the sample's mean age and the population's mean age of forty-six years old?

Step 1: State the null and alternative hypotheses.

H_o: There is no statistically significant difference between the sample and population with regard to their mean age.

$\mu = 46$

H_a: There is a statistically significant difference between the sample and population with regard to their mean age.

$\mu \neq 46$

---

[1]Siegel & Castellan (1988).

In this hypothesis, the dependent variable is age (Age) and is measured at the ratio level of measurement. It is tested against the constant, 46. Thus, given this information, we will utilize the one-sample case *t*-test to examine the null hypothesis.

Step 2: Set the criteria for rejecting H_0.
Set alpha at .05 (α = .05). Reject H_0 only if $p \leq .05$.

Step 3: Select the appropriate statistical test.
Prior to conducting the one-sample case *t*-test, we should evaluate the test's assumptions to ensure that it is appropriate to test the null hypotheses. The following is evaluation of these assumptions:

1. LEVEL OF MEASUREMENT: The dependent variable must be interval or ratio. Here, age, the dependent variable, is measured at the ratio level of measurement.

2. NORMALITY OF DISTRIBUTION: The shape of the distribution of the dependent variable must approach the shape of a normal curve. To evaluate this assumption, compute measures of skewness and create a histogram and a normal Q-Q plot for age (see chapter 5).

    Table 8.3, figure 8.2, and figure 8.3 display the descriptive statistics and graphs for age. Evaluation of the Pearson's skewness coefficient [(44.70 − 45)/12.01 = −.025] and Fisher's skewness coefficient (.015/.162 = .09), and inspection of both histogram and normal Q-Q plot for age, show that the distribution approaches the shape of a normal curve, perhaps with minor deviation (see chapter 5 for skewness coefficients).

3. SAMPLE SIZE: In this study, 230 newly arrived refugees completed the study. This sample size is larger than the minimum thirty cases need for this test

Table 8.3: Descriptive Statistics for Age

			Statistic	Std. Error
AGE	Mean		44.6991	.79857
	95% Confidence	Lower Bound	43.1255	
	Interval for Mean	Upper Bound	46.2727	
	5% Trimmed Mean		44.6131	
	Median		45.0000	
	Variance		144.122	
	Std. Deviation		12.00510	
	Minimum		18.00	
	Maximum		76.00	
	Range		58.00	
	Interquartile Range		17.00	
	Skewness		.015	.162
	Kurtosis		−.621	.322

Figure 8.2:   Histogram for Age

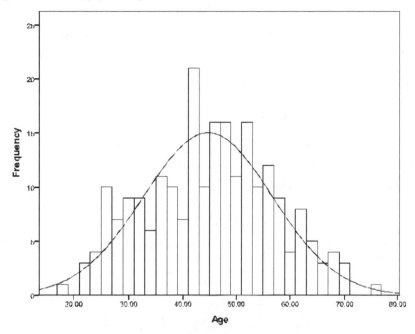

Figure 8.3:   Normal Q-Q Plot of Age

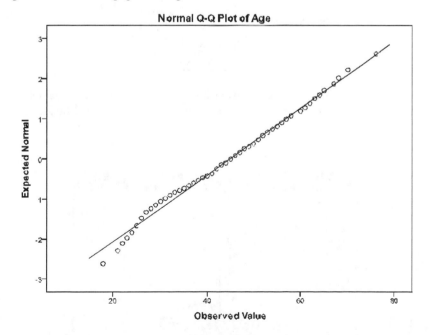

and larger than the thirty-four cases needed to achieve a power of .80 with a two-tailed alpha of .05 and a moderate effect size (see table 8.1 above).

To conclude, data for age met all assumptions for the one-sample case *t*-test. Next, compute the test statistic.

Step 4: Compute the test statistic (using SPSS).
Recall that the variable under study is age and is tested against the constant 46. Now use SPSS to compute the test statistic.

How to compute the one-sample case *t*-test in SPSS.   To run the analysis, follow these steps:

1. Open the SPSS PTSD data file.

2. Click on *Analyze* in the SPSS main toolbar, click on *Compare Means*, and click on *One-Sample T Test* (see screen 8.1). This is the main menu for the two-sample case *t*-test, two-repeated measures *t*-test (see chapter 9), and one-way ANOVA (see chapter 10).

Screen 8.1:   SPSS Compare Means Main Menu

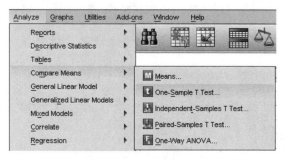

3. In the "One-Sample T Test" dialog box, scroll down in the variables list, click on *Age*, and click on the middle arrow to move *Age* in the *Test Variable(s)* box (see screen 8.2).

Screen 8.2:   SPSS One-Sample T Test Main Dialog Box

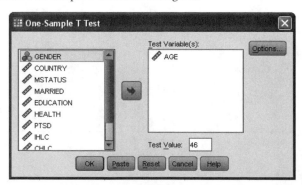

4. Type "46" (this is the population's age) in the *Test Value* box.
5. Click on *OK*.

SPSS One-Sample Case *t*-Test Syntax

T-TEST

/TESTVAL=46

/MISSING=ANALYSIS

/VARIABLES=AGE

/CRITERIA=CI(.95).

Interpreting the output of the one-sample case *t*-test.   The execution of the SPSS commands or syntax produces two tables. The first reports the descriptive statistics for age (see table 8.4) and the second displays the inferential statistics including the *t* and *p* values (see table 8.5).

Table 8.4 shows that 226 participants reported their age (recall than N = 230, see appendix A). The mean age was 44.70 with a standard deviation of 12.00, and a standard error of .80 (values rounded to the nearest two decimals). Remember, standard error is the standard deviation divided by the square root of N; that is, $12.00/\sqrt{226} - .798$.

Table 8.5 conveys the results of the one-sample case *t*-test. The table displays the *t* value (*t* = −1.629); the degrees of freedom (df = N − 1 = 226 − 1 = 225); the *p* value [Sig. (2-tailed) = .105)]; the mean difference (44.6991 − 46 = −1.30088); and the 95th confidence interval for the mean difference (Lower boundary = −2.8745 and upper boundary = .2727).

The results presented in table 8.5 show that the difference between the sample's mean (44.70) and the population's mean (46) is only 1.3 points. The

Table 8.4:   One-Sample Case *t*-Test Descriptive Statistics

One-Sample Statistics

	N	Mean	Std. Deviation	Std. Error Mean
Age	226	44.6991	12.00510	.79857

Table 8.5:   One-Sample Case *t*-Test Values

One-Sample Test

	Test Value = 46					
					95% Confidence Interval of the Difference	
	t	df	Sig. (2-tailed)	Mean Difference	Lower	Upper
Age	−1.629	225	.105	−1.30088	−2.8745	.2727

table shows this mean difference is not large enough to be considered statistically significant (Sig. = .105).

Step 5: Decide whether to reject the null hypothesis.

The results of the one-sample case *t*-test presented in table 8.5 show no statistically significant difference between the sample and the population with regard to age ($p > .05$). Therefore, do not reject the null hypothesis.

Writing the results.   As stated earlier, the one-sample case *t*-test is rarely used in social science research for hypothesis testing, especially since it is often hard to know the actual population's parameter. However, researchers may use it to examine if the sample is similar to the population with regard to some known characteristics, such as age, to justify generalizing their findings to the larger population. When used, like in our example, we may report the findings as follows:

The one-sample case *t*-test was utilized to examine if our sample is similar to the refugee population with regard to their age. The results show no statistically significant difference between our sample of refugees and the population from which it was selected with regard to their age ($t_{(df=225)} = -1.63$; $p > .05$). Therefore, we do not reject the null hypothesis. The mean age of the sample and the population are similar (44.70 and 46.00, respectively); a difference of only 1.3 points. In other words, it seems that the sample represents the population on this regard.

Example 2: Independent *t*-Test—PTSD by Country

Use the SPSS PTSD data file (appendix A) to examine the difference between refugees from Africa and Asia with regard to their levels of post-traumatic stress disorder.

RESEARCH QUESTION: Is there a statistically significant difference between African and Asian refugees (Country) with regard to their levels of post-traumatic stress disorder (PTSD)?

Step 1: State the null and alternative hypotheses (using a one-tailed hypothesis).

H_o: There is no statistically significant difference between African refugees (μ_{AF}) and Asian refugees (μ_{AS}) with regard to their levels of PTSD.

$\mu_{AF} = \mu_{AS}$

H_a: African refugees will have statistically significant higher levels of PTSD than Asian refugees.

$\mu_{AF} > \mu_{AS}$

This is a one-tailed research hypothesis, where country is the independent variable and PTSD is the dependent variable.

Step 2: Set the criteria for rejecting H_0.
Set alpha at .05 (α = .05). Reject H_0 only if $p \leq .05$.

Step 3: Select the appropriate statistical test.

In this hypothesis, the independent variable, country of origin, consists of two groups (Asia and Africa) and is compared on continuous data (PTSD). Thus, we will utilize independent *t*-test and/or the Mann-Whitney *U* test to compare both groups on the dependent *t*-test. First, however, we should evaluate the assumptions of the independent *t*-test to ensure they are met. Otherwise, we should use the Mann-Whitney *U* test as an alternative. These assumptions are as follows:

1. LEVEL OF MEASUREMENT: The dependent variable must be interval or ratio level of measurement, and the independent variable must be dichotomous (nominal with only two groups). In this study, the dependent variable, PTSD, consists of continuous data and is measured at the interval level of measurement. The independent variable, country of origin, is dichotomous (Asia and Africa).

2. NORMALITY OF DISTRIBUTION: The shape of the distribution of the dependent variable must approach that of a normal curve. To evaluate this assumption, compute measures of skewness and create a histogram and a normal Q-Q plot for PTSD.

Table 8.6 and figures 8.4 and 8.5 display the descriptive statistics and graphs for PTSD.

Evaluation of the Pearson's skewness coefficient [(13.54 − 11)/8.63 = .29] and Fisher's skewness coefficient (1.175/.17 = 6.91), and inspection of both histogram and normal Q-Q plot for PTSD show that the distribution is

Table 8.6:   Descriptive Statistics for PTSD

			Statistic	Std. Error
PTSD	Mean		13.5415	.60298
	95% Confidence	Lower Bound	12.3526	
	Interval for Mean	Upper Bound	14.7303	
	5% Trimmed Mean		12.8984	
	Median		11.0000	
	Variance		74.534	
	Std. Deviation		8.63330	
	Minimum		1.00	
	Maximum		46.00	
	Range		45.00	
	Interquartile Range		10.50	
	Skewness		1.175	.170
	Kurtosis		1.353	.338

Figure 8.4:   Histogram for PTSD

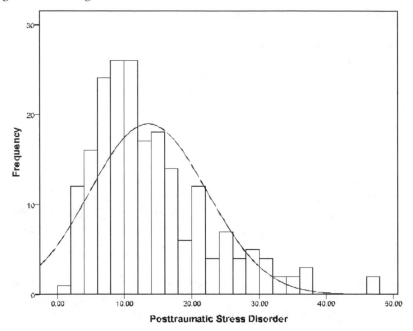

Figure 8.5:   Normal Q-Q Plot of PTSD

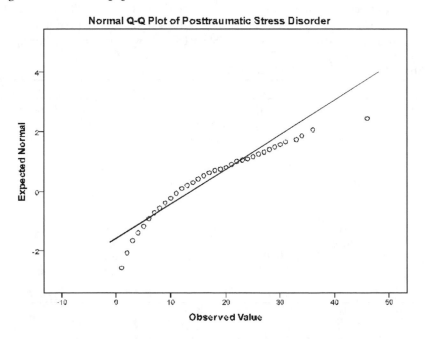

severely skewed to the right (positive severe skewness), thus violating the assumption of normality. Therefore, before we move forward with the analysis, we should transform PTSD to the square root and reevaluate its shape (see chapter 5 for transformation).

Table 8.7 and figures 8.6 and 8.7 display the descriptive statistics and graphs for the square root of PTSD. Evaluation of the Pearson's skewness coefficient $[(3.50 - 3.32)/1.13 = .16]$ and Fisher's skewness coefficient $(.417/.170 = 2.45)$, and inspection of both histogram and normal Q-Q plot for the square root of PTSD show that the distribution now approaches the shape of a normal curve, thus satisfying the assumption of normality.

Note: If transformation to square root does not produce a normal curve, try transformation to logarithm. If still severely skewed, use the nonparametric Mann-Whitney U test to test the hypothesis instead of the independent t-test.

---

4. HOMOGENEITY OF VARIANCES: The variances of both groups under comparison must be equal. To evaluate this assumption, check the results of Levene's test of equality of variance. This test is performed simultaneously with the independent t-test. SPSS uses two formulas to compute the t value for the independent t-test; one assumes that the variances are equal, and the second assumes that the variances are significantly different (this is discussed in the next step).

5. SAMPLE SIZE: As stated above, 230 subjects participated in this study. This sample size is larger than the minimum requirement $(N = 60)$. Furthermore, it is larger than the fifty-one per group $(N = 102)$ needed to achieve

Table 8.7:   Descriptive Statistics for Square Root of PTSD

			Statistic	Std. Error
SQRT_PTSD	Mean		3.5017	.07920
	95% Confidence	Lower Bound	3.3455	
	Interval for Mean	Upper Bound	3.6578	
	5% Trimmed Mean		3.4730	
	Median		3.3166	
	Variance		1.286	
	Std. Deviation		1.13400	
	Minimum		1.00	
	Maximum		6.78	
	Range		5.78	
	Interquartile Range		1.54	
	Skewness		.417	.170
	Kurtosis		−.135	.338

Figure 8.6:   Histogram for Square Root of PTSD

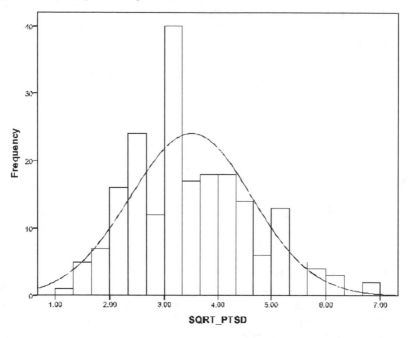

Figure 8.7:   Normal Q-Q Plot of Square Root of PTSD

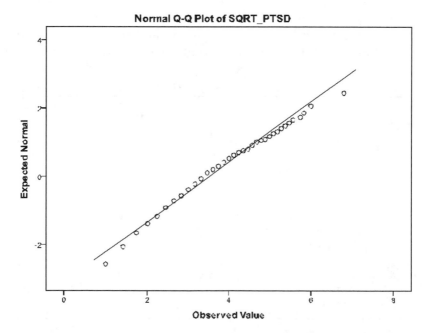

a power of .80, considering a one-tailed hypothesis, alpha of .05, and a moderate effect size (see table 8.2).

To conclude, our data met all assumptions for the independent *t*-test. Next, compute the test statistic. Also compute the Mann-Whitney *U* test to check if results are consistent.

Step 4: Compute the test statistic (using SPSS).

Recall that the dependent variable is the square root of PTSD (SQRT_PTSD) and the independent variable is Country (0 = Asia, 1 = Africa). Now use SPSS to compute the test statistic.

How to compute the independent *t*-test in SPSS.   Unlike with the Pearson's and Spearman's *rho* correlation tests, SPSS does not perform the independent *t*-test and Mann-Whitney *U* simultaneously. They have different SPSS toolbars and commands. First, utilize the independent *t*-test and then the Mann-Whitney *U*. To run the independent *t*-test in SPSS, follow these steps:

1.   Open the SPSS PTSD data file.

2.   Click on *Analyze* in the SPSS main toolbar, click on *Compare Means*, and click on *Independent-Sample T Test* (see screen 8.1 above).

3.   Scroll down in the variables list in the "Independent Samples T Test" dialog box, click on *SQRT_PTSD* (dependent variable), and click on the upper arrow button to move it into the *Test Variable(s)* box (see screen 8.3).

4.   Scroll down in the variables list, click on *Country* (independent variable), and click on the lower arrow button to move it into the *Grouping Variable* box.

5.   Click on *Define Groups.* A new dialog box called "Define Groups" will open (see screen 8.4).

Screen 8.3:   SPSS Independent-Samples T Test Dialog Box

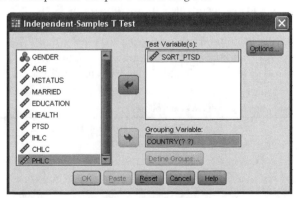

Screen 8.4:   SPSS Define Groups Dialog Box

6. Type "0" for *Group 1* and type "1" for *Group 2* under "Use Specified Values." *Remember:* These are the values for the variable Country (0 = Asia and 1 = Africa). These values will replace the two question marks in screen 8.3 under "Grouping Variable." If you do not remember these values, click on *Cancel* to close "Define Groups," point the mouse on *Country*, right-click, then click on *Variable Information*. A new box displaying the variable name and value labels for Country will open.

7. Click on *Continue* to close the "Define Groups" dialog box.

8. Click on *OK.*

SPSS Two-Sample Case *t*-Test Syntax

T-TEST GROUPS=COUNTRY(0 1)

/MISSING=ANALYSIS

/VARIABLES=SQRT_PTSD

/CRITERIA=CI(.95).

Interpreting the output of the independent *t*-test.   Tables 8.8 and 8.9 display the results of the independent *t*-test. They include two parts: Group Statistics (table 8.8) and Independent Samples Test (table 8.9).

Table 8.8, Group Statistics, displays the number of participants, mean score, standard deviation, and standard error for each group. The table includes sixty-two refugees from Asia and 117 from Africa. The mean PTSD for Asians is 3.27 and standard deviation is 1.24. For Africans, the mean is 3.72 and stan-

Table 8.8:   Group Statistics—PTSD by Country

	Group Statistics				
	Country of Origin	N	Mean	Std. Deviation	Std. Error Mean
SQRT_PTSD	0 Asia	62	3.2689	1.23799	.15722
	1 Africa	117	3.7236	1.08200	.10003

Table 8.9:   Independent *t*-Test   PTSD by Country

Independent Samples Test

| | Levene's Test for Equality of Variances | | *t*-test for Equality of Means | | | | | | |
| | | | | | | | | 95% Confidence Interval of the Difference | |
	F	Sig.	t	df	Sig. (2-tailed)	Mean Difference	Std. Error Difference	Lower	Upper
Equal variances assumed	2.700	.102	−2.543	177	.012	−.45467	.17879	−.80751	−.10183
Equal variances not assumed			−2.440	110.829	.016	−.45467	.18635	−.82394	−.08540

dard deviation is 1.08. Remember, these are square root values. Based on the two means, it appears that African refugees have higher levels of PTSD than Asian refugees. Is this difference statistically significant?

The Independent Samples Test, table 8.9, answers this question. However, before we answer the question, we should understand how to read the table.

The table has two parts: Levene's test for equality of variances and the *t*-test for equality of means. Levene's test for equality of variances examines whether the variances of the two groups (Africa and Asia) on the dependent variable are equal; that is, whether the assumption of homogeneity of variances is met.

Table 8.9 shows that the *F* value (first column) under Levene's test of equality of variances is 2.700 and the *p* value is .102 (second column; Sig. = .102). This *p* value is greater than an alpha of .05, which indicates the two variances are not significantly different; the variances are equal. Thus, data met the assumption of homogeneity of variances.

> *Note*: If the *p* value of Levene's test of equality of variances is greater than .05, then the two variances are not significantly different and, thus, the assumption of homogeneity of variances is met.
>
> If the *p* value is less than or equal to .05, then the two variances are significantly different, so the assumption of homogeneity of variances is not met.

The second part of the table, *t*-test for equality of means, examines whether the two means are significantly different. Notice that there are two lines.

1. If the variances are equal (Levene's *p* value > .05), then read and report the results of the top line (equal variances assumed row) under *t*-test for equality of means (third column *t*; fourth column df; fifth column Sig. 2-tailed; sixth column Mean Difference). That is, the results of the Equal Variances Assumed row.

2. If the variances are not equal (Levene's *p* value ≤ .05), then read and report the results of bottom line (equal variances not assumed row) under *t*-test for equality of means.

   In our case, read the top line, because the variances are equal, which shows that the *t* statistic is −2.543; df is 177; Sig. (2-tailed) is .012 (*p* value); and the mean difference is −.455 ($\mu_{AS} - \mu_{AF}$).

Note: Unlike the Pearson's and Spearman's *rho*, the independent *t*-test and Mann-Whitney *U* always produce a two-tailed statistic, even if the alternative hypothesis is one-tailed. Divide the *p* value by two only if you have a one-tailed research hypothesis, as seen in our example. In this case, the *p* value is .012/2 = .006.

How to compute the Mann-Whitney *U* test in SPSS.   The independent variable is country of origin (Country) and the dependent variable is PTSD (PTSD). To run the Mann-Whitney *U* in SPSS, follow these steps:

1. Open the SPSS PTSD data file.

2. Click on *Analyze* in the SPSS main toolbar, click on *Nonparametric Tests*, click on *Legacy Dialogs,* and click on *2 Independent Samples* (see screen 8.5). This is the main menu for all nonparametric tests used in this book.

Screen 8.5:   SPSS Nonparametric Main Menu

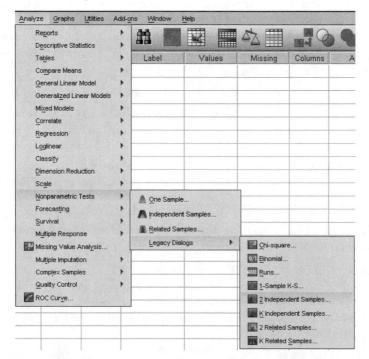

3. Scroll down in the variables list in the "Two-Independent-Samples Tests" dialog box, click on *SQRT_PTSD*, and click on the upper arrow button to move it into the *Test Variable List* box (see screen 8.6).

Screen 8.6: SPSS Two Independent Samples Tests Dialog Box

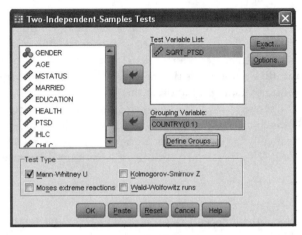

4. Scroll down in the variables list, click on *Country*, and click on the lower arrow button to move it into the *Grouping Variable* box.
5. Click on *Define Groups,* type "0" for *Group 1*, and type "1" for *Group 2* (see screen 8.7).

Screen 8.7: SPSS Two Independent Samples Define Groups Dialog Box

6. Click on *Continue.*
7. Make sure that *Mann-Whitney U* box is checked under "Test Type." This is SPSS default. If not checked, check it.
8. Click on *OK.*

SPSS Mann-Whitney *U* Test Syntax

NPAR TESTS

/M-W = PTSD BY COUNTRY(0 1)

/MISSING ANALYSIS.

Interpreting the output of the Mann-Whitney *U*.   Like the independent *t*-test, by default, SPSS produces two tables for the Mann-Whitney *U*. These include a Ranks table and a Test Statistics table. They are presented in tables 8.10 and 8.11, respectively.

Table 8.10 displays the number of refugees from Africa (n = 117) and Asia (n = 62). The table shows that the mean rank for Asian refugees is 78.29 compared to 96.21 for African refugees. Recall that Mann-Whitney *U* first ranks scores for both groups, computes the mean rank for each group, and then uses the *z* distribution (see chapter 5 for *z* scores) to examine if the mean ranks difference is statically significant. Is the mean ranks difference in our example statistically significant? Table 8.11 answers this question.

Table 8.11 shows that the *z* value (third line) is −2.20 with a significance level of .028 (fourth line, Asymp. Sig. 2-tailed). As with the independent *t*-test, divide this *p* value by two, because our research hypothesis is one-tailed. Thus, the *p* value is .028/2 = .014, which indicates a significant difference between the two groups.

Step 5: Decide whether to reject the null hypothesis.

The results of the independent *t*-test presented in table 8.9 (and the results of the Mann-Whitney *U* presented in table 8.11) show a statistically significant difference between African and Asian refugees with regard to their levels of PTSD ($p < .05$). Therefore, reject the null hypothesis.

Writing the results.   Similar to Pearson's correlation, when writing the results of the independent *t*-test or Mann-Whitney *U* test, first discuss the normality of distributions, data transformation, if any, and homogeneity of variances.

Table 8.10:   Mann-Whitney *U* Mean Ranks Table—PTSD by Country

	Ranks			
	Country of Origin	N	Mean Rank	Sum of Ranks
SQRT_PTSD	0 Asia	62	78.29	4854.00
	1 Africa	117	96.21	11256.00
	Total	179		

Table 8.11:   Mann-Whitney *U* Test Statistics—PTSD by Country

Test Statistics[a]	
	SQRT_PTSD
Mann-Whitney U	2901.000
Wilcoxon W	4854.000
Z	−2.203
Asymp. Sig. (2-tailed)	.028

[a]Grouping Variable: Country (Country of Origin).

Then, report the t and p values for the independent t-test or the z and p for the Mann-Whitney U test, the mean for each group, and mean difference. Next, present the results in a summary table. In our example, the results may be summarized as follows:

Before conducting group comparison, data were evaluated for normality and homogeneity of variances. Evaluation of measures of skewness, histogram, and normal Q-Q plot for PTSD scores indicated severe skewness, and thus scores were transformed to the square root. On the other hand, evaluation of the distribution of the square root of PTSD indicated that it approached the shape of a normal curve, thus satisfying the assumption of normality. In addition, the results of the Levene's test of equality of variances show no significant difference between the two groups with regard to their variance (F = 2.70; p > .05). Therefore, the independent t-test was utilized to examine levels of (square root of) post-traumatic stress disorder among refugees based on their country of origin.

> *Note*: You may state that "the Mann-Whitney U test was utilized because" normality was violated, transformation was not successful to fix the shape of the distribution, the dependent variable was measured at the ordinal level of measurement, and/or the sample size was too small to conduct the independent t-test.

The results of the independent t-test show a significant difference between African and Asian refugees with regard to their levels of PTSD ($t_{(df=177)}$ = −2.54; p < .010).[2] In this study, refugees from Africa reported statistically significant higher levels of PTSD ($\bar{X}$ = 3.72) than refugees from Asia ($\bar{X}$ = 3.27); a mean difference of .45. These results are supported by the results of the Mann-Whitney U, which also show a significant difference between African and Asian refugees with regard to their levels of PTSD (z = −2.20; p < .05).

Presentation of results in summary table.   The results of the independent t-test should be presented in a summary table that includes results of the two SPSS tables, the Group Statistics and the independent t-test. The table should report the number of cases for each group, the means and standard deviations, overall test statistic, and p value. Table 8.12 presents the results of the independent t-test for PTSD by country of origin.

Example 3: Independent t-Test—PHLC by Married

Use the SPSS PTSD data file (appendix A) to examine the difference between married and not married refugees with regard to their powerful health locus of control.

---

[2] p = .012/2 = .006, which is less than .010.

Table 8.12:   Results of the Independent *t*-Test—PTSD by Country of Origin

Variable	N	$\bar{X}$	SD	*t*	*p*[*]
PTSD[a]					
Asia	62	3.27 (12.19)[b]	1.23 (8.48)[b]	−2.54	.006
Africa	117	3.72 (15.03)	1.08 (8.91)		

*One-tailed *p* value.
[a]Square Root of PTSD.
[b]Numbers in parentheses are actual means and standard deviations.

RESEARCH QUESTION: Is there a statistically significant difference between married and not married refugees (Married) with regard to their levels of powerful health locus of control (PHLC)?

Step 1: State the null and alternative hypotheses (using a two-tailed hypothesis).

H_o: There is no statistically significant difference between married (μ_M) and not married (μ_{NM}) refugees with regard to their levels of PHLC.

$\mu_M = \mu_{NM}$

H_a: There is a statistically significant difference between married (μ_M) and not married (μ_{NM}) refugees with regard to their levels of PHLC.

$\mu_M \neq \mu_{NM}$

This is a two-tailed research hypothesis in which Married is the independent variable and PHLC is the dependent variable.

Step 2: Set the criteria for rejecting H_0.
Set alpha at .05 ($\alpha = .05$). Reject H_0 only if $p \leq .05$.

Step 3: Select the appropriate statistical test.
In this hypothesis, the independent variable, Married, consists of two groups (married and not married) and is compared on continuous data (PHLC). Thus, we will utilize the independent *t*-test and/or the Mann-Whitney *U* test to compare both groups on the dependent *t*-test. To choose which one is more appropriate, we should evaluate the assumptions of the independent *t*-test to ensure they are met. Otherwise, we should use the Mann-Whitney *U* test as an alternative. These are as follows:

1. LEVEL OF MEASUREMENT: PHLC is continuous data and is measured at the interval level of measurement. The independent variable, Married, is dichotomous (married and not married).

2. NORMALITY OF DISTRIBUTION: The shape of the distribution of PHLC should approach the shape of a normal curve. Inspection of the Pearson's skewness coefficient [(18.54 − 18)/5.41 = .10] and Fisher's skewness coefficient (.141/ .161 = .88) (see table 8.13), and reviewing the histogram (see figure 8.8),

Table 8.13: Descriptive Statistics for PHLC

			Statistic	Std. Error
PHLC	Mean		18.54	.359
	95% Confidence	Lower Bound	17.84	
	Interval for Mean	Upper Bound	19.25	
	5% Trimmed Mean		18.47	
	Median		18.00	
	Variance		29.306	
	Std. Deviation		5.414	
	Minimum		6	
	Maximum		32	
	Range		26	
	Interquartile Range		8	
	Skewness		.141	.161
	Kurtosis		−.449	.321

Figure 8.8: Histogram for PHLC

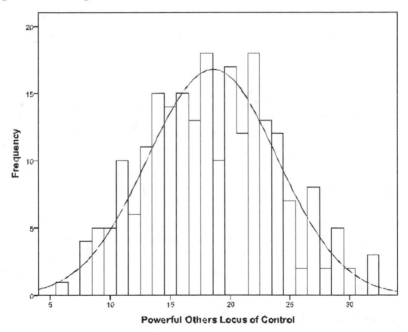

and normal Q-Q plot (see figure 8.9) for PHLC show that the distribution of PHLC approaches the shape of a normal curve.

3. HOMOGENEITY OF VARIANCES: As we said above, the SPSS independent *t*-test generates two sets of analyses, one for equal variances assumed and another for equal variances not assumed. We will return to this under interpreting the SPSS output.

Figure 8.9:   Normal Q-Q Plot of PHLC

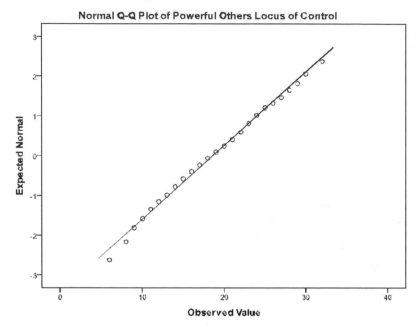

4.   SAMPLE SIZE: Table 8.2 (above) shows a minimum sample size of sixty-four cases per group (total 128) is needed in order to achieve a power of .80, given a moderate effect size and a two-tailed alpha of .05. Here, our sample is 230, which exceeds the minimum requirement.

To conclude, our data met all assumptions for the independent *t*-test. Now compute the independent *t*-test and Mann-Whitney *U* test.

Step 4: Compute the test statistic.

Follow the same SPSS steps discussed under example 2 to run both the independent *t*-test and the Mann-Whitney *U* test. Tables 8.14 and 8.15 display the SPSS output for the independent *t*-test, and tables 8.16 and 8.17 display the SPSS output for the Mann-Whitney *U* test.

Results of the independent *t*-test.   Table 8.14 shows that fifty-seven participants are not married compared to 171 who are married. That table shows that the mean score for not married is 17.00 (SD = 4.39) compared to 19.06 (SD = 5.63) for married. Is this mean difference statistically significant? Table 8.15 examines this question. However, first inspect the results of the Levene's test for equality of variances.

Table 8.14:   Group Statistics—PHLC by Married

				Std.	Std. Error
	MARRIED	N	Mean	Deviation	Mean
PHLC	0 No	57	17.00	4.392	.582
	1 Yes	171	19.06	5.632	.431

Group Statistics

The results of Levene's test for equality of variances presented in table 8.15 indicate that there is a significant difference between the two variances (F = 4.282, p = .040, which is smaller than .05). The assumption of homogeneity of variances is thus violated. Therefore, read the bottom line (equal variances not assumed) for the t-test for equality of means in table 8.15.

The results of the t-test for equality of means show that the t is –2.84; df is 122.13; Sig. (two-tailed) is .005 (p value); and the mean difference is –2.06. Remember, there is no need to divide the p value by two, since our hypothesis is two-tailed. Therefore, there is a significant difference between the two groups on their levels of PHLC (p < .05).

Results of the Mann-Whitney U Test

As with the independent t-test, table 8.16 shows that there are fifty-seven not married refugees and 171 married refugees. The mean rank for married is 120.89, which is higher than for not married refugees. Is this mean ranks difference statistically significant? Table 8.17 examines this question.

Table 8.17 shows that the z value is –2.54 (z = –2.537) with a p value of .011 [Asymp. Sig. (2-tailed) = .011], thus indicating significant difference between the two groups (p < .05).

Table 8.15:   Independent t-Test—PHLC by Married

	Levene's Test for Equality of Variances		t-test for Equality of Means					95% Confidence Interval of the Difference	
	F	Sig.	t	df	Sig. (2-tailed)	Mean Difference	Std. Error Difference	Lower	Upper
Equal variances assumed	4.282	.040	–2.515	226	.013	–2.058	.818	–3.671	–.446
Equal variances not assumed			–2.844	122.130	.005	–2.058	.724	–3.491	–.626

Independent Samples Test

Table 8.16:   Mann-Whitney U Mean Ranks Table—PHLC by Married

		Ranks		
	MARRIED	N	Mean Rank	Sum of Ranks
PHLC	0 No	57	95.33	5434.00
	1 Yes	171	120.89	20672.00
	Total	228		

Table 8.17:   Mann-Whitney U Test Statistics—PHLC by Married

Test Statistics[a]	
	PHLC
Mann-Whitney U	3781.000
Wilcoxon W	5434.000
z	−2.537
Asymp. Sig. (2-tailed)	.011

[a]Grouping Variable: Married.

Step 5: Decide whether to reject the null hypothesis.

The results of the independent *t*-test presented in table 8.15 (and the results of the Mann-Whitney U test presented in table 8.17) show a significant difference between married and not married refugees with regard to their levels of powerful health locus of control ($p < .05$). Therefore, we reject the null hypothesis.

Writing the results.   The independent *t*-test was utilized to examine levels of powerful health locus of control (PHLC) among married and not married refugees. Evaluation of measures of skewness and reviewing the histogram and the normal Q-Q plot showed that the shape of the distribution of PHLC approached the shape of a normal curve. On the other hand, the results of the Levene's test of equality of variances show that the variances of the two groups were significantly different (F = 4.28, $p <.05$). Therefore, the results of the independent *t*-test for unequal variances are reported.

The results of the independent *t*-test show a significant difference between married and not married refugees with regard to their levels of PHLC ($t_{(df=122.13)}$ = −2.84; $p < .010$). In this study, married refugees reported statistically significant higher levels of PHLC ($\overline{X} = 19.06$) than not married refugees ($\overline{X} = 17.00$); a mean difference of 2.06. In other words, married refugees have significantly greater belief that their health/illness is determined by powerful other factors than not married refugees. These results are supported by the results of the Mann-Whitney U test ($z = −2.54$; $p < .05$). Table 8.18 displays these results.

Table 8.18:   Results of the Independent t-Test—PHLC by Married

Variable	N	$\overline{X}$	SD	t	p*
PHLC					
Not Married	57	17.00	4.39	−2.84	.005
Married	171	19.06	5.63		

*Two-tailed p value.

SUMMARY

One primary goal of practitioners is to ensure that their practice meets the expectations of their clients. A group therapist's goal, for example, is to show that participation in therapy significantly improves the lives of clients. To accomplish this goal, therapists will observe clients who participate in therapy (experimental group) versus clients who do not participate (control group), then examine differences between the two groups. Others may be interested in the differences among clients based on their group affiliation: males versus females, African Americans versus Caucasians, immigrants versus native, etc. Whatever the purpose is, practitioners also need to show that their samples represent the populations to which generalizations will be made, especially when nonprobability sampling methods are utilized.

Chapter 8 introduced the Student's t-tests. These are a group of statistical techniques which examine the difference between two mean scores and whether it is statically significant. These include the one-sample case and two-sample case t-tests, the independent t-tests. The first examines if the sample's measures are significantly different than those known in the population, and the second examines if the two groups under study are significantly different.

The chapter discussed the purpose and assumptions of the one-sample case and two-sample case t-tests and then discussed the nonparametric version of the independent t-test, the Mann-Whitney U test. Next, chapter 8 presented three examples illustrating step-by-step how to evaluate the data; use the SPSS to compute the test statistics, p values, and mean differences for these tests; and how to interpret, write, and present the results in a readable table.

Chapter 9 introduces another Student's t-test suitable to examine the mean difference for two repeated measures or two related topics for the same subjects. The chapter presents the dependent t-test and its nonparametric version, the Wilcoxon signed ranks test. The chapter discusses the purpose and assumptions underlying the dependent t-test and Wilcoxon signed ranks test. Two examples that illustrate how to compute the test statistics, interpret the output, and write and present results are also presented.

PRACTICAL EXERCISES

Part I: Access the Job Satisfaction SPSS data file (appendix A) and examine the following research questions:

a. Given the mean age of the population was thirty-seven years old, is there a statistically significant difference between the sample and the population regarding their age (Age)?

b. Is there a statistically significant difference in the levels of comfort (Comfort) based on workers' ethnicity (Ethnicity)?

1. Follow the steps in hypothesis testing and examine each hypothesis (use one-tailed hypotheses). Discuss all steps in detail.

2. Write the SPSS syntax for data transformation, if any.

3. Present the results of the second research question in a summary table.

Part II: Use the self-esteem data you entered in chapter 2 and examine the following research question:

Is there a significant difference between U.S.-born and not U.S.-born older immigrants on their levels of self-esteem?

1. Follow the steps in hypothesis testing and examine the hypothesis (use a one-tailed hypothesis). Discuss all steps in detail.

2. Present the results in a summary table.

CHAPTER 9

Dependent *t*-Test:
Two-Paired Observations

LEARNING OBJECTIVES

1. Understand the purpose of the dependent *t*-test
2. Understand the assumptions underlying the dependent *t*-test
3. Understand the alternative nonparametric Wilcoxon signed ranks test
4. Understand how to use SPSS to compute the statistics
5. Understand how to interpret, write, and present the results of the tests

DATA SET (APPENDIX A)

Anxiety

Elderly

INTRODUCTION

Chapter 8 introduced Student's *t*-tests. As stated, Student's *t*-tests are suitable for examining the difference between two means and whether these differences are statistically significant. Chapter 8 presented two situations in which Student's *t*-tests are appropriate. The first was the one-sample case, which examines the difference between an observed mean and a known population mean. The second was the two-sample case *t*-test, or independent *t*-test, which examines the difference between the means of two groups.

Sometimes, however, we are interested not only in examining the differences between two groups on one measure, but also in examining the difference between two measures within one group. Consider the following three cases:

CASE 1: A clinician working in the center for victims of torture develops a *pre-experimental one-group pretest-posttest design*[1] therapy aiming to increase levels of

---

[1]For more on experimental designs, see Rubin & Babbie (2011).

self-worth among victims of torture. At the beginning, all participants complete a twenty-item standardized measure of self-worth (pretest) and then participate in a ten-session group therapy. At the conclusion of the therapy, they complete the twenty-item self-worth measure (posttest). The clinician believes that participants' levels of self-worth will improve after they complete the therapy. If this proves correct, the clinician may conclude therapy is effective. Statistically, the clinician hypothesizes that levels of self-worth at the posttest (μ_{Post}) will be significantly higher than levels of self-worth at the pretest (μ_{Pre}). That is,

$$\mu_{Post} > \mu_{Pre}$$

CASE 2: A mental health practitioner believes that older people tend to be more emotionally balanced than cognitively. To test this, the practitioner administers a standardized measure of emotional balance and cognitive status to a sample of one hundred older individuals and then compares levels of emotional balance with levels of cognitive status. Here, the practitioner hypothesizes that levels of emotional balance (μ_{EB}) among older people will be significantly higher than their levels of cognitive status (μ_{CS}). That is,

$$\mu_{EB} > \mu_{CS}$$

CASE 3: A psychology professor believes that graduate students are more likely to pass oral exams than written exams. To test her belief, the professor administers a written exam to students enrolled in her psychology course and then conducts an oral exam of every student. Next, the professor compares students' results of both exams. In this case, the professor hypothesizes that the results of the oral exams (μ_O) will be significantly higher than the results of the written exams (μ_W). That is,

$$\mu_W < \mu_O$$

In the first example, each subject is tested twice: once before administering the therapy and again after the therapy is completed, that is *two-repeated measures* (pretest and posttest). In the second example, each subject is also tested twice, however on *two related topics* (emotional balance and cognitive status). In the third example, again each subject is tested twice, but under *two different conditions* (written exam and oral exam).

Each subject in all three cases has two observations, *two-paired observations*, and researchers are interested in differences between these two observations; that is, *within-subjects* differences. The question is, then, what statistical test(s) are most suitable to examine the hypotheses postulated under each case?

This chapter presents the third Student's *t*-test, dependent *t*-test, its purpose, and its underlying assumptions. The alternative nonparametric Wilcoxon signed ranks test is then presented, along with two practical examples describing in detail how to utilize SPSS to compute the test statistics and levels of significance, and how to interpret, write, and present the results in summary tables.

PURPOSE OF DEPENDENT *T*-TEST

The dependent *t*-test is also known as paired-samples *t*-test, *t*-test for pairs, *t*-test for matched samples, and *t*-test for related samples. It is a parametric statistical test that examines (1) changes in a dependent variable measured at two times among same subjects, *two-repeated measures*; (2) changes in a dependent variable measured under *two conditions*; or (3) differences among *two related topics* (two related variables), such as subjects' performance, views, or attitudes. In other words, the dependent *t*-test examines *within-subjects* differences, whereas the independent *t*-test examines *between-subjects* differences.

In some cases, however, it may not be practicable to observe the same subjects twice, and therefore researchers may compare data on the same variable from two similar samples collected at two different occasions. This situation is known as *two-matched samples*. For example, a research professor has recently developed a new teaching method that is believed to increase students' performance in statistics. To examine the effect of the new teaching method, the professor may compare grades of students enrolled in her statistics course under the new teaching method with grades of students who previously completed the same course under the old teaching methods. The dependent *t*-test can be used then to examine the differences between these two-matched samples on their grades in statistics.

EXAMPLE RESEARCH QUESTION FOR TWO-REPEATED MEASURES: Is there a statistically significant difference between the number of alcohol consumptions before and after participants completed an Alcoholics Anonymous group therapy?

EXAMPLE RESEARCH QUESTION FOR TWO-RELATED TOPICS: Is there a statistically significant difference between students' performance in statistics and psychopathology courses?

EXAMPLE RESEARCH QUESTION FOR TWO CONDITIONS: Is there a statistically significant difference in the depressive symptoms among participants with bipolar depression disorder after completing a psychotherapy treatment and after taking antidepressant medications?

Like the one-sample case and two-sample case *t*-tests, the dependent *t*-test produces a test statistic called *t*, which measures how far apart the two paired means are in standard deviation units. The larger the difference between the two means (also known as mean difference), the more likely it is statistically significant. Again, we will utilize the SPSS program to compute the *t* and *p* values, as well as the means difference.

ASSUMPTIONS OF DEPENDENT *T*-TEST

Recall that the dependent *t*-test is a parametric test, and, thus, it follows the same assumptions. In addition, it makes its own assumptions about the data. These are the following:

1. LEVEL OF MEASUREMENT: The dependent and independent variables (two-paired observation) must be continuous data and measured at the interval or ratio level of measurement.

2. OBSERVATIONS: The two variables must be either repeated measures for the same subjects (Time 1 and Time 2), two conditions, or two related topics, performances, views, or attitudes for the same subjects or two-matched samples.

3. NORMALITY OF DISTRIBUTIONS: The shape of the distributions of the two measures must approximate the shape of a normal curve.

    As we discussed in previous chapters, evaluate this assumption by creating histograms and normal Q-Q plots, and inspecting measures of central tendency and skewness coefficients for both measures. If departure from normality for either or both variables exists, consider data transformation. If still severely skewed, consider the nonparametric Wilcoxon signed ranks test to examine the means differences.

4. RANGE OF SCORES: The two measures must have equal possible ranges (minimum and maximum scores) and similar interpretations. That is, if high scores in one measure indicate greater value, they should also indicate high value in the second measure. If not, data should be transformed into standard scores so they have similar scales.

5. SAMPLE SIZE: The sample size should be large enough to conduct an examination of the test hypothesis.

    As with other bivariate parametric tests, a sample size as low as thirty subjects is considered adequate for the dependent *t*-test. Yet again, researchers should choose a sample size based on the purpose of their study and hypothesis. Table 9.1 displays the minimum sample size needed to utilize the dependent *t*-test. Notice that this table is identical to table 8.1 (in chapter 8) for the one-sample case *t*-test.

    As it is shown in table 9.1, a sample size as low as thirty-four cases will be sufficient to produce a power of .80 with a moderate effect size (ES = .50) and a two-tailed alpha of .05. Furthermore, a sample of only twenty-seven cases is needed with a one-tailed hypothesis, given other factors held constant.

Table 9.1:   Minimum Sample Size for Dependent *t*-Test (Power = .80)

Alpha	Two-Tailed Hypothesis			One-Tailed Hypothesis		
	ES = .20	ES = .50	ES = .80	ES = .20	ES = .50	ES = .80
.050	198	34	15	156	27	12
.010	295	51	22	254	43	19
.001	432	74	33	391	67	29

WILCOXON SIGNED RANKS TEST

The Wilcoxon signed ranks test,[2] also known as the Wilcoxon matched-pairs signed ranks test, is the nonparametric version of the dependent t-test. Like Spearman's rho correlation test, the Wilcoxon signed ranks test ranks each pair of raw scores for the two measures, or the two-matched samples. The test computes the difference within each pair and gives more weight to pairs that show a large difference than pairs that show a small difference. The Wilcoxon signed ranks test is based on the distribution of the z score. Thus, it produces a z value that is compared with a pre-established z score (known as critical value). A z value above $+1.96$ or below -1.96 (for a two-tailed hypothesis) will be significant at .05 alpha (see chapter 5).

Like the Spearman's rho correlation, the Wilcoxon signed ranks test is appropriate to examine the difference between the mean ranks of two-paired observation when data do not meet the assumptions of the dependent t-test, especially the assumption of normality. Yet, the Wilcoxon signed ranks test requires that the sample be representative of the population, data are continuous, and the two measures be repeated measures or paired observations of the same subjects or matched samples.

PRACTICAL EXAMPLES

We will use SPSS to compute the means difference, t, and p values for the dependent t-test and the z and p values for the Wilcoxon signed ranks test. Two examples are presented; the first demonstrates two repeated measures, and the second demonstrates two paired observations.

Example 1—Two Repeated Measures

To demonstrate the use of the dependent t-test and Wilcoxon signed ranks test, use the pre-experimental one group pretest-posttest control group design data from the Anxiety SPSS data file (appendix A) to examine the following research questions:

RESEARCH QUESTION: Is there a statistically significant difference between levels of anxiety at the pretest (Anxiety_Pre) and levels of anxiety at the posttest (Anxiet_Post) among women exposed to interpersonal violence?

Step 1: State the null and alternative hypotheses.

H_0: There is no statistically significant difference between levels of anxiety at the pretest (μ_{Pre}) and levels of anxiety at the posttest (μ_{Post}) among women exposed to interpersonal violence.

$\mu_{Pre} = \mu_{Post}$

---

[2]Named after Frank Wilcoxon, an American chemist and statistician (1892–1965) known for the development of statistical tests.

H_a: Posttest levels of anxiety among women exposed to interpersonal violence will be significantly lower than their pretest levels of anxiety. Or, there will be a statistically significant decrease in levels of anxiety among women exposed to interpersonal violence after they complete the therapy.

$\mu_{Post} < \mu_{Pre}$

In this one-tailed research hypothesis, the dependent variable (levels of anxiety) is measured twice among the same subjects, once before therapy, and then after therapy is implemented; that is two-repeated measures. Thus, we will use either the dependent *t*-test or the Wilcoxon signed ranks test to examine changes in subjects' scores before and after therapy.

Step 2: Set the criteria for rejecting the null hypothesis.
Set alpha at .05 (α = .05). Reject H_0 only if $p \leq .05$.

Step 3: Select the appropriate statistical test.
As stated, we will utilize the dependent *t*-test or Wilcoxon signed ranks test to examine whether a significant decrease in women's levels of anxiety occurred after therapy was completed. To select which one, first we should evaluate the assumptions of the dependent *t*-test to ensure they are met. If not, we would select the Wilcoxon signed ranks test as an alternative. The following is an evaluation of these assumptions:

1. LEVEL OF MEASUREMENT: The two variables must be interval or ratio level of measurement. Levels of anxiety at both pretest and posttest were measured using a twenty-item scale, and their scores were summed to generate total scores for each time. Thus, scores of pretest and posttest are interval level of measurement.

2. OBSERVATIONS: The two variables must be either repeated measures or paired observations. Levels of anxiety at pretest and posttest are two-repeated measures for the same subjects.

3. NORMALITY OF DISTRIBUTION: The distributions of both pretest and posttest scores should be normal. To evaluate the distributions of levels of anxiety at pretest and posttest, run measures of central tendency and skewness coefficients and create histograms and normal Q-Q plots for the two variables (see chapter 5).

   Table 9.2 and figures 9.1 through 9.4 display the descriptive statistics and graphs for levels of anxiety at both pretest and posttest. Evaluation of the Pearson's skewness coefficient [(78.86 − 78.50)/11.76 = .03] and Fisher's skewness coefficient (−.052/.337 = −.15) for levels of anxiety at pretest, and inspection of both histogram (see figure 9.1) and normal Q-Q plot (see figure 9.2), show that the distribution of levels of anxiety at pretest approaches the shape of a normal curve. Also, evaluation of the Pearson's skewness coefficient [(72.36 − 72.50)/9.54 = −.01] and Fisher's skewness coefficient (−.019/.337 = −.06) for levels of anxiety at posttest, and inspection of both histogram (see figure 9.3) and normal Q-Q plot (see figure 9.4),

Table 9.2:   Descriptive Statistics for Pretest and Posttest Anxiety

			Statistic	Std. Error
Anxiety_Pre	Mean		78.86	1.664
	95% Confidence	Lower Bound	75.52	
	Interval for Mean	Upper Bound	82.20	
	5% Trimmed Mean		78.89	
	Median		78.50	
	Variance		138.368	
	Std. Deviation		11.763	
	Minimum		55	
	Maximum		100	
	Range		45	
	Interquartile Range		20	
	Skewness		−.052	.337
	Kurtosis		−.837	.662
Anxiety_Post	Mean		72.36	1.349
	95% Confidence	Lower Bound	69.65	
	Interval for Mean	Upper Bound	75.07	
	5% Trimmed Mean		72.33	
	Median		72.50	
	Variance		91.051	
	Std. Deviation		9.542	
	Minimum		50	
	Maximum		90	
	Range		40	
	Interquartile Range		15	
	Skewness		−.019	.337
	Kurtosis		−.647	.662

Figure 9.1:   Histogram for Pretest Levels of Anxiety

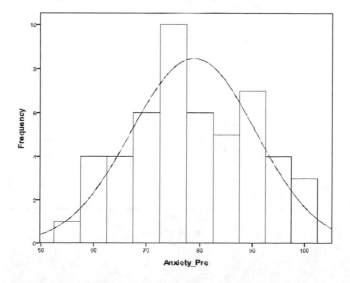

Figure 9.2:   Normal Q-Q Plot of Pretest Levels of Anxiety

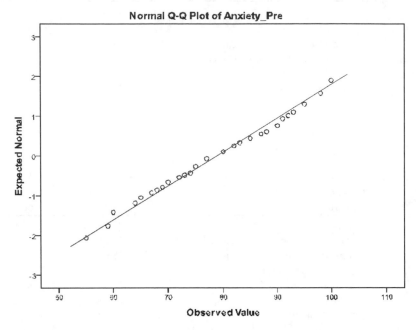

Figure 9.3:   Histogram for Posttest Levels of Anxiety

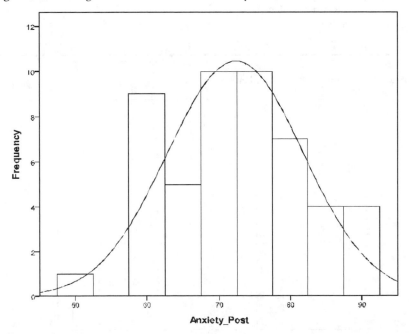

Figure 9.4:   Normal Q-Q Plot of Posttest Levels of Anxiety

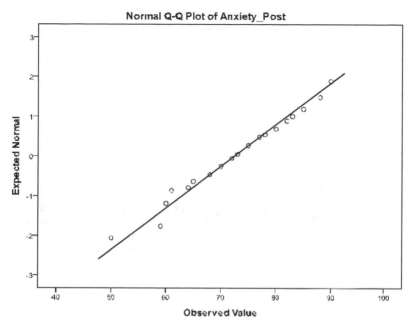

show that the distribution of levels of anxiety at posttest approaches the shape of a normal curve. Therefore, both distributions satisfy the assumption of normality.

4.   RANGE OF SCORES: Measures of both variables must have equal possible ranges and similar interpretations. Levels of anxiety at pretest and posttest range between 20 and 100, with higher scores indicating greater levels of anxiety (see appendix A), thus satisfying this assumption.

5.   SAMPLE SIZE: The sample size should be large enough to conduct an examination of the test hypothesis. Fifty women participated in the Anxiety study, which is larger than thirty cases. Furthermore, this sample size is larger than the minimum twenty-seven cases required to detect a power of .80, given a one-tailed alpha of .05 and a moderate effect size (see table 9.1).

To conclude, our data met all assumptions for the dependent *t*-test. Next, run the dependent *t*-test. Also run the Wilcoxon signed ranks test to examine if the results are consistent.

Note: If normality was violated for one or both measures, try data transformation. If this still exists and/or sample size is too small, use the Wilcoxon signed ranks test to examine the hypothesis.

Step 4: Compute the test statistic (using SPSS).

The two measures in the Anxiety study are Anxiety_Pre and Anxiety_Post. Now use SPSS to compute the test statistic.

How to compute the dependent *t*-test in SPSS.   To run the dependent *t*-test in SPSS, follow these steps:

1.   Open the SPSS Anxiety data file.

2.   Click on *Analyze* in the SPSS main toolbar, click on *Compare Means*, and click on *Paired-Sample T-Test* (see chapter 8, screen 8.1). This opens the "Paired Samples T Test" main dialog box (see screen 9.1).

Screen 9.1:   SPSS Paired-Samples T Test Dialog Box

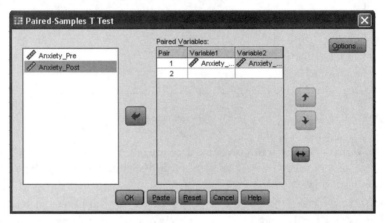

3.   Click on *Anxiety-Pre* in the variables list, and click on the middle arrow button to move it into the *Paired Variables* box. This moves *Anxiety_Pre* under *Variable 1* for *Pair 1*.

4.   Repeat step 3 to move *Anxiety_Post* in the *Paired Variables* box. This moves *Anxiety_Post* under *Variable 2* for *Pair 1*.

5.   Click on *OK*.

SPSS Dependent *t*-Test Syntax

T-TEST PAIRS=Anxiety_Pre WITH Anxiety_Post (PAIRED)
/CRITERIA=CI(.9500)
/MISSING=ANALYSIS.

Interpreting the output of the dependent *t*-test.   SPSS produces three tables for the dependent *t*-test. The first table is called "Paired Samples Statistics," the second is "Paired Samples Correlations," and the third table is "Paired Samples Test." These tables are 9.3, 9.4, and 9.5, respectively.

Table 9.3 displays the mean, number of cases, standard deviation, and standard error of the mean for levels of anxiety at the pretest and posttest. The table shows that the number of cases at pretest and posttest is equal (N = 50). Remember that the same subjects pretested are also posttested. Each subject must have two scores: one at pretest and another at posttest.

The table shows that the mean of the pretest levels of anxiety is 78.86 compared to 72.36 at the posttest, a decrease of 6.50 points on average (78.86 − 72.36 = 6.50). Is this means difference large enough to claim a statistical significance?

Table 9.4 displays the results of the Pearson's correlation coefficient (see chapter 7). The table shows that there is a significant (Sig. = .000; $p < .05$) positive correlation between pretest scores and posttest scores ($r = .79$). This simply indicates that participants who experienced high levels of anxiety at the pretest also experienced high levels of anxiety at the posttest, but does not mean that their levels of anxiety increased.

Table 9.5 displays the results of the dependent t-test. This table compares the mean score of levels of anxiety at the pretest with the mean score of levels of

Table 9.3: Descriptive Statistics—Pretest-Posttest Levels of Anxiety

		Paired Samples Statistics			
		Mean	N	Std. Deviation	Std. Error Mean
Pair 1	Anxiety_Pre	78.86	50	11.763	1.664
	Anxiety_Post	72.36	50	9.542	1.349

Table 9.4: Correlation between Pretest-Posttest Levels of Anxiety

		Paired Samples Statistics		
		N	Correlation	Sig.
Pair 1	Anxiety_Pre & Anxiety_Post	50	.790	.000

Table 9.5: Dependent t-Test—Pretest-Posttest Levels of Anxiety

		Paired Samples Test								
		Paired Differences								
					95% Confidence Interval of the Difference					
			Std.	Std. Error						Sig.
		Mean	Deviation	Mean	Lower	Upper	t	df		(2-tailed)
Pair 1	Anxiety_Pre − Anxiety_Post	6.500	7.223	1.022	4.447	8.553	6.363	49		.000

anxiety at the posttest. The first column displays the pairs being compared (Anxiety_Pre – Anxiety_Post). The second column displays the mean difference (Mean = 6.50). The table also displays the standard deviation, standard error, and the 95 percent confidence interval of the mean difference, respectively.

The last three columns include the values for the dependent *t*-test: the *t* value, degrees of freedom,[3] and the level of significance (two-tailed hypothesis).[4] The *t* value is 6.363 with 49 degrees of freedom and a *p* value (Sig.) of .000. Because the hypothesis is one-tailed, technically this two-tailed *p* value should be divided by two. However, since this *p* value is already significant, with an alpha of .05, dividing it by two is not necessary. These results show a statistically significant decrease in the levels of anxiety among participants from pretest to posttest.

Results of the Wilcoxon Signed Ranks Test

Next, this chapter will illustrate how to compute the Wilcoxon signed ranks test in SPSS and interpret its results.

How to compute the Wilcoxon signed ranks test in SPSS.   To run the Wilcoxon signed ranks test in SPSS, follow these steps:

1.   Open the SPSS Anxiety data file.

2.   Click on *Analyze* in the SPSS main toolbar, click on *Nonparametric Tests*, click on *Legacy Dialogs,* and click on *2 Related Samples* (see chapter 8, screen 8.5). This opens the SPSS "Two-Related-Samples Tests" main dialog box (see screen 9.2).

Screen 9.2:   SPSS Wilcoxon Two-Related-Samples Tests Dialog Box

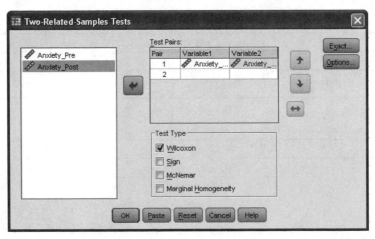

---

[3]df = N – 1; N = sample size.

[4]By default, except with the Pearson's *r*, SPSS produces a two-tailed *p* value. Thus, for a one-tailed hypothesis, divide the *p* value by two.

3. Click on *Anxiety_Pre* in the variables list, and click on the middle arrow button to move it into the *Test Pairs* box. This moves *Anxiety_Pre* under *Variable 1* for *Pair 1*.

4. Repeat step 3 to move *Anxiety_Post* into the *Test Pairs* box. This moves *Anxiety_Post* under *Variable 2* for *Pair 1*.

5. Make sure that *Wilcoxon* is checked under "Test Type" (SPSS default). If not, check it.

6. Click on *Options* in the upper right corner to request *Descriptive Statistics*. This opens the "Two-Related-Samples Tests Options" dialog box (see screen 9.3).

7. Check *Descriptive* under *Statistics*.

8. Click on *Continue*, then click on *OK*.

Screen 9.3:   SPSS Two-Related-Samples Options Dialog Box

SPSS Wilcoxon Signed Ranks Test Syntax

NPAR TESTS

/WILCOXON=Anxiety_Pre WITH Anxiety_Post (PAIRED)

/STATISTICS DESCRIPTIVES

/MISSING ANALYSIS.

Interpreting the output of the Wilcoxon signed ranks test.   As with the dependent *t*-test, SPSS produces three tables for the Wilcoxon signed ranks test. The first table is called "Descriptive Statistics," the second is "Ranks," and the third one is "Test Statistics." These are tables 9.6, 9.7., and 9.8., respectively.

Table 9.6:   Descriptive Statistics—Pretest-Posttest Levels of Anxiety

			Descriptive Statistics		
	N	Mean	Std. Deviation	Minimum	Maximum
Anxiety_Pre	50	78.86	11.763	55	100
Anxiety_Post	50	72.36	9.542	50	90

Table 9.7:   Wilcoxon Ranks—Pretest-Posttest Levels of Anxiety

		Ranks		
		N	Mean Rank	Sum of Ranks
Anxiety_Post –	Negative Ranks	40[a]	24.85	994.00
Anxiety_Pre	Positive Ranks	6[b]	14.50	87.00
	Ties	4[c]		
	Total	50		

[a]Anxiety_Post < Anxiety_Pre
[b]Anxiety_Post > Anxiety_Pre
[c]Anxiety_Post = Anxiety_Pre

Table 9.7 displays the number of participants at each measure (Anxiety_Pre and Anxiety_Post), the mean score, standard deviation, and range of scores of levels of anxiety. This table is similar to table 9.3 of the dependent *t*-test, except the dependent *t*-test table does not report the minimum and maximum scores. Remember, however, that you need to instruct SPSS to compute this table in the "Options" dialog box.

Table 9.7 displays the sum of the negative, positive, and tie mean ranks, which is how this test computes the level of significance. The negative mean rank is 40. This indicates the number of subjects whose posttest scores are smaller than their pretest scores (lower levels of anxiety at posttest than pretest). The positive mean rank is 6. This indicates the number of subjects whose posttest scores are smaller than their corresponding pretest scores (higher levels of anxiety at posttest than pretest). The tie mean rank is 4. This indicates the number of subjects whose posttest scores are equal to their corresponding pretest scores.

Overall, the table shows that forty out of the fifty women have lower levels of anxiety at posttest (mean rank = 24.85) compared to pretest (mean rank = 14.50). Is this mean ranks difference statistically significant?

Table 9.8 displays the *z* value and level of significance of the Wilcoxon signed ranks test. As you may recall from chapters 5 and 6, a *z* score above +1.96 or below −1.96 will fall at the rejection area, which indicates a significant value. Table 9.8 shows the *z* value as −4.96 (*z* = −4.959), which is beyond a *z* of −1.96. The Sig. (two-tailed) confirms that this value is significant at .001 alpha. In

Table 9.8:   Wilcoxon Test—Pretest-Posttest Levels of Anxiety

Test Statistics[b]	
	Anxiety_Post – Anxiety_Pre
Z	−4.959[a]
Asymp. Sig. (2-tailed)	.000

[a]Based on positive ranks.
[b]Wilcoxon Signed Ranks Test.

other words, the results show the mean ranks difference observed in table 9.7 is statistically significant.

Step 5: Decide whether to reject the null hypothesis.

The results of the dependent *t*-test presented in table 9.5 show a significant change in levels of anxiety among participants in the study (p = .000, which is < .001), and therefore we reject the null hypothesis.

Writing the results.   Writing the results of the dependent *t*-test or Wilcoxon signed ranks test is the same as the independent *t*-test and Mann-Whitney *U* test. First discuss the normality of the distributions of the two measures and whether data transformation was conducted. Then, report the *t* and *p* values for the dependent *t*-test or the *z* and *p* value for the Wilcoxon signed ranks test, the mean for each measure, and means difference. Next, present the results in a summary table. The following illustrates writing the results obtained in this example:

This study examined whether there was a significant decrease in levels of anxiety among women exposed to interpersonal violence after they completed therapy. Evaluation of Pearson's and Fisher's skewness coefficients and inspecting the histograms and normal Q-Q plots for the distributions of the two measures indicated that both approached the shape of a normal curve.

> *Note*: You may state that "the Wilcoxon signed ranks test was utilized because" normality was violated, transformation was not successful to fix the shape of the distribution(s), variable(s) were measured at the ordinal level of measurement, and/or sample size was too small to conduct the dependent *t*-test.

The results of the dependent *t*-test show significant changes in levels of anxiety among women exposed to interpersonal violence ($t_{(df=49)}$ = −6.36; p < .001). Participants in this therapy significantly decreased their levels of anxiety from 78.86 (SD = 11.76) at pretest to 72.36 (SD = 9.54) at posttest; a decrease of 6.5 points on average. These findings were supported by the findings of the Wilcoxon signed ranks test (z = −4.96; p < .001). These findings provide statistical evidence that the therapy is effective.

Presentation of results in a summary table.   Next, present the results of the dependent *t*-test in a summary table similar to that of the independent *t*-test. The table should include results of the SPSS descriptive table and dependent *t*-test. In the table, report the number of cases for each measure, the means and standard deviations, overall test statistic, and *p* value. Table 9.9 presents the results of the dependent *t*-test for levels of anxiety at pretest and posttest.

Table 9.9:   Results of the Dependent *t*-Test for Levels of Anxiety (N = 50)

Variable	$\overline{X}$	SD	*t*	*p*[a]
Levels of Anxiety				
Pretest	78.86	11.76	−6.36	<.001
Posttest	72.36	9.54		

[a]One-tailed *p* value.

Example 2—Two Related Topics (Variables)

To demonstrate the use of the dependent *t*-test and the Wilcoxon signed ranks test with two related variables, use the SPSS Elderly data file (appendix A) to examine the following research question:

RESEARCH QUESTION: Is there a statistically significant difference between levels of emotional balance (EB) and cognitive status (CS) among the elderly population?

Step 1: State the null and alternative hypotheses.

H_0: There is no statistically significant difference between levels of emotional balance (μ_{EB}) and levels of cognitive status (μ_{CS}) among elderly people.

$$\mu_{EB} = \mu_{CS}$$

H_a: Levels of emotional balance among elderly people will be significantly higher than their levels of cognitive status.

$$\mu_{EB} > \mu_{CS}$$

In this one-tailed research hypothesis, the two variables under study are emotional balance and cognitive status for the same subjects; that is two related topics. Therefore, we will use either the dependent *t*-test or the Wilcoxon signed ranks test to examine the means difference.

Step 2: Set the criteria for rejecting the null hypothesis.
Set alpha at .05 (α = .05). Reject H_0 only if $p \leq .05$.

Step 3: Select the appropriate statistical test.
In order to select which paired observations test statistic should be used to examine the hypothesis, we first evaluate the data and whether they meet the assumptions of the dependent *t*-test. These are as follows:

1. LEVEL OF MEASUREMENT: The two variables must be interval or ratio level of measurement. Levels of emotional balance and cognitive status are total scores for two subscales. Thus, both variables are measured at the interval level of measurement.

2.   OBSERVATIONS: The two variables must be either repeated measures or paired observations. Each subject in the Elderly study completed one measure for emotional balance and another for cognitive status. The two measures are thus paired observations.

3.   NORMALITY OF DISTRIBUTION: The distributions of cognitive status and emotional balance must be normal. To evaluate the distributions of emotional balance and cognitive status, run measures of central tendency and skewness coefficients, and create histograms and normal Q-Q plots for the two variables (see chapter 5).

   We already evaluated the distribution of cognitive status in chapter 7 and found it to be normal (see chapter 7, table 7.3 and figures 7.3 through 7.6). Now we evaluate the distribution of emotional balance. Table 9.10 conveys the descriptive statistics for emotional balance. Also, figures 9.5 and 9.6 display the graphs for emotional balance.

   Evaluation of the Pearson's skewness coefficient [(23.18 − 24.00)/6.16 = −.13] and Fisher's skewness coefficient (−.399/.243 = −.16), and inspection of both histogram (see figure 9.5) and normal Q-Q plot (see figure 9.6) show that the shape of the distribution of emotional balance approaches the shape of a normal curve, perhaps with a minor deviation to the left (minor negative skewness). That is, the distributions of both emotional balance and cognitive status satisfy the assumption of normality.

4.   RANGE OF SCORES: Measures of both variables must have equal possible ranges and similar interpretations. In the Elderly study, emotional balance and cognitive status were measured by the Iowa Self-Assessment Inventory (IOWA) (Morris & Buckwalter, 1988). In addition to emotional balance and cognitive status, IOWA also measures physical health, economic resources, trusting others, mobility, and social support. The possible total score for

Table 9.10:   Descriptive Statistics for Emotional Balance

			Statistic	Std. Error
EB Emotional	Mean		23.18	.619
Balance	95% Confidence	Lower Bound	21.95	
	Interval for Mean	Upper Bound	24.41	
	5% Trimmed Mean		23.37	
	Median		24.00	
	Variance		37.885	
	Std. Deviation		6.155	
	Minimum		10	
	Maximum		32	
	Range		22	
	Interquartile Range		10	
	Skewness		−.399	.243
	Kurtosis		−.771	.481

Figure 9.5:   Histogram for Emotional Balance

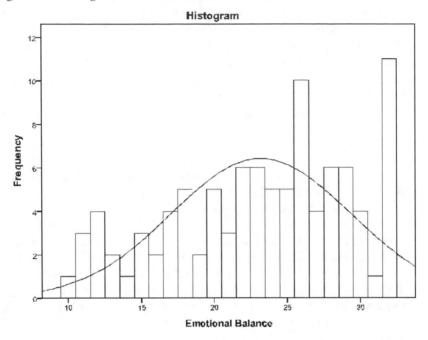

Figure 9.6:   Normal Q-Q Plot of Emotional Balance

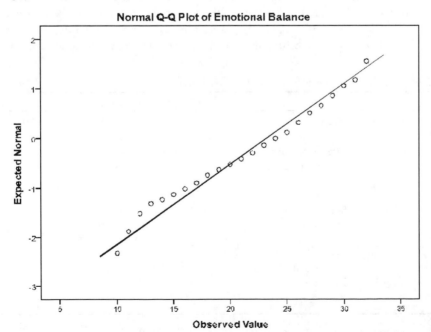

each variable ranges between 8 and 32, with higher scores indicating greater value: greater emotional balance and greater cognitive status (see appendix A). Therefore, data for both variables satisfy this assumption.

5. SAMPLE SIZE: The sample size should be large enough to conduct an examination of the test hypothesis. Ninety-nine subjects participated in the Elderly study, which is larger than the thirty cases needed to conduct bivariate parametric tests. Also, it is larger than the minimum twenty-seven cases needed for power of .80 with a one-tailed alpha of .05 and a moderate effect size (see table 9.1).

To conclude, data for both cognitive status and emotional balance satisfy all assumptions for the dependent *t*-test. Therefore, we will utilize the dependent *t*-test to examine the means difference between the two variables.

Note: If normality was violated for one or both variables, try data transformation. If severe skewness still exists and/or the sample size is too small, use the Wilcoxon signed ranks test to examine the hypothesis.

Step 4: Compute the test statistic (using SPSS).
Now run the dependent *t*-test. Also run the Wilcoxon signed ranks test to examine if results are consistent. Follow the same steps discussed under Example 1 to run the test statistics.

Interpreting the output of the dependent *t*-test.   Tables 9.11 through 9.13 display the results of the dependent *t*-test generated by SPSS.

Table 9.11 displays the means, number of cases, standard deviations, and standard errors of the mean for emotional balance and cognitive status. The table shows that the levels of emotional balance ($\overline{X}$ = 23.18) among the elderly are greater than their levels of cognitive status ($\overline{X}$ = 21.72), that is, a means difference of 1.47. Is this increase significant?

Table 9.12 shows a significant (Sig. = .018) positive correlation between emotional balance and cognitive status (r = .24). In other words, elderly with

Table 9.11:   Descriptive Statistics—Emotional Balance and Cognitive Status

		Mean	N	Std. Deviation	Std. Error Mean
Pair 1	Emotional Balance	23.18	99	6.155	.619
	Cognitive Status	21.72	99	5.608	.564

Table 9.12:   Correlation between Emotional Balance and Cognitive Status

		N	Correlation	Sig.
Pair 1	Emotional Balance and Cognitive Status	99	.238	.018

higher levels of emotional balance tend to have higher levels of cognitive status. This relationship is considered very weak (see chapter 7). In this study, however, we are less interested in the relationship between the two measures and more interested in the difference between the two in the elderly population.

Table 9.13 shows that the means difference is 1.465 (that is, 23.18 − 21.72). The *t* value is 2.004 with 98 degrees of freedom (99 − 1 = 98). This *t* value is significant at the .05 alpha (p = .048). Remember, however, that our hypothesis is one-tailed, and thus we should divide this *p* value by two; that is, .048/2 = .024. Overall, these results show a significant difference between emotional balance and cognitive status ($p < .05$).

Results of the Wilcoxon signed ranks test.   Tables 9.14 through 9.16 display the results of the Wilcoxon signed ranks test generated by SPSS.

Table 9.14 displays the descriptive statistics for emotional balance and cognitive status. It is similar to table 9.11 of the dependent *t*-test.

Table 9.15 shows that of the ninety-nine cases, forty have negative ranks (emotional balance is smaller than cognitive status). On the other hand, fifty

Table 9.13:   Dependent *t*-Test—Emotional Balance and Cognitive Status

		Paired Differences							
					95% Confidence Interval of the Difference				
			Std.	Std. Error					Sig.
		Mean	Deviation	Mean	Lower	Upper	t	df	(2-tailed)
Pair 1	Emotional Balance – Cognitive Status	1.465	7.274	.731	.014	2.915	2.004	98	.048

Table 9.14:   Descriptive Statistics—Emotional Balance and Cognitive Status

	N	Mean	Std. Deviation	Minimum	Maximum
Cognitive Status	99	21.72	5.608	8	32
Emotional Balance	99	23.18	6.155	10	32

Table 9.15:   Wilcoxon Ranks—Emotional Balance and Cognitive Status

		N	Mean Rank	Sum of Ranks
Emotional Balance –	Negative Ranks	40[a]	40.56	1622.50
Cognitive Status	Positive Ranks	50[b]	49.45	2472.50
	Ties	9[c]		
	Total	99		

[a]Emotional Balance < Cognitive Status
[b]Emotional Balance > Cognitive Status
[c]Emotional Balance = Cognitive Status

Table 9.16:   Wilcoxon Test—Emotional Balance and Cognitive Status

Test Statistics[b]	
	Emotional Balance – Cognitive Status
Z	−1.712[a]
Asymp. Sig. (2-tailed)	.087

[a]Based on negative ranks.
[b]Wilcoxon Signed Ranks Test.

cases have positive ranks (emotional balance is greater than cognitive status). Nine cases have tied scores (emotional balance equals cognitive status). Overall, the table shows that the positive mean rank is 49.45, and the negative mean rank is 40.56, a difference of 8.89. Is this means ranks difference statistically significant?

Table 9.16 shows that the z value is −1.71 and the level of significance (Sig.) is .087. Recall, however, that our hypothesis is one-tailed, and thus we need to divide this p value by two; that is, .087/2 = .043, which indicates a significant difference between the mean scores of two variables.

Note: If the hypothesis was two-tailed, the results will not be significant. Also, they will not be consistent with the results of the dependent t-test, which shows significant results. When this occurs, report the results of the test you chose under step 3, here, the dependent t-test.

Step 5: Decide whether to reject the null hypothesis.

The results of the dependent t-test presented in table 9.13 show a significant difference between levels of emotional balance and levels of cognitive status among elderly people ($p < .05$). Therefore, we will reject the null hypothesis.

Writing the results.   We utilized the dependent t-test to examine the differences in levels of emotional balance and cognitive status among elderly individuals. Inspection of both Pearson's and Fisher's skewness coefficients and reviewing the histograms and normal Q-Q plots for emotional balance and cognitive status showed that the distributions of the two variables appear normal.

The results of the dependent t-test are presented in table 9.17. These results show a significant difference in the levels of emotional balance and cognitive status ($t_{(df=98)} = 2.00$; $p < .05$). Elderly participants in this study reported higher levels of emotional balance ($\bar{X} = 23.18$) than cognitive status ($\bar{X} = 21.72$), a means difference that is significant, even though it is small—1.47 points on average. These findings were supported by the findings of the Wilcoxon signed ranks test ($z = −1.71$; $p < .05$).

Table 9.17:   Results of the Dependent *t*-Test for Emotional Balance and Cognitive Status
              (N = 99)

Variable	$\overline{X}$	SD	t	p^a
Emotional Balance	23.18	6.16	2.00	< .05
Cognitive Status	21.72	5.61		

ᵃOne-tailed *p* value.

SUMMARY

This chapter introduced the dependent *t*-test and the Wilcoxon signed ranks test, also known as tests for pairs. These tests provide another statistical way for social science researchers and professionals to evaluate their own practice. They are suitable to examine within-subjects changes or differences on two-repeated measures or two related observations. The tests are also useful to examine differences between two-matched samples measured on two related topics or under two conditions.

Chapter 9 presented and discussed the purpose and assumptions of the dependent *t*-test and its corresponding nonparametric Wilcoxon signed ranks test. The chapter then presented two research examples using real data illustrating the use of the dependent *t*-test and the Wilcoxon signed ranks test. The first illustrated use of the tests with two repeated measures (pretest and posttest); the second illustrated use of the tests with two related topics (emotional balance and cognitive status). The chapter also discussed how to use SPSS to compute the test statistics followed by a discussion of how to interpret the results of the dependent *t*-test and Wilcoxon signed ranks test, how to write them, and how to present the results in a summary table.

Chapter 10 introduces two statistical tests suitable to examine differences between three or more groups on one continuous variable. The chapter presents the one-way analysis of variance (ANOVA) and its nonparametric version, the Kruskal-Wallis *H* test. The chapter also introduces the one-way analysis of covariance (ANCOVA). The chapter then discusses the assumptions underlying the one-way ANOVA and ANCOVA, as well as the Kruskal-Wallis *H* test and the importance of post hoc tests in groups' comparison. The chapter ends with a presentation of two examples illustrating how to compute the test statistics, interpret the output, write the results, and present the results in summary tables.

PRACTICAL EXERCISES

Part 1: A local Office of Refugee Resettlement offered a three-month English as a Second Language (ESL) course to thirty-two refugees to improve their English proficiency in reading, writing, and speaking. As part of its course evaluation, the office administered the ESL proficiency test to all participants at the start of the course (Before) and then after they completed the course (After). Total scores range between 0 and 100, with higher scores indicating greater English proficiency. The followings are participants' scores before and after the course:

Case #	Before	After	Case #	Before	After
1	46	64	17	40	65
2	69	91	18	61	93
3	58	77	19	51	83
4	49	69	20	48	75
5	54	50	21	48	74
6	64	88	22	50	65
7	63	85	23	45	64
8	37	64	24	30	68
9	68	98	25	55	75
10	51	77	26	42	56
11	58	86	27	60	80
12	54	77	28	45	60
13	43	67	29	55	75
14	61	85	30	50	80
15	51	51	31	68	68
16	47	77	32	70	82

Enter these data in SPSS program and examine the following research question:

Is there a significant improvement in refugees' English proficiency?

1. Follow the steps in hypothesis testing and examine the hypothesis (use a one-tailed hypothesis). Discuss all steps in detail.
2. Write the SPSS syntax for the test statistic.
3. Present the results in a summary table.

Part 2: Access the PTSD SPSS data file (appendix A) and examine the following research question:

RESEARCH QUESTION: Is there significant difference between the chance health locus of control (CHLC) and the powerful other health locus of control (PHLC) among refugees?

1. Follow the steps in hypothesis testing and examine the hypothesis (use a two-tailed hypothesis). Discuss all steps in detail.
2. Present the results in a summary table.

CHAPTER 10

K Group Comparisons:
One-Way Analysis of Variance
and Covariance

LEARNING OBJECTIVES

1. Understand the purpose of the one-way ANOVA and ANCOVA
2. Understand the assumptions of the one-way ANOVA and ANCOVA
3. Understand the post hoc tests
4. Understand the nonparametric Kruskal-Wallis *H* test
5. Understand how to use SPSS to compute the test statistics
6. Understand how to interpret, write, and present results of the tests

DATA SET (APPENDIX A)

Job Satisfaction

INTRODUCTION

Chapter 8 presented the independent *t*-test and the Mann-Whitney *U* test. As stated, these tests are appropriate to examine the difference between *only* two groups (independent variable) on a continuous variable (dependent variable) and whether this means difference is statistically significant. Social science researchers often, however, are interested in the means differences among more than two groups, simultaneously, and whether these means differences are significantly different. Also, researchers sometimes may be interested in whether a third variable may impact the relationship between the independent and dependent variables and lead to significant differences. Consider the following two cases:

CASE 1: The researcher of the Job Satisfaction study (appendix A) was interested in the impact of marital status (independent variable) on employees' levels of turnover (dependent variable). For this purpose, the researcher classifies

Figure 10.1:   Turnover by Marital Status

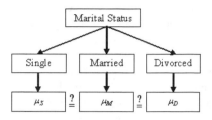

marital status as single, married, and divorced, then compares levels of turnover among all three marital status groups. In this case, the researcher conducts three pairs of comparisons: single (μ_S) versus married (μ_M); single (μ_S) versus divorced (μ_D); and married (μ_M) versus divorced (μ_D). Figure 10.1 illustrates these group comparisons.

Statistically, the researcher hypothesizes that there will be statistically significant differences between single, married, and divorced social services employees with regard to their levels of turnover. That is, $\mu_S \neq \mu_M \neq \mu_D$; group means of turnover are not equal.

CASE 2: The same researcher was also interested in the levels of job satisfaction differences based on employees' location of employment (north, south, and center). However, believing that job satisfaction can be affected by quality of supervision in the workplace, the researcher decides to control for it, so it does not impact the relationship between job satisfaction and location of employment. Here, the researcher also conducts three pairs of comparisons, however, while controlling (adjusting) for employees' quality of supervision: (1) north (μ'_N) versus south (μ'_S); (2) north (μ'_N) versus center (μ'_C); and (3) south (μ'_S) versus center (μ'_C). Figure 10.2 displays these group comparisons. The μ' represents the adjusted mean of job satisfaction for the particular group.

Statistically, the researcher hypothesizes that there will be statistically significant job satisfaction differences among social services employees based on their location of employment (north, center, and south) while controlling for the effect of their quality of supervision. That is, $\mu'_N \neq \mu'_C \neq \mu'_S$; adjusted group means of job satisfaction are not equal.

Figure 10.2:   Job Satisfaction by Location Controlling for Supervision

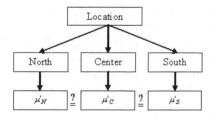

In these two examples, the researchers are interested in comparing multiple groups on a single variable: turnover (dependent variable) by marital status (independent variable) in the first case, and job satisfaction (dependent variable) by location of employment (independent variable) in the second one. In both cases, the independent variables consist of multiple groups (marital status = single, married, and divorced; Location = north, center, and south) and the dependent variables (outcome) consist of continuous data.

Unlike in the first example, the researcher in the second example believes there is a third variable (quality of supervision) that may affect the relationship between job satisfaction and location of employment, and therefore he/she decides to control for its effect. Given this information, the question is, then, what statistical test(s) are most suitable to examine differences between group mean scores in both cases?

This chapter presents the one-way analysis of variance (ANOVA) and one-way analysis of covariance (ANCOVA) followed by the nonparametric Kruskal-Wallis *H* test, and the post hoc tests. The chapter then presents two practical examples describing in detail the utilization of these test statistics in hypothesis testing and the use of SPSS to compute the tests, and then interpret, write, and present the results in summary tables and graphs. The chapter, however, begins with a discussion of why not to use the independent *t*-test to compare group means differences.

WHY NOT USE THE INDEPENDENT *T*-TEST?

There are three main reasons for not using the independent *t*-test (two-sample case *t*-test) to compare the means or adjusted means of categorical variables with more than two groups.

As discussed in chapter 8, the independent *t*-test is suitable to compare the means difference of *only* two groups (males vs. females; undergraduate vs. graduate; etc.) on one continuous outcome variable. Therefore, when a variable consists of more than two groups, multiple independent *t*-tests would be required to examine differences among all possible pairs of groups. For example, in case 1, there are three marital status groups, so the researcher would need *three* independent *t*-tests to examine all possible pairs: (1) single versus married; (2) single versus divorced; and (3) married versus divorced. Also, since there are three locations of employment in the second case, the researcher would also need *three* independent *t*-tests to examine all possible pairs: (1) north versus south; (2) north versus center; and (3) center versus south.

Now imagine that you want to examine the means differences of attitudes toward abortion among registered voters based on the four political party affiliations (Republican, Democratic, independent, and other). To examine these differences, you would conduct *six* independent *t*-tests to compare all possible pairs: (1) Republican versus Democrat; (2) Republican versus independent; (3) Republican versus other; (4) Democrat versus independent; (5) Democrat versus other; and (6) independent versus other.

In other words, the number of comparisons depends on the number of groups (levels) in the independent variable; the more groups, the more independent *t*-tests are required to compare all possible pairs. Mathematically, the number of independent *t*-tests required to compare all possible pairs is as follows:

Number of Independent *t*-Tests for Multiple Comparisons

$$\frac{K * (K - 1)}{2}$$

K = Number of groups

For example, if a researcher wants to examine the impact of religious affiliation (1 = Muslim, 2 = Christian, 3 = Jewish, 4 = Buddhist, 5 = no preference, and 6 = other) on levels of life satisfaction among immigrants, then the researcher will need fifteen independent *t*-tests to compare all possible religious pairs with regard to their self-esteem. That is,

$$\text{Number of independent } t\text{-tests} = \frac{6 * (6 - 1)}{2} = \frac{30}{2} = 15$$

The second reason for not using the independent *t*-test is derived from the first one. By using multiple independent *t*-tests, the probability of making a type I error (alpha) is higher. If alpha is set up at, for example, .05 with one independent *t*-test, it will be greater (inflated) if multiple independent *t*-tests are used. In other words, the more tests that are used, the greater the likelihood of making a type I error; that is, rejecting the null hypothesis when it is true.

Therefore, if the independent *t*-test is utilized to conduct multiple group comparisons, researchers ideally should adjust alpha to a higher level to avoid making a type I error. To adjust alpha, first compute the number of independent *t*-tests required to compare all possible pairs and then adjust alpha as follows:

Adjusting Alpha for Multiple Comparisons

Adjusted $\alpha = 1 - (1 - \alpha)^K$

α = Level of significance (e.g., .05)
K = Number of independent *t*-tests

For example, if the researcher decides to use multiple independent *t*-tests to compare the three marital status groups or the three locations, he or she should set alpha at .14. That is, $\alpha = 1 - (1 - .05)^3 = 1 - (.95)^3 = .14$.

Also, if the researcher decides to use multiple independent *t*-tests to compare the six religious groups with regard to self-esteem, the researcher should set alpha at .54. That is, $\alpha = 1 - (1 - .05)^{15} = 1 - (.95)^{15} = .54$.

Lastly, as stated, the independent *t*-test examines the relationship between only two variables in which one is a dichotomous variable and the second is a continuous variable. Thus, it is not suitable to control for the impact of a third variable on the relationship between the independent and dependent variables.

This chapter therefore presents two new statistical techniques that overcome the problems of multiple independent *t*-tests and inflation of alpha and allow researchers to control for an extraneous effect on the relationship between the independent and dependent variables. These are the one-way analysis of variance and covariance.

ANALYSIS OF VARIANCE: AN OVERVIEW

Analysis of variance (ANOVA) and covariance (ANCOVA) are a collection of statistical techniques that examines one or more categorical (independent) variables on one or more dependent variables. In addition, analysis of covariance controls for the effect of one or more extraneous variables believed to affect the relationship between the independent and dependent variables. These tests include the one-way ANOVA/ANCOVA, two-way ANOVA/ANCOVA, factorial ANOVA/ANCOVA, and multivariate ANOVA/ANCOVA (MANOVA/MANCOVA). Table 10.1 compares these tests with regard to the number of variables.

PURPOSE OF ONE-WAY ANOVA AND ANCOVA

One-Way ANOVA

One-way ANOVA was developed by Ronald Aylmer Fisher (1890–1962), an English statistician and scientist, in 1915. It is a univariate general linear model (GLM).

Table 10.1:   Types of Analysis of Variance and Covariance

Test	# of IVs	# of DV	# of COV
One-Way ANOVA	1 Categorical	1 Continuous	None
One-Way ANCOVA	1 Categorical	1 Continuous	1+ Continuous
Two-Way ANOVA	2 Categorical	1 Continuous	None
Two-Way ANCOVA	2 Categorical	1 Continuous	1+ Continuous
Factorial ANOVA	3+ Categorical	1 Continuous	None
Two-Way ANCOVA	3+ Categorical	1 Continuous	1+ Continuous
One-Way MANOVA	1 Categorical	2+ Continuous	None
One-Way MANCOVA	1 Categorical	2+ Continuous	1+ Continuous
Two-Way MANOVA	2 Categorical	2+ Continuous	None
Two-Way MANCOVA	2 Categorical	2+ Continuous	1+ Continuous
Factorial MANOVA	3+ Categorical	2+ Continuous	None
Two-Way MANCOVA	3+ Categorical	2+ Continuous	1+ Continuous

The purpose of one-way ANOVA is to examine differences between the mean scores of three or more groups (one independent variable, three or more groups) and whether these differences are statistically significant. For example, one-way ANOVA can help determine whether there are statistically significant differences in levels of turnover among social services employees based on their marital status or if there are statistically significant differences in levels of job satisfaction based on their location of employment.

The one-way ANOVA produces a test statistic called the F ratio. Like the t value in the independent t-test, the F ratio measures how far apart the means of the groups are in standard error units. The larger the F ratio is, the more likely that the differences between the group means are statistically significant. Mathematically, F is the square of t; ($F = t^2$).

One-Way ANCOVA

One-way ANCOVA is an extension version of the one-way ANOVA. It is a combination of the one-way ANOVA and multiple linear regression analysis (see chapter 12).

The purpose of the one-way ANCOVA is to examine differences between the mean scores of multiple groups (one independent variable) and whether these differences are statistically significant (like the one-way ANOVA), while controlling for the effect of one or more extraneous variables (like multiple regression). In other words, one-way ANCOVA examines if there are statistically significant differences between *two* or more groups regarding the dependent variable after removing the effect of (or adjusting for) one or more variables on the dependent variable. These variables are called control variables, covariates, or covariances.

For example, one-way ANCOVA can be used to examine whether there are statistically significant differences in levels of job satisfaction among social services employees based on their location of employment while controlling for (or removing) the effect of quality of supervision on job satisfaction. Quality of supervision, in this case, serves as the control variable, or covariate.

As with ANOVA, the one-way ANCOVA uses the F distribution to measure how far apart the means of the groups are in standard error units after adjusting these means for variability due to the control variable (covariate). The larger the F ratio is, the more likely that the difference between the adjusted group means is statistically significant.

SOURCES OF VARIATIONS IN ANOVA AND ANCOVA

The variance (SS) in one-way ANOVA is partitioned into two sources of variability: *between-groups variability (SS_B)* and *within-groups variability (SS_W)*. In one-way ANCOVA, a third source of variability is added due to the covariance, *covariate variability (SS_{COV})*.

The between-groups variability is the variance in the dependent variable due to differences between groups (e.g., differences in job satisfaction between employees in the north vs. south; north vs. center, and south vs. center). The within-groups variability is the error variance (residuals) due to differences between subjects within a particular level of the independent variable (e.g., differences in job satisfaction among employees within each location: north, south, and center). The covariate variability is the variance in the dependent variable due to the inclusion of the covariate, control variable, in the analysis (e.g., variability in job satisfaction accounted for by quality of supervision).

In one-way ANOVA, the total variance (SS_T) is the sum of both within-groups variance and between-groups variance ($SS_T = SS_B + SS_W$). In one-way ANCOVA, the total variance (SS_T) is the sum of the between-groups variance, within-groups variance, and the covariate variance ($SS_T = SS_B + SS_W + SS_{COV}$). Figure 10.3 illustrates the sources of variability in ANOVA and ANCOVA.

Figure 10.3:   Variability in ANOVA and ANCOVA

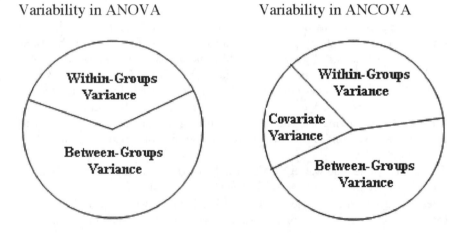

ANOVA and ANCOVA.

ASSUMPTIONS OF ANOVA AND ANCOVA

One-way ANOVA and ANCOVA require the same set of assumptions as the independent *t*-tests. These are the following:

1. The independent variable must be nominal level of measurement (categorical data) and consist of three or more groups. Technically, the one-way ANOVA and ANCOVA can be used to compare the means difference of two groups.

2. The independent and dependent variables must be paired observations. That is, data for all groups must be collected at the same time.

3. The dependent variable must be continuous data and measured at the interval level of measurement or higher (ratio).

4. The shape of the distribution of the dependent variable must approach the shape of a normal curve.

   To evaluate the assumption of normality, compute measures of central tendency, variability, and skewness, and inspect the histogram and normal Q-Q plot of the variable under study. If data are severely skewed, consider different data transformation methods.

5. The variances of all groups on the dependent variable should be equal. This is known as the assumption of homogeneity of variances, equality of variances, or homoscedasticity (or homoskedasticity).

   As with the independent t-test, this assumption can be evaluated by inspecting the results of the Levene's test of homogeneity of variances (also called Levene's test of equality of error variances). A p value greater than .05 (alpha = .05) indicates the assumption is met (or a more conservative level of .001).

   If variances are not equal in ANOVA, report the results of the Welch statistic given other assumptions are met. This test can be requested in SPSS, along with the one-way ANOVA (discussed later). On the other hand, if variances are not equal in ANCOVA, you may exclude the covariate from the analysis, treat it as a second independent variable, and conduct a multiple linear regression analysis (see chapter 12).

6. The sample size should be large enough to utilize the one-way ANOVA or ANCOVA. As with other bivariate parametric tests, a sample size of thirty cases should be sufficient for means comparisons. For statistical power consideration, however, we recommend a sample size that would increase the likelihood of accurately rejecting a false hypothesis (make a correct decision). As we discussed in the previous chapters, the sample size is affected by four criteria: type of hypothesis, level of significance, power, and effect size. In addition to these criteria, the number of groups under analysis also impacts the sample size for ANOVA and ANCOVA.

   Given Cohen's (1988) definition of effect size for means difference (small = .20, moderate = .50, and large = .80) and a two-tailed hypothesis, we used SPSS Sample Power and computed the minimum sample size needed per group to detect a power of .80 for three-, four-, and five-group comparisons.

   Table 10.2 presents the results of the SPSS Sample Power. As it appears in the table, a minimum sample size of forty-two cases is needed to compare the means differences among three groups (14×3 groups = 42) in order to achieve a power of .80, given a moderate effect size and two-tailed alpha of .05. On the other hand, a sample size as low as twenty-one cases (7×3 groups) will be needed to achieve a power of .80, given a larger effect size (ES = .80) with other criteria are held constant.

   Yet, when a smaller sample size is used to compare multiple groups, it is recommended that researchers conduct power analysis, given the observed effect size and sample size.

Table 10.2:   Sample Size Per Group for ANOVA and ANCOVA
(Power = .80; Two-Tailed Alpha)

	3 Groups			4 Groups			5 Groups		
Alpha	ES = .20	ES = .50	ES = .80	ES = .20	ES = .50	ES = .80	ES = .20	ES = .50	ES = .80
.050	82	14	7	70	12	6	61	11	5
.010	118	21	9	99	17	8	86	15	7
.001	167	29	13	137	24	11	118	21	10

In addition to these assumptions, one-way ANCOVA requires four additional assumptions. They are as follows:

7. The control variable (covariate) must be continuous data and measured at the interval or ratio level of measurement.

8. The shape of the distribution of the covariate must approach the shape of a normal curve.

    As with the dependent variable, evaluate this assumption by inspecting measures of skewness coefficients and reviewing the histogram and normal Q-Q plot of covariate. If data are severely skewed, consider data transformation.

9. The relationship between the covariate and the dependent variable should be a linear relationship. This is the assumption of linearity.

    To evaluate this assumption, compute the Pearson's correlation coefficient and create a scatterplot with a fit line displaying the relationship between the dependent and control variables. When a linear relationship between variables exists, scores should cluster around the fit line (see chapter 7).

    If a nonlinear relationship or no significant correlations exist between the covariate and dependent variable, stop and consider a one-way ANOVA or its alternative Kruskal-Wallis *H* test to examine the means differences. The inclusion of the covariate in the analysis will not impact the relationship between the independent and dependent variables.

10. The relationship between the dependent variable and covariate should be the same for each group of the independent variable. In other words, there should be no interaction between the independent variable and covariate. This is the assumption of homogeneity of regression.

    Homogeneity of regression is evaluated by inspecting the interaction effect between the independent variable and the covariate on the dependent variable. A *p* value greater than .05 indicates the assumption to be met. If this assumption is violated, stop; ANCOVA is not the appropriate technique. In this case, treat the covariate as another independent variable and conduct multiple regression analysis (see chapter 12). Also, you may recode the covariate into groups, treat it as a second independent variable, and conduct a two-way ANOVA.[1]

---

[1] See Abu-Bader (2010) for two-way ANOVA.

KRUSKAL-WALLIS *H* TEST

The Kruskal-Wallis *H* test,[2] also known as Kruskal-Wallis one-way analysis of variance, is the nonparametric version of the one-way ANOVA. It is the extension of the Mann-Whitney *U* test for multiple groups. Like the Mann-Whitney *U* test, Kruskal-Wallis *H* test first ranks scores for each group, computes the mean rank for each group, and then determines whether there is a statistically significant difference between at least two means rank.

The Kruskal-Wallis *H* test is appropriate to compare three or more groups when data violate the assumptions for one-way ANOVA (interval level of measurement, normality of distribution, homogeneity of variances, and sufficient sample size). As with one-way ANOVA, Kruskal-Wallis *H*, however, still requires the sample is representative of the population, dependent and independent variables are paired observations, and the independent variable is nominal with three or more levels.

POST HOC TESTS

Unlike the independent *t*-test and Mann-Whitney *U*, the one-way ANOVA and ANCOVA examine whether there is an overall significant difference between three or more groups on the dependent variable. Yet, when a significant difference is detected, neither ANOVA nor ANCOVA pinpoint which pair(s) of groups are significantly different. Further statistical tests are thus required to precisely detect which pairs are significantly different with regard to the dependent variable. These tests are known as post hoc tests.

Like the independent *t*-test and Mann-Whitney *U*, post hoc tests examine whether there is a statistically significant difference between the means of each possible pair of groups. The SPSS program provides eighteen post hoc tests for one-way ANOVA; fourteen of them are suitable when data meet the assumption of homogeneity of variances, and four are suitable when this assumption is not met. The four most frequently reported post hoc tests when equality of variances is assumed include the LSD (least significant difference), Bonferroni (also known as Bonferroni correction), Scheffe, and Tukey. The Tamhane's T2 is another post hoc test that is based on the independent *t*-test and is most appropriately utilized when equality of variances is not assumed. On the other hand, SPSS provides only three post hoc tests for one-way ANCOVA. These are LSD, Bonferroni, and Sidak.

Each post hoc test uses different statistical formulas to examine the difference between the means of each possible pair of groups. All these tests, except the LSD, adjust the level of significance (alpha) based on the number of comparisons.

---

[2]Named after William H. Kruskal (1919–2005), an American mathematician and statistician, and Wilson A. Wallis (1912–1998), an American economist and statistician.

PRACTICAL EXAMPLES

To illustrate the utilization of the one-way ANOVA, Kruskal-Wallis *H* test, and the one-way ANCOVA in social science research, we present two examples. The first utilizes the one-way ANOVA and Kruskal-Wallis *H* test to examine levels of turnover based on marital status among social services employees. The second example utilizes the one-way ANCOVA to examine levels of job satisfaction based on location of employment among social services employees while controlling (adjusting) for their quality of supervision. Both examples are based on the Job Satisfaction study (appendix A).

Example 1: Turnover by Marital Status (One-Way ANOVA)

We will use the SPSS *Job Satisfaction* data file (appendix A) and follow steps in hypothesis testing to examine the differences between single, married, and divorced social services employees with regard to their levels of turnover. In other words, we will examine the following research question:

RESEARCH QUESTION: Are there statistically significant differences between single, married, and divorced social services employees with regard to their levels of turnover?

Step 1: State the null and alternative hypotheses.

H_0: There are no statistically significant differences in the levels of turnover among single, married, and divorced social services employees. That is,

$\mu_S = \mu_M = \mu_D$

H_a: There are statistically significant differences in the levels of turnover among single, married, and divorced social services employees. That is,

$\mu_S \neq \mu_M \neq \mu_D$, for at least two marital status groups.

In this two-tailed research hypothesis, marital status (MStatus) is the independent variable, and turnover (Turnover) is the dependent variable.

Step 2: Set the criteria for rejecting the null hypothesis.
Set alpha at .05 ($\alpha = .05$). Reject H_0 only if $p \leq .05$.

Step 3: Select the appropriate statistical test.
In the above hypothesis, the independent variable (marital status) is nominal level of measurement and consists of three groups (single, married, divorced), and the dependent variable (turnover) is continuous data and measured at the interval level of measurement. These are the basic requirements for both the one-way ANOVA and Kruskal-Wallis *H* test. Next, we evaluate the data for normality, homogeneity of variances, and sample size.

1. NORMALITY OF DISTRIBUTION: The shape of the distribution of the dependent variable (turnover) must approach that of a normal curve.

    To evaluate this assumption, compute measures of skewness and create a histogram and a normal Q-Q plot for turnover. Table 10.3 and figures 10.4 and 10.5 display the descriptive statistics and graphs for turnover.

Table 10.3: Descriptive Statistics for Levels of Turnover

			Statistic	Std. Error
Turnover	Mean		18.83	.312
	95% Confidence	Lower Bound	18.21	
	Interval for Mean	Upper Bound	19.44	
	5% Trimmed Mean		18.80	
	Median		19.00	
	Variance		21.269	
	Std. Deviation		4.612	
	Minimum		2	
	Maximum		34	
	Range		32	
	Interquartile Range		6	
	Skewness		−.007	.165
	Kurtosis		.882	.328

Figure 10.4: Histogram for Levels of Turnover

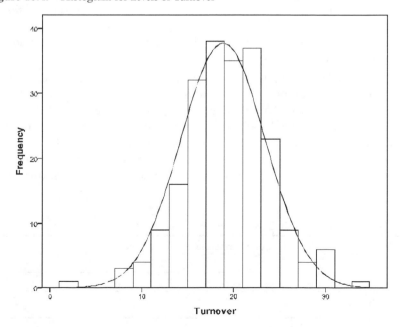

Figure 10.5:   Normal Q-Q Plot of Levels of Turnover

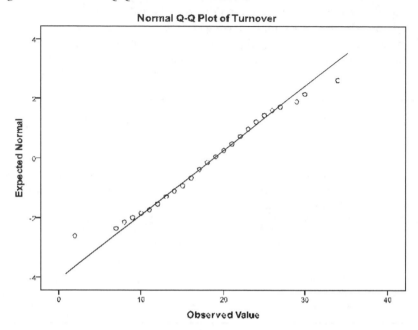

Evaluation of the Pearson's skewness coefficient [(18.83 − 19.00)/4.61 = −.04] and Fisher's skewness coefficient (−.007/.165 = .04), and inspection of the histogram (figure 10.4) and normal Q-Q plot (figure 10.5) for the distribution of levels of turnover show that it approaches the shape of a normal curve and, thus, satisfies the assumption of normality.

2. HOMOGENEITY OF VARIANCES: The variances of all groups must be equal. To evaluate this assumption, check the results of the Levene's test of homogeneity of variance. This test can be requested along with the one-way ANOVA. Table 10.4 displays the results of the Levene's test of homogeneity of variances. Because the *p* value is greater than .05 (Sig. = .163), we conclude that there are no statistically significant differences between the variances of the three marital status groups. That is, data met the assumption of homogeneity of variances.

Table 10.4:   Levene's Test for Turnover by Marital Status

Test of Homogeneity of Variances			
Turnover			
Levene Statistic	df1	df2	Sig.
1.830	2	215	*.163*

3. SAMPLE SIZE: In this study, 218 social services employees completed the surveys. As table 10.2 above shows, we only needed forty-two subjects to detect a power of .80 for a three-group comparison, given a two-tailed alpha of .05 and a moderate effect size. In other words, our sample size exceeded the minimum requirement for a one-way ANOVA.

To conclude, data for both marital status and burnout satisfied all assumptions for the one-way ANOVA. We will also use the Kruskal-Wallis *H* test to demonstrate how to use this test and to examine whether results of both tests are consistent.

Step 4: Compute the test statistic (using SPSS).

Recall that the dependent variable is turnover (Turnover), and the independent variable is marital status (MStatus). Also, remember that marital status is classified as married = 1, single = 2, and divorced = 3 (you need this information for SPSS). Now, use SPSS to compute the test statistic.

How to compute the one-way ANOVA in SPSS. The steps used to run the one-way ANOVA are similar to the steps for the independent *t*-test. To run the one-way ANOVA in SPSS, follow these steps:

1. Open the SPSS Job Satisfaction data file.

2. Click on *Analyze* in the SPSS main toolbar, click on *Compare Means*, and click on *One-Way ANOVA* (see chapter 8, screen 8.1).

3. Scroll down in the variables list in the "One-Way ANOVA" dialog box, click on *Turnover* (dependent variable), and click on the upper arrow button to move it into the *Dependent List* box (see screen 10.1)

4. Scroll down in the variables list, click on *MStatus* (independent variable), and click on the lower arrow button to move it into the *Factor* box.

Screen 10.1:   SPSS One-Way ANOVA Main Dialog Box

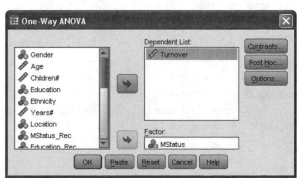

5.   Click on *Post Hoc* to choose one or more post hoc tests. This will open the "One-Way ANOVA: Post Hoc Multiple Comparisons" dialog box (see screen 10.2). These tests are organized in two groups: *Equal Variances Assumed* and *Equal Variances Not Assumed*.

Note: If you decide to use the nonparametric Kruskal-Wallis *H* test as the main test statistic under step 3, you still need to run the post hoc test(s) using the ANOVA dialog boxes since they cannot be computed along with the Kruskal-Wallis *H* test.

Screen 10.2:   SPSS One-Way ANOVA Post Hoc Multiple Comparisons Dialog Box

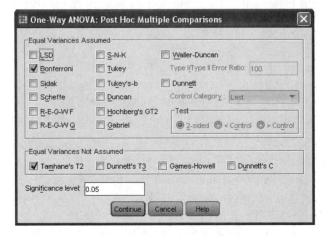

6.   Check the box corresponding with *Bonferroni* under "Equal Variances Assumed" and *Tamhane's T2* under "Equal Variances Not Assumed" (you need the *Tamhane's T2* only if the variances are not equal).

7.   Click on *Continue* to return to the "One-Way ANOVA" dialog box.

8.   Click on *Options* in the "One-Way ANOVA" dialog box. A new dialog box called "One-Way ANOVA: Options" will open (see screen 10.3).

9.   Check the boxes corresponding with *Descriptive* (this generates descriptive statistics for each group), *Homogeneity of variance test* (this is the Levene's test of homogeneity of variances), *Welch* (this is the alternative for ANOVA when equal variances are not assumed), and *Means plot* (this creates a means plot comparing the means of all groups).

10.   Click on *Continue* then click on *OK*.

Interpreting the SPSS Output of the One-Way ANOVA.   The execution of the SPSS commands generates five tables and one graph. They include

Screen 10.3:   SPSS One-Way ANOVA Options Dialog Box

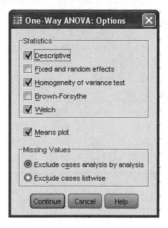

SPSS One-Way ANOVA Syntax

ONEWAY Turnover BY MStatus

/STATISTICS DESCRIPTIVES HOMOGENEITY WELCH

/PLOT MEANS

/MISSING ANALYSIS

/POSTHOC=BONFERRONI T2 ALPHA(0.05).

Note: To request another post hoc test, replace Bonferroni with that test's name, such as LSD, Scheffe, etc.

---

descriptive statistics (table 10.5), test of homogeneity of variances (table 10.4 discussed above under "Assumptions"), ANOVA (table 10.6), Welch test (table 10.7), multiple comparisons (table 10.8), and a means plot (figure 10.6). They are discussed below.

Table 10.5 displays the descriptive statistics. It conveys the number of participants (N), mean, standard deviation, standard error, 95 percent confidence interval (lower bound and upper bound), and minimum and maximum scores for turnover (dependent variable) for each marital status in the independent variable and for the sample as a whole. The table shows that of the 218 (total N = 218) participants in the study, 141 are married, forty-seven are single, and thirty are divorced. The table shows that single social services employees have the highest level of turnover ($\overline{X}$ = 19.87), followed by married ($\overline{X}$ = 19.29), then divorced ($\overline{X}$ = 15.00). Are the differences between these means statistically significant?

Table 10.6 conveys results of the overall one-way ANOVA test. The table shows the sum of square deviations (SS) (see chapter 4 for SS), the degrees of

Table 10.5:   One-Way ANOVA Descriptive—Turnover by Marital Status

Descriptives

Turnover

	N	Mean	Std. Deviation	Std. Error	95% Confidence Interval for Mean		Minimum	Maximum
					Lower Bound	Upper Bound		
Married	141	19.29	4.386	.369	18.56	20.02	8	34
Single	47	19.87	4.412	.643	18.58	21.17	10	29
Divorced	30	15.00	4.177	.763	13.44	16.56	2	27
Total	218	18.83	4.612	.312	18.21	19.44	2	34

Table 10.6:   One-Way ANOVA—Turnover by Marital Status

ANOVA

Turnover

	Sum of Squares	df	Mean Square	F	Sig.
Between Groups	521.064	2	260.532	13.681	.000
Within Groups	4094.312	215	19.043		
Total	4615.376	217			

freedom[3] (df), and the mean square deviations for both between groups (MS_B) and within groups (MS_W). The table also shows the F ratio and the level of significance (Sig., or p value). Mathematically, the F ratio is defined as the mean square between groups (MS_B) divided by the mean square within groups (MS_W); that is, $F = \frac{MS_B}{MS_W}$.

The table shows that the F ratio is 13.68 with a p value (two-tailed) of .000, which is smaller than alpha of .05. That is, the results show a significant difference between at least two groups.

Note: As with the *t*-tests, divide the p value (Sig.) by two if you have a one-tailed hypothesis.

Table 10.7 conveys the results of the Welch statistic. This is the alternative for one-way ANOVA when the assumption of homogeneity of variances is violated. As with table 10.6, the results of the Welch test show a significant difference between at least two pairs of marital status. However we do not need to report the results of Welch here since the assumption of homogeneity was satisfied.

---

[3]One-way ANOVA has two parts of degrees of freedom; one is between groups, and the other is within groups. They are (K − 1) and (N − K), respectively. K = number of groups and N = sample size. In this case, df = K − 1 and N − K = 3 − 1 and 218 − 3 = 2 and 215.

Table 10.7:   Welch Test for Unequal Variances—Turnover by Marital Status

Robust Tests of Equality of Means

Turnover

	Statistic[a]	df1	df2	Sig.
Welch	14.537	2	67.701	.000

[a]Asymptotically *F* distributed.

Now, which groups are significantly different? To find out, examine the results of the Bonferroni post hoc test (or Tamhane's T2 if you report the results of Welch statistic).

Tables 10.8 and 10.9 display the results of both Bonferroni and Tamhane's T2 post hoc multiple comparisons, respectively. Report results of Bonferroni (see table 10.8) along with the results of the one-way ANOVA when the assumption of homogeneity of variances is met. When the assumption is violated, report the results of the Tamhane's T2 (see table 10.9) along with the results of the Welch test. Reading the results of Tamhane's T2 is the same as reading the results of Bonferroni. Here we read the results of Bonferroni because the assumption of homogeneity of variances is met.

Table 10.8 conveys the results of the Bonferroni multiple comparisons for all possible marital status pairs. These pairs are shown in the first two columns [(I) MStatus and (J) MStatus]. The table has three rows corresponding with the three levels of marital status (independent variable). Each row has two lines. Each line displays the means difference for each pair (third column: Mean Difference), standard error (fourth column: Standard Error), the *p* value (fifth column: Sig.), and the 95 percent confidence interval for the means difference (last two columns: Lower Bound and Upper Bound).

Table 10.8:   Bonferroni Multiple Comparisons—Turnover by Marital Status

Multiple Comparisons

Turnover
Bonferroni

(I) MStatus	(J) MStatus	Mean Difference (I-J)	Std. Error	Sig.	95% Confidence Interval Lower Bound	95% Confidence Interval Upper Bound
Married	Single	−.582	.735	1.000	−2.36	1.19
	Divorced	4.291[*]	.877	.000	2.17	6.41
Single	Married	.582	.735	1.000	−1.19	2.36
	Divorced	4.872[*]	1.020	.000	2.41	7.33
Divorced	Married	−4.291[*]	.877	.000	−6.41	−2.17
	Single	−4.872[*]	1.020	.000	−7.33	−2.41

*The mean difference is significant at the 0.05 level.

Table 10.9: Tamhane's T2 Multiple Comparisons—Turnover by Marital Status

Multiple Comparisons

Turnover
Tamhane

(I) MStatus	(J) MStatus	Mean Difference (I-J)	Std. Error	Sig.	95% Confidence Interval	
					Lower Bound	Upper Bound
Married	Single	−.582	.742	.820	−2.39	1.23
	Divorced	4.291*	.847	.000	2.19	6.39
Single	Married	.582	.742	.820	−1.23	2.39
	Divorced	4.872*	.998	.000	2.43	7.32
Divorced	Married	−4.291*	.847	.000	−6.39	−2.19
	Single	−4.872*	.998	.000	−7.32	−2.43

*The mean difference is significant at the 0.05 level.

The first row compares married versus single (first line), and married versus divorced (second line) on their levels of turnover. The table shows the mean difference between married and single as −.58 with a standard error of .74. This means difference is not statistically significant at the .05 level (Sig. = 1.000). The first row also shows that the means difference between married and divorced is 4.29 with a standard error of .88. This means difference is statistically significant at the .05 level[4] (Sig. = .000). In other words, married social services employees reported significantly higher (because the means difference, 4.29, is positive) levels of turnover than their counterpart divorced social services employees ($p < .05$).

The second row compares single versus married (first line). This line is redundant of the first line in the first row. The second row also compares single versus divorced (second line). The table shows the means difference between the two groups as 4.87 with a standard error of 1.02 and a *p* value (Sig.) of .000. This *p* value indicates a significant difference between the two groups. In other words, single social services employees reported significantly higher (because the means difference, 4.87, is positive) levels of turnover than their counterpart divorced social services employees ($p < .05$).

The third row compares divorced versus married, and divorced versus single. These results are redundant of the first two rows. Notice that in both cases the means differences are negative and the *p* values are .000. This indicates that divorced social services employees reported significantly less levels of turnover than married and single social services employees, respectively.

The last part of the output is a means plot (see figure 10.6) displaying the mean scores for all levels of the independent variable, three marital status

---

[4]By default, results that are significant at .05 or less are marked by a single asterisk.

Figure 10.6:   Means Plot for Turnover by Marital Status

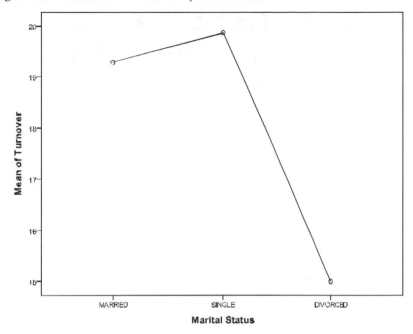

groups. As it appears in the figure, the mean score for divorced social services employees is considerably lower than the mean scores of single and married employees. The graph also shows that the mean score for married is slightly lower than the mean score for singles.

Now we illustrate how to compute the Kruskal-Wallis H test in SPSS and interpret its results.

How to compute the Kruskal-Wallis H test in SPSS.   Like with the Mann-Whitney U test (chapter 8), you need to know the numeric value associated with the first group and the numeric value associated with the last group in the independent variable. In this example, marital status (MStatus) is coded as 1 = married, 2 = single, 3 = divorced; that is, minimum = 1 and maximum = 3. To run the Kruskal-Wallis H in SPSS, follow these steps:

1. Open the SPSS Job Satisfaction data file.

2. Click on *Analyze* in the SPSS main toolbar, click on *Nonparametric Tests*, click on *Legacy Dialogs,* and click on *K Independent Samples* (see chapter 8, screen 8.5).

3. A dialog box called "Tests for Several Independent Samples" will open.

4. Scroll down in the variables list in the "Tests for Several Independent Samples" dialog box, click on *Turnover*, and click on the upper arrow button to move it into the *Test Variable List* box (see screen 10.4).

Screen 10.4:   SPSS Tests for Several Independent Samples Dialog Box

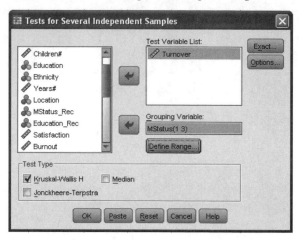

5.   Scroll down in the variables list, click on *MStatus*, and click on the lower arrow button to move it into the *Grouping Variable* box.

6.   Click on *Define Groups*, type "1" for *Minimum*, and type "3" for *Maximum* (see screen 10.5).

Screen 10.5:   SPSS Several Independent Samples Define Groups Dialog Box

7.   Click on *Continue.*

8.   Make sure that *Kruskal-Wallis H* box is checked under "Test Type." This is the SPSS default. If not checked, check it.

9.   Click *OK* on the main "Tests for Several Independent Samples" dialog box.

SPSS Kruskal-Wallis *H* Test Syntax

NPAR TESTS

/K-W=Turnover BY MStatus(1 3)

/MISSING ANALYSIS.

Interpreting the SPSS output of the Kruskal-Wallis H test. Tables 10.10 and 10.11 display the results of the Kruskal-Wallis H test generated by SPSS. These tables include descriptive statistics (mean ranks) for levels of turnover by marital status and the results of the test statistics.

Table 10.10 displays the number of participants and their mean rank for each level of the independent variable (marital status) on the dependent variable (turnover). The table shows that the mean rank for married social services employees (n = 141) is 116.18, compared to 126.83 for singles (n = 47) and 50.97 for divorced (n = 30) social services employees. Again, the question is whether the differences between these means ranks are statistically significant. The answer is found in table 10.11.

Table 10.11 conveys the results of the Kruskal-Wallis H test. Unlike the Mann-Whitney U, which uses the z distribution to calculate the means rank difference (see chapter 8, table 8.11), the Kruskal-Wallis H test uses the chi-square test to examine the overall differences between the means ranks. In this example, table 10.11 shows chi-square (χ^2) as 31.137 with two degrees of freedom.[5] The level of significance (Sig.) is .000 (two-tailed). That is, the results of Kruskal-Wallis H test show a significant difference among the three means. Which groups are significantly different?

As with one-way ANOVA, a post hoc test is needed to determine which groups are significantly different. To conduct a post hoc test, use the SPSS ANOVA menu to run either the Bonferroni or Tamhane's T2. Again, report the

Table 10.10: Means Rank for Turnover by Marital Status

Ranks			
	MStatus	N	Mean Rank
Turnover	Married	141	116.18
	Single	47	126.83
	Divorced	30	50.97
	Total	218	

Table 10.11: Kruskal-Wallis H Test for Turnover by Marital Status

Test Statistics[a,b]	
	Turnover
Chi-square	31.137
df	2
Asymp. Sig.	.000

[a] Kruskal Wallis Test
[b] Grouping Variable: MStatus

---

[5] df = K − 1, where K = number of groups. In this case, df = K − 1 = 3 − 1 = 2.

results of Bonferroni if the assumption of homogeneity of variances is met and the results of Tamhane's T2 if it is not. We report here the results of Tamhane's T2 since we already reported the results of Bonferroni.

The results of the Tamhane's T2 presented in table 10.9 are similar to results for the Bonferroni presented in table 10.8. The table shows that married and single social services employees reported similar (not significant) levels of turnover (first line, first row; Sig. = .820). On the other hand, the table shows that married employees reported significantly higher levels of turnover than divorced employees (second line, first row; Sig. = .000), and that singles reported significantly higher levels of turnover than divorced (second line, second row; Sig. = .000).

Step 5: Decide whether to reject the null hypothesis.

The results of the one-way ANOVA presented in table 10.6 show an over-all significant difference in levels of turnover among married, single, and divorced social workers ($p < .001$). Therefore, reject the null hypothesis.

Note: You may report the results of the Welch test or Kruskal-Wallis *H* test, depending on which one is used to examine the means differences between the groups.

Writing the results.   As we did in the previous tests, begin the results of the one-way ANOVA with a discussion of the test's assumptions, especially normality of distribution and homogeneity of variances. If data violate the assumption of normality, discuss whether data transformation is utilized and whether it improves the shape of the distribution. Also, if homogeneity of variances is not met, indicate if the results of the Welch test are reported instead of the ANOVA. Next, report the overall *F* ratio, degrees of freedom, and *p* values for the one-way ANOVA, Welch test, or the chi-square and *p* values for the Kruskal-Wallis *H* test. Then report the results of the post hoc test and the mean and standard deviation for each group. Finally, present the results in summary tables and perhaps a means plot. In our example, the results of the one-way ANOVA are as follows:

We utilized the one-way ANOVA to examine whether there were statisti-cally significant differences in the levels of turnover among social services employees based on their marital status (married, single, and divorced). At the beginning, data were inspected for normality and homogeneity of variances. Evaluation of measures of skewness and reviewing the histogram and normal Q-Q plot for the distribution of turnover indicated that it approached the shape of a normal curve. Moreover, the results of the Levene's test of homogeneity of variances showed no significant difference between the groups with regard to their variance ($F = 1.83; p > .05$).

Note: You may state that "the Kruskal-Wallis test was utilized because" normality was violated, transformation was not successful to fix the shape of the distribution, the dependent variable was measured at the ordinal level of measurement, and/or the sample size was too small to conduct the one-way ANOVA.

The results of the one-way ANOVA show an overall significant difference between married, single, and divorced social services employees with regard to their levels of turnover ($F_{(df=2,215)}$ = 13.68, $p < .001$).

The Bonferroni post hoc test was conducted to evaluate pairwise differences between married, single, and divorced social services employees on their levels of turnover. The results of the Bonferroni test show that divorced social services employees reported significantly ($p < .05$) lower levels of turnover ($\bar{X}$ = 15.00) than their counterpart married employees ($\bar{X}$ – 19.29) or single employees ($\bar{X}$ = 19.87). On the other hand, no significant difference was detected between single and married social services employees with regard to levels of turnover (mean difference = .58). These results were supported by the results of Kruskal-Wallis H ($\chi^2_{(df = 2)}$ = 31.14; $p < .001$) and the Tamhane's T2 tests.

Presentation of results in summary table and graph.   Unlike the independent *t*-test, analysis of variance requires two tests to examine the means differences: a one-way ANOVA and a post hoc test. Accordingly, the results of these tests should be presented in two tables, respectively. First, report the results of the one-way ANOVA in a summary table that displays the sources of variability (between-groups, within-groups, and total), their sum of squares of variation (SS), degrees of freedom (df), and mean squares of variations (MS) followed by the overall F ratio and p value. In the second table, report the number of cases, mean, and standard deviation for each level of the independent variable and the sample as a whole. The table should also report the mean difference for each pair of groups and indicate significant differences. These values can be found in tables 10.5 and 10.8, respectively. Lastly, to help readers visualize these results, present group means in a graph. Tables 10.12 and 10.13 and figure 10.6 (above) present the results of the one-way ANOVA and Bonferroni post hoc test.

Table 10.12:   One-Way ANOVA Summary Table—Turnover by Marital Status

Source	SS	df	MS	F	p^*
Between Groups	521.06	2	260.532	13.68	<.001
Within Groups	4094.31	215	19.043		
Total	4615.38	217			

*Two-tailed p.

Table 10.13:   Bonferroni Multiple Comparisons —Turnover by Marital Status

Variable	N	Mean	SD	Mean Difference		
				Married	Single	Divorced
Turnover	218	18.83	4.61			
Married	141	19.29	4.39	——		
Single	47	19.87	4.41	–.58	——	
Divorced	30	15.00	4.18	4.29*	4.87*	——

*$p < .001$.

Example 2: Job Satisfaction by Location by Supervision (One-Way ANCOVA)

We will use the SPSS Job Satisfaction data file (appendix A) and follow steps in hypothesis testing to examine the difference between social services employees employed in the north, south, and center districts with regard to their levels of job satisfaction while removing (controlling for) the effect of quality of supervision on job satisfaction. That is, we will examine the following research question:

RESEARCH QUESTION: Are there statistically significant differences in levels of job satisfaction (Satisfaction) among social services employees based on location of employment (Location: north, south, and center) while controlling for the effect of quality of supervision?

Step 1: State the null and alternative hypotheses.

H_0: Controlling for the effect of quality of supervision, there are no statistically significant differences between social services employees in the north (μ'_N), south (μ'_S), and center (μ'_C) with regard to levels of job satisfaction.

$\mu'_N = \mu'_S = \mu'_C$, adjusted group means are equal

H_a: Controlling for the effect of quality of supervision, there are statistically significant differences between social services employees in the north (μ'_N), south (μ'_S), and center (μ'_C) with regard to levels of job satisfaction.

$\mu'_N \neq \mu'_S \neq \mu'_C$, adjusted group means are not equal for at least two locations

In this two-tailed research hypothesis, location (Location) is the independent variable, job satisfaction (Satisfaction) is the dependent variable, and quality of supervision (Supervision) is the control variable.

Step 2: Set the criteria for rejecting the null hypothesis.
Set alpha at .05 ($\alpha = .05$). Reject H_0 only if $p \leq .05$.

Step 3: Select the appropriate statistical test.

In this research hypothesis, the independent variable (location) is a nominal level of measurement and consists of three groups (north, south, and center), the dependent variable (job satisfaction) is continuous data and is measured at the interval level of measurement, and the covariate is also continuous data and is measured at the interval level of measurement. These are the basic requirements for the one-way ANCOVA. However, before utilizing the one-way ANCOVA in hypothesis testing, we must ensure that data satisfy the assumptions of normality, linearity, homogeneity of variances, homogeneity of regression, and sample size. The following evaluate these assumptions:

1. NORMALITY OF DISTRIBUTIONS: The shape of the distribution of job satisfaction (dependent variable) and quality of supervision (control variable) should approach that of a normal curve. To evaluate this assumption, compute measures of skewness and create histograms and normal Q-Q plots for job satisfaction and quality of supervision.

   In chapter 5, we evaluated the shape of the distribution of quality of supervision and found it to be severely skewed to the left (see chapter 5, table 5.3 and figures 5.11 and 5.12). Then, we reversed the distribution and transformed it to the square root. Evaluation of the transformed distribution revealed a distribution with a normal curve (see chapter 5, table 5.5 and figures 5.15 and 5.16). Thus, we will use the square root of supervision (SQRT_Super) in our current one-way ANCOVA.

   Now, we evaluate the shape of the distribution of job satisfaction. Table 10.14 and figures 10.7 and 10.8 display the descriptive statistics and graphs for job satisfaction. Evaluation of both Pearson's skewness coefficient [(66.16 − 67.00)/8.83 = −.10] and Fisher's skewness coefficient (−.392/.165 = −2.38),

Table 10.14:   Descriptive Statistics for Job Satisfaction

			Statistic	Std. Error
Satisfaction	Mean		66.16	.598
	95% Confidence	Lower Bound	64.98	
	Interval for Mean	Upper Bound	67.37	
	5% Trimmed Mean		66.37	
	Median		67.00	
	Variance		77.887	
	Std. Deviation		8.825	
	Minimum		39	
	Maximum		85	
	Range		46	
	Interquartile Range		11	
	Skewness		−.392	.165
	Kurtosis		.148	.328

Figure 10.7:   Histogram for Job Satisfaction

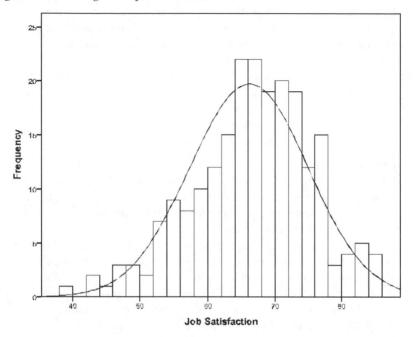

Figure 10.8:   Normal Q-Q Plot of Job Satisfaction

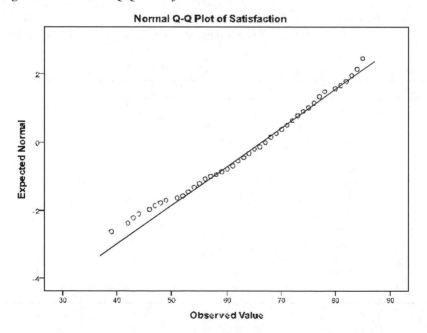

and a review of the histogram (see figure 10.7) and normal Q-Q plot (see figure 10.8) for the distribution of job satisfaction show that the shape of the distribution approaches the shape of a normal curve, with minor departure from normality perhaps due to some minor outlier case in the lower end of the distribution. Thus, we conclude that the shape of the distribution of job satisfaction satisfies the assumption of normality.

2. HOMOGENEITY OF VARIANCES: The variances of all locations on job satisfaction must be equal. To evaluate this assumption, check the results of Levene's test of homogeneity of variance.

    Table 10.15 displays the results of the Levene's test of equality of error variances for job satisfaction by location of employment while controlling for quality of supervision (SQRT_Super). The results of the Levene's test of equality of error variances show no significant differences between the three locations of employment with regard to their variances on job satisfaction (F = 1.329, Sig. = .267; $p > .05$); thus satisfying the assumption of homogeneity of variances (we will discuss how to generate this table under "Step 4: Compute the Test Statistic").

3. SAMPLE SIZE: As we discussed under Example 1, 218 social services employees participated in the Job Satisfaction study which exceeded the minimum requirement for a one-way ANCOVA (see table 10.1).

4. ASSUMPTION OF LINEARITY: The relationship between the (square root) quality of supervision (covariate) and job satisfaction (dependent variable) should be linear. To examine this assumption, we inspect the results of the Pearson's correlation coefficient and look at the scatterplot of both variables (see chapter 7 for Pearson's correlation and scatterplot).

    Table 10.16 conveys the Pearson's correlation coefficient between job satisfaction and (square root) quality of supervision. Figure 10.9 is a scatterplot displaying these results. The table and scatterplot show a significant negative linear relationship between job satisfaction and quality of supervision.[6] Notice that most scores fall around the fit line in figure 10.9, indicating a linear relationship.

Table 10.15:   Levene's Test for Levels of Job Satisfaction by Location

Levene's Test of Equality of Error Variances[a]			
Dependent Variable: Satisfaction			
F	df1	df2	Sig.
1.329	2	210	.267

Tests the null hypothesis that the error variance of the dependent variable is equal across groups.
[a]Design: Intercept + SQRT_Super + Location

---

[6]Remember that since supervision was reversed, the interpretation was reversed also; that is, the higher the score, the lower quality of supervision.

Table 10.16:   Correlation between Job Satisfaction and Supervision

Correlations

		Satisfaction	SQRT_Super
Satisfaction	Pearson Correlation	1.00	
	Sig. (2-tailed)		
	N	218	
SQRT_Super	Pearson Correlation	−.356[**]	1.00
	Sig. (2-tailed)	.000	
	N	214	214

**Correlation is significant at the 0.01 level (2-tailed).

Figure 10.9:   Scatterplot for Job Satisfaction and Square Root of Supervision

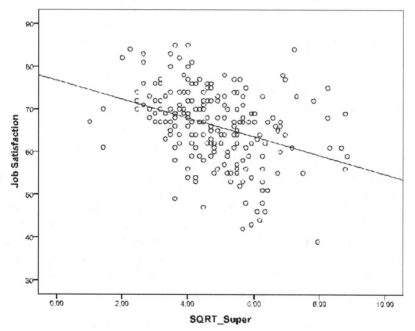

5. HOMOGENEITY OF REGRESSION: The relationship between job satisfaction (dependent variable) and quality of supervision (covariate) should be the same for all three locations (independent variable).

To evaluate this assumption, examine the results of the SPSS Univariate General Linear Model custom table and look for a p value greater than .05 for location (independent variable) by square root of supervision (dependent variable). Table 10.17 conveys the results of the ANCOVA custom table (we will discuss how to generate this table under the next step).

Table 10.17:   ANCOVA Custom Table—Homogeneity of Regression

Tests of Between-Subjects Effects

Dependent Variable: Satisfaction

Source	Type III Sum of Squares	df	Mean Square	F	Sig.
Corrected Model	3090.079[a]	5	618.016	9.601	.000
Intercept	85156.568	1	85156.568	1322.942	.000
Location	.737	2	.368	.006	.994
SQRT_Super	1901.609	1	1901.609	29.542	.000
Location * SQRT_Super	89.461	2	44.731	.695	.500
Error	13324.399	207	64.369		
Total	946620.000	213			
Corrected Total	16414.479	212			

[a]R Squared = .188 (Adjusted R Squared = .169)

We are only interested in the results of the fifth row under Source: Location * SQRT_Super. This row examines if there is a significant interaction between the independent variable (Location) and the control variable (SQRT_Super) on the dependent variable (Satisfaction). The table shows that the p value is greater than .05 (Sig.: last column, fifth row = .500).

In other words, there is no statistically significant interaction between location of employment and quality of supervision among social services employees with regard to their job satisfaction. Since the p value is greater than .05, we conclude that the relationship between job satisfaction and quality of supervision is the same for all three locations. That is, the assumption of homogeneity of regression is fulfilled.

> *Note*: If the assumption is violated (that is, $p < .05$), STOP! ANCOVA is not the right test. Consider conducting multiple regression analysis by treating the covariate as a second independent variable. Or, recode the covariate to a categorical variable and conduct a two-way ANOVA.

To sum up, data for job satisfaction by location of employment and quality of supervision met the assumptions for one-way ANCOVA. Now, compute the test statistic.

Step 4: Compute the test statistic (using SPSS).

As we said, in this example the dependent variable is job satisfaction (Satisfaction), the independent variable is location of employment (Location), and the covariate is quality of supervision (SQRT_Super). Now use SPSS to compute the test statistic. First, we will demonstrate how to use SPSS to examine the assumptions of homogeneity of regression.

How to use SPSS to examine the assumption of homogeneity of regression.   To use SPSS to examine this assumption, follow these SPSS steps:

1. Open the SPSS Job Satisfaction data file.

2. Click on *Analyze* in the SPSS main toolbar, scroll down, click on *General Linear Model*, and click on *Univariate* (see screen 10.6).

Screen 10.6:   SPSS General Linear Model Main Menu

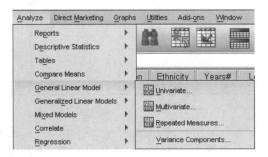

3. In the main "Univariate" dialog box, scroll down in the variables list, click on *Satisfaction* (dependent variable), and click on the upper arrow button to move it into the *Dependent Variable* box (see screen 10.7).

4. Scroll down in the variables list, click on *Location* (independent variable), and click on the second arrow button to move it into the *Fixed Factor(s)* box.

5. Scroll down in the variables list, click on *SQRT_Super* (Control variable), and click on the fourth arrow button to move it into the *Covariate(s)* box.

Screen 10.7:   SPSS Univariate Main Dialog Box

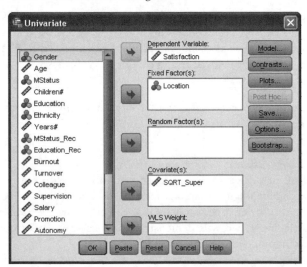

6. Click on *Model* at the upper right corner, then check *Custom* under "Specify Model" in the "Univariate: Model" dialog box (see screen 10.8).

7. Click on *Location* in the *Factors and Covariates* box and click on the arrow under "Build Term(s)" to move it into the *Model* box. Repeat this step to move *SQRT_Super* in the *Model* box.

8. While holding down the control button on the keyboard, click on *Location* and *SQRT*_Super, then click on the arrow to move both into the *Model* box.

9. Click on *Continue* and click *OK*.

Screen 10.8:   SPSS Univariate Custom Model Dialog Box

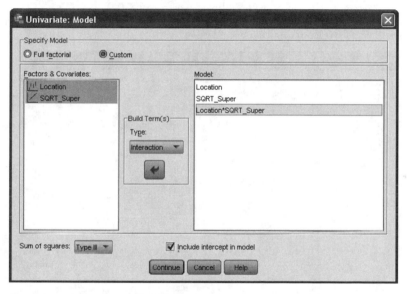

```
              SPSS Homogeneity of Regression Syntax

UNIANOVA Satisfaction BY Location WITH SQRT_Super
/METHOD=SSTYPE(3)
/INTERCEPT=INCLUDE
/CRITERIA=ALPHA(.05)
/DESIGN=Location SQRT_Super
Location*SQRT_Super.
```

The execution of these SPSS commands produces two tables. The first is labeled as "Between-Subjects Factors." It only displays the number of subjects in each level of the independent variable (Location). The second table is labeled as

"Tests of Between-Subjects Effects." It tests the assumption of homogeneity of regression, which was already discussed (see table 10.17). Now, we use SPSS to compute the one-way ANCOVA.

How to compute ANCOVA in SPSS.   To use SPSS to compute the one-way ANCOVA, follow these steps:

1.   Follow steps 1 to 6 above to enter the dependent, independent, and covariate in their respective boxes, and to open the "Univariate: Model" dialog box.

2.   Click on *Full Model* under "Specify Model." This will dim all variables in *Factors & Covariates* and *Model* boxes (see screen 10.9).

Screen 10.9:   SPSS Univariate Full Model Dialog Box

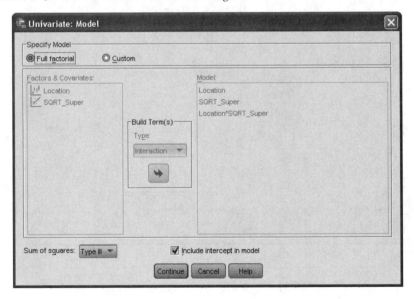

3.   Click on *Continue* to return to the main "Univariate" dialog box.

4.   Click on *Options*. A new dialog box called "Univariate: Options" will open (see screen 10.10).

5.   Click on *Overall* in the *Factor(s) and Factor Interactions* box and click on the arrow to move it in the *Display Means for* box. Repeat step to move *Location* into the *Display Means for* box.

6.   Check the *Compare main effects* box.

7.   Click on the drop down arrow under *Confidence interval adjustment* and click on *Bonferroni* (this is the post hoc test in ANCOVA).

8.   Check the boxes associated with *Descriptive statistics*, *Estimates of effect size*, and *Homogeneity tests* under "Display."

Screen 10.10:   SPSS Univariate Options Dialog Box

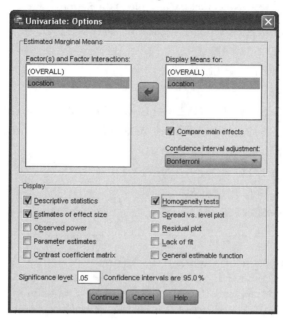

9.   Click on *Continue* to return to the "Univariate" dialog box, then click on *Plots*. This opens a "Univariate Profile Plots" dialog box (see screen 10.11).

10.   Click on *Location* and move it into the *Horizontal Axis* box, then click on *Add* to add location in the *Plots* box.

11.   Click on *Continue* and click *OK*.

Screen 10.11:   SPSS Univariate Profile Plots Dialog Box

SPSS One-Way ANCOVA Syntax

UNIANOVA Satisfaction BY Location WITH SQRT_Super

/METHOD=SSTYPE(3)

/INTERCEPT=INCLUDE

/PLOT=PROFILE(Location)

/EMMEANS=TABLES(OVERALL) WITH(SQRT_Super=MEAN)

/EMMEANS=TABLES(Location) WITH(SQRT_Super=MEAN)

COMPARE ADJ(BONFERRONI)

/PRINT=ETASQ HOMOGENEITY DESCRIPTIVE

/CRITERIA=ALPHA(.05)

/DESIGN=SQRT_Super Location.

Interpreting the SPSS output of the one-way ANCOVA.   The execution of the SPSS commands generates eight tables and one graph. Two of these tables are unnecessary and thus not discussed. The remaining SPSS outputs include descriptive statistics (see table 10.18), Levene's test of equality of error variances (see table 10.15 discussed above under assumptions), tests of between-subjects effects—ANCOVA (see table 10.19), grand mean (see table 10.20), estimates (see table 10.21), pairwise comparisons (see table 10.22), and a means plot (see figure 10.10). These are the following:

Table 10.18 conveys the descriptive statistics for job satisfaction based on participants' location of employment. It displays the actual mean for each group (unadjusted means). The table shows the mean (second column: Mean), standard deviation (third column: Standard Deviation), and number of cases (fourth column: N) for each location (First Column, Location: North, Center, and South) and for the entire sample (Total). As it appears in the table, social services employees in the south have the highest level of job satisfaction ($\bar{X} = 68.42$, SD = 8.662), followed by employees in the center ($\bar{X} = 64.72$, SD = 8.817), and then employees in the north ($\bar{X} = 63.02$, SD = 7.875). Now, adjusting for employees'

Table 10.18:   Descriptive Statistics—Unadjusted Means

Descriptive Statistics

Dependent Variable: Satisfaction

Location	Mean	Std. Deviation	N
North	63.02	7.875	51
Center	64.72	8.817	60
South	68.42	8.662	102
Total	66.08	8.799	213

quality of supervision, are there statistically significant differences between these means? Table 10.19 examines this question.

Table 10.19 displays the results of the one-way ANCOVA. It has seven columns, all of which provide valuable information about the relationship between the independent, dependent, and control variables. These are the source of variations (first column: Source), sum of square deviations (second column: Type III Sum of Squares), degrees of freedom (third column: df), mean square deviations (fourth column: Mean Square), F ratio (fifth column: F), level of significance (sixth column: Sig.), and the proportion of variance explained by each source (seventh column: Partial Eta Squared), symbolized as η^2 (eta squared). The table also has seven rows corresponding with sources of variability: Corrected Model, Intercept, SQRT_Super, Location, Error, Total, and Corrected Total. We are only interested in the results of two rows. These are as follows:

SQRT_Super Row: This row displays the results of the one-way ANCOVA for the covariate (quality of supervision). It examines the relationship between quality of supervision and job satisfaction (dependent variable). The results show a significant relationship between the two variables ($F = 28.859, p = .000$ which is smaller than .05). Recall that this is one of the assumptions for ANCOVA (assumption of linearity). Partial eta squared conveys the proportion (%) of variance in the dependent variable that is accounted for by the corresponding source of variability. It is equivalent to the coefficient of determination in correlations (see chapter 7). In this case, quality of supervision (covariate) accounted for 12.1 percent of the variance in job satisfaction (partial eta squared = .121).

Location Row: This row displays the results of the one-way ANCOVA for the independent variable (Location). It examines the null hypothesis that the adjusted job satisfaction mean scores for the three locations are equal (not significantly different). The results of this row show significant differences between at least two locations with regard to job satisfaction ($F = 7.227, p = .001$, which is smaller than .05) and thus the null hypothesis should be rejected. Partial eta

Table 10.19:   Tests of Between-Subjects Effects—One-way ANCOVA

Tests of Between-Subjects Effects

Dependent Variable: Satisfaction

Source	Type III Sum of Squares	df	Mean Square	F	Sig.	Partial Eta Squared
Corrected Model	3000.618[a]	3	1000.206	15.584	.000	.183
Intercept	94360.302	1	94360.302	1470.218	.000	.876
SQRT_Super	1852.175	1	1852.175	28.859	.000	.121
Location	927.693	2	463.847	7.227	.001	.065
Error	13413.861	209	64.181			
Total	946620.000	213				
Corrected Total	16414.479	212				

[a] R Squared = .183 (Adjusted R Squared = .171)

squared indicates that location (independent variable) accounted for 6.5 percent of the variance in job satisfaction after controlling for quality of supervision (partial eta squared = .065).

Table 10.19 also displays the total proration of variance in the dependent variable that is accounted by the ANCOVA model in the last line as footnote a (R squared = .183). In this example, both quality of supervision and location of employment accounted for 18.3 percent of the variance in job satisfaction.

Table 10.20 displays the adjusted grand (total) mean for levels of job satisfaction. The table shows that the mean of job satisfaction after removing the effect of quality of supervision is 65.45, slightly below the actual grand mean reported in Table 10.18 (total mean = 66.08).

Table 10.21 displays the adjusted mean score for levels of job satisfaction for each location (north, center, and south). It also reports the standard error and the 95th confidence interval for each location. Notice that these means are slightly, but not significantly, different than those means reported in table 10.18 after controlling for the effect of quality of supervision.

Table 10.22 reports the results of the Bonferroni post hoc test. It is similar to table 10.8 in one-way ANOVA. Here, however, it examines the means differences in job satisfaction after removing the effect of quality of supervision on job satisfaction. The table shows a significant difference between north and south (first row, second line: Sig. = .002) with north experiencing lower levels of job satisfaction than south (first row, second line: Mean Difference = −4.859). The table also shows a significant difference between center and south (second row, second line: Sig. = .032) with center also experiencing lower levels of job

Table 10.20: Adjusted Grand (Total) Mean

Grand Mean

Dependent Variable: Satisfaction

Mean	Std. Error	95% Confidence Interval	
		Lower Bound	Upper Bound
65.455[a]	.573	64.324	66.585

[a]Covariates appearing in the model are evaluated at the following values: SQRT_Super = 4.8267.

Table 10.21: Adjusted Group Means

Estimates

Dependent Variable: Satisfaction

Location	Mean	Std. Error	95% Confidence Interval	
			Lower Bound	Upper Bound
North	63.335[a]	1.123	61.121	65.550
Center	64.834[a]	1.034	62.795	66.874
South	68.194[a]	.794	66.628	69.760

[a]Covariates appearing in the model are evaluated at the following values: SQRT_Super = 4.8267.

Table 10.22: Bonferroni Post Hoc Pairwise Comparison

Pairwise Comparisons

Dependent Variable: Satisfaction

(I) Location	(J) Location	Mean Difference (I-J)	Std. Error	Sig.ᵃ	95% Confidence Interval for Differenceᵃ	
					Lower Bound	Upper Bound
North	Center	−1.499	1.526	.982	−5.182	2.185
	South	−4.859*	1.378	.002	−8.184	−1.534
Center	North	1.499	1.526	.982	−2.185	5.182
	South	−3.360*	1.305	.032	−6.510	−.211
South	North	4.859*	1.378	.002	1.534	8.184
	Center	3.360*	1.305	.032	.211	6.510

Based on estimated marginal means

ᵃAdjustment for multiple comparisons: Bonferroni.

*The mean difference is significant at the .05 level.

satisfaction than south (second row, second line: Mean Difference = −3.360). No significant difference, however, is detected between north and center with regard to their levels of job satisfaction (first row, first line: Mean Difference = −1.499, Sig. = .982).

The last part of the SPSS output is a means plot displayed in figure 10.10. It provides a visual picture of what is going on with our study. The line represents

Figure 10.10: Adjusted Means Plot

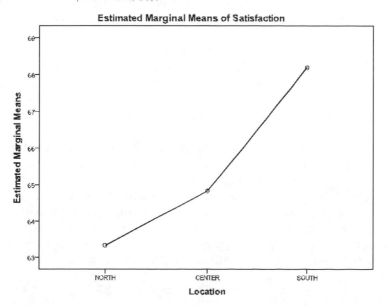

the estimated marginal means for levels of job satisfaction for each location. As we see, social services employees in the south have the highest level of job satisfaction, followed by employees in the center, and then in the north. These means correspond to those found in table 10.20.

Step 5: Decide whether to reject the null hypothesis.

The results of the one-way ANCOVA presented in table 10.19 show a significant difference between social services employees in at least two locations of employment with regard to their job satisfaction while controlling for their quality of supervision ($p < .001$). Therefore, we reject the null hypothesis.

Writing the results.   Similar to the one-way ANOVA and other test statistics, begin the results of the one-way ANCOVA with a statement about data evaluation and whether assumptions are fulfilled. In particular, discuss the assumptions of normality, linearity, homogeneity of variances, and homogeneity of regression. Then, report the overall F ratio, degrees of freedom, and p values for both covariate and independent variable. Next, report the results of the post hoc test and the adjusted mean and standard error for each group. Finally, present the results in summary tables and a means plot. In our example, the results of the one-way ANCOVA can be presented as follows:

The one-way analysis of covariance (ANCOVA) was utilized to examine the differences in levels of job satisfaction among social services employees based on their location of employment (north, center, and south) while controlling for quality of supervision. A preliminary evaluation of measures of skewness, histograms, and normal Q-Q plots indicated that job satisfaction (dependent variable) was normally distributed. However, the covariate, quality of supervision, had severe negative skewness and thus was reversed and then transformed to the square root. Evaluation of the square root of supervision revealed a normal distribution.

Next, the results of the Pearson's correlation and the scatterplot showed a linear relationship between job satisfaction and square root of supervision, indicating the assumption of linearity was met. In addition, the assumptions of homogeneity of variances and regression were fulfilled as indicated by the results of the Levene's test ($F = .498, p = .777$) and the one-way ANCOVA custom table ($F = 2.079, p > .05$), respectively.

The results of the one-way ANCOVA show overall significant differences in levels of job satisfaction among social services employees based on their location of employment after adjusting for the effect of their quality of supervision ($F_{(df=2,209)} = 28.86, p < .001$). However, location accounted only for 6.5 percent of the variance in job satisfaction ($\eta^2 = .065$). Overall, about 18 percent of the variance in job satisfaction was accounted for by this model ($R^2 = .18$).

The Bonferroni multiple comparisons post hoc test was utilized to examine what locations were significantly different regarding their adjusted levels of job

Table 10.23: One-Way ANCOVA Summary Table—Job Satisfaction by Location Controlling for Supervision

Source of Variability	SS	df	MS	F	p*
Supervision (Covariate)[a]	1852.175	1	1852.175	28.859	< .001
Location[b]	927.693	2	463.847	7.227	< .010
Error	13413.861	209	64.181		
Total	16414.479	212			

*Two-tailed p.
[a]η^2 = .121.
[b]η^2 = .065.

Table 10.24: Bonferroni Multiple Comparisons—Job Satisfaction by Location Controlling for Supervision

Variable	N	Mean	Adjusted Mean	Mean Difference North	Center	South
Job Satisfaction	213	66.08	65.46			
North	51	63.02	63.34	——		
Center	60	64.72	64.83	−1.50	——	
South	102	68.42	68.19	−4.86**	−3.36*	——

**p < .01, *p < .05.

satisfaction. The results of the Bonferroni test show that social services employees in the north ($\overline{X}$ − 63.34) and in the center ($\overline{X}$ = 64.72) reported significantly (p < .05) lower levels of job satisfaction than employees in the south ($\overline{X}$ = 68.42). On the other hand, no significant difference was found between north and center with regard to job satisfaction (means difference = 1.50).

Presentation of results in summary tables and graph.   As with a one-way ANOVA, the results of the one-way ANCOVA should be presented in two tables (summary table and multiple comparisons table) and a graph. Unlike the one-way tables, the tables and graph should be adjusted to account for the covariate. In our example, tables 10.23 and 10.24 and figure 10.10 (above) present the results of the one-way ANCOVA.

SUMMARY

This chapter introduced the one-way analysis of variance (ANOVA) and the Kruskal-Wallis H tests; these powerful statistical techniques are extended versions of the independent t-test and the Mann-Whitney U test, respectively. They are most suitable for examining the differences between three or more groups on one outcome variable without the need for adjusting the level of significance for multiple tests. The chapter also introduced the one-way analysis of covariance

(ANCOVA). It is an extension of the one-way ANOVA that allows researchers to control for extraneous variables that are believed to affect the relationship between the independent and dependent variables.

Chapter 10 discussed the purposes and assumptions underlying the one-way ANOVA, one-way ANCOVA, and the nonparametric Kruskal-Wallis *H* test. The chapter also presented the Welch test, which is an alternative statistic to the one-way ANOVA when the assumption of homogeneity is not met.

The chapter then demonstrated how to use the one-way ANOVA and ANCOVA, Kruskal-Wallis *H* tests, and two post hoc tests, Bonferroni and Tamhane's T2, in hypothesis testing.

Chapter 10 next presented two practical examples using real social science data detailing how to utilize the SPSS program to compute the test statistics followed by a presentation of how to interpret, write, and present the results of the one-way ANOVA and ANCOVA in summary tables and graphs.

Chapter 11 introduces the chi-square test of association and the goodness-of-fit. The chapter discusses the purpose and assumptions of chi-square tests along with how to compute the statistics, interpret the output, and write and present the results.

PRACTICAL EXERCISES

Part I: Access the Elderly SPSS data file (appendix A) and examine the following research question:

Is there a statistically significant difference in the levels of emotional balance (EB) among elderly based on their marital status (MStatus)?

1. Follow the steps in hypothesis testing and examine the hypothesis. Discuss all steps in detail.

2. Present the results in summary tables and a graph.

Part II: Now control for elderly levels of depression (CESD) and re-examine the relationship between marital status and emotional balance.

1. Rewrite the research question.

2. Follow the steps in hypothesis testing and examine the hypothesis. Discuss all steps in detail.

3. Are there any differences between these results and those in Part I?

4. Write the SPSS syntax for the test statistic.

5. Present the results in summary tables and a graph.

CHAPTER 11

Chi-Square Tests: Goodness-of-Fit Test and Test of Association

LEARNING OBJECTIVES

1. Understand the purpose of the chi-square goodness-of-fit-test
2. Understand the purpose of the chi-square test of association
3. Understand the contingency table
4. Understand the difference between observed and expected frequencies
5. Understand the assumptions of the chi-square tests
6. Understand the *phi* and Cramer's *V* coefficients
7. Understand how to use SPSS to create a contingency table and compute the test statistics
8. Understand how to interpret and present the results of the test statistics

DATA SET (APPENDIX A)

Elderly

Job Satisfaction

Well-Being

INTRODUCTION

So far, this book has presented a number of parametric and nonparametric tests that examine the relationships between one independent variable or a constant (given score) and one dependent variable. Tests such as the independent *t*-test, Mann-Whitney *U*, one-way ANOVA/ANCOVA, and Kruskal-Wallis *H* require a categorical independent variable (nominal), while others such as the Pearson's *r* correlation, Spearman's *rho* correlation, one-sample case *t*-test, dependent *t*-test, and Wilcoxon signed ranks test require a continuous independent variable (ordinal or higher) or a constant in the case of the one-sample case *t*-test. All these tests, however, share one requirement; the dependent variable must be continuous data and is measured at the ordinal level of measurement or higher.

None of these tests is appropriate when the dependent variable consists of categorical data; that is, nominal variables.

Sometimes, however, social science researchers are interested in the association (relationship) between two categorical variables, one dependent and one independent or constant. Consider these two cases:

CASE 1: In the Job Satisfaction study (appendix A), the researcher was interested to find out if social services employees who participated in the study represent the population from which they were selected. For this purpose, the researcher decides to compare participants' levels of education (B.A./B.S.W., M.A., and other) and ethnicity (Arab and Jewish) observed in his study, with the overall levels of education and ethnicity of social services employees known in the general population.

CASE 2: The researcher of the Well-Being study (appendix A) was interested to find out if there is an association between participants' gender (male and female) or race (African American, Caucasian, and other) and their body mass index (BMI: under weight, normal weight, overweight, and obese).

All variables in both cases consist of categorical (nominal) data (education, ethnicity, gender, race, and BMI); each with two or more groups or levels. In case 1, the distribution of one observed variable (education or ethnicity) is compared with a known, given distribution of the same variable in the population (education or ethnicity). In this case, the researcher wants to examine this research question: is there a statistically significant difference between the sample and the population with regard to their levels of education and ethnicity?

On the other hand, in case 2, the researcher is interested in the relationship between two observed variables, (gender and BMI), and whether this relationship can be generalized to the population. Here, the researcher wants to examine this research question: is there a statistically significant association (relationship) between participants' gender and their BMI in the population? Now, the question is: what test statistic(s) are most suitable to examine each research question?

This chapter begins with a presentation of the chi-square goodness-of-fit and test of association and their purposes, followed by the contingency table. Next, the chapter discusses the underlying assumptions of the test statistics and presents the *phi* and Cramer's *V* measures of association. The chapter then presents two practical examples illustrating in detail how to create contingency tables and compute both chi-square test statistics and levels of significance in SPSS. The chapter also discusses how to interpret, write, and present the results of chi-square test statistics in tables.

CHI-SQUARE TEST

The chi-square (pronounced "kai") test is probably the most used nonparametric test in social science research. It is also known as Pearson's chi-square test, named after Karl Pearson (1857–1936), who also developed the Pearson's correlation test and other statistics. It is symbolized by the Greek letter χ^2.

Chi-square test can be used to compare the distribution of one variable with a known distribution or the relationship (association) between two variables. In a sense, it is similar to the Student's *t*-test, one-sample case *t*-test, and two-sample case *t*-test. Unlike the Student's *t*-test, variables to be analyzed by chi-square must be categorical variables. Two chi-square tests are discussed, chi-square goodness-of-fit test and chi-square test of association.

CHI-SQUARE GOODNESS-OF-FIT TEST

The purpose of the chi-square goodness-of-fit test is to examine the distribution of one categorical variable observed in a sample with a theoretical or a known distribution in the population. In other words, it examines whether there are statistically significant differences between the frequency of each level of the categorical variable (e.g., males and females) and the corresponding frequency in the population. The latter is called "expected frequency" (discussed later in this chapter). In a sense, chi-square goodness-of-fit examines how well a sample *fits* the population. Therefore, like the one-sample case *t*-test, the chi-square goodness-of-fit can be used to examine whether a sample represents the population.

Mathematically, the chi-square goodness-of-fit test compares the observed frequency of each level in the dependent variable with its corresponding expected frequency in the population. The larger the difference between the observed and expected frequencies (also known as residuals or errors) is, the larger the chi-square value and the smaller the level of significance (*p* value).

For example, the chi-square test can be used to examine the research question in Case 1; that is, if there are statistically significant differences between the frequency of each level of education or each ethnicity observed in the sample and those corresponding frequencies known in the population, respectively.

The chi-square goodness-of-fit test is an alternative test to the Anderson-Darling and the Kolmogorov-Smirnov goodness-of-fit tests (not covered in this book), which are used with continuous distributions. The Binomial test is another alternative to the chi-square goodness-of-fit test, however, it is used with dichotomous data (only two groups).[1]

CHI-SQUARE TEST OF ASSOCIATION

The purpose of the chi-square test of association is to examine the association (relationship) between two variables (independent and dependent) measured at the nominal level of measurement. It examines the frequency of each level of the dependent variable (e.g., BMI) on each level of the independent variable (gender) and whether these frequencies (observed frequencies) are significantly different from those frequencies expected (expected frequencies) in the population. Again, the larger the difference (residual) between the observed and expected frequencies is, the larger the chi-square value and the smaller the level of significance.

---

[1] See Siegel & Castellan (1988).

For example, the chi-square test of association can be utilized to examine the research question in case 2; that is, if the observed frequencies of BMI by gender in Case 2 are significantly different from their corresponding expected frequencies.

Unlike the chi-square goodness-of-fit test, expected frequencies for the chi-square test of association are unknown and therefore must be estimated based on the actual observed frequencies. To better help you understand the process of estimating the expected frequencies and the terminology used by chi-square tests, we first must discuss the contingency table.

CONTINGENCY TABLE

A contingency table, also called a cross-tabs table, cross-tabulation, chi-square table, or two-way table, is a frequency table that presents the observed frequencies of one categorical variable (dependent variable) as a function of another categorical variable (independent variable). A contingency table presents the frequencies of two categorical variables simultaneously (e.g., BMI by gender).

Constructing a Contingency Table

To construct a contingency table, first list all the values (groups) in the first variable in the rows of the table (also called row variable) and the values (groups) in the second variable in the columns (also called column variable). Second, find the frequency for each cell (intersection). Third, sum all cell frequencies for each row and place it in the corresponding row margin. Fourth, sum all cell frequencies for each column and place it in the corresponding column margin. Fifth, sum all row margins, as well as all column margins. The sum of all row margins and the sum of all column margins each should equal the number of all cases in the sample size (N).

Example: Table 11.1 displays the frequencies for BMI by gender. As stated, BMI is defined as underweight (UW), normal weight (NW), overweight (OW), and obese (OB); and gender is defined as male (M) and female (F).

BMI is placed in four rows, and gender is placed in two columns. The fifth row in table 11.1 displays the total *column margins* (C_1 and C_2) and the third column displays the total *row margins* (R_1, R_2, R_3, and R_4). The joint cell of column

Table 11.1: Contingency Table—BMI by Gender

BMI	Male	Female	Total
Underweight	O_1	O_2	$R_1 = N_{UW}$
Normal weight	O_3	O_4	$R_2 = N_{NW}$
Overweight	O_5	O_6	$R_3 = N_{OW}$
Obese	O_7	O_8	$R_4 = N_{OB}$
Total	$C_1 = N_M$	$C_2 = N_F$	N

margins and row margins (N) displays the total number of cases in the study; that is, the sample size.

Each joint cell in table 11.1 displays the frequency for only one level of BMI by only one gender. For example, the joint cell of male and normal weight displays the number of males who are considered normal weight (O_3), and the joint cell of female and overweight displays the number of females who are considered overweight (O_6).

Number of cells.   The number of cells in a contingency table is determined by multiplying the number of levels (groups) in the first variable (number of rows) by the number of levels (groups) in the second variable (number of columns). In our example, because gender has two levels and BMI has four levels, the number of cells is eight cells ($2 \times 4 = 8$). The number of rows and columns is used to label a contingency table; in this example, a 2×4 table. This is especially important for computing the sample size (this will be discussed later under "Assumptions").

Row and column margins.   Each row margin represents the total number of cases within a particular row. For example, R_1 (N_{UW}) represents the first-row margin; the number of all participants who are considered underweight ($R_1 = O_1 + O_2$). R_2 (N_{NW}) represents the second-row margin; the number of all participants who are considered normal weight ($R_2 = O_3 + O_4$). R_3 (N_{OW}) represents the third-row margin; the number of all participants who are considered overweight ($R_3 = O_5 + O_6$). R_4 (N_{OB}) represents the fourth-row margin; the number of all participants who are considered obese ($R_4 = O_7 + O_8$). The sum of R_1, R_2, R_3, and R_4 is equal to the number of all cases in the study (N).

The same explanation applies to columns. Each column margin represents the total number of cases within a particular column. For example, C_1 (N_M) represents the first-column margin, the number of all participants who are males ($C_1 = O_1 + O_3 + O_5 + O_7$); and C_2 (N_F) represents the second column margin, the number of all participants who are females ($C_2 = O_2 + O_4 + O_6 + O_8$). The sum of C_1 and C_2 is equal to the number of all cases in the study (N).

Row, column, and total percentages.   Sometimes, along with the observed frequencies, it is useful to present the row, column, and total percentages for each cell. Table 11.2 is an extension of table 11.1.

In table 11.2, O stands for the observed frequency, RP stands for row percentage, CP stands for column percentage, TP stands for total percentage, and N stands for the overall number of cases in the study (sample size).

The row percentage (RP) conveys the percentage of cases in a particular cell within the corresponding row (row margin). For example, in table 11.2, RP_1 conveys the percentage of participants that are considered *underweight* who are *males*, RP_6 conveys the percentage of participants that are considered *overweight* who are *females*, and PR_7 conveys the percentage of participants that are considered *obese* who are *males*.

Table 11.2: Contingency Table—BMI by Gender

BMI	Male	Female	Total
Underweight	O_1	O_2	O_{UW}
	RP_1	RP_2	RP_{UW}
	CP_1	CP_2	CP_{UW}
	TP_1	TP_2	TP_{UW}
Normal weight	O_3	O_4	O_{NW}
	RP_3	RP_4	RP_{NW}
	CP_3	CP_4	CP_{NW}
	TP_3	TP_4	TP_{NW}
Overweight	O_5	O_6	O_{OW}
	RP_5	RP_6	RP_{OW}
	CP_5	CP_6	CP_{OW}
	TP_5	TP_6	TP_{OW}
Obese	O_7	O_8	O_{OB}
	RP_7	RP_8	RP_{OB}
	CP_7	CP_8	CP_{OB}
	TP_7	TP_8	TP_{OB}
Total	O_M	O_F	N
	RP_M	RP_F	RP_N
	CP_M	CP_F	CP_N
	TP_M	TP_F	TP_N

Note: To compute the row percentage for a specific cell, divide the number of cases in that cell by the corresponding row margin and multiply it by 100 percent. For example: $RP_4 = O_4 / O_{NW} * 100\%$.

The column percentage (CP) conveys the percentage of cases in a particular cell within the corresponding column (column margin). For example, CP_2 conveys the percentage of *females* who are considered *underweight*, CP_5 conveys the percentage of *males* who are considered *overweight*, and CP_8 conveys the percentage of *females* who are considered *obese*.

Note: To compute the column percentage for a specific cell, divide the number of cases in that cell by the corresponding column margin and multiply it by 100 percent. For example: $CP_6 = O_6 / O_F * 100\%$.

The total percentage (TP) conveys the percentage of cases in a particular cell of the total number of cases in the study (N). For example, TP_3 in table 11.2 conveys the overall percentage of *males* who are considered *normal weight*, TP_6

conveys the overall percentage of *females* who are considered *overweight*, and TP_7 conveys the overall percentage of *males* who are considered *obese*.

> *Note*: To compute the total percentage for a specific cell, divide the number of cases in that cell by the sample size (N) and multiply it by 100 percent. For example: $TP_7 = O_7 / N * 100\%$.

Example: Now we illustrate the observed frequency, row, column, and total percentages for BMI (Weight) by gender (Gender) from the Well-Being study (appendix A).

Table 11.3 displays the frequencies and percentages of levels of BMI by gender. In this table, three rows correspond with the three BMI levels (in this study, none of the participants was underweight) and two columns correspond with the two levels of gender, forming a 2 × 3 table (six cells).

Each row in table 11.3 has four lines. The first line, Count, represents the observed frequency (O) for the particular cell. For example, the frequency of the first joint cell, *Male* and *Normal weight*, is 28, which indicates that of the 182 participants in the study (*Total* with *Total*: N = 182), twenty-eight are males who are normal weight compared to sixty-five females who are normal weight (second joint cell, *Female* and *Normal weight*). Also, the third joint cell (*Male* and *Overweight*) shows that thirty-seven participants are males who are overweight, compared to twenty-five females who are overweight (fourth joint cell, *Female* and *Overweight*).

Table 11.3:   BMI by Gender

		Gender		
		Male	Female	*Total*
Normal weight	Count	28	65	93
	% within Weight	30.1%	69.9%	100.0%
	% within Gender	35.9%	62.5%	51.1%
	% of Total	15.4%	35.7%	51.1%
Overweight	Count	37	25	62
	% within Weight	59.7%	40.3%	100.0%
	% within Gender	47.4%	24.0%	34.1%
	% of Total	20.3%	13.7%	34.1%
Obese	Count	13	14	27
	% within Weight	48.1%	51.9%	100.0%
	% within Gender	16.7%	13.5%	14.8%
	% of Total	7.1%	7.7%	14.8%
Total	Count	78	104	182
	% within Weight	42.9%	57.1%	100.0%
	% within Gender	100.0%	100.0%	100.0%
	% of Total	42.9%	57.1%	100.0%

The second line, % within Weight, represents the row percentage. This conveys the percentage of cases in a particular cell within the corresponding Weight (BMI). For example, the second line in the second joint cell, *Female* and *Normal weight,* indicates that 69.9 percent of all participants who are considered normal weight (normal weight = 93) are females. That is:

row percentage = 65 / 93 × 100% = .699 × 100% = 69.9%

The third line, % within Gender, represents the column percentage. This conveys the percentage of cases in a particular cell within the corresponding gender. For example, the third line in the fifth joint cell, *Male* and *Obese*, indicates that 16.7 percent of all participants who are males (males = 78) are obese. That is:

column percentage = 13 / 78 × 100% = .167 × 100% = 16.7%

The fourth line, % of Total, represents the total percentage. This conveys the percentage of cases in a particular cell of the total number of cases (N = 182). For example, the fourth line in the fourth joint cell, *Female* and *Overweight*, indicates that 13.7 percent of all participants in the study (N = 182) are females who are overweight. That is:

total percentage = 25/182 × 100% = .318 × 100% = 13.7%

The table also displays the total count and percentages for the rows and the total count and percentages for the columns.

The *Total* rows show that ninety-three participants are normal weight (joint cell, *Normal Weight* and *Total*), sixty-two are overweight (joint cell, *Overweight* and *Total*), and twenty-seven are obese (joint cell, *Obese* and *Total*). In terms of percentages, 51.1 percent are normal weight (93/182 × 100% = 51.1%); 34.1 percent are overweight (62/182 × 100% = 34.1%), and 14.8 percent are obese (27/182 × 100% = 14.8%).

The *Total* columns show that seventy-eight participants are males (joint cell, *Male* and *Total*) and 104 are females (joint cell, *Female* and *Total*). That is, 42.9 percent of participants are males (78/182 × 100% = 42.9%) and 57.1 percent are females (104/182 × 100% = 57.1%).

Observed and expected frequencies.   Observed frequencies (O) are the actual number of cases in each cell obtained by direct observation of a sample presumed to represent the population from which it is selected. In table 11.3, Count represents the observed, actual, frequencies for each cell. For example, in the Well-Being study, the researcher observed twenty-eight males who are normal weight. Also, in the same study, the researcher observed seventy-eight males and 104 females (ratio male to female = 42.9:57.1).

Expected frequencies (E) are the frequencies or number of cases in each cell that the researcher would expect to occur if the row and column variables were unrelated and/or if the study represents the population from which it is drawn. In other words, expected frequencies are those frequencies the researcher expects if the null hypothesis is correct. In our previous example, if no association exists between BMI and gender, then the expected frequency of males who are normal weight should be 28 or close to 28. Also, if the sample represents the population from which it is selected, then the ratio of male to female in the population should be somewhat similar to that observed in the sample (42.9:57.1).

Unlike observed frequencies, expected frequencies are either hypothetical numbers, estimated by using the actual row and column margins and the total sample size from a contingency table, or known in the general population.

To illustrate computation of expected frequencies (E), use the observed frequencies of BMI and gender from table 11.3. Table 11.4 is similar to table 11.3; it displays the observed (O) frequencies, but does not present row, column, and total percentages.

The expected frequency for each cell is computed simply by multiplying the corresponding row margin by the corresponding column margin for each cell and dividing the product by the total number of cases (N). The formula for the expected frequency is as follows:

Formula for Expected Frequency

$$E_i = \frac{R_i * C_i}{N}$$

E_i = expected frequency for i^{th} cell
R_i = row margin for the ith cell
C_i = column margin for the ith cell
N = sample size

Table 11.4:   Observed Frequencies—BMI by Gender

	Gender		
	Male	Female	Total
Normal weight	$O_1 = 28$	$O_2 = 65$	$R_1 = 93$
Overweight	$O_3 = 37$	$O_4 = 25$	$R_2 = 62$
Obese	$O_5 = 13$	$O_6 = 14$	$R_3 = 27$
Total	$C_1 = 78$	$C_2 = 104$	$N = 182$

Using this formula, the expected frequencies for cell 1 to cell 6 in table 11.4 are as follows:

Formula for Expected Frequency
$$E_i = \frac{R_i * C_i}{N}$$

$E_1 = \dfrac{93 * 78}{182} = 39.9$	$E_2 = \dfrac{93 * 104}{182} = 53.1$
$E_3 = \dfrac{62 * 78}{182} = 26.6$	$E_4 = \dfrac{62 * 104}{182} = 35.4$
$E_5 = \dfrac{27 * 78}{182} = 11.6$	$E_6 = \dfrac{27 * 104}{182} = 15.4$

Table 11.5 is a reproduction of table 11.4, yet it displays, in addition to the observed frequencies, the expected frequencies, as well as the differences between the two. As is evidenced in the table, there are differences between the observed and expected frequencies in all six cells, ranging from 1.4 points to 11.9 points. For example, the table shows that the observed frequency for females who are normal weight is 65, whereas the expected frequency is 53.1, a difference of 11.9. On the other hand, the observed frequency for females who are obese is 14, whereas the expected frequency is 15.4, a difference of only 1.4. The question is, then, are these differences statistically significant? The chi-square test of association addresses this question.

Table 11.5: Observed and Expected Frequencies—BMI by Gender

		Gender		
		Male	Female	Total
Normal weight	Observed	28	65	93
	Expected	39.9	53.1	93
	Difference	−11.9	11.9	
Overweight	Observed	37	25	62
	Expected	26.6	35.4	62
	Difference	10.4	−10.4	
Obese	Observed	13	14	27
	Expected	11.6	15.4	27
	Difference	1.4	−1.4	
Total	Observed	78	104	182
	Expected	78	104	182

ASSUMPTIONS OF CHI-SQUARE TESTS

As stated, the chi-square test is a nonparametric test and, thus, does not follow the same set of assumptions for parametric tests. In other words, data need not be continuous nor approach the shape of a normal curve. On the other hand, the chi-square test makes some assumptions about the data and the sample size. These assumptions are as follows:

1. LEVEL OF MEASUREMENT: Variables under analysis must be measured at the nominal level. That is, each variable must have at least two mutually exclusive and exhaustive levels or groups.

2. INDEPENDENCY: For the chi-square test of association, the two variables must be independent one from another; that is, a response to one variable has nothing to do with a response to the other variable.

3. TYPES OF DATA: Unlike the previous test statistics, data analyzed by a chi-square test must be frequencies (number of cases for each cell), not scores. As you may recall, all previous tests examine the relationship between means (parametric tests) or means rank (nonparametric tests).

4. SAMPLE SIZE: As a rule of thumb, no more than 20 percent of cells should have expected frequencies of less than five cases per cell. For example, in a 3×5 table (total fifteen cells) no more than three cells ($15 \times 20\%$) should have expected frequencies less than five cases. All other cells (twelve cells) should have a minimum of five cases per cell. In a 2×2 table, however, all cells must have expected frequencies of five cases or more per cell.

    This assumption can be evaluated simply by inspecting the results of the chi-square tests. When data violate this assumption, it is recommended to collapse cells together, especially those with small expected frequencies. It is also recommended to use the *Yates's continuity correction* or *Fisher's exact test* to examine the association between two dichotomous variables (2×2 tables). These tests are appropriate with a small sample size and small expected frequencies.

5. SAMPLE SIZE AND POWER: When a small sample size is used, the results of the chi-square may not have an adequate power (e.g., .80). As discussed in previous chapters, power is a function of four criteria: sample size, the direction of the research hypothesis (one-tailed versus two-tailed), level of significance (alpha .05, .01, etc.), and effect size (small, moderate, or large). Cohen (1988) defines effect size (ES) for chi-square as the proportion of the difference between the observed and expected frequency: small ES = .10; moderate ES = .30; and large ES = .50. In addition to these criteria, the number of degrees of freedom entered in the analysis also impacts the sample size. In chi-square tests, number of degrees of freedom is defined as follows:

Degrees of Freedom for Chi-Square Goodness-of-Fit Test

df = (R − 1)

df = Degrees of freedom

R = Number of groups in the observed variable

Degrees of Freedom for Chi-Square Test of Association:

df = (R − 1) * (C − 1)

R = Number of groups in the first variable (row variable)

C = Number of groups in the second variable (column variable)

Table 11.6:   Sample Size for Chi-Square Tests (Power = .80; Two-Tailed Alpha)

Alpha	df = 1			df = 2			df = 3		
	ES = .10	ES = .30	ES = .50	ES = .10	ES = .30	ES = .50	ES = .10	ES = .30	ES = .50
.050	785	88	32	964	108	39	1090	122	44
.010	1168	130	47	1389	155	56	1546	172	62
.001	1708	190	69	1967	219	79	2155	240	87

For example, in the BMI by gender (table 11.3), there are three BMI groups (normal weight, overweight, and obese) and two genders (male and female). In other words, R = 3 and C = 2; that is df = (3 − 1) * (2 − 1) = 2. In a 2 × 2 table, for example, df = (2 − 1) * (2 − 1)=1.

Based on the above criteria, we used SPSS Sample Power to calculate the sample size required to achieve a power of .80 for 1 (2 × 2 table), 2 (2 × 3 table), and 3 (2 × 4 table) degrees of freedom given a two-tailed alpha of .05, and small, moderate, and large effect sizes. Table 11.6 conveys the results of SPSS Sample Power.

As it appears in table 11.6, a minimum sample size of thirty-two subjects is required to conduct a chi-square test for a 2 × 2 table (df = 1) in order to achieve a power of .80 given a two-tailed alpha of .05 and a large effect size. On the other hand, a sample size of eighty-eight cases will be needed to achieve a power of .80 for a medium effect size given other criteria held constant. Notice that the larger the number of degrees of freedom is, the larger the sample size required to achieve a power of .80, given all other criteria are held constant. Therefore, when a small sample size is used, consider collapsing small cells together to increase the expected frequencies, reduce the degrees of freedom, and, in turn, reduce the sample size required.

MEASURES OF ASSOCIATION

Like the Pearson's correlation test, when the chi-square test of association reveals significant results, it is necessary to examine the strength of the association, or relationship between the independent and dependent variables; in other words, the variance in the dependent variable that is accounted for by the independent variable.

Two measures of association can be produced simultaneously with chi-square test of association. These are the *phi* and Cramer's *V* coefficients, which are both interpreted in the same way as the Pearson's correlation coefficient. Both coefficients convey the simple correlation between the independent and dependent variables. Squaring the *phi* or Cramer's *V* coefficients is interpreted in the same way as the coefficient of determination (r^2) (see chapter 7, table 7.1: Interpretations of Correlation Coefficients).

$(phi)^2$ or (Cramer's $V)^2$ = proportion of variance in the dependent variable that is accounted for by the independent variable

---

The difference between the *phi* and Cramer's *V* is simple. *Phi* is used to convey the correlation between two dichotomous variables, where each variable has only two groups: a 2 × 2 table. The Cramer's *V* is used with all other contingency tables such as 3 × 3, 3 × 4, 4 × 4 tables, and so on. Report the *phi* or the Cramer's *V* only if the results of the chi-square test of association are statistically significant.[2]

PRACTICAL EXAMPLES

In the following sections, three practical examples illustrate in detail the utilizations of chi-square tests in hypothesis testing. The first example illustrates the use of the chi-square goodness-of-fit test. The second illustrates the use of the chi-square test of association in examining a 2 × 2 table, and the third example illustrates the use of the chi-square test of association with a 2 × 3 table.

Example 1: Chi-Square Goodness-of-Fit Test

First, we illustrate how to use the chi-square goodness-of-fit to examine how well a set of observations fits a population from which the sample was selected. For this purpose, we use the SPSS Job Satisfaction data file to examine if the distribution of levels of education observed in the sample is similar to that known, or expected, in the population. To do so, first assume, based on data made available by the National Association of Social Workers, that 80 percent of social services employees have B.A or B.S.W. degrees, 15 percent have M.S.W. degrees, and the remaining 5 percent have other degrees. Now, given this distribution of levels of education among social services employees in general, examine the following research question:

---

[2]See Siegel & Castellan (1988).

RESEARCH QUESTION: Is there a statistically significant difference between the social services employees who participated in the Job Satisfaction study and social services employees in general with regard to their levels of education?

Or, how well do levels of education observed in the Job Satisfaction study fit the population of social services employees?

Step 1: State the null and alternative hypotheses.

H_o: There are no statistically significant differences between the sample and population with regard to their levels of education. That is, the sample is similar to the population.

H_a: There are statistically significant differences between the sample and population with regard to their levels of education. That is, the sample is not similar to the population.

In this hypothesis, the dependent variable is level of education (Education) and is measured at the nominal level of measurement. It consists of three levels (1 = B.A./B.S.W., 2 = M.S.W., and 3 = others). Given that the ratio of these levels in the population is .80:.15:.05, we will utilize the chi-square goodness-of-fit test to examine the null hypothesis.

Step 2: Set the criteria for rejecting H_0.
Set alpha at .05 (α = .05). Reject H_0 only if $p \leq .05$.

Step 3: Select the appropriate statistical test.
First, we need to ensure that data meet the assumptions for the chi-square goodness-of-fit test. These assumptions are as follows:

1. LEVEL OF MEASUREMENT: The dependent variable must be categorical. As stated, the dependent variable in this example is level of education and is measured at the nominal level of measurement. It consists of three groups.

2. TYPES OF DATA: Data analyzed by a chi-square test must be frequencies and not scores. Here, the frequency of each level of education in the sample is being compared with those frequencies expected in the population. We will use the ratio .80:.15:.05 to calculate the expected frequency for each level of education.

3. SAMPLE SIZE: No more than 20 percent of cells should have expected frequencies of less than five cases per cell. However, given that there are only three cells (groups) in the dependent variable, all three must have at least five cases per level.

Table 11.7 displays the observed and expected frequency for each level of education. Calculations of expected frequencies for the chi-square goodness-of-fit is simple; multiply the expected proportion for each cell (level) by total sample size (remember, 218 subjects completed the Job Satisfaction

Table 11.7:   Observed and Expected Frequencies for Levels of Education

	Observed	Expected
B.S.W./B.A.	180	174.4
M.S.W.	32	32.7
Other	6	10.9
Total	218	218

survey). That is, B.S.W./B.A. = .80 * 218 = 174.4; M.S.W. = .15 * 218 = 32.7; and Other = .05 * 218 = 10.9.

As it is shown in table 11.7, none of the expected frequencies is less than 5. The smallest is 10.9. We will also return to this table under the next step.

4. SAMPLE SIZE AND POWER: Sample size should be sufficient to achieve a power of .80. According to table 11.6, a minimum sample size of 108 is needed for chi-square test to achieve a power of .80, given a medium effect size (ES = .30), a two-tailed alpha of .05, and two degrees of freedom (df = 3 levels − 1 = 2). In our example, 218 subjects participated in the study and therefore exceeded the minimum requirement to achieve a power of .80 given our predetermined criteria.

To conclude, data for levels of education met all assumptions for the chi-square goodness-of-fit test. Next, compute the test statistic.

Step 4: Compute the test statistic (using SPSS).

Recall that the variable under study is education (Education) and is classified as 1 = B.A./B.S.W, 2 = M.S.W., and 3 = other. Also, remember, that the ratio of these levels in the population is .80:.15:.05, respectively. You need these values for SPSS. Now use SPSS to compute the test statistic.

How to compute the chi-square goodness-of-fit test in SPSS.   To run the analysis, follow these steps:

1. Open the SPSS Job Satisfaction data file.

2. Click on *Analyze* in the SPSS main toolbar, click on *Nonparametric Tests*, click on *Legacy Dialogs,* and click on *Chi-square* (see chapter 8, screen 8.5).

3. Scroll down in the variables list in the "Chi-Square Test" dialog box, click on *Education*, and click on the middle arrow button to move it into the *Test Variable List* box (see screen 11.1).

4. Click on *Values* under "Expected Values." Here, you need to enter the expected proportion for each level in the same order as they appear in SPSS. Total proportions must equal 1.00.

    Note: If all groups are equal in the population (same proportion for B.A./B.S.W., M.S.W., and other—33.3% each), keep *All categories equal* as is under "Expected Values" and click on *OK*.

5. Now enter ".80" (proportion for the first level, 1 = B.A./B.S.W.) in the *Values* box and click on *Add* to confirm your entry. Next, type ".15" (proportion for the second level, 2 = M.S.W.) and click on *Add* to confirm it. Then, type ".05" (proportion for the third level, 3 = other) and click on *Add* to confirm it.

    Note: If you made an error (for example, typed ".50" instead of ".05"), click on the error, type the correct value in the *Values* box, and click on *Change* to change the error with the correct value.

Screen 11.1:   SPSS Chi-Square Goodness-of-Fit Dialog Box

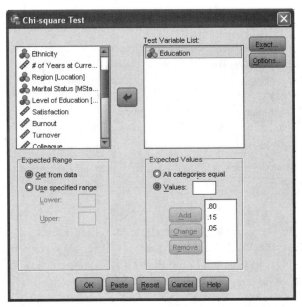

6. Click on *OK*.

Chi-Square Goodness-of-Fit Test SPSS Syntax

NPAR TESTS
/CHISQUARE=Education
/EXPECTED=.80 .15 .05
/MISSING ANALYSIS.

Interpreting the SPSS output of the chi-square goodness-of-fit test. The execution of these SPSS commands or syntax produces two tables. These include the Frequencies Table and the Test Statistics Table. They are presented in tables 11.8 and 11.9, respectively.

Table 11.8: Frequencies for Levels of Education

	Education		
	Observed N	Expected N	Residual
1 BSW/BA	180	174.4	5.6
2 MSW	32	32.7	−.7
3 OTHER	6	10.9	−4.9
Total	218		

Table 11.8 is the same as table 11.7. It displays the observed and expected frequency for each level of education. It also displays the residuals; difference between observed and expected. A positive residual indicates that the number of participants in a particular level is more than expected. A negative residual indicates that the number of participants in a particular level is less than expected.

In this study, the number of social services employees who have B.A./B.S.W. is more than expected (residual = 5.6) while the number of those with other degrees is less than expected (residual = −.49). The number of employees with M.S.W. degrees is about the same. The question is, then, are these residuals statistically significant? The answer is found in the next table.

Table 11.9 displays the results of the chi-square goodness-of-fit. It shows the chi-square value (chi-square = 2.398), number of degrees of freedom (df = 3 − 1 = 2), and the level of significance (Asymp. Sig. = .302).

The table also reports the number of cells that have expected frequencies less than 5. As it appears in the table, none of the cells (0%) have expected frequencies that are less than 5, thus satisfying the assumption of expected frequency per cell.

Step 5: Decide whether to reject the null hypothesis.

The results of the chi-square goodness-of-fit presented in table 11.9 show no statistically significant difference between the sample and the population with regard to their levels of education ($p > .05$). Therefore, do not reject the null hypothesis. In other words, levels of education observed in the sample of social services employees fit well the population.

Table 11.9: Chi-Square Test Statistics

Test Statistics	
	Education
Chi-Square	2.398[a]
df	2
Asymp. Sig.	.302

[a] 0 cells (.0%) have expected frequencies less than 5. The minimum expected cell frequency is 10.9.

Writing the results.   Like the one-sample case t-test, researchers may use the chi-square goodness-of-fit test to justify that their sample's characteristics (e.g., gender, race, education, etc.) are similar to those known in the population, and they are representative of the population to which study results will be generalized. In such cases, researchers my report their findings as follows:

The chi-square goodness-of-fit test was utilized to examine how well levels of education observed in a sample of 218 social services employees fit the general population. The results show no statistically significant difference between the sample and the population with regard to their levels of education ($\chi^2_{(df=2)}$ = 2.40; $p > .05$). Therefore, do not reject the null hypothesis. The results show that levels of education fit well the population of social services employees and therefore the sample and population are similar. (*Note:* You probably need to show that the sample is similar to the population on multiple characteristics before concluding it is representative of the population.)

Presentations of results in a summary table.   You may present the results of the chi-square goodness of fit test in a summary table. The table should display the observed and expected frequency for each cell, as well as their residuals. Next, report the overall chi-square and p values. Table 11.10 displays the results of the chi-square goodness-of-fit test for levels of education.

Example 2: Chi-Square Test of Association—A 2 × 2 Table

Use the data from the SPSS Elderly data file (appendix A) to examine the following research question:

RESEARCH QUESTION: Is there a statistically significant association between race and sickness among the elderly population?

Step 1: State the null and alternative hypotheses.

H_o: There is no statistically significant association between race and sickness among the elderly. That is, the two variables are uncorrelated in the population.

H_a: There is a statistically significant association between race and sickness among the elderly. That is, the two variables are correlated in the population.

Table 11.10:   Results of Chi-Square Goodness-of-fit Test (N = 218)

Education	Observed	Expected	Residual	χ^2	p*
BSW/BA	180	174.40	5.6	2.40	.301
MSW	32	32.70	−.7		
Other	6	10.90	−4.9		

*Two-tailed alpha (df = 2).

In this hypothesis, the dependent variable is sickness (Sick), and the independent variable is race. Both variables are dichotomous; each consists of two levels (Race: 0 = Not White and 1 = White; Sick: 0 = No and 1 = Yes). That is, the two variables form a 2 × 2 contingency table, or four cells. Therefore, we will utilize the chi-square test of association to examine the relationship between the two variables.

Step 2: Set the criteria for rejecting H_0.
Set alpha at .05 (α = .05). Reject H_0 only if $p \leq .05$.

Step 3: Select the appropriate statistical test.
As in Example 1, first we need to examine the test assumptions. These assumptions are as follows:

1. LEVELS OF MEASUREMENT: The dependent and independent variables must be categorical. Both race and sickness are categorical data and are measured at the nominal level of measurement.

2. INDEPENDENCY: The two variables must be independent one from another. Observations from race and sickness are made independently.

3. TYPES OF DATA: Data analyzed by a chi-square test must be frequencies and not scores. In this example, the observed frequencies in the 2 × 2 table are used to compute the expected frequencies and then examine the association between race and sickness.

4. SAMPLE SIZE: No more than 20 percent of cells should have expected frequencies of less than five cases per cell. In a 2 × 2 table, however, all cells must have expected frequencies of five or more. Table 11.11 displays the observed and expected frequencies for sickness by race.

   As it appears in the table, one cell out of four has an expected frequency smaller than five (Not White by Yes = 2.6), thus violating this assumption and possibly leading to an inaccurate conclusion. In this case and since this is a 2 × 2 table, report the results of the *Yates's continuity correction* or *Fisher's exact test*. However, if the results of these tests are consistent with the results of the chi-square, then report the results of chi-square test.

Table 11.11:   Observed and Expected Frequencies—Sick by Race

		Sick * Race Cross tabulation			
			Race		
			0 Not White	1 White	Total
Sick	0 No	Count	8	74	82
		Expected Count	12.4	69.6	82.0
	1 Yes	Count	7	10	17
		Expected Count	2.6	14.4	17.0
Total		Count	15	84	99
		Expected Count	15.0	84.0	99.0

5. SAMPLE SIZE AND POWER: For a 2 × 2 table, a sample size of eighty-eight is needed for chi-square test to achieve a power of .80, given a medium effect size (ES = .30), a two-tailed alpha of .05, and one degree of freedom [df = (2 − 1) × (2 − 1) = 1] (see table 11.6). In the elderly study, ninety-nine subjects completed the survey, thus exceeding the minimum requirement to achieve a power of .80, given the preestablished criteria.

To conclude, data for sickness by race met all but one assumption for the chi-square test of association. Next, compute the test statistic.

Step 4: Compute the test statistic (using SPSS).
Remember that the variables under study are race (Race: 0 = Not White, 1 = White) and sickness (Sick: 0 = No, 1 = Yes). Now use SPSS to compute the chi-square test of association.

How to run the chi-square test of association in SPSS.   Unlike the previous tests, the chi-square test of association can be executed through the *Analyze* and *Descriptives* SPSS main menu. To run the chi-square test of association, follow these steps:

1. Open the SPSS Elderly data file.

2. Click on *Analyze* in the SPSS main toolbar, click on *Descriptive Statistics*, and click on *Crosstabs* (see screen 11.2). This opens the "Crosstabs" dialog box.

Screen 11.2:   SPSS Crosstabs Main Menu

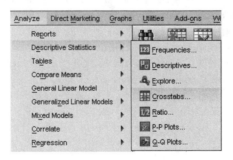

3. Scroll down in the variables list in the "Crosstabs" dialog box, click on *Sick*, and click on the upper arrow button to move it into the *Row(s)* box.

4. Scroll down in the variables list, click on *Race*, and click on the middle arrow button to move it into the *Column(s)* box (see screen 11.3). *Note:* It makes no difference what variable is entered in the *Row(s)* box or the *Column(s)* box.

5. Click on *Statistics* to open the "Crosstabs: Statistics" dialog box.

Screen 11.3: SPSS Crosstabs Dialog Box

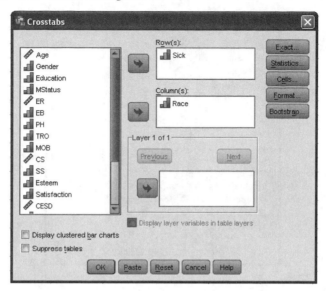

6. Check *Chi-square* and then check *Phi and Cramer's V* under "Nominal" (see screen 11.4).

7. Click on *Continue* to return to the "Crosstabs" dialog box and click on *Cells*. This opens a new dialog box called "Crosstabs: Cell Display" (see screen 11.5).

Screen 11.4: SPSS Crosstabs Statistics Dialog Box

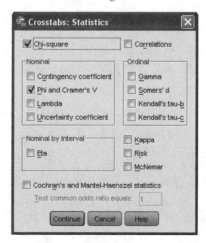

Screen 11.5:   SPSS Crosstabs Cell Display Dialog Box

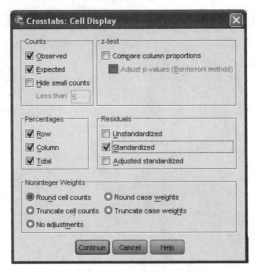

8. Check *Expected* under "Counts" (*Observed* is checked by default. If not checked, do so), check *Row*, *Column*, and *Total* under "Percentages," and check *Standardized* under "Residuals."

9. Click on *Continue* and then click on *OK*.

Chi-Square Test of Association SPSS Syntax

CROSSTABS
/TABLES=Sick BY Race
/FORMAT=AVALUE TABLES
/STATISTICS=CHISQ PHI
/CELLS=COUNT EXPECTED ROW COLUMN TOTAL SRESID
/COUNT ROUND CELL.

Interpreting the chi-square test of association in SPSS output.   The following output presents the results of the chi-square test of association generated by SPSS. They include four tables (tables 11.12 through 11.15).

Table 11.12 displays the number of valid, missing, and total cases and their respective percentages. The valid number is the number of cases included in the analysis. The missing number is the number of cases excluded from the analysis due to missing data in one or both variables. The total number is the number of all participants in the study. As the table shows, there are ninety-nine cases in this analysis, none of which has missing data. Thus, all cases are included in the analysis (N = 99).

Table 11.12: Case Processing Summary Table—Sickness by Race

				Case Processing Summary				
		Cases						
		Valid		Missing		Total		
		N	Percent	N	Percent	N	Percent	
Sick * Race		99	100.0%	0	.0%	99	100.0%	

Table 11.13 is a 2 × 2 contingency table. It is an extended table of table 11.11. It has two columns and two rows. Each row has six lines. They are as follows:

The *first two lines*, Count and Expected Count, display the observed and expected frequencies for each level of the dependent variable (Sick) by the independent variable (Race). These are the same frequencies as in table 11.11.

The *third line*, % within Sick, displays the row percentage. The table shows that 9.8 percent of all participants who said they are not sick (Total No = 82) are not white (joint cell of No and Not White). On the other hand, 90.2 percent of all participants who said they are not sick are white. The table also shows that 41.2 percent of all participants who said they are sick (Total Yes = 17) are not white (joint cell of Yes and Not White), while 58.8 percent of all participants who are sick are white (joint cell Yes and White).

The *fourth line*, % within Race, displays the column percentage. The table shows that 53.3 percent of not white elderly (Total Not White = 15) said they

Table 11.13: 2 × 2 Contingency Table—Sickness by Race

| | | | Sick * Race Crosstabulation | | |
| | | | Race | | |
			Not White	White	Total
Sick	No	Count	8	74	82
		Expected Count	12.4	69.6	82.0
		% within Sick	9.8%	90.2%	100.0%
		% within Race	53.3%	88.1%	82.8%
		% of Total	8.1%	74.7%	82.8%
		Std. Residual	−1.3	.5	
	Yes	Count	7	10	17
		Expected Count	2.6	14.4	17.0
		% within Sick	41.2%	58.8%	100.0%
		% within Race	46.7%	11.9%	17.2%
		% of Total	7.1%	10.1%	17.2%
		Std. Residual	2.8	−1.2	
Total		Count	15	84	99
		Expected Count	15.0	84.0	99.0
		% within Sick	15.2%	84.8%	100.0%
		% within Race	100.0%	100.0%	100.0%
		% of Total	15.2%	84.8%	100.0%

are not sick (joint cell of Not White and No). On the other hand, 88.1 percent of all white elderly (Total White = 84) said they are not sick. The table also shows that 46.7 percent of all not white elderly said they are sick (joint cell of Not White and Yes), compared to only 11.9 percent of all white elderly who said they are sick (joint cell White and Yes).

The *fifth line*, % of Total, displays the total percentage for a specific cell. The table shows that 8.1 percent of all participants (N = 99) are not white elderly who said they are not sick (joint cell of Not White and No), compared to 74.7 percent of all participants who are white and said they are not sick (joint cell White and No). On the other hand, 46.7 percent of all participants are not white who said they are sick (joint cell Not White and Yes), compared to only 11.9 percent who are white and said they are sick (joint cell White and Yes).

The fifth line, % of Total, also reports the overall percentage for each group (not to confuse with a cell). Overall, 82.2 percent of all participants said they are not sick (first row, No, fifth line, % of Total with Total column), compared to 17.2 percent of all participants who said they are sick (second row, Yes, fifth line, % of Total with Total column).

Also, overall, 15.2 percent of all participants are not white (Total row, Not White, fifth line, % of Total) compared to 84.8 percent who are white (Total row, White, fifth line, % of Total).

The *sixth line*, Std. Residual, displays the standardized residual for each cell. This is the residuals in each cell (difference between observed and expected frequencies) divided by its standard error. Standardized residuals are like post hoc tests in one-way ANOVA and ANCOVA; they indicate what cell(s) contribute to the significant results.

As a general rule, a standardized residual greater than +1.96 or smaller than −1.96 (two-tailed alpha = .05) indicates a significant difference between the observed and expected frequencies for a specific cell. Notice that only one cell has a standardized residual greater than 1.96; Not White with Yes (Std. Residual = 2.8). This indicates a significant difference between the observed (O = 7) and expected (E = 2.6) frequencies of not white elderly who are sick (Yes). Since this standardized residual is positive, it indicates that not white elderly who are sick are overrepresented in this sample. A negative standardized residual indicates that a particular cell is underrepresented in the sample.

Table 11.14 displays the results of the chi-square test. This table examines whether there is a statistically significant difference between the observed and expected frequencies. Table 11.14 has six rows. The number of rows will be smaller for tables that are greater than 2 × 2 (see practical example 3).

The *first row*, Pearson Chi-Square, displays the value (χ^2), degrees of freedom (df), and the level of significance (*p* value) for the chi-square test. The chi-square value is 10.813 with one degree of freedom and a *p* value of .001 (two-tailed *p*), which is smaller than alpha of .05.

Table 11.14:   Chi-Square Test of Association—Sickness by Race

	Chi-Square Tests				
	Value	df	Asymp. Sig. (2-sided)	Exact Sig. (2-sided)	Exact Sig. (1-sided)
Pearson Chi-Square	10.813[a]	1	.001		
Continuity Correction[b]	8.507	1	.004		
Likelihood Ratio	8.751	1	.003		
Fisher's Exact Test				.004	.004
Linear-by-Linear Association	10.704	1	.001		
N of Valid Cases	99				

[a]1 cell (25.0%) has expected count less than five. The minimum expected count is 2.58.
[b]Computed only for a 2 × 2 table.

Footnote a at the lower left side of the chi-square table shows that one cell (25%) has an expected count (frequency) of less than five. The minimum expected count is 2.58. This indicates a violation of the assumption of expected frequency per cell; five cases per cell for a 2 × 2 table.

The *second row*, Continuity Correction, displays the value, degrees of freedom, and level of significance for the continuity-correction formula (not covered in this book). It is computed for a 2 × 2 table to improve the approximation of the chi-square test when the expected frequency in any cell is less than five, as in our example. It is also known as Yates's continuity correction. In this case, the corrected chi-square value is 8.507, with one degree of freedom and a *p* value of .004 (*p* < .05).

The *third row*, Likelihood Ratio, displays the value, degrees of freedom, and level of significance for the likelihood ratio test (not covered in this book). This test is similar to the chi-square test. It is useful for smaller sample sizes. The likelihood ratio and chi-square tests are equivalent when used with large sample sizes. The table shows that the likelihood value is 8.751 with one degree of freedom and a *p* value of .003 (*p* < .05).

The *fourth row*, Fisher's exact test, only displays one-tailed and two-tailed levels of significance for the Fisher's exact test. This test is only computed for 2 × 2 tables. It is more appropriate when a small sample size is used. The table shows that the two-tailed *p* value (fifth column, Exact Sig. 2-sided) is .004 (*p* < .05).

The *fifth row*, Linear-by-Linear Association, displays the value, degrees of freedom, and levels of significance for a linear-by-linear association (not covered in this book). This test is also known as the Mantel-Haenszel chi-square test. It is *not* appropriate for use with nominal variables.

The *sixth row*, N of Valid Cases, displays the number of valid cases in the analysis. In this case, the sample includes 99 cases.

To conclude, Table 11.14 provides the results of various statistical techniques. Because one cell has an expected frequency less than five, the results of the

Table 11.15:   Measures of Association—Sickness by Race

Symmetric Measures		Value	Approx. Sig.
Nominal by Nominal	*Phi*	−.330	.001
	Cramer's *V*	.330	.001
N of Valid Cases		99	

chi-square may be inaccurate. In such cases, we would report the results of either Yates's continuity correction or Fisher's exact test. However, since the results of both continuity correction and Fisher's exact test are consistent with the results of the chi-square, then it is safe to report the results of the chi-square test. These results show a significant association between race and sickness ($p < .05$).

Because the results of the chi-square test presented in table 11.14 show a significant association between race and sickness ($p < .05$), it is recommended to examine the strength of this association. Table 11.15 presents the results of *phi* and Cramer's *V* measures of association. It has three rows: *phi*, Cramer's *V*, and N.

In this case, because this is a 2 × 2 table, examine the *phi* coefficient. Table 11.15 shows that the correlation coefficient between race and sickness as −.33 (*phi* = −.330) with a *p* value of .001. The minus sign indicates that the two variables have a negative correlation; that is, the higher the value of race (0 = Not White, 1 = White), the lower the sickness (1 = Yes, 0 = No). Squaring the *phi* coefficient produces the variance in the dependent variable (Sick) that is accounted for by the independent variable (Race). That is, $(phi)^2 = (−.33)^2 = .1089 = 10.89$ percent, thus indicating a weak relationship (see chapter 7, table 7.1).

Step 5: Decide whether to reject the null hypothesis.

The results of the chi-square test of association (as well as Yates's continuity correction and Fisher's exact test) presented in table 11.14 show a significant association between race and sickness ($p < .01$). Therefore, reject the null hypothesis.

Writing the results.   When reporting the results of the chi-square test (χ^2), first you discuss if the test assumptions are met, especially the assumption of expected frequencies. Then, report the chi-square value (Yates's continuity correction or Fisher's exact test), number of degrees of freedom, and the *p* value. Next report what cell(s) contribute to the significant results followed by the results of the *phi* or Cramer's *V* and the frequencies of cells. In our example, the results are as follows:

The chi-square test of association was utilized to examine the association between race (white vs. not white) and perceived sickness (yes vs. no) among a sample of ninety-nine elderly participants. Inspection of the 2 × 2 table shows that one cell (25%) has an expected frequency less than five. However, since the results of Fisher's exact test and Yates's continuity correction test are consistent with the results of the chi-square test, the results of the latter are reported here.

The results of the chi-square test show a significant association between race and sickness ($\chi^2_{(df=1)}$ = 10.81; p < .01). In other words, these results indicate that sickness is related to race in the population.

The results of the contingency table show that the number of elderly who are not white and said they are sick (n = 7) is significantly greater than expected (n = 2.6) (Standardized Residual = 2.8, p <.05). On the other hand, there are no statically significant differences between the observed and expected frequencies in any of the other three cells.

The *phi* measure of symmetric coefficient shows a significant negative association between race and sickness; that is, white elderly are more likely to perceive themselves as not sick while not white elderly are more likely to perceive themselves as sick. Race, however accounted for only about 11 percent (*phi*^{2} = .1085) of the variance in sickness, thus indicating a weak relationship between the two variables. In other words, more than 89 percent of the variance in sickness is unaccounted for.

Presentation of results in a summary table.   When presenting the results of the chi-square test of association in a summary table, report the observed frequency for each level in the dependent variable by each level in the independent variable; that is, the frequency for each joint cell. In addition, present the total percentages for each cell (some researchers may present either the row percentages or the column percentages instead. It is a personal preference). Then, report the chi-square value and the level of significance for each analysis, as well. For a 2 × 2 table, it is also useful to report the results of the Fisher's exact test or Yates's continuity correction as a footnote, especially when a small sample size is used.

Table 11.16 presents the results of the chi-square test for sickness by race. It shows the observed frequency and total percentage for each cell. The sum of the total percentages of all cells must equal 100 percent.

Table 11.16:   Results of Chi-Square Test—Sickness by Race

Sick	Not White n	Not White %	White n	White %	Total N	Total %	χ^{2a}	p^b
Yes	7[c]	7.1	10	10.1	17	17.2	10.81	< .01
No	8	8.1	74	74.7	82	82.8		
Total	15	15.2	84	84.8	99	100.0		

[a]Yates's continuity correction ($\chi^2_{(df=1)}$ = 8.51, p < .01).
[b]Two-tailed alpha.
[c]Standardized Residual = 2.8 (p < .05).

Example 3: Chi-Square Test of Association—A 2 × 3 Table

Now we will use the SPSS Well-Being data file (appendix A) to examine the association between gender and BMI (Case 2). The research question is as follows:

RESEARCH QUESTION: Is there a statistically significant association between gender (male and female) and body mass index (BMI: normal weight, over-weight, and obese) among college students?

Step 1: State the null and alternative hypotheses.

H_o: There is no statistically significant association between gender and BMI among college students.

H_a: There is a statistically significant association between gender and BMI among college students.

In this hypothesis, the dependent variable is BMI (Weight) and the independent variable is gender (Gender). BMI is classified as normal weight, over-weight, and obese. Gender is classified as male and female. That is, the two variables form a 2 × 3 contingency table or six cells and, thus, we will use the chi-square test of association to examine the effect of gender on students' BMI.

Step 2: Set the criteria for rejecting H_0.
Set alpha at .05 (α = .05). Reject H_0 only if $p \leq .05$.

Step 3: Select the appropriate statistical test.
As we did in the previous example, first examine the test assumptions. These assumptions are as follows:

1. LEVEL OF MEASUREMENT: The dependent and independent variables must be categorical variables. Gender and BMI are classified in two and three groups, respectively.

2. INDEPENDENCY: The two variables must be independent one from another. The observations of gender and BMI were made independently.

3. TYPES OF DATA: Data analyzed by the chi-square test must be frequencies and not scores. Here, we use the observed and expected frequencies in the 2 × 3 table to examine the effect of gender on BMI.

4. SAMPLE SIZE: No more than 20 percent of cells should have expected frequencies of less than five cases per cell. Table 11.17 displays the observed and expected frequencies for gender by BMI. As it is shown in table 11.17, all expected frequencies are greater than five. The smallest expected frequency is 11.6 and, thus, satisfies this assumption.

5. SAMPLE SIZE AND POWER: Table 11.6 shows that a sample size of 108 is needed for the chi-square test to achieve a power of .80 for a 2 × 3 table [df = $(2 - 1) \times (3 - 1) = 2$], given a medium effect size (ES = .30) and a two-tailed

Table 11.17:   Observed and Expected Frequencies—Weight by Gender

Weight * Gender Crosstabulation

| | | | Gender | | Total |
			Male	Female	
Weight	Normal weight	Count	28	65	93
BMI		Expected Count	39.9	53.1	93.0
	Over weight	Count	37	25	62
		Expected Count	26.6	35.4	62.0
	Obese	Count	13	14	27
		Expected Count	11.6	15.4	27.0
Total		Count	78	104	182
		Expected Count	78.0	104.0	182.0

alpha of .05. As table 11.17 shows, a total of 182 subjects participated in the Well-Being study, thus exceeding the minimum requirement of 108.

To conclude, data for BMI by gender met all assumptions for the chi-square test of association. Next compute the test statistic.

Step 4: Compute the test statistic (using SPSS).
Recall that the dependent variable is BMI (Weight) and the independent variable is gender (Gender). Now follow the steps discussed under practical example 2 and compute the chi-square test of association.

Interpreting the chi-square test of association SPSS output.   Tables 11.18 through 11.21 convey the SPSS outputs for the chi-square test of association.

Table 11.18 shows that all 182 participants completed the study (0% is missing).

Table 11.19 is a 2 × 3 contingency table. It displays the observed and expected frequency for each level of BMI for each gender followed by the row, column, and total percentages. The table also displays the standardized residuals for each cell. This table is the same as table 11.3, however, it also reports the standardized residuals. Notice here that two cells have standardized residuals of 1.9 and above. These are normal weight males and overweight males. In this

Table 11.18:   Case Processing Summary Table—BMI by Gender

Case Processing Summary

| | Cases | | | | | |
| | Valid | | Missing | | Total | |
	N	Percent	N	Percent	N	Percent
Weight * Gender	182	100.0%	0	.0%	182	100.0%

Table 11.19: 2 × 3 Contingency Table—BMI by Gender

		Weight * Gender Crosstabulation			
			Gender		
			Male	Female	Total
Weight	Normal weight	Count	28	65	93
		Expected Count	39.9	53.1	93.0
		% within Weight	30.1%	69.9%	100.0%
		% within Gender	35.9%	62.5%	51.1%
		% of Total	15.4%	35.7%	51.1%
		Std. Residual	−1.9	1.6	
	Over weight	Count	37	25	62
		Expected Count	26.6	35.4	62.0
		% within Weight	59.7%	40.3%	100.0%
		% within Gender	47.4%	24.0%	34.1%
		% of Total	20.3%	13.7%	34.1%
		Std. Residual	2.0	−1.8	
	Obese	Count	13	14	27
		Expected Count	11.6	15.4	27.0
		% within Weight	48.1%	51.9%	100.0%
		% within Gender	16.7%	13.5%	14.8%
		% of Total	7.1%	7.7%	14.8%
		Std. Residual	.4	−.4	
Total		Count	78	104	182
		Expected Count	78.0	104.0	182.0
		% within Weight	42.9%	57.1%	100.0%
		% within Gender	100.0%	100.0%	100.0%
		% of Total	42.9%	57.1%	100.0%

study, twenty-eight male students are of normal weight where there should be forty students (E = 39.9); that is, normal weight males in this study appear to be underrepresented (Standardized residuals = −1.9). On the other hand, thirty-seven males are overweight where there should be only twenty-seven (E = 26.6) males who are overweight; that is, overweight males are overrepresented in this study (Standardized residuals = 2.0).

Table 11.20 displays the results of the chi-square test of association. Unlike table 11.14 in the previous example, this table has four rows. In table 11.14, there were two extra rows, Continuity correction and Fisher's exact test, that are produced by default only with 2 × 2 tables. From this table, we are interested in the results of the Pearson chi-square and the number of cells with expected frequencies less than five.

As we can see, footnote "a" indicates that none of the cells (0%) have an expected count (frequency) less than five. It shows that the smallest expected frequency is 11.57 (see assumption 4 under step 3). *Note:* Always inspect this table to evaluate the assumption for sample size. If the % in parentheses (%) is

Table 11.20:   Chi-Square Test of Association—BMI by Gender

Chi-Square Tests			
	Value	df	Asymp. Sig. (2-sided)
Pearson Chi-Square	13.644[a]	2	.001
Likelihood Ratio	13.783	2	.001
Linear-by-Linear Association	7.461	1	.006
N of Valid Cases	182		

[a]0 cells (.0%) have expected count less than five. The minimum expected count is 11.57.

equal to or less than 20 percent for any contingency table other than a 2 × 2 table, then this indicates the assumption is met.

Table 11.20 shows the chi-square is 13.64 with two degrees of freedom and a p value of .001. This indicates a statistically significant association between BMI and gender.

Table 11.21 presents the results of *phi* and Cramer's V measures of association. It is similar to table 11.15. Here, however, we report the results of the Cramer's V coefficient because this is a 2 × 3 table (remember to report the *phi* coefficient with a 2 × 2 table).

Table 11.21 shows that Cramer's V coefficient is .274 with a p value of .001 (notice that it is the same as the *phi* coefficient, but this is not always the case). This indicates a statistically significant positive association between gender and BMI. That is, female students (0 = male, 1 = female) are more likely to have higher levels of BMI (2 = normal weight, 3 = overweight, and 4 = obese) than male students. Squaring the Cramer's V here conveys the variance in BMI that is accounted for by gender; that is, $(.274)^2 = .0751$ or 7.51 percent.

Step 5: Decide whether to reject the null hypothesis.

The results of the chi-square test of association presented in table 11.20 show a significant association between gender and BMI ($p < .01$). Therefore, reject the null hypothesis.

Writing the results.   The chi-square test of association was utilized to examine the association between gender and body mass index among a sample of 182 college students. Preliminary inspection of the 2 × 3 contingency table indicates no violation of the assumption of sample size.

Table 11.21:   Measures of Association—BMI by Gender

Symmetric Measures			
		Value	Approx. Sig.
Nominal by Nominal	*Phi*	.274	.001
	Cramer's V	.274	.001
N of Valid Cases		182	

Table 11.22:   Results of Chi-Square Test—BMI by Gender

Sick	Male n	Male %	Female n	Female %	Total N	Total %	χ^2	p^a
Normal Weight	28[b]	15.4	65	35.7	93	51.1	13.64	< .01
Overweight	37[c]	20.3	25	13.7	62	34.1		
Obese	13	7.1	14	7.7	27	14.8		
Total	78	42.9	104	57.1	182	100.0		

[a]Two-tailed alpha.
[b]Standardized Residual = -1.9 ($p = .05$).
[c]Standardized Residual = 2.0 ($p < .05$).

The results of the chi-square test show a significant association between gender and body mass index ($\chi^2_{(df=2)} = 13.64$, $p < .01$). In other words, the two variables are related in the population.

The results of the contingency table show that the number of overweight male students (n = 37) is significantly higher (Standardized residual = 2, $p < .05$) than expected (n = 26.6), while the number of normal weight male students (n = 28) is significantly less (Standardized residual = -1.9, $p \leq .05$) than expected (39.9). Furthermore, the number of overweight female students (n = 25) is much smaller than expected (n = 35.4), yet it is not statistically significant (Standardized residual = -1.8). On the other hand, the frequencies of obese male students (n = 13), as well as female students (n = 14), are as expected (n = 11.6 and 15.6, respectively). Table 11.22 presents the results of the chi-square test of association.

The results of the Cramer's V measure of symmetry coefficient show a significant positive association between gender and BMI (Cramer's $V = .27$, $p < .001$). In other words, female students are more likely to have higher levels of BMI than their counterpart male students. Gender, however, accounted for less than 8 percent (Cramer's $V^2 = .073$) of the variance in BMI, thus indicating a very weak relationship between the two variables.

SUMMARY

Unlike previous bivariate test statistics, which examine scores, this chapter introduced new statistical tests that examine the frequency observed in the sample and whether it is different than the expected frequency in the population from which the sample is selected. This is especially important for social science practitioners and researchers who are more favorable of categorical data rather than continuous data.

This chapter presented two chi-square tests: chi-square goodness-of-fit test and chi-square test of association. First, the chapter discussed the purpose of each test and then discussed the contingency table, defined its elements, how to construct it, and how to compute the expected frequencies. The chapter next discussed the assumptions underlying the chi-square test statistics. Two measures of association appropriate for examining the strengths and directions of the results of the chi-square test of association were then presented: the *phi* and Cramer's *V* coefficients. In addition, three practical examples illustrated in detail how to use the chi-square goodness-of-fit and chi-square test of association, and how to use SPSS to create a contingency table and compute the chi-square values and levels of significance were presented. Finally, the chapter discussed how to interpret the SPSS output and write and present the results of the contingency table and the results of the chi-square tests in summary tables.

The final chapter in this book will introduce multiple regression analysis, an advanced statistical technique widely used among social science researchers to predict a single outcome. The chapter will discuss the purpose of multiple regression analysis, the regression equation, and the coefficients produced by this analysis, as well as the assumptions underlying multiple regression analysis and the process in selecting variables to be entered in the analysis. The chapter will also discuss differences among forward, stepwise, and backward regression methods and how to produce the coefficients in SPSS, how to interpret the output, and how to write and present the results of multiple regression analysis.

PRACTICAL EXERCISES

Part I: Access the Mental Health data file (appendix A) and examine the following research question:

Given that the distribution of gender among refugees is distributed equally (ratio 1:1), is there a statistically significant difference between the sample and the population with regard to their gender (Gender)?

1. Follow the steps in hypothesis testing and examine the null hypothesis. Discuss all steps in detail.
2. Present the results in a summary table.

Part II: Recode levels of depression (CESD) from the Mental Health data file (appendix A) to a new variable called Depression as follows: (0–15 = Not depressed) and (16 and above = Depressed). Then examine the following research question:

Is there a statistically significant association between owning a home (Home) and levels of depression (Depression) among refugees?

1. Follow the steps in hypothesis testing and examine the null hypothesis. Discuss all steps in detail.
2. Write the SPSS syntax for the recode function and test statistic.
3. Present the results of the test statistic in a summary table.

Part III: Access the Well-Being data file (appendix A) and examine the following research question:

Is there a significant association between race (Race) and overall level of financial status (Financialstatus) among college students?

1. Follow the steps in hypothesis testing and examine the null hypothesis. Discuss all steps in detail.
2. Present the results in a summary table.

CHAPTER 12

Multiple Regression Analysis

LEARNING OBJECTIVES

1. Understand the purpose of multiple regression analysis
2. Understand the regression equation
3. Understand the coefficients of multiple regression
4. Understand the assumptions underlying multiple regression
5. Understand how to choose variables to be entered in multiple regression
6. Understand forward, stepwise, and backward regression methods
7. Understand how to use SPSS to run multiple regression
8. Understand how to interpret, write, and present the results of multiple regression

DATA SET (APPENDIX A)

Job Satisfaction

INTRODUCTION

The previous chapters presented statistical techniques that examine the overall relationship between one dependent variable and one independent variable (Pearson's correlation test, independent and dependent t-tests, one-way ANOVA and ANCOVA, and chi-square test of association) or one constant (one-sample case t-test and chi-square goodness-of-fit test). These techniques are known as bivariate statistics. For instance, by using the Pearson's correlation or the chi-square tests, researchers may determine whether independent and dependent variables are significantly correlated and how much of the variance (r^2, phi, Cramer's V, etc.) in the dependent variable can be explained by the independent variable.

However, researchers may wish to know more than whether two variables are significantly correlated. By learning certain conditions or characteristics (independent variables) in the population, researchers might be able to predict a specific outcome (dependent variable). For example, a director of a graduate school admissions office wants to predict prospective graduate students' GPA based on their undergraduate GPA, GRE scores (verbal and analytical), and letters of recommendation. Prospective students with the highest predicted graduate GPA will be admitted to the graduate school. A social work clinician/researcher wants to predict levels of depression among welfare recipients based on their age, education, social support, and physical health. Welfare recipients with the highest predicted levels of depression will be considered for intervention. An organization administrator wants to predict levels of burnout among social services employees based on their gender, age, salary, physical environment, and workload. Employees with the highest predicted levels of burnout will be referred for intervention.

In these three examples, the purpose is to predict a single outcome (graduate GPA, depression, or burnout) based on multiple conditions (independent variables). An early prediction of the outcome can help clinicians, practitioners, and professionals to plan treatment or intervention strategies in advance. In such cases, bivariate statistics are no longer appropriate because the relationship among multiple independent variables and one dependent variable is being examined. Advanced and multivariate statistics will be more appropriate (Abu-Bader, 2010). These statistics examine the relationship among multiple independent variables and one or more dependent variables. These techniques include multiple regression analysis, logistic regression analysis, multivariate analysis of variance and covariance, canonical correlation analysis, factor analysis, and others.

This chapter introduces multiple regression analysis. It discusses the purpose of the test statistic and the regression equation. Next, the chapter presents the coefficients associated with multiple regression analysis, discusses the assumptions underlying it, and shows how to select the variables that should be entered in multiple regression. In addition, the chapter describes three regression methods of data entry: forward, stepwise, and backward. Finally, the chapter discusses how to use SPSS to compute the coefficients of multiple regression analysis and how to interpret, write, and present the results in a summary table.

PURPOSE OF MULTIPLE REGRESSION

Multiple regression analysis is an advanced statistical technique. It is an extension of the Pearson's correlation test (see chapter 7) and simple linear regression analysis (Abu-Bader, 2010), and was first used by Karl Pearson in 1908. It is perhaps the most used advanced statistical technique in social sciences research.

The purpose of multiple regression analysis is to examine the effect of multiple independent variables (two or more) on only one dependent variable. The independent variables are known as factors or predictors, and the dependent variable is known as a criterion or outcome. The criterion is symbolized by the English capital letter "Y," and each predictor is symbolized by the capital letter "X" with a subscript "i" that represents the number of each factor. For example, X_1 represents the first factor, X_2 represents the second factor, and X_i represents the

i^{th} factor. In general, multiple regression analysis estimates a model of multiple factors that best predicts the criterion. Thus, multiple regression analysis allows researchers to answer the following general research question:

What set of the following factors best predicts Y: X_1, X_2, X_3, . . . , X_i?

Y = Criterion, Outcome

X_1 = 1st factor; X_2 = 2nd factor; X_3 = 3rd factor; X_i = i^{th} factor.

Example: What set of the following factors best predicts levels of depression (criterion) among welfare recipients: age, marital status, race, level of education, number of years on welfare, physical health, and social support (factors)?

By using multiple regression analysis, the researcher's aim is to predict levels of depression among welfare recipients based on their age, marital status, race, level of education, number of years on welfare, physical health, and social support. In other words, the researcher wants to know which set of these factors best predicts recipients' levels of depression. This can help practitioners and therapists plan early intervention and prevention strategies for recipients who are likely to experience higher levels of depression.

EQUATION OF MULTIPLE REGRESSION

The results of multiple regression analysis are expressed in a regression equation that represents a combination of the best factors predicting the criterion. This equation simply follows a straight-line equation. It can be either unstandardized scores (based on raw scores) or standardized scores (based on z score). They are expressed as follows:

Unstandardized Regression Equation

$Y = a + b_1X_1 + b_2X_2 + b_3X_3 + . . . + b_iX_i$

Y = Criterion (dependent variable)

a = Y intercept (the value of Y when all X values are zero)

b = Unstandardized regression coefficient

X = Factors (independent variables)

Standardized Regression Equation

$Z_Y = \beta_1Z_{X1} + \beta_2Z_{X2} + \beta_3Z_{X3} + . . . + \beta_iZ_{Xi}$

Z_Y = z score for criterion (dependent variable)

β (beta) = standardized regression coefficient

Z_X = z score for each factor (independent variable)

For example, levels of depression could be expressed as follows:

1. Unstandardized Regression Equation:

   Depression = a + (b_1 * Age) + (b_2 * Marital status) + (b_3 * Race) + (b_4 * Education) + (b_5 * Years on welfare) + (b_6 * Physical health) + (b_7 * Social support)

2. Standardized Regression Equation:

   $Z_{Depression}$ = (β_1 * Z_{Age}) + (β_2 * $Z_{Marital\ status}$) + (β_3 * Z_{Race}) + (β_4 * $Z_{Education}$) + (β_5 * $Z_{Years\ on\ welfare}$) + (β_6 * $Z_{Physical\ health}$) + (β_7 * $Z_{Social\ support}$)

The purpose of a multiple regression analysis is thus to find out what set of the seven factors best predicts depression and what their regression coefficients are.

COEFFICIENTS OF MULTIPLE REGRESSION

Multiple regression analysis generates several coefficients in which each provides valuable information. They are: correlation coefficient (R); R square (R^2); adjusted R square (adjusted R^2); regression constant (a); unstandardized regression coefficient (B); and standardized regression coefficient (β).

While there will be only one R, one R^2, one adjusted R^2, and one a, there will be one B and one β for each factor. The interpretations of these coefficients are as follows:

1. MULTIPLE CORRELATION COEFFICIENT (R): This represents the correlation coefficient between the criterion (Y) and all factors entered in the regression equation (X's). It ranges between "0" (no linear relationship) to "1" (perfect linear relationship).

   In order to find the size and the direction of the relationship between the criterion and each factor, simply look at the size and the sign (plus or minus) of the standardized regression coefficients (beta).

2. MULTIPLE R SQUARE (R^2): This is the proportion of the variance in the criterion that is explained by the multiple factors in the regression equation. The complement of R^2 (that is, $1 - R^2$) represents the proportion of the unexplained variance in the criterion.

3. ADJUSTED R SQUARE (ADJUSTED R^2): The adjusted R^2 is based on the number of factors entered in the regression analysis as opposed to the sample size. The greater the number of factors entered compared to the sample size, the smaller it becomes. Since in multiple regression analysis multiple factors are examined, adjusted R^2 is more appropriate than the standard R^2. Simply report both.

4. R SQUARE CHANGE (R^2 CHANGE): This represents the amount of variance in the criterion due to the addition of another factor. If only one factor is entered in the analysis, then R square change and R square values will be identical (0% change).

5. F CHANGE AND SIGNIFICANCE OF CHANGE: These represent the F ratio (ANOVA) and whether the R^2 change is statistically significant.

6. REGRESSION CONSTANT (a): This is the Y axis intercept; the value of Y when the values of all X's are zero.

7. UNSTANDARDIZED REGRESSION COEFFICIENTS (b): These are the unstandardized regression coefficients between the criterion and each factor, the slope of the regression line. They are computed using raw scores.

8. STANDARDIZED REGRESSION COEFFICIENTS (β): These represent linear correlation coefficients between the criterion and each factor while controlling for the effects of all other factors in the analysis. They are computed using standard z scores.

ASSUMPTIONS OF MULTIPLE REGRESSION

Because multiple regression analysis is an extension of the Pearson's correlation test, it requires the same set of assumptions. These assumptions include the following:

1. SAMPLE REPRESENTATIVENESS: The sample must represent the population from which it is selected and to which generalization will be made.

2. LEVEL OF MEASUREMENT: THE criterion (dependent variable) must be continuous data and measured at the interval or ratio levels of measurement.

3. NORMAL DISTRIBUTION: The shape of the distribution of the criterion must approximate the shape of a normal curve.

    To evaluate the assumption of normality, examine measures of skewness and inspect the histogram and normal Q-Q plot for the dependent variable. If measures of skewness and plots show severe departure from normality, consider transforming the data to the square root, logarithm, or other transformation methods (see chapter 5).

In addition to these assumptions, multiple regression analysis requires the following:

4. FACTORS (INDEPENDENT VARIABLES): While the criterion must be measured at the interval or ratio levels of measurement, the factors can be measured at any level of measurement (nominal, ordinal, interval, or ratio). However, if a nominal variable (categorical) is used in multiple regression analysis, it must be recoded to dummy variables prior to entering it in the analysis.

    Dummy Variable: A dummy variable is a dichotomous variable that is coded as "0" and "1." It is simply expressed in terms of "X" versus "Not X." For example, if gender were coded as "1" for males and "2" for females, then you may recode "2" to "0" (not males) and keep "1" as is. You may also recode "1" to "0" (males) and "2" to "1" (not males) prior to entering gender in the regression analysis.

Furthermore, a nominal variable with three or more levels must be recoded to one or more dummy variables. For example, if Race is classified as 1 = Whites, 2=African Americans, 3=Asian Americans, and 4=Hispanics, then you may create up to four dummy variables as follows: (1) 1 = Whites versus 0 = Not Whites; (2) 0 = African Americans versus 1 = Not African Americans; (3) 0 = Asians versus 1 = Not Asians; and (4) 0 = Hispanics versus 1 = Not Hispanics.

5. NORMALITY OF RESIDUALS: The shape of the distribution of the residuals must approach the shape of a normal curve. Residuals refer to the differences between the observed (actual) scores and the predicted scores. If the analysis is perfect, the differences between the observed scores and predicted scores will be zero.

To examine this assumption, create a histogram and normal probability plot for the residual scores. These are available in most statistical software. In SPSS, you can request a histogram and normal probability plot for the residuals (see figures 12.3 and 12.4 under "Practical Example") simultaneously, along with the results of multiple regression analysis. If a distribution is normal, data will form a straight diagonal line on the normal probability plot. If not, consider transforming the data to the square root, logarithm, or other methods of transformation.

6. LINEARITY: The relationship between the criterion and all factors is assumed to be a linear relationship.

Practically, it is almost impossible to confirm this assumption. However, it is recommended to examine linearity by creating a scatterplot for each factor with the criterion and then reviewing each scatterplot. Minor deviation from linearity does not greatly affect the results of multiple regression analysis. If a curvilinear relationship exists in one or more scatterplots, consider transforming the data to a square root, logarithm, or other methods of transformation.

7. HOMOSCEDASTICITY: For each value of the independent variables (factors), the dependent variable (criterion) should be normally distributed. In other words, the variance around the regression line should be the same for all values of the independent variables. This is also known as the assumption of homogeneity (equality) of variances.

To examine the assumption of homoscedasticity, plot the residuals against the predicted values. This plot also can be generated simultaneously along with the results of multiple regression analysis. If the distribution is normally distributed (homoscedastic), data will be distributed equally around a horizontal (reference) line (see figure 12.9 under "Practical Example"). Again, if data are heteroscedastic (not homoscedastic), consider transforming the data to a square root, logarithm, or other method of transformation.

8. MULTICOLLINEARITY: Multicollinearity occurs when two independent variables (factors) are highly correlated. When this occurs, both variables measure essentially the same thing.

    a. DETECTING MULTICOLLINEARITY: To check the data for multicollinearity, use one of these two options:

        i. Run and examine the Pearson's correlation coefficient for each pair of independent variables (factors). A correlation coefficient that is greater than .80 ($r > .80$) indicates a multicollinearity problem.

        ii. Check the variance inflation factor (VIF) and tolerance. VIF is the reciprocal of tolerance, which is the proportion of variance in one factor that is unexplained by the other factors ($1 - R^2$). They can be computed along with the multiple regression coefficients in SPSS or any other statistical program. A VIF value that is greater than ten usually indicates a multicollinearity problem. A tolerance value smaller than .10 also indicates a multicollinearity problem.

$$Tolerance = \frac{1}{VIF}$$

Multicollinearity exists if VIF > 10 or tolerance < .10

---

    b. SOLVING THE PROBLEM: When two variables appear to be highly correlated, you may consider one of the following two methods:

        i. REMOVING ONE VARIABLE: If you believe that one of the two variables that are highly correlated doesn't appear to be necessary for the regression analysis, consider removing it from the regression analysis. For example, if physical health and mental health were to be used in predicting life satisfaction among elderly and both are highly correlated, you may consider removing the one that you believe is less important for life satisfaction and enter the second one in the regression analysis.

        ii. CREATING COMPOSITE VARIABLES: If it is feasible, consider creating a new variable that combines the scores of both variables. In the above example, you may merge the scores of physical health and mental health to create a new variable (e.g., health in general). However, if the two variables have different units of measures (e.g., 1 to 10 for physical health and 10 to 50 for mental health), you should transform their raw scores to standard scores (z scores) before creating the new variable.

9. SAMPLE SIZE: There is no clear agreement among researchers on the sample size required to utilize multiple regression analysis.

Researchers have used anywhere between ten to fifty cases per each factor entered in the regression analysis. However, as discussed in previous chapters, sample size greatly affects the power of a test statistic; the larger the sample size is, the greater the power. Power is also affected by three more factors, the direction of the research hypothesis (one-tailed vs. two-tailed), the level of significance (alpha .05, .01, etc), and effect size. Cohen (1988) defines effect size (ES) in multiple regression analysis as the proportion of variance in the dependent variable that is accounted for by the factors (that is, R^2). He defines $R^2 = .02$ as small effect size, $R^2 = .15$ as medium effect size, and $R^2 = .35$ as large effect size. In regression analysis, the number of factors entered in the analysis also affect the power and, in turn, the sample size.

Therefore, as a rule of thumb, a sample size of at least $50 + 8m$ (that is, $N \geq 50 + 8m$, where m = number of factors) is needed for multiple regression analysis to achieve a power of .80, given a two-tailed alpha .05 and a medium effect size (Tabachnick & Fidell, 2007). For example, to examine the relationship between one criterion and six factors, we need at least ninety-eight subjects; that is, $N \geq 50 + 8 \times 6 \geq 50 + 48 \geq 98$. Keep in mind, however, when a smaller effect size or alpha is used, a larger sample size is needed to detect a power of .80. Using Cohen's definition of effect size and a two-tailed alpha, we used SPSS Sample Power to compute the sample size needed to achieve a power of .80, given the level of significance (.05, .01, and .001) and number of independent variables (1 to 10). Table 12.1 conveys the results of SPSS Sample Power.

Table 12.1 shows that a sample size of eighty-four cases is needed to achieve a power of .80, given a two-tailed alpha .05, a medium effect size of .15, and six factors. As you may notice, this number (84) is smaller than that we computed using the rule-of-thumb formula above (98). Remember,

Table 12.1:   Sample Size for Multiple Regression (Power = .80; Two-Tailed Alpha)

#IV	$\alpha = .050$			$\alpha = .010$			$\alpha = .001$		
	ES = .02	ES = .15	ES = .35	ES = .02	ES = .15	ES = .35	ES = .02	ES = .15	ES = .35
1	387	47	17	576	70	26	843	103	38
2	476	58	22	685	84	31	971	119	44
3	539	66	25	764	94	35	1064	131	49
4	590	73	28	828	102	39	1142	141	53
5	635	79	30	884	109	42	1209	149	56
6	674	84	33	934	116	44	1270	157	60
7	711	89	35	979	122	47	1325	165	63
8	744	94	37	1022	128	49	1377	171	66
9	776	98	39	1061	133	52	1425	178	68
10	806	102	41	1099	138	54	1471	184	71

however, that the rule of thumb is a general guideline that helps researchers to estimate how large their sample should be. Also, different computer software may produce slightly different results. As a recommendation, always seek a larger sample size when possible.

SELECTING APPROPRIATE FACTORS FOR MULTIPLE REGRESSION

Because the purpose of multiple regression analysis is to produce the most significant set of factors that predicts a criterion, it is logical to assume that each factor to be entered in the regression analysis should have a significant bivariate relationship with the criterion. If the two do not have a significant relationship to begin with, it is unlikely that one will predict the other. In fact, this is the assumption of linearity.

Selecting only factors that are significantly correlated with the criterion could decrease the number of factors entered in the regression analysis and, in turn, decrease the required sample size. Thus, prior to entering factors in the regression analysis, researchers should examine the bivariate relationship between each factor and the criterion. In order to examine this relationship, first determine the appropriate bivariate statistical test to examine the relationship (Pearson's correlation, t-test, ANOVA, etc.) and then run the test. Factors that are significantly correlated with the criterion then are entered in the regression analysis, while factors that are not significantly correlated with the criterion should not be entered in the analysis.

METHODS OF DATA ENTRY IN MULTIPLE REGRESSION

While some researchers may decide to enter all factors in the regression analysis at once, others may decide to enter them based on specific criteria. There is a number of ways in which researchers choose to enter the factors in the regression analysis. The most common methods are as follows:

Forward Method

At the beginning, the bivariate correlation coefficient between each factor and the criterion is computed. Next, the factor with the largest correlation coefficient is entered in the regression analysis. The next factor entered in the equation is the one that has the second largest correlation coefficient. In this method, once a factor is entered in the regression analysis, it remains in the equation. This procedure continues until no more factors contribute significantly to the variance in the criterion.

Backward Method

This method begins with entering all factors at once in the regression analysis. Then, multiple R square (R^2) and partial correlation coefficients (beta's) are computed. In the next step, the factor that has the smallest partial correlation coefficient with the criterion is removed from the analysis. Then, the factor that has the second smallest partial correlation coefficient is removed. This procedure stops when the variance in the criterion significantly drops.

Stepwise Method

This method perhaps is the most used method of regression analysis. It combines both the forward and backward methods, and thus it overcomes the problems that arise by these two methods. Like the forward method, in the stepwise method, factors are entered based on the size of their partial correlation coefficients; the one with the largest correlation coefficient is entered first in the analysis. The second factor with the largest correlation coefficient is entered next. Unlike the forward method, after a new factor is entered in the analysis, the contribution of the factors that are already in the analysis is reassessed. Like the backward method, factors that no longer contribute significantly to the variance in the criterion are removed from the regression equation. The procedure stops when no more factors contribute significantly to the variance in the criterion. The stepwise method will be used in this chapter.

PRACTICAL EXAMPLE

We will use the Job Satisfaction SPSS data file (appendix A) to predict levels of job satisfaction among social services employees based on a number of factors. In particular, we will examine the following research question:

RESEARCH QUESTION: What set of the following factors best predicts levels of job satisfaction among social services employees: gender, ethnicity, level of education, region of employment, working with colleagues, quality of supervision, promotion, and workload?

In this research question, job satisfaction (Satisfaction) is the dependent variable (criterion) and is measured at the interval level of measurement. Gender (Gender), ethnicity (Ethnicity), level of education (Education_REC), region of employment (Location), working with colleagues (Colleague), quality of supervision (Supervision), promotion (Promotion), and workload (Workload) are the independent variables (factors). We thus will use multiple regression analysis to examine which set of these factors best predicts levels of job satisfaction.

Step 1: State the null and alternative hypotheses.
Unlike in previous test statistics, in multiple regression analysis, it is unnecessary to state a null and alternative hypothesis simply because the researchers' aim is not to verify or falsify a research hypothesis but rather to develop a regression model that best predicts a criterion. Thus, in multiple regression analysis, simply state the research question under study. In this case, the research question is as follows:

RESEARCH QUESTION: What set of the following factors best predicts levels of job satisfaction among social services employees: gender, ethnicity, level of education, region of employment, working with colleagues, quality of supervision, promotion, and workload?

Step 2: Choose alpha.

We will set alpha at .05 (α = .05). That is, results will be statistically significant only if $p \leq .05$.

Step 3: Select the appropriate statistical test.

Because the purpose here is to predict a single outcome based on a number of factors, we obviously will utilize multiple regression analysis. However, before starting this analysis, we need to evaluate the data and examine whether they meet the assumptions for multiple regression analysis.

1. LEVEL OF MEASUREMENT: The dependent variable must be measured at the interval or ratio level of measurement. In this research question, job satisfaction is the criterion and is measured at the interval level of measurement.

2. NORMAL DISTRIBUTION: The shape of the distribution of the criterion must approach the shape of a normal curve. To evaluate this assumption, inspect measures of skewness and create a histogram and a normal Q-Q plot for job satisfaction (see chapter 5). Table 12.2 and figures 12.1 and 12.2 display the descriptive statistics and graphs for job satisfaction.

   Evaluation of Fisher's skewness coefficient ($-.392/.165 = -2.38$) shows that the distribution is severely skewed to the left, yet it is still within the normal range given an alpha of .01 (normal range of ± 2.56). Also, evaluation of Pearson's skewness coefficient $[(66.16 - 67)/8.825 = -.09]$ and inspection of the histogram (see figure 12.1) and normal Q-Q plot (see figure 12.2) for job satisfaction show that it approaches the shape of a normal

Table 12.2: Descriptive Statistics for Job Satisfaction

			Statistic	Std. Error
Satisfaction	Mean		66.16	.598
	95% Confidence	Lower Bound	64.98	
	Interval for Mean	Upper Bound	67.34	
	5% Trimmed Mean		66.37	
	Median		67.00	
	Variance		77.887	
	Std. Deviation		8.825	
	Minimum		39	
	Maximum		85	
	Range		46	
	Interquartile Range		11	
	Skewness		−.392	.165
	Kurtosis		.148	.328

Figure 12.1:   Histogram for Job Satisfaction

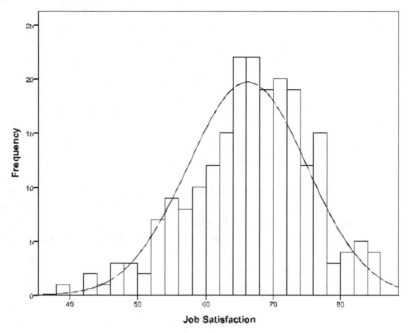

Figure 12.2:   Normal Q-Q Plot of Job Satisfaction

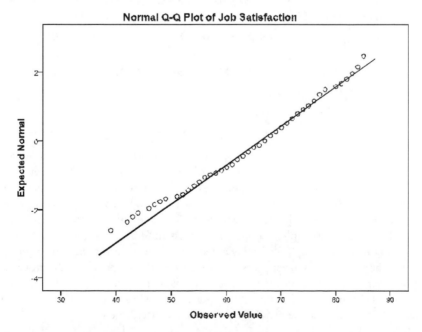

curve. Therefore, we conclude that the dependent variable met the assumption of normality.

3.   FACTORS: Factors to be entered in the regression analysis can be measured at any level of measurement (nominal, ordinal, interval, or ratio). However, if nominal variables (categorical) are used in multiple regression analysis, they must be recoded to dummy variables before they are entered in the analysis.

The factors (independent variables) in this research question are gender, ethnicity, level of education, region of employment, working with colleagues, quality of supervision, promotion, and workload. The variables working with colleagues, quality of supervision, promotion, and workload are all continuous variables and are measured at the interval level of measurement.

On the other hand, gender, ethnicity, level of education, and region of employment are categorical variables. Thus, they must be coded as "0" and "1." Looking at the SPSS data file, gender, ethnicity, and level of education (Education_REC) are all coded as "0" and "1." Region of employment (Location), however, is coded as "1 = North," "2 = Center," and "3 = South." In this case, it must be recoded to three dummy variables as follows: North (1 = North, 0 = Others); Center (1 = Center, 0 = Others); and South (1 = South, 0 = Others).

SPSS Syntax for Recoding Location to Three New Variables

RECODE LOCATION (SYSMIS=SYSMIS) (1=1) (2=0) (3=0) INTO NORTH.

RECODE LOCATION (SYSMIS=SYSMIS) (1=0) (2=1) (3=0) INTO CENTER.

RECODE LOCATION (SYSMIS=SYSMIS) (1=0) (2=0) (3=1) INTO SOUTH.

EXECUTE.

---

4.   NORMALITY OF RESIDUALS: The shape of the distribution of the residuals must approach the shape of a normal curve. As mentioned earlier, this assumption is evaluated by inspecting the histogram of the residuals and the normal P-P (probability) plot. This plot can be produced in SPSS along with the results of the multiple regression analysis (we will illustrate this under "How to Run Multiple Regression Analysis in SPSS").

Figures 12.3 and 12.4 display a histogram and a normal probability plot for the residuals. As it appears in figure 12.3, the shape of the distribution of the residuals follows the shape of a normal curve. Also, figure 12.4 shows that the points fall on a straight diagonal line. Thus, both figures 12.3 and 12.4 indicate that the residuals are normally distributed.

Figure 12.3:   Histogram for the Residuals

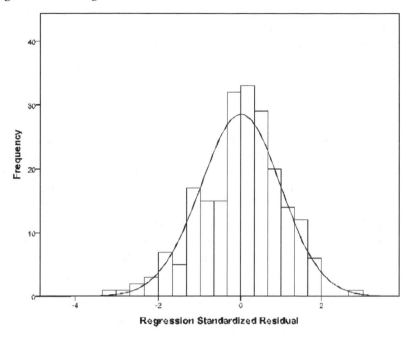

Figure 12.4:   Normal Probability Plot for the Residuals

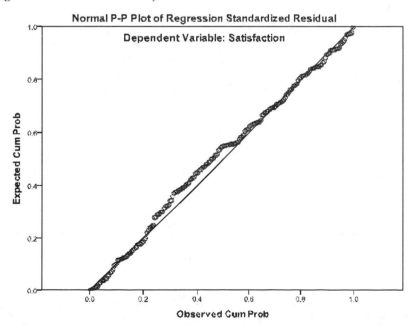

5. LINEARITY: The relationship between the criterion and the factors is assumed to be linear. As stated earlier, this assumption can be evaluated by looking at the scatterplot for each factor with the criterion. Here, we should only consider factors with continuous data. In this case, there are four continuous factors: working with colleagues, quality of supervision,[1] promotion, and workload. Use SPSS *Graphs*, *Legacy Dialog*, and *Scatter/Dot* main menu to create scatterplots (see chapter 7).

    Figures 12.5, 12.6, 12.7, and 12.8 display the scatterplots for job satisfaction with working with colleagues, square root of supervision, promotion, and workload, respectively. A review of these scatterplots shows a linear relationship (a straight line with the points clustered around it) between job satisfaction and working with colleagues, quality of (square root) supervision, and promotion, perhaps with minor deviation (a few points appear to be far from the line). Figure 12.8, on the other hand, shows little, if any, linear relationship between job satisfaction and workload.

6. HOMOSCEDASTICITY: The variance around the reference line should be the same for all values of the independent variables; that is, distributed evenly above and below the line. This assumption can be evaluated by looking at

Figure 12.5:   Scatterplot for Job Satisfaction with Working with Colleagues

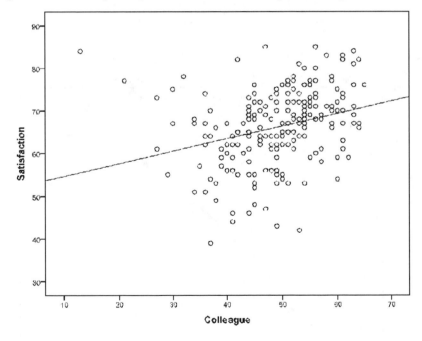

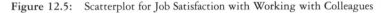

[1]Recall from chapter 5 that Quality of Supervision was reflected and transformed into the Square Root (SQRT_Super). Thus, low scores indicate better supervision.

Figure 12.6:   Scatterplot for Job Satisfaction with Quality of Supervision

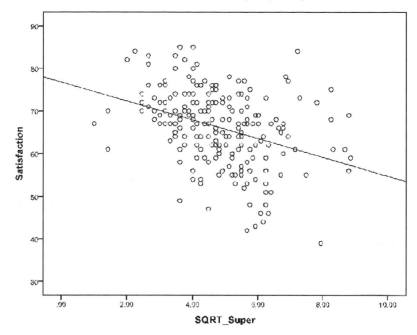

Figure 12.7:   Scatterplot for Job Satisfaction with Promotion

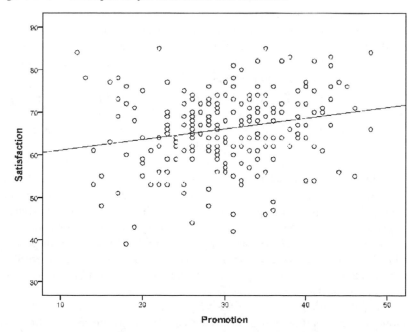

Figure 12.8:   Scatterplot for Job Satisfaction with Workload

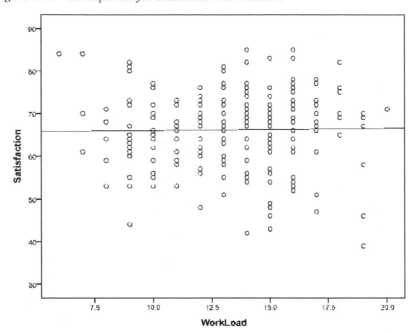

the scatterplot of the residuals against the predicted values. Figure 12.9 displays a scatterplot for the residuals with the predicted scores (we will illustrate this under "How to Run Multiple Regression Analysis in SPSS").

As it appears in figure 12.9, the points appear to distribute equally along the horizontal line for each level of the multiple factors (X axis), thus indicating that the data are homoscedastic.

7.   MULTICOLLINEARITY: The relationship between all pairs of the independent variables must not exceed .80. To examine this assumption, we will run Pearson's correlation coefficients between all factors (do not include the dependent variable). Table 12.3 displays the Pearson's correlation coefficients between all factors.

Table 12.3 shows that the correlation coefficients between the independent variables range between –.006 (gender and location) and –.487 (working with colleagues and square root supervision). No correlation coefficient exceeds .80, thus indicating no multicollinearity exists among the factors.

Also, we can evaluate the assumption of multicollinearity by inspecting the VIF and tolerance values produced by the regression analysis (described later). Table 12.4 displays these values. It shows the VIF and tolerance values for each factor with all other factors.

The table shows that none of the VIF exceeds the cutoff value of 10. Also, none of the tolerance value is smaller than .10. Thus, no multicollinearity problem exists.

Figure 12.9:   Scatterplot for the Residuals and Predicted Scores

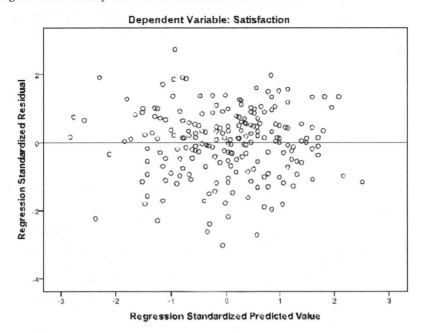

8.   SAMPLE SIZE: There are eight factors in this research question (gender, ethnicity, region, education, supervision, colleagues, promotion, and workload). Applying the sample size formula, a sample size of 114 cases or more $(50 + 8m = 50 + 8 \times 8 = 114)$ is needed for multiple regression analysis to detect a power of .80, given a two-tailed alpha of .05 and a medium effect size. In this case, 218 social services employees completed and returned the Job Satisfaction survey, which exceeds the minimum required sample size.

Table 12.3:   Pearson's Correlation Coefficients

		Gender	Ethnicity	Location	Education	Colleague	SQRT_Super	Promotion	WorkLoad
Gender	Pearson Correlation	1							
	Sig. (2-tailed)								
Ethnicity	Pearson Correlation	-.475	1						
	Sig. (2-tailed)	.000							
Location	Pearson Correlation	-.006	-.388	1					
	Sig. (2-tailed)	.934	.000						
Education	Pearson Correlation	-.053	-.053	.033	1				
	Sig. (2-tailed)	.432	.436	.629					
Colleague	Pearson Correlation	.133	-.232	.082	-.092	1			
	Sig. (2-tailed)	.050	.001	.232	.178				
SQRT_Super	Pearson Correlation	-.024	.174	-.077	.118	-.487	1		
	Sig. (2-tailed)	.730	.011	.265	.084	.000			
Promotion	Pearson Correlation	-.146	-.042	.215	-.122	.449	-.321	1	
	Sig. (2-tailed)	.031	.542	.001	.071	.000	.000		
WorkLoad	Pearson Correlation	.174	-.123	.043	.041	-.045	.051	-.060	1
	Sig. (2-tailed)	.010	.069	.525	.547	.509	.456	.381	

Table 12.4:   VIF and Tolerance Values for Each Factor

	Collinearity Statistics	
	Tolerance	VIF
(Constant)		
Gender	.685	1.461
Ethnicity	.587	1.704
Education_Rec	.961	1.040
Location	.768	1.302
Colleague	.623	1.605
SQRT_Super	.734	1.362
Promotion	.706	1.417
Workload	.958	1.044

Step 4: Select factors that will be entered in the analysis.

The next step after evaluating the assumptions is to select what factors should be entered in the regression analysis. This is especially important because (1) if the variable shows no bivariate relationship with the criterion, it will likely not contribute to the variance in the criterion, and (2) the less the number of factors entered in the analysis is, the smaller the sample size required for the regression analysis.

In our example, there are eight factors in which four are categorical variables and four are continuous variables. Of the four categorical variables, three are dichotomous (gender, ethnicity, and education), and one has three groups (region of employment).

Recall that the criterion (job satisfaction) is measured at the interval level of measurement and is normally distributed. Thus, we will run three independent t-tests to examine the relationship between job satisfaction and gender, ethnicity, and education (see chapter 8). We will also run a one-way ANOVA to test the relationship between region and job satisfaction (see chapter 10). The results of the three independent t-tests and ANOVA are presented in Tables 12.5 to 12.12.

Table 12.6 shows no significant difference (Sig. = .276) between male and female social services employees with regard to their levels of job satisfaction. Both males and females have similar mean scores in job satisfaction, 64.69 and 66.45, respectively (table 12.5). This variable, thus, will not be included in the regression analysis.

Table 12.5:   Descriptive Statistics for Job Satisfaction by Gender

	Gender	N	Mean	Std. Deviation	Std. Error Mean
Satisfaction	0 MALE	36	64.69	8.783	1.464
	1 FEMALE	182	66.45	8.829	.654

Table 12.6:   Independent *t*-Test for Job Satisfaction by Gender

Independent Samples Test

		Levene's Test for Equality of Variances		t-test for Equality of Means						
		F	Sig.	t	df	Sig. (2-tailed)	Mean Difference	Std. Error Difference	95% Confidence Interval of the Difference	
									Lower	Upper
Satisfaction	Equal variances assumed	.036	.849	-1.091	216	.276	-1.756	1.609	-4.928	1.415
	Equal variances not assumed			-1.095	50.005	.279	-1.756	1.603	-4.977	1.464

Table 12.8 shows a significant difference (Sig. = .000) between Arab and Jewish social services employees with regard to their levels of job satisfaction. Table 12.7 shows that Jewish employees have significantly higher levels of job satisfaction (mean = 67.69) than Arab employees (mean = 63.03). This variable, thus, will be included in the regression analysis.

Assuming a one-tailed hypothesis, table 12.10 shows a significant difference (Sig. = .088/2 = .044) between undergraduate and graduate social services employees with regard to their levels of job satisfaction. Table 12.9 shows that graduate employees have significantly higher levels of job satisfaction (mean = 68.58) than undergraduate employees (mean = 65.73). This variable will also be included in the regression analysis.

Table 12.7:   Descriptive Statistics for Job Satisfaction by Ethnicity

	Ethnicity	N	Mean	Std. Deviation	Std. Error Mean
Satisfaction	0 JEWS	145	67.69	8.156	.877
	1 ARABS	72	63.03	9.391	1.107

Table 12.8:   Independent *t*-Test for Job Satisfaction by Ethnicity

Independent Samples Test

		Levene's Test for Equality of Variances		t-test for Equality of Means						
		F	Sig.	t	df	Sig. (2-tailed)	Mean Difference	Std. Error Difference	95% Confidence Interval of the Difference	
									Lower	Upper
Satisfaction	Equal variances assumed	2.292	.132	3.767	215	.000	4.662	1.238	2.223	7.101
	Equal variances not assumed			3.593	125.4	.000	4.662	1.298	2.094	7.230

Table 12.9:   Descriptive Statistics for Job Satisfaction by Education

	Education_Rec	N	Mean	Std. Deviation	Std. Error Mean
Satisfaction	0 Undergraduate	185	65.73	8.798	.647
	1 Graduate	33	68.58	8.718	1.518

Table 12.10:   Independent *t*-Test for Job Satisfaction by Education

Independent Samples Test

| | | Levene's Test for Equality of Variances | | t-test for Equality of Means | | | | | | |
| | | | | | | | | | 95% Confidence Interval of the Difference | |
		F	Sig.	t	df	Sig. (2-tailed)	Mean Difference	Std. Error Difference	Lower	Upper
Satisfaction	Equal variances assumed	.198	.657	-1.714	216	.088	-2.846	1.660	-6.118	.426
	Equal variances not assumed			-1.725	44.428	.091	-2.846	1.650	-6.170	.478

Table 12.11 shows a significant overall difference (Sig. = .000) between the three regions of employment (north, center, and south) with regard to levels of job satisfaction. The post hoc Bonferroni test (table 12.12) shows that there is no significant difference between north and center regions (Sig. = .652). On the other hand, there is a significant difference between north and south (Sig. = .000). The second row shows a significant difference between the center and south regions (Sig. = .021). These findings suggest that social services employees in the south are significantly different than their counterpart employees from the other two regions.

Recall that a categorical variable with three or more levels must be recoded to one or more dummy variables prior to entering it in the regression analysis. In this case, because the one-way ANOVA and the post hoc test show that the south is significantly different than the other two regions, we should create a new dummy variable that has "South" as one group (coded as "1") and

Table 12.11:   One-Way ANOVA for Job Satisfaction by Region

ANOVA

Satisfaction

	Sum of Squares	df	Mean Square	F	Sig.
Between Groups	1294.728	2	647.364	8.885	.000
Within Groups	15591.843	214	72.859		
Total	16886.571	216			

Table 12.12:   Post Hoc Bonferroni for Job Satisfaction by Region

Multiple Comparisons

Satisfaction
Bonferroni

| | | Mean Difference (I-J) | Std. Error | Sig. | 95% Confidence Interval | |
| | | | | | Lower Bound | Upper Bound |
(I) Location	(J) Location					
1 NORTH	2 CENTER	-1.993	1.611	.652	-5.88	1.89
	3 SOUTH	-5.750*	1.450	.000	-9.25	-2.25
2 CENTER	1 NORTH	1.993	1.611	.652	-1.89	5.88
	3 SOUTH	-3.757*	1.377	.021	-7.08	-.44
3 SOUTH	1 NORTH	5.750*	1.450	.000	2.25	9.25
	2 CENTER	3.757*	1.377	.021	.44	7.08

*. The mean difference is significant at the 0.05 level.

"All Others" as the second group (coded as "0"). Recall that we already created three new dummy variables. However, we will only enter South in the regression analysis.

Next, we will select the continuous factors that will be entered in the analysis. To select these factors, we simply run a simple Pearson's correlation between job satisfaction (criterion) and each factor (supervision, colleagues, promotion, and workload). Table 12.13 presents the Pearson's correlation coefficients generated by SPSS.

Table 12.13 shows that job satisfaction has a significant correlation with working with colleagues (r = .283, p < .01), promotion (r = .213, p <.01), and quality of (square root) supervision (r = −.356, p < .01). On the other hand, no significant correlation is found between job satisfaction and workload (r = .016, p > .05), which supports figure 12.8. Thus, workload will not be entered in the regression analysis.

To conclude, the variables ethnicity, education, south, colleagues, square root of supervision, and promotion have significant bivariate relationships with job satisfaction. Thus, they will be entered in the regression analysis. The variables gender and workload have no significant relationships with job satisfaction. Therefore, they will be excluded from the analysis.

Step 5: Run multiple regression analysis.

Recall that the dependent variable is job satisfaction (Satisfaction) and the independent variables are ethnicity (Ethnicity), education (Education_REC), region (South), supervision (SQRT_Super), colleagues (Colleague), and promotion (Promotion). Now, use SPSS to run multiple regression analysis.

How to run multiple regression analysis in SPSS. The multiple regression procedures in SPSS enable us to select and compute many statistics and coefficients and create various plots in which each can provide valuable information. For our purpose here, we will only request the statistics, coefficients, and plots that we discussed. To run the multiple regression analysis in SPSS, follow these steps:

Table 12.13:   Pearson's Correlation between Job Satisfaction and Factors

		Satisfaction	Colleague	Promotion	WorkLoad	SQRT_Super
Satisfaction	Pearson Correlation	1				
	Sig. (2-tailed)					
Colleague	Pearson Correlation	.283**	1			
	Sig. (2-tailed)	.000				
Promotion	Pearson Correlation	.213**	.449**	1		
	Sig. (2-tailed)	.002	.000			
WorkLoad	Pearson Correlation	.016	-.045	-.060	1	
	Sig. (2-tailed)	.815	.509	.381		
SQRT_Super	Pearson Correlation	-.356**	-.487**	-.321**	.051	1
	Sig. (2-tailed)	.000	.000	.000	.456	

**. Correlation is significant at the 0.01 level (2-tailed).

1. Open the SPSS Job Satisfaction data file.
2. Click on *Analyze* in the SPSS main toolbar, scroll down to and click on *Regression*, and click on *Linear* (see screen 12.1).

Screen 12.1: SPSS Linear Regression Main Menu

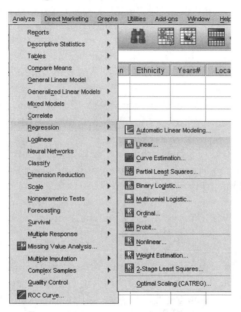

3. A dialog box called "Linear Regression" will open (see screen 12.2).

Screen 12.2: SPSS Linear Regression Dialog Box

4. Scroll down in the *Variables List*, click on *Satisfaction*, and click on the upper arrow button to move it into the *Dependent* box.

5. Scroll down in the *Variables List*, click on *Ethnicity*, and click on the arrow button corresponding with *Independent(s)* to move it into the *Independent(s)* box. Repeat this step to move *South*, *Education_REC*, *SQRT_Super*, *Colleague*, and *Promotion* into the *Independent(s)* box.

6. Click on the drop down arrow button associated with *Method* to select the method of data entry in the regression (*Forward*, *Stepwise*, *Backward*, etc.). Select *Stepwise* (you may choose any other method).

7. Click on *Statistics* in the upper right corner of the "Linear Regression" dialog box. A new dialog box called "Linear Regression: Statistics" will open (see screen 12.3).

Screen 12.3:   SPSS Linear Regression: Statistics Dialog Box

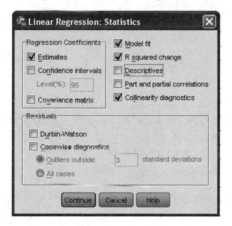

8. Make sure that the box of *Estimates* under "Regression Coefficients" is checked. This is the SPSS default. If not, check it. This computes the standardized (β) and unstandardized (b) regression coefficients, their levels of significance (*t* and *p* values), and the regression constant (a).

9. Also, make sure that the box of *Model Fit* is checked (this is also the SPSS default). This computes the multiple correlation coefficient (R), R square, and adjusted R square. It also computes the ANOVA table and the level of significance for the overall model.

10. Check the box of *R Squared Change*. This command computes the change in the proportion of the variance in the criterion due to the addition of a new factor and whether the change is significant.

11. Check the box of *Collinearity diagnostics*. This command computes the *Tolerance* and the *Variance Inflation Factor* (VIF). You need this to evaluate the assumption of multicollinearity (discussed earlier).

12.   Click on *Continue* to return to the "Linear Regression" dialog box.

13.   Click on *Plots*. A new dialog box called "Linear Regression: Plots" will open (see screen 12.4).

Screen 12.4:   SPSS Linear Regression: Plots Dialog Box

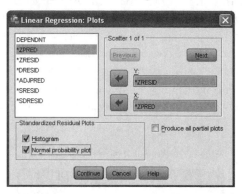

14.   Under *Standardized Residual Plots*, check the boxes of *Histogram* and *Normal Probability Plot*. You need these plots to check the assumption of normality of residuals.

15.   Click on *ZRESID* and click on the top arrow to move it into the *Y* box. Also, click on *ZPRED* and the second arrow to move it in the *X* box. This will create a scatterplot for the predicted and the residuals. You need this to evaluate the assumption of homoscedasticity.

16.   Click on *Continue* and click on *OK*.

You can also request these output using the SPSS syntax commands. These commands are as follows:

SPSS Syntax for Stepwise Multiple Regression Analysis

REGRESSION
/MISSING LISTWISE
/STATISTICS COEFF OUTS R ANOVA COLLIN TOL CHANGE
/CRITERIA=PIN(.05) POUT(.10)
/NOORIGIN
/DEPENDENT Satisfaction
/METHOD=STEPWISE Ethnicity Education_Rec South Colleague SQRT_Super Promotion
/SCATTERPLOT=(*ZRESID, *ZPRED)
/RESIDUALS HIST(ZRESID) NORM(ZRESID).

Note: To select a different regression method, change STEPWISE (fifth line) to BACKWARD or FORWARD.

Reading the output.   The following output presents the results of multiple regression procedures. These results include four tables (12.14 to 12.17) and three graphs (12.3, 12.4, and 12.9, discussed earlier). Other tables that were produced by SPSS were omitted because they are not necessary for our purpose at this level.

Table 12.14 displays the number, order, and the regression method in which factors are entered in and removed from the regression equation. It has four columns:

1. The Model column shows the number of steps the regression method utilized to produce the best regression model predicting the dependent variable (criterion). Table 12.14 shows (under Model) that the regression method utilized three steps to produce a final regression model, equation.

2. The second column in table 12.14, Variables Entered, shows the order in which the factors were entered in the regression equation. As discussed earlier, in the stepwise method, the variable that has the largest correlation coefficient with the dependent variable will be entered first, followed by the second, the third, and so on. The process stops when no more independent variables contribute significantly to the variance in the criterion.

   Table 12.14 (second column, Variables Entered) shows that in all only three factors were entered: Quality of Supervision (SQRT_Super) was entered first, then Region (South), and lastly Level of Education (Education_REC).

   Notice that no other factor was entered after education because ethnicity, promotion, and colleague (recall that six variables were entered in the analysis) did not contribute significantly to the variance in job satisfaction.

   This column thus displays the number and order of the factors that best predict job satisfaction. In this example, three factors are shown: supervision, region, and education.

3. The third column, Variables Removed, summarizes the variables that no longer contribute significantly to the variance in job satisfaction after a new variable is entered in the regression equation. In this example, the list is empty because all variables entered in the regression equation remain significant after each entry (e.g., supervision remained significant after south was entered; supervision and south remained significant after education was entered).

Table 12.14:   Multiple Regression Analysis—Methods of Variables Entry

Variables Entered/Removed[a]

Model	Variables Entered	Variables Removed	Method
1	SQRT_Super	.	Stepwise (Criteria: Probability-of-F-to-enter <= . 050, Probability-of-F-to-remove >= .100).
2	South	.	Stepwise (Criteria: Probability-of-F-to-enter <= . 050, Probability-of-F-to-remove >= .100).
3	Education_Rec	.	Stepwise (Criteria: Probability-of-F-to-enter <= . 050, Probability-of-F-to-remove >= .100).

a. Dependent Variable: Satisfaction

4. The fourth column, Method, describes the regression method in which variables are entered in the regression equation (stepwise, forward, backward, etc.). In this case, variables were entered based on the stepwise method. The column also shows that variables are entered only if their correlation with the criterion is significant at an alpha of .05 or less.

Table 12.15 has ten columns of which *six* are appropriate for our discussion at this level:

1. The Model (first) column conveys the number and order of the best factors entered in the regression equation; predicting the criterion.

2. The R (second) column conveys the correlation coefficient between the criterion and the factor(s) at each step.

3. The R Square (third) column conveys the proportion of the variance in the criterion that is accounted for by all factors entered in the equation at each step. This is also known as effect size.

4. The Adjusted R Square (fourth) column conveys the adjusted proportion of the variance in the criterion due to sample size and number of factors.

5. The R Square Change column (sixth) conveys the change in the proportion of the variance in the criterion as a result of entering a new factor. When only one factor is entered, R square and R square change are identical.

6. The Sig. F Change (tenth) column conveys the level of significance for the R square change. A Sig. value of .05 or less indicates a significant change in the R square.

Table 12.15 shows that there were three steps in which factors were entered in the regression equation:

1. MODEL 1: Quality of supervision (SQRT_Super) was entered at the first step. The first row and second column (R=.355) show that the correlation between supervision and job satisfaction is .355. The R Square column shows that supervision contributes 12.6 percent to the variance in job satisfaction (first row and third column, $R^2=.1265$). The fourth column shows

Table 12.15: Multiple Regression Analysis—Model Summary

Model Summary[d]

Model	R	R Square	Adjusted R Square	Std. Error of the Estimate	Change Statistics				
					R Square Change	F Change	df1	df2	Sig. F Change
1	.355[a]	.126	.122	8.244	.126	30.498	1	211	.000
2	.423[b]	.179	.171	8.011	.053	13.492	1	210	.000
3	.454[c]	.206	.195	7.896	.027	7.148	1	209	.008

a. Predictors: (Constant), SQRT_Super
b. Predictors: (Constant), SQRT_Super, South
c. Predictors: (Constant), SQRT_Super, South, Education_Rec
d. Dependent Variable: Satisfaction

that the adjusted R Square is 12.2 percent (first row, fourth column, adjusted $R^2 = .122$). The sixth column (R Square Change) shows that supervision added 12.6 percent to the variance in job satisfaction. Since this is the first step in the analysis, the R^2 and R^2 Change are the same (only one variable is in the regression equation, supervision). The tenth column shows that this proportion (R^2 Change) is significant at an alpha of .05 (first row and 10th column, Sig. F Change = .000).

2. MODEL 2: Region of employment (*South*) was entered at the second step. Table 12.15 shows that the multiple correlation between all variables in the equation at Model 2 (Step 2) and job satisfaction is .423 (second row and second column, R = .423). These factors are supervision (entered at step 1) and region of employment (entered at step 2). The two variables together accounted for 17.9 percent of the variance in job satisfaction (second row and third column, R Square = .179). The adjusted R square is still similar to the standard R square (second row, fourth column, Adjusted R Square = .171). The second variable (region of employment) added 5.3 percent to the variance in job satisfaction (second row and sixth column, R Square Change = .053).[2] This R Square Change is still significant at an alpha of .05 (second row and 10th column, F Change = .000).

3. MODEL 3: Finally, level of education (Education_REC) was entered at the third step. Table 12.15 shows that the multiple correlation between all factors in the equation and job satisfaction is .454 (third row and second column, R = .454). These variables are supervision (entered at step 1), region of employment (entered at step 2), and level of education (entered at step 3). The three variables accounted for 20.6 percent of the variance in job satisfaction (third row and third column, R Square = .206). This R square is still similar to the adjusted R square (third row, fourth column, Adjusted R Square = .195). The third variable (level of education) added 2.7 percent to the variance in job satisfaction (third row and sixth column, R Square Change = .027). This R square change is still significant at an alpha of .05 (third row and 10th column, Sig. F Change = .018).

The Model Summary table is followed by footnotes. The first three footnotes list the variables in each step (a = SQRT_Super, b = SQRT_Super, South, etc.). The last footnote shows the dependent variable (Satisfaction).

To sum up, this table shows that quality of supervision is the best predictor of job satisfaction, followed by region of employment and level of education.

Table 12.16 displays the results of the one-way ANOVA. Multiple regression analysis uses one-way ANOVA to examine the overall level of significance for each regression model. There will be one ANOVA test for each model.

---

[2]You can also compute the variance that each variable contributes simply by subtracting the R square at the previous step from the R square at the current step.

Table 12.16:   Multiple Regression Analysis—ANOVA

ANOVA^d

Model		Sum of Squares	df	Mean Square	F	Sig.
1	Regression	2072.925	1	2072.925	30.498	.000^a
	Residual	14341.554	211	67.969		
	Total	16414.479	212			
2	Regression	2938.719	2	1469.360	22.898	.000^b
	Residual	13475.760	210	64.170		
	Total	16414.479	212			
3	Regression	3384.337	3	1128.112	18.095	.000^c
	Residual	13030.142	209	62.345		
	Total	16414.479	212			

a. Predictors: (Constant), SQRT_Super
b. Predictors: (Constant), SQRT_Super, South
c. Predictors: (Constant), SQRT_Super, South, Education_Rec
d. Dependent Variable: Satisfaction

Table 12.16 conveys the results of the overall ANOVA for each model (see chapter 10 for these terms). The table lists the order of the models at the first column (Model) and then provides the Sum of Squares (second column), Degrees of Freedom (third column), Mean Square (fourth column), the ANOVA *F* ratio (fifth column), and the overall Level of Significance (sixth column). Here, we are only interested in the last two columns.

1. MODEL 1: The first row shows the results of ANOVA for the first model (supervision). With only one factor in (supervision), the model is a significant predictor of job satisfaction (first row and last two columns, *F* = 30.498, Sig. = .000).

2. MODEL 2: The second row shows the results of ANOVA for the second model (supervision and region). With these two factors in, the model is also a significant predictor of job satisfaction (second row and last two columns, *F* = 22.898, Sig. = .000).

3. MODEL 3: The third row shows the results of ANOVA for the third model (supervision, region, and education). With these three factors in, the model is still a significant predictor of job satisfaction (third row and last two columns, *F* = 18.095, *Sig.* = .000).[3]

To sum up, the results of ANOVA show that the three-factor model (Model 3) significantly predicts job satisfaction (*F* = 18.10, *p* < .001).

Table 12.17 displays the unstandardized and standardized regression coefficients, their levels of significance, and the collinearity statistics. It has eight columns:

---

[3]Notice that the more variables entered into the analysis, the smaller the *F* value.

Table 12.17: Multiple Regression Analysis: Coefficients

Coefficients[a]

Model		B	Std. Error	Beta	t	Sig.	Tolerance	VIF
		Unstandardized Coefficients		Standardized Coefficients			Collinearity Statistics	
1	(Constant)	76.686	2.001		38.321	.000		
	SQRT_Super	-2.197	.398	-.355	-5.522	.000	1.000	1.000
2	(Constant)	74.243	2.055		36.126	.000		
	SQRT_Super	-2.092	.388	-.338	-5.398	.000	.995	1.005
	South	4.047	1.102	.230	3.673	.000	.995	1.005
3	(Constant)	74.167	2.026		36.610	.000		
	SQRT_Super	-2.211	.385	-.358	-5.748	.000	.981	1.019
	South	4.124	1.086	.235	3.796	.000	.994	1.006
	Education_Rec	4.078	1.525	.166	2.673	.008	.985	1.015

a. Dependent Variable: Satisfaction

1. The first column, Model, conveys the number and order of the models and lists the variables that entered in the regression equation in each step (model). This is consistent with the previous two tables.

2. The second and third columns, B and Std. Error, convey the unstandardized regression coefficients (b's) and their standard errors for each factor entered in the analysis. It also reports the constant (a) for each model.

3. The fourth column, Beta, conveys the standardized regression coefficients (β). This reports the size and direction of the partial correlation between each factor and the criterion (in this case, job satisfaction).

4. The fifth and sixth columns, t and Sig., convey the t value and the level of significance (p) for each regression coefficient. This examines whether the partial correlation between the criterion and the corresponding factor is significant.

5. The seventh and eighth columns, Tolerance and VIF, convey the collinearity measures. These measures evaluate the assumption of multicollinearity. These were presented and discussed earlier in table 12.4.

These coefficients and statistics are reported for each factor entered in the regression equation and reassessed once a new variable is entered. We only need the last row, which displays the coefficients for all factors that best contribute to the variance in the criterion (Job Satisfaction); that is, Model 3.

1. The first line in Model 3 (Constant) conveys the regression constant (the "a" value in the unstandardized regression equation). The second column shows that the constant for this Model is 74.167 (first line in third row and second column, B = 74.167) with a standard error of 2.026 (first line in third row and third column, Std. Error = 2.026).

Table 12.17 does not report the standardized coefficient for the constant (first line in third row and fourth column, *Beta* =). This is because, as you may recall from the formula of the regression equation, the constant (a) for a standardized regression equation is zero.

2. The second line in Model 3 reports the coefficients and statistics for the strongest factor in the equation, supervision. The unstandardized regression coefficient for supervision is −2.211 with a standard error of .385 (that is, $b_{SUPERVISION} = -2.211$).

   Table 12.17 shows that the partial correlation (*Beta*) between supervision and job satisfaction is −.358 (that is, $\beta_{SUPERVISION} = -.358$). This indicates a negative partial correlation between supervision and job satisfaction; the better the supervision is, the higher the levels of job satisfaction. This correlation is significant (second line in Model 3 and fifth and sixth columns; $t = -5.748$, Sig. = .000).

3. The third line in Model 3 reports the coefficients and statistics for the second strongest factor in the equation, region of employment (South). The unstandardized regression coefficient is 4.124 with a standard error of 1.086 (that is, $b_{SOUTH} = 4.124$).

   The partial correlation (*Beta*) between region of employment and job satisfaction is .235 ($\beta_{SOUTH} = .235$) which indicates that social services employees from the south (coded as "1") tend to be more satisfied than those from other regions (coded as "0"). This correlation is significant (third line in Model 3 and fifth and sixth columns; $t = 3.796$, Sig. = .000).

4. Finally, the fourth line in Model 3 reports the coefficients and statistics for the third and last strongest factor in the equation, level of education. The unstandardized regression coefficient is 4.078 with a standard error of 1.525 (that is, $b_{EDUCATION} = 4.078$).

   The partial correlation (*Beta*) between level of education and job satisfaction is .166 ($\beta_{EDUCATION} = .166$) which indicates that graduate social services employees (coded as "1") tend to be more satisfied than undergraduate employees (coded as "0"). This correlation is significant (fourth line in Model 3 and fifth and sixth columns; $t = 2.673$, Sig. = .008).

Next, SPSS commands produce one table labeled as "Excluded Variables" and three graphs. The table displays the factors that are excluded from the analysis at each step (Model). It is not of importance. The three graphs include a histogram (figure 12.3) and normal probability plot for the residuals (figure 12.4) which are used to evaluate the assumption of normality of residuals and a scatterplot for the residuals with the predicted scores (figure 12.9), which is used to evaluate the assumption of homoscedasticity. These graphs were discussed earlier under step 3, "Select the appropriate statistical test." SPSS, however, does not insert a horizontal (reference) line in the scatterplot. You may do so through the Chart Viewer (see chapter 7, "How to Create a Scatterplot in SPSS").

WRITING THE RESULTS

As with previous tests, prior to reporting the results, show that you have examined the assumptions of multiple regression analysis, especially normality, linearity, homoscedasticity, and multicollinearity. In addition, report whether a transformation was carried out and how it changed the variable(s).

Next, you should report the number of factors that best predicts the criterion, their order from the most significant to the least significant, the proportion of the variance each contributes to the criterion, their partial correlation coefficients, and the level of significance. In our example, the results can be summarized as follows:

Evaluation of Assumptions

A stepwise multiple regression analysis was conducted to estimate a regression model that best predicts levels of job satisfaction among social services employees based on six factors: ethnicity, education, location, working with colleagues, quality of supervision, and opportunities for promotion.

Prior to conducting the analysis, several descriptive statistics and graphs were generated to examine the test assumptions, including normality of distributions, linear relationship between job satisfaction and factors, normality of residuals, homoscedasticity, and multicollinearity.

Measures of skewness and kurtosis, histograms, and Q-Q plots show that the shapes of the distributions of job satisfaction, working with colleagues, and promotions approach that of a normal curve. On the other hand, supervision was significantly skewed to the left (see chapter 5). Therefore, a square root transformation was conducted on supervision after it was reflected due to the negative skewness. Evaluation of the transformed supervision indicates it was close to a normal curve.

Pearson's correlation coefficients and scatterplots show a linear relationship between job satisfaction and all factors, except workload. In addition, inspections of both the histogram and the normal probability plots of the residuals indicate that the errors were normally distributed. Moreover, inspection of the scatterplot of predicted scores against the residuals confirms that the assumption of homoscedasticity was met. Finally, evaluation of the correlation matrix and both VIF and tolerance values show no multicollinearity exists among the six factors.

Results of Multiple Regression Analysis

The results of the stepwise multiple regression analysis revealed that three of the six factors emerged as significant predictors of job satisfaction ($F = 18.10$, $p < .001$). With a beta of $-.36$ ($p < .001$), quality of supervision emerged as the strongest predictor of job satisfaction accounting for 12.6 percent of the variance in job satisfaction. The second strongest factor was region of employment (β = .24, p < .001) accounting for an additional 5.3 percent of the variance in job satisfaction. The third strongest factor was level of education (β = .17, p < .001). Education however accounted only for 2.7 percent of the variance in job satisfaction.

These results indicate that higher job satisfaction among social services employees is a function of better quality of supervision, employed in the south region, and having higher levels of education. Overall, the model explains almost 21 percent of the variance in job satisfaction (R = .45). On the other hand, about 79 percent of the variance in job satisfaction is still uncounted for by this model.

Presentation of Results in a Summary Table

When presenting the results of multiple regression analysis in a summary table, report the multiple correlation coefficient and R Square for each factor (from the Model Summary Table), the partial correlation coefficient (β's), the t value, and the level of significance for each factor (from the Coefficients Table), and the overall F ratio and level of significance for each model (from the ANOVA table). The table should be part of the results section. Factors should be presented based on their partial correlation; from the largest to the smallest beta. For example, Table 12.18 presents the results of the multiple regression analysis for job satisfaction.

In this table, the first two columns (R and R^2) are from the Model Summary Table (table 12.15), the second three columns (β, t, and p) are from the Coefficients Table (table 12.17), and the last two columns (F and p) are from the ANOVA Table (table 12.16).

Writing the Regression Equation

Once a regression model has been estimated and all coefficients have been computed, you should be able to write the regression equation. This helps you to compute the level of job satisfaction for an individual employee. Recall that job satisfaction was found to be a function of quality of supervision, region of

Table 12.18:   Multiple Regression Analysis—Predictors of Job Satisfaction

Factor	R	R^{2a}	β	t	p	F	p
Supervision[b]	.36	.13	−.36	−5.75	<.001	30.50	<.001
Region—South	.42	.18	.24	3.80	<.001	22.90	<.001
Education	.45	.21	.17	2.67	<.010	18.10	<.001

[a]Adjusted R^2 = .20.
[b]Square Root of Supervision.

employment, and level of education. The regression equation for job satisfaction is thus as follows:

Regression Equation:

$$Y = a + b_1X_1 + b_2X_2 + b_3X_3 + \ldots + b_iX_i$$
Job Satisfaction = 74.17 + (−2.21 × Square Root of Supervision) + (4.12 × South) + (4.08 × Education)

QUESTION:

If John (a social services employee) is employed in the southern region (a score of "1"), has a BSW (a score of "0"), and has a score of "60" on the supervision scale, then what will be John's level of job satisfaction?

ANSWER:

First we have to reflect and compute the square root for supervision using the same methods we used in reflecting and transforming the scores of supervision (see chapter 5). (*Remember:* Always use in the equation the same type of scores used in the regression analysis).

Reflect: John's Score = 80 − 60 = 20

Square Root: John's Score = $\sqrt{20}$ = 4.47
Job Satisfaction = 74.17 + (−2.21 × 4.47) + (4.12 × 1) + (4.08 × 0) = 68.41

SUMMARY

Multiple regression analysis perhaps is the most used advanced statistical technique in social sciences research. It allows researchers and practitioners to predict a specific outcome (criterion) based on several observed factors (independent variables). For example, by predicting what clients are more likely to be drug addicts, clinically depressed, or to experience anxiety, clinicians and practitioners can plan early intervention techniques that will result in reducing or preventing such problems from occurring.

This chapter began with an introduction and a discussion of the purpose of multiple regression analysis and the regression equation. Two equations were introduced, the unstandardized and the standardized regression equations. The unstandardized regression equation is based on the actual raw scores, while the standardized regression equation is based on the transformation of the scores of all factors to standard scores (z scores).

The chapter then introduced and discussed major coefficients that are produced by the regression analysis. These coefficients include the unstandardized regression coefficient (b), standardized regression coefficient (beta), multiple correlation coefficient (R), multiple R square (R^2), adjusted R square (adjusted R^2), and the regression constant (a).

The chapter also presented and discussed the assumptions underlying multiple regression analysis. These assumptions include the level of measurement of the dependent variable, normality of the distributions of the criterion and the residuals, linearity of the relationship between the criterion and the factors, multicollinearity, homoscedasticity, and the assumption for the sample size. The chapter also discussed various methods for evaluating each assumption.

Because multiple regression analysis predicts one criterion based on multiple factors, the chapter discussed how to select only the factors that are more likely to contribute to the variance in the criterion to be included in the regression analysis. This section was followed by a discussion of the different regression methods. These methods include forward, stepwise, and backward regression methods. Finally, the chapter presented a practical example based on actual research data to illustrate the use of multiple regression analysis in social sciences research. This chapter then discussed how to use SPSS to analyze the data and how to interpret the output and write and present the results of multiple regression analysis.

PRACTICAL EXERCISE

Access the Elderly SPSS data file (appendix A) and examine the following research question:

What factors predict self-esteem (Esteem) among the elderly: gender (Gender), age (Age), race (Race), sickness (Sick), emotional balance (EB), physical health (PH), trusting others (TRO), mobility (MOB), cognitive status (CS), and social support (SS)?

1. Follow the steps in hypothesis testing and examine the research question. Discuss all steps in detail.

2. Write the SPSS syntax for the test statistic.

3. Present the results in a summary table.

4. Write the regression equation for self-esteem.

5. Jim is an eighty-seven-year-old white male. He considers himself as a sick person. What would be Jim's level of self-esteem if he scored 14 on emotional balance; 13 on physical health; 22 on trusting others; 15 on mobility; 21 on cognitive status; and 23 on social support?

APPENDIX A

SPSS Data Files

Download files from www.lyceumbooks.com.

DATA FILE 1: ANXIETY (N = 50)

This file contains data collected from fifty women who were exposed to inter-personal violence. All women participated in a ten-session group therapy to reduce their levels of anxiety. Prior to administering the therapy, all women completed a twenty-item self-administered survey measuring levels of anxiety on a five-point Likert scale (Anxiety_Pre). They also completed the anxiety survey after they completed the therapy (Anxiety_Post). Total scores range from 20 to 100, with higher scores indicating greater levels of anxiety.

DATA FILE 2: ELDERLY (N = 99)

This file contains data collected from a random sample of ninety-nine elderly people ages sixty years and older. Participants indicated their age, gender, race, education, marital status, and whether they perceived themselves as sick or not. They also completed the Center for Epidemiologic Studies Depression Scale (CESD) (Radloff, 1977), the Rosenberg Self-Esteem Scale (Royse, 1999), the Life Satisfaction Index (Wood, Wylie, & Sheafor, 1969), the Iowa Self-Assessment Inventory (Morris & Buckwalter, 1988), and the Geriatric Scale of Recent Life Events (Kiyak, Liang, & Kahana, 1976). Table A.1 describes the Elderly variables list.

DATA FILE 3: JOB SATISFACTION (N = 218)

This file contains data collected from a random sample of 218 Arab and Jewish social services employees in Israel. Participants answered questions related to their gender, age, marital status, number of children, education, ethnicity, time at current job, and region of employment. They also completed the Index of Job Satisfaction (Brayfield & Rothe, 1951) and Correlates of Work Satisfaction (Abu-Bader, 1998). In addition, participants completed a number of items related to autonomy and role conflict (Quinn & Staines, 1979), comfort (Quinn & Shepard, 1974), and workload (Caplan, Cobb, French, Harrison, & Pinneau, 1975). Table A.2 describes the Job Satisfaction variables list.

Table A.1:   Elderly SPSS Variable List

Variable Name	Variable Label	Range	Value Labels
Age		60–101	Actual age
Gender		0–1	0 = Female
			1 = Male
Race		0–1	0 = Not White
			1 = White
Education	Level of education	1–4	1 = Less than high school
			2 = High school
			3 = Some business/college
MStatus	Marital Status	1–3	1 = Widow
			2 = Married
			3 = Divorced/separated
Sick	Consider self sick	0–1	0 = No
			1 = Yes
ER	Economic resources	5–32	Scale (from low to high)[1]
EB	Emotional balance	10–32	Scale (from low to high)
PH	Physical health	7–26	Scale (from low to high)
TRO	Trusting others	13–32	Scale (from low to high)
MOB	Mobility	5–30	Scale (from low to high)
CS	Cognitive status	8–32	Scale (from low to high)
SS	Social support	10–32	Scale (from low to high)
Esteem	Levels of self-esteem	18–40	Scale (from low to high)
Satisfaction	Life satisfaction	3–14	Scale (from low to high)
CESD	Levels of depression	0–47	Scale (from low to high)
NRLEV	Negative life events	0–11	Number of events
REV_SS	Reverse of SS	1–23	Scale (from high to low)[2]
LG10_SS	Log10 for SS	0–1.36	Scale (from high to low)
ZER	Z-Score for ER	−2.9–1.58	Scale (from low to high)
Depress	Depression	0–1	0 = Not depressed
			1 = Depressed

[1]Low scores indicate lower value of the corresponding scale. (The lower the scores in economic resources, the less the economic resources; the lower the scores in depression, the lower the levels of depression).
[2]Low scores indicate higher value of the corresponding scale.

DATA FILE 4: MENTAL HEALTH (N = 155)

This file contains data collected from a sample of 155 immigrant Muslims aged fifty and above. Participants in the study were recruited from the Washington, D.C., metropolitan area and the Middle East using various recruitment methods. Participants were asked to indicate their gender, age, and whether they owned their home. They were also asked to complete the Center for Epidemiologic Studies Depression Scale (CESD) (Radloff, 1977). Total scores for CESD range between 0 and 60, with higher scores indicating greater depression. Participants were also asked to complete the Iowa Self-Assessment Inventory (IOWA) (Morris & Buckwalter, 1988). The IOWA contains seven subscales measuring participants' emotional balance (EB), physical health (PH), cognitive status (CS), economic resources (ER), trusting others (TRO), mobility (MOB), and social support

Table A.2:   Job Satisfaction SPSS Variables List

Variable Name	Variable Label	Range	Value Labels
Gender		0–1	0 = Male
			1 = Female
Age		22–62	Actual age
MStatus	Marital status	1–3	1 = Married
			2 = Single
			3 = Divorced
Children#	Number of children	0–8	Actual number
Education	Levels of education	1–3	1 = B.S.W./B.A.
			2 = M.S.W.
			3 = Other
Ethnicity		0–1	0 = Jews
			1 = Arabs
Years#	Years at job	1–35	Number of years
Location	Region	1–3	1 = North
			2 = Center
			3 = South
MStatus_Rec	Marital status (Recoded)	0–1	0 = Married
			1 = Never Married
Education_Rec	Level of Education (Recoded)	0–1	0 = Undergraduate
			1 = Graduate
Satisfaction	Levels of job satisfaction	39–85	Scale (from low to high)
Burnout	Levels of burnout	8–49	Scale (from low to high)
Turnover	Levels of turnover	2–34	Scale (from low to high)
Colleague	Satisfaction with colleagues	13–65	Scale (from low to high)
Supervision	Satisfaction with supervisor	2–19	Scale (from low to high)
Salary	Satisfaction with salary	4–35	Scale (from low to high)
Promotion	Satisfaction with promotion	12–48	Scale (from low to high)
Autonomy	Autonomy at work	6–22	Scale (from high to low)[3]
RoleConflict	Role conflict	2–15	Scale (from low to high)
Comfort	Comfort at work	7–25	Scale (from high to low)[4]
Workload	Load at work	6–20	Scale (from low to high)

[3]Higher scores in autonomy indicate lower levels of autonomy at work.
[4]Higher scores in comfort indicate lower levels of comfort at work.

(SS). Total scores for each subscale range between 8 and 32, with higher scores indicating greater value with respect to each subscale. Finally, participants were asked to complete the Rosenberg Self-Esteem Scale (Royse, 1999) and the Life Satisfaction Index (Wood, Wylie, & Sheafor, 1969). Table A.3 describes the Mental Health variables list.

DATA FILE 5: PTSD (N = 230)

This file contains data collected from a sample of 230 newly arrived refugees from Africa and Asia in the Washington, D.C., metropolitan area. Participants answered questions about their gender, age, marital status, level of education, and country of origin. They also completed self-report measures on physical

Table A.3:   Mental Health SPSS Variables List

Variable Name	Variable Label	Range	Value Labels
Gender		0–1	0 = Male
			1 = Female
Home	Own home?	0–1	0 = No
			1 = Yes
Age		50+	Actual age
EB	Emotional balance	8–32	Scale (from low to high)[5]
PH	Physical health	8–32	Scale (from low to high)
CS	Cognitive status	8–32	Scale (from low to high)
ER	Economic resources	8–32	Scale (from low to high)
TRO	Trusting others	8–32	Scale (from low to high)
MOB	Mobility	8–32	Scale (from low to high
SS	Social support	8–32	Scale (from low to high)
CESD	Levels of depression	0–47	Scale (from low to high)
SelfEsteem	Levels of self-esteem	18–40	Scale (from low to high)
Satisfaction	Life satisfaction	3–14	Scale (from low to high)

[5]Low scores indicate lower value of the corresponding scale (the lower the scores in emotional balance, the less the levels of emotional balance; the lower the scores in depression, the lower the levels of depression).

health and post-traumatic stress disorder. In addition, they completed the Multidimensional Health Locus of Control Scale (MHLC) (Wallston, Wallston, & DeVellis, 1978).

Higher scores on physical health, PTSD, and health locus of control indicate better physical health, greater PTSD, and more belief on internal, chance, and powerful others health locus of control, respectively. Table A.4 describes the PTSD variables list.

Table A.4:   PTSD SPSS Variables List

Variable Name	Variable Label	Range	Value Labels
Gender		0–1	0 = Male
			1 = Female
Age		18–76	Actual age
Country	Country of origin	0–1	0 = Asia
			1 = Africa
MStatus	Marital status	1–3	1 = Married
			2 = Widowed/divorced
			3 = Never married
Education	Level of education	1–3	1 = > 3 Year college
			2 = Undergraduate degree
			3 = Graduate degree
Health	Overall physical health	10–50	Scale (from low to high)
PTSD	Post-traumatic stress disorder	0–60	Scale (from low to high)
IHLC	Internal health locus of control	6–32	Scale (from low to high)
CHLC	Chance health locus of control	6–32	Scale (from low to high)
PHLC	Powerful other health locus of control	6–32	Scale (from low to high)

DATA FILE 6: WELFARE (N = 107)

This file contains data collected from a random sample of 107 former welfare recipients in Prince George's County, Maryland. Participants completed a number of demographic, health, and job-related questions. They also completed the Rosenberg Self-Esteem Scale (Royse, 1999), the Center for Epidemiologic Studies Depression Scale (CESD) (Radloff, 1977), and a nineteen-item social support scale (Barusch, Taylor, & Abu-Bader, 1999). Table A.5 describes the Welfare variables list.

Table A.5:   Welfare SPSS Variable List

Variable Name	Variable Label	Range	Value Labels
Age		21–61	Actual age
Gender		0–1	0 = Male
			1 = Female
Race		1–6	1 = African Americans
			2 = Asian or Pacific Islander
			3 = Hispanic
			4 = Native American
			5 = White
			6 = Mix or multiracial
School	Highest level of school completed	1–8	1 = Less than high school
			2 = High school/GED
			3 = Some vocational/business school
			4 = Certificate from vocational/business school
			5 = Less than 2 year college
			6 = More than 2 year college
			7 = College
			8 = Graduate school or higher
MStatus	Marital status	1–6	1 = Married
			2 = Single, never married
			3 = Divorced
			4 = Widowed
			5 = Separated
			6 = Living together unmarried
House	Any government assistance for housing	0–1	0 = No
			1 = Yes
PHealth	Physical health	1–5	1 = Poor
			2 = Fair
			3 = Good
			4 = Very good
			5 = Excellent
GHealth	Health in general	1–5	1 = Much worse
			2 = Somewhat worse
			3 = About the same
			4 = Somewhat better
			5 = Much better
JOB1	Time off of welfare		Number of months

Table A.5:   Welfare SPSS Variable List—(*Continued*)

Variable Name	Variable Label	Range	Value Labels
JOB2	Employment status	0–1	0 = No
			1 = Yes
JOB3	Participated in job training	0–1	0 = No
			1 = Yes
Esteem	Levels of self-esteem	22–40	Scale (from low to high)
CESD	Levels of depression	0–47	Scale (from low to high)
Support	Social support	0–11	Scale (from low to high)
Race_REC	Race (Recoded)	0–1	0 = Others
			1 = African Americans
MStatus_REC	Recoded MStatus	0–1	0 = Others
			1 = Single, never married
Education	Levels of education	0–1	0 = Less than high school
			1 = High school or higher
Depression	Depression	0–1	0 = Not depressed
			1 = Depressed

DATA FILE 7: WELL-BEING (N = 182)

This file contains data collected from a random sample of 182 college students selected from two universities in the Washington, D.C., area. Participants in the study were asked to indicate their gender, age, race, marital status, financial status, weight, and height. Students were also asked to rate their physical health on a single, five-point Likert scale, and complete the Satisfaction with Life Scale (Diener, Emmons, Larsen, & Griffin, 1985), Rosenberg Self-Esteem Scale (Royse, 1999), and the CESD (Radloff, 1977). In addition, they were asked to complete a self-perception scale developed for this purpose. Total scores for life satisfaction range between 7 and 35, self-esteem 10 and 50, depression 0 and 60, and self-perception between 12 and 60. Greater scores indicated greater satisfaction with life, higher self-esteem, greater depression, and greater self-perception. Finally, for this study, weight and height were used to compute students' Body Mass Index (BMI). Table A.6 describes the Well-Being variables list.

Table A.6: Well-Being SPSS Variables List

Variable Name	Variable Label	Range	Value Labels
Gender		0–1	0 = Male
			1 = Female
Age		18–45	Actual age
Race		1–3	1 = African American
			2 = White
			3 = Other
MaritalStatus	Marital status	1–3	1 = Single
			2 = Married
			3 = Other
FinancialStatus	Financial status	1–3	1 = Over extended
			2 = Making ends meet
			3 = Comfortable
PhysicalHealth	Overall physical health	1–5	1 = Poor
			2 = Fair
			3 = Good
			4 = Very good
			5 = Excellent
LifeSatisfaction	Satisfaction with life	7–35	Scale (from low to high)
SelfEsteem	Levels of self-esteem	10–50	Scale (from low to high)
Depression	Levels of depression (CESD)	0–60	Scale (from low to high)
SelfPerception	Levels of self-perception	12–60	Scale (from low to high)
Weight	Body Mass Index (BMI)	1–4	1 = Under weight
			2 = Normal weight
			3 = Over weight
			4 = Obese
Overweight	Are you overweight?	0–1	0 = No
			1 = Yes

APPENDIX B

Welfare Survey

ID #: _____

When were you born? ____/____/____

What is your gender?
- ❑ Male
- ❑ Female

What race are you?
- ❑ African American
- ❑ Asian or Pacific Islander
- ❑ Hispanic
- ❑ Native American (American Indian)
- ❑ White
- ❑ Mix or Multi-racial, Please specify: _____
- ❑ Other, Please specify: _____

How many years of education do you have? _____ Years

Do you receive government assistance to help pay for your housing?
- ❑ No
- ❑ Yes

> If YES, what type of housing assistance?
> - ❑ Section 8
> - ❑ Public housing
> - ❑ Other, Please specify: _____

How would you describe your physical health?
- ❑ Excellent
- ❑ Very good
- ❑ Good
- ❑ Fair
- ❑ Poor

Please circle the number for each statement that best describes how often you felt or behaved this way during the past week (*this is the CESD Scale*).

    0 = Rarely or none of the time (Less than 1 day)

    1 = Some or a little of the time (1-2 days)

    2 = Occasionally or a moderate amount of time (3-4 days)

    3 = Most or all of the time (5-7 days)

1.	I was bothered by things that usually don't bother me.	0	1	2	3
2.	I did not feel like eating; my appetite was poor.	0	1	2	3
3.	I felt that I could not shake off the blues even with help from my family or friends.	0	1	2	3
4.	I felt that I was just as good as other people.	0	1	2	3
5.	I had trouble keeping my mind on what I was doing.	0	1	2	3
6.	I felt depressed.	0	1	2	3
7.	I felt that everything I did was an effort.	0	1	2	3
8.	I felt hopeful about the future.	0	1	2	3
9.	I thought my life had been a failure.	0	1	2	3
10.	I felt fearful.	0	1	2	3
11.	My sleep was restless.	0	1	2	3
12.	I was happy.	0	1	2	3
13.	I talked less than usual.	0	1	2	3
14.	I felt lonely.	0	1	2	3
15.	People were unfriendly.	0	1	2	3
16.	I enjoyed life.	0	1	2	3
17.	I had crying spells.	0	1	2	3
18.	I felt sad.	0	1	2	3
19.	I felt that people disliked me.	0	1	2	3
20.	I could not get "going."	0	1	2	3

Rosenberg Self-Esteem Scale

Below is a list of statements dealing with your general feelings about yourself.

If you STRONGLY AGREE with the statement, circle SA.

If you AGREE with the statement, circle A.

If you DISAGREE with the statement, circle D.

If you STRONGLY DISAGREE with the statement, circle SD.

1	On the whole, I am satisfied with myself.	SA	A	D	SD
2.	At times I think I am no good at all.	SA	A	D	SD
3.	I feel that I have a number of good qualities.	SA	A	D	SD
4.	I am able to do things as well as most other people.	SA	A	D	SD
5.	I feel I do not have as much to be proud of.	SA	A	D	SD
6.	I certainly feel useless at times.	SA	A	D	SD
7.	I feel that I am a person of worth, at least on an equal plane with others.	SA	A	D	SD
8.	I wish I could have more respect for myself.	SA	A	D	SD
9.	All in all, I am inclined to feel that I am a failure.	SA	A	D	SD
10.	I take a positive attitude toward myself.	SA	A	D	SD

APPENDIX D

z Scores Table

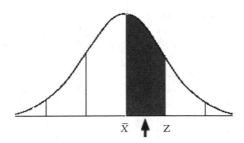

Area between the Mean and Z

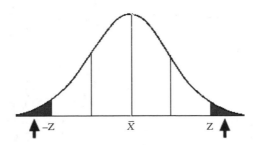

Area beyond –Z or beyond +Z

Z (+ or −)	Area between $\overline{X}$ and Z	Area beyond Z	Z (+ or −)	Area between $\overline{X}$ and Z	Area beyond Z
.00	.0000	.5000	.45	.1736	.3264
.01	.0040	.4960	.46	.1772	.3228
.02	.0080	.4920	.47	.1808	.3192
.03	.0120	.4880	.48	.1844	.3156
.04	.0160	.4840	.49	.1879	.3121
.05	.0199	.4801	.50	.1915	.3085
.06	.0239	.4761	.51	.1950	.3050
.07	0279	.4721	.52	.1985	.3015
.08	.0319	.4681	.53	.2019	.2981
.09	.0359	.4641	.54	.2054	.2946
.10	.0398	.4602	.55	.2088	.2912
.11	.0438	.4562	.56	.2123	.2877
.12	.0478	.4522	.57	.2157	.2843
.13	.0517	.4483	.58	.2190	.2810
.14	.0557	.4443	.59	.2224	.2776
.15	.0596	.4404	.60	.2257	.2743
.16	.0636	.4364	.61	.2291	.2709
.17	.0675	.4325	.62	.2324	.2676
.18	.0714	.4286	.63	.2357	.2643
.19	.0753	.4247	.64	.2389	.2611
.20	.0793	.4207	.65	.2422	.2578
.21	.0832	.4168	.66	.2454	.2546
.22	.0871	.4129	.67	.2486	.2514
.23	.0910	.4090	.68	.2517	.2483
.24	.0948	.4052	.69	.2549	.2451
.25	.0987	.4013	.70	.2580	.2420
.26	.1026	.3974	.71	.2611	.2389
.27	.1064	.3936	.72	.2642	.2358
.28	.1103	.3897	.73	.2673	.2327
.29	.1141	.3859	.74	.2704	.2296
.30	.1179	.3821	.75	.2734	.2266
.31	.1217	.3783	.76	.2764	.2236
.32	.1255	.3745	.77	.2794	.2206
.33	.1293	.3707	.78	.2823	.2177
.34	.1331	.3669	.79	.2852	.2148
.35	.1368	.3632	.80	.2881	.2119
.36	.1406	.3594	.81	.2910	.2090
.37	.1443	.3557	.82	.2939	.2061
.38	.1480	.3520	.83	.2967	.2033
.39	.1517	.3483	.84	.2995	.2005
.40	.1554	.3446	.85	.3023	.1977
.41	.1591	.3409	.86	.3051	.1949
.42	.1628	.3372	.87	.3078	.1922
.43	.1664	.3336	.88	.3106	.1894
.44	.1700	.3300	.89	.3133	.1867

Z (+ or −)	Area between $\overline{X}$ and Z	Area beyond Z	Z (+ or −)	Area between $\overline{X}$ and Z	Area beyond Z
.90	.3159	.1841	1.35	.4115	.0885
.91	.3186	.1814	1.36	.4131	.0869
.92	.3212	.1788	1.37	.4147	.0853
.93	.3238	.1762	1.38	.4162	.0838
.94	.3264	.1736	1.39	.4177	.0823
.95	.3289	.1711	1.40	.4192	.0808
.96	.3315	.1685	1.41	.4207	.0793
.97	.3340	.1660	1.42	.4222	.0778
.98	.3365	.1635	1.43	.4236	.0764
.99	.3389	.1611	1.44	.4251	.0749
1.00	.3413	.1587	1.45	.4265	.0735
1.01	.3438	.1562	1.46	.4279	.0721
1.02	.3461	.1539	1.47	.4292	.0708
1.03	.3485	.1515	1.48	.4306	.0694
1.04	.3508	.1492	1.49	.4319	.0681
1.05	.3531	.1469	1.50	.4332	.0668
1.06	.3554	.1446	1.51	.4345	.0655
1.07	.3577	.1423	1.52	.4357	.0643
1.08	.3599	.1401	1.53	.4370	.0630
1.09	.3621	.1379	1.54	.4382	.0618
1.10	.3643	.1357	1.55	.4394	.0606
1.11	.3665	.1335	1.56	.4406	.0594
1.12	.3686	.1314	1.57	.4418	.0582
1.13	.3708	.1292	1.58	.4429	.0571
1.14	.3729	.1271	1.59	.4441	.0559
1.15	.3749	.1251	1.60	.4452	.0548
1.16	.3770	.1230	1.61	.4463	.0537
1.17	.3790	.1210	1.62	.4474	.0526
1.18	.3810	.1190	1.63	.4484	.0516
1.19	.3830	.1170	1.64	.4495	.0505
1.20	.3849	.1151	1.65	.4505	.0495
1.21	.3869	.1131	1.66	.4515	.0485
1.22	.3888	.1112	1.67	.4525	.0475
1.23	.3907	.1093	1.68	.4535	.0465
1.24	.3925	.1075	1.69	.4545	.0455
1.25	.3944	.1056	1.70	.4554	.0446
1.26	.3962	.1038	1.71	.4564	.0436
1.27	.3980	.1020	1.72	.4573	.0427
1.28	.3997	.1003	1.73	.4582	.0418
1.29	.4015	.0985	1.74	.4591	.0409
1.30	.4032	.0968	1.75	.4599	.0401
1.31	.4049	.0951	1.76	.4608	.0392
1.32	.4066	.0934	1.77	.4616	.0384
1.33	.4082	.0918	1.78	.4625	.0375
1.34	.4099	.0901	1.79	.4633	.0367

Z (+ or −)	Area between $\overline{X}$ and Z	Area beyond Z	Z (+ or −)	Area between $\overline{X}$ and Z	Area beyond Z
1.80	.4641	.0359	2.25	.4878	.0122
1.81	.4649	.0351	2.26	.4881	.0119
1.82	.4656	.0344	2.27	.4884	.0116
1.83	.4664	.0336	2.28	.4887	.0113
1.84	.4671	.0329	2.29	.4890	.0110
1.85	.4678	.0322	2.30	.4893	.0107
1.86	.4686	.0314	2.31	.4896	.0104
1.87	.4693	.0307	2.32	.4898	.0102
1.88	.4699	.0301	2.33	.4901	.0099
1.89	.4706	.0294	2.34	.4904	.0096
1.90	.4713	.0287	2.35	.4906	.0094
1.91	.4719	.0281	2.36	.4909	.0091
1.92	.4726	.0274	2.37	.4911	.0089
1.93	.4732	.0268	2.38	.4913	.0087
1.94	.4738	.0262	2.39	.4916	.0084
1.95	.4744	.0256	2.40	.4918	.0082
1.96	.4750	.0250	2.41	.4920	.0080
1.97	.4756	.0244	2.42	.4922	.0078
1.98	.4761	.0239	2.43	.4925	.0075
1.99	.4767	.0233	2.44	.4927	.0073
2.00	.4772	.0228	2.45	.4929	.0071
2.01	.4778	.0222	2.46	.4931	.0069
2.02	.4783	.0217	2.47	.4932	.0068
2.03	.4788	.0212	2.48	.4934	.0066
2.04	.4793	.0207	2.49	.4936	.0064
2.05	.4798	.0202	2.50	.4938	.0062
2.06	.4803	.0197	2.51	.4940	.0060
2.07	.4808	.0192	2.52	.4941	.0059
2.08	.4812	.0188	2.53	.4943	.0057
2.09	.4817	.0183	2.54	.4945	.0055
2.10	.4821	.0179	2.55	.4946	.0054
2.11	.4826	.0174	2.56	.4948	.0052
2.12	.4830	.0170	2.57	.4949	.0051
2.13	.4834	.0166	2.58	.4951	.0049
2.14	.4838	.0162	2.59	.4952	.0048
2.15	.4842	.0158	2.60	.4953	.0047
2.16	.4846	.0154	2.61	.4955	.0045
2.17	.4850	.0150	2.62	.4956	.0044
2.18	.4854	.0146	2.63	.4957	.0043
2.19	.4857	.0143	2.64	.4959	.0041
2.20	.4861	.0139	2.65	.4960	.0040
2.21	.4864	.0136	2.66	.4961	.0039
2.22	.4868	.0132	2.67	.4962	.0038
2.23	.4871	.0129	2.68	.4963	.0037
2.24	.4875	.0125	2.69	.4964	.0036

Z (+ or −)	Area between $\overline{X}$ and Z	Area beyond Z	Z (+ or −)	Area between $\overline{X}$ and Z	Area beyond Z
2.70	.4965	.0035	3.11	.4991	.0009
2.71	.4966	.0034	3.12	.4991	.0009
2.72	.4967	.0033	3.13	.4991	.0009
2.73	.4968	.0032	3.14	.4992	.0008
2.74	.4969	.0031	3.15	.4992	.0008
2.75	.4970	.0030	3.16	.4992	.0008
2.76	.4971	.0029	3.17	.4992	.0008
2.77	.4972	.0028	3.18	.4993	.0007
2.78	.4973	.0027	3.19	.4993	.0007
2.79	.4974	.0026	3.20	.4993	.0007
2.80	.4974	.0026	3.21	.4993	.0007
2.81	.4975	.0025	3.22	.4994	.0006
2.82	.4976	.0024	3.23	.4994	.0006
2.83	.4977	.0023	3.24	.4994	.0006
2.84	.4977	.0023	3.25	.4994	.0006
2.85	.4978	.0022	3.26	.4994	.0006
2.86	.4979	.0021	3.27	.4995	.0005
2.87	.4979	.0021	3.28	.4995	.0005
2.88	.4980	.0020	3.29	.4995	.0005
2.89	.4981	.0019	3.30	.4995	.0005
2.90	.4981	.0019	3.31	.4995	.0005
2.91	.4982	.0018	3.32	.4995	.0005
2.92	.4982	.0018	3.33	.4996	.0004
2.93	.4983	.0017	3.34	.4996	.0004
2.94	.4984	.0016	3.35	.4996	.0004
2.95	.4984	.0016	3.36	.4996	.0004
2.96	.4985	.0015	3.37	.4996	.0004
2.97	.4985	.0015	3.38	.4996	.0004
2.98	.4986	.0014	3.39	.4997	.0003
2.99	.4986	.0014	3.40	.4997	.0003
3.00	.4987	.9993	3.41	.4997	.0003
3.01	.4987	.9993	3.42	.4997	.0003
3.02	.4987	.9992	3.43	.4997	.0003
3.03	.4988	.9992	3.44	.4997	.0003
3.04	.4988	.9992	3.45	.4997	.0003
3.05	.4989	.9992	3.46	.4997	.0003
3.06	.4989	.9991	3.47	.4997	.0003
3.07	.4989	.9991	3.48	.4997	.0003
3.08	.4990	.9991	3.49	.4998	.0002
3.09	.4990	.9990	3.50	.4998	.0002
3.10	.4990	.0010			

References

Abu-Bader, S. H. (1998). *Predictors of work satisfaction between Arab and Jewish social workers in Israel.* Unpublished doctoral dissertation, University of Utah, Salt Lake City.

Abu-Bader, S. H. (2010). *Advanced & multivariate statistical methods in social science research.* Chicago: Lyceum Books.

Barusch, A., Taylor, M. J., & Abu-Bader, S. H. (1999). *Understanding families with multiple barriers to self-sufficiency.* Salt Lake City, UT: Social Research Institute, University of Utah.

Bloom, M., Fischer, J., & Orme, J. G. (2003). *Evaluating practice: Guidelines for the accountable professional (4th ed.).* Boston: Allyn and Bacon.

Brayfield, A. H., & Rothe, H. F. (1951). An index of job satisfaction. *Journal of Applied Psychology, 35*(5), 307–311.

Caplan, R., Cobb, S., French, J. R. P., Harrison, R. V., & Pinneau, S. R. (1975). *Job demands and workers health.* Washington, DC: U.S. Department of Health, Education, and Welfare.

Cohen, J. (1988). *Statistical power analysis for the behavioral sciences (2nd ed.).* New York: Psychology Press.

Crocker, L., & Algina, J. (1986). *Introduction to classical and modern test theory.* Fort Worth, TX: Harcourt Brace Jovanovich College Publishers.

DeVellis, R. F. (2003). *Scale development: Theory and application (2nd ed).* Thousand Oaks, CA: Sage.

Diener, E., Emmons, R. A., Larsen, R. J., & Griffin, S. (1985). The Satisfaction with Life Scale. *Journal of Personality Assessment, 49,* 71–75.

Fisher, R. A. (1915). Frequency distributions of values of the correlation coefficient in samples of an infinitely large population. *Biometrika, 10,* 507–521.

Fortune, A. E., & Reid, W. J. (1999). *Research in social work (3rd ed.).* New York: Columbia University Press.

Gilmore, J. (2004). *Painless Windows: A handbook for SAS users (3rd ed.).* Cary, NC: SAS Publishing.

Hair, J. F., Black, W. C., Babin, B. J., & Anderson, R. E. (2010). *Multivariate data analysis (7th ed.).* Upper Saddle River, NJ: Prentice Hall.

Hildebrand, D. K. (1986). *Statistical thinking for behavioral scientists.* Boston: Duxbury.

Hinkle, D. E., Wiersma, W., & Jurs, S. G. (2003). *Applied statistics for the behavioral sciences (5th ed.).* Boston: Houghton Mifflin.

Kiyak, A., Liang, J., & Kahana, E. (1976). A methodological inquiry into the schedule of recent life events. In D. J. Mangen & W. A. Peterson (Eds.), *Research instruments in social gerontology, Vol. 1: Clinical and social psychology.* Minneapolis: University of Minnesota Press.

Morris, W. W., & Buckwalter, K. C. (1988). Functional assessment of the elderly: The Iowa self-assessment inventory. In C. F. Waltz & O. L. Strickland (Eds.), *Measurement of nursing outcomes, Volume 1: Measuring client outcomes* (328–351). New York: Springer.

Munro, B. H. (2005). *Statistical methods for health care research (5th ed.).* Philadelphia: Lippincott.

Pearson, K. (1895). Contributions to the mathematical theory of evolution, II: Skew variation in homogeneous material. *Philosophical Transactions of the Royal Society of London, 186,* 343–414.

Quinn, R. P., & Shepard, L. J. (1974). *The 1972–73 quality of employment survey.* Ann Arbor, MI: Institute for Social Research.

Quinn, R. P., & Staines, G. L. (1979). *The 1977 quality of employment survey.* Ann Arbor, MI: Institute for Social Research.

Radloff, L. S. (1977). The CES-D Scale: A self-report depression scale for research in the general population. *Applied Psychological Measurement, 1*(3), 385–401.

Royse, D. (1999). *Research methods in social work (3rd ed.).* Chicago: Nelson-Hall.

Rubin, A., & Babbie, E. (2011). *Research methods for social work (7th ed.).* Pacific Grove, CA: Brooks/Cole.

SAS Publishing. (2001). *Step-by-step programming with base SAS software.* Cary, NC: Author.

SAS Publishing. (2006). *SAS learning edition 41.* Cary, NC: Author.

Siegel, S., & Castellan, N. J. (1988). *Nonparametric statistics for the behavioral sciences (2nd ed.).* New York: McGraw-Hill.

SPSS Inc. (1999). *Intermediate topics: SPSS for Windows 10.0.* Chicago: Author.

SPSS Inc. (2001). *Advanced techniques: ANOVA.* Chicago: Author.

SPSS Inc. (2001). *Advanced techniques: Regression.* Chicago: Author.

SPSS Inc. (2001). *Statistical analysis using SPSS.* Chicago: Author.

SPSS Inc. (2002). *Syntax I: Introduction to syntax.* Chicago: Author.

Stinson, C., & Dodge, M. (2007). *Microsoft Excel 2007 inside out.* Redmond, WA: Microsoft Press.

Tabachnick, B. G., & Fidell, L. S. (2007). *Using multivariate statistics (5th ed.).* Boston: Allyn and Bacon.

Tukey, J. (1977). *Exploratory data analysis.* Upper Saddle River, NJ: Pearson Education.

Walkenbach, J. (2007). *Microsoft Office Excel 2007 bible.* Indianapolis: Wiley Publishing.

Wallston, K. A., Wallston, B. S., & DeVellis, R. (1978). Development of the multidimensional health locus of control (MHLC) scales. *Health Education Monographs, 6*(2), 160–170.

Weinbach, R. W., & Grinnell, R. M. (2010). *Statistics for social workers (8th ed.).* Boston: Allyn and Bacon.

Wood, V., Wylie, M. L., & Sheafor, B. (1969). An analysis of a short self-report measure of life satisfaction: Correlation with rater judgments. *Journal of Gerontology, 24,* 465–469.

Index

About the Author

Soleman H. Abu-Bader (PhD, University of Utah; MSW, Augsburg College) is a professor in the School of Social Work at Howard University. He has worked as a social work practitioner, researcher, and teacher. He is the author of *Advanced and Multivariate Statistical Methods for Social Science Research with a Complete SPSS Guide* (2010), as well as several articles that focus on the elderly, mental health, gerontology, and organized behavior. He also serves on the editorial boards of a number of peer-reviewed journals, including *Best Practices in Mental Health: An International Journal.*